International Investment Protection within Europe

The steadily rising number of investor-State arbitration proceedings within the EU has triggered an extensive backlash and an increased questioning of the international investment law regime by different Member States as well as the EU Commission. This has resulted in the EU's assertion of control over the intra-EU investment regime by promoting the termination of bilateral intra-EU investment treaties (intra-EU BITs) and by opposing the jurisdiction of arbitral tribunals in intra-EU investor-State arbitration proceedings. Against the backdrop of the landmark *Achmea* decision of the European Court of Justice, the book offers an in-depth analysis of the interplay of international investment law and the law of the European Union with regard to intra-EU investments, i.e. investments undertaken by an investor from one EU Member State within the territory of another EU Member State.

It specifically analyses the conflict between the two investment protection regimes applicable within the EU with a particular emphasis on the compatibility of the international legal instruments with the law of the European Union. The book thereby addresses the more general question of the relationship between EU law and international law and offers a conceptual framework of intra-European investment protection based on the analysis of all intra-EU BITs, the Energy Charter Treaty and EU law, as well as the arbitral practice in more than 180 intra-EU investor-State arbitration proceedings.

Finally, the book develops possible solutions to reconcile the international legal standards of protection with the regionalized transnational law of the European Union.

Julien Berger is a lawyer specialized in public international law and the law of the European Union. He completed his legal studies at the Humboldt-Universität zu Berlin and holds a Maître en Droit (Paris II – Panthéon-Assas), a Magister Juris (University of Oxford) as well as a PhD from the Universität Potsdam. Julien Berger is currently completing his legal clerkship at the Higher Regional Court of Berlin.

Routledge Research in International Economic Law

For more information about this series, please visit www.routledge.com/Routledge-Research-in-International-Economic-Law/book-series/INTECONLAW

International Investment Protection within Europe

The EU's Assertion of Control

Julien Berger

Routledge
Taylor & Francis Group

LONDON AND NEW YORK

First published 2021
by Routledge
2 Park Square, Milton Park, Abingdon, Oxon OX14 4RN

and by Routledge
52 Vanderbilt Avenue, New York, NY 10017

Routledge is an imprint of the Taylor & Francis Group, an informa business

British Library Cataloguing-in-Publication Data
A catalogue record for this book is available from the British Library

Library of Congress Cataloging-in-Publication Data
Names: Berger, Julien, author.
Title: International investment protection within Europe : the EU's assertion of control / Julien Berger.
Description: Milton Park, Abingdon, Oxon ; New York, NY : Routledge, 2021. | Series: Routledge research in finance and banking law | Includes bibliographical references and index.
Identifiers: LCCN 2020026954 (print) | LCCN 2020026955 (ebook) | ISBN 9780367610630 (hardback) | ISBN 9781003103080 (ebook)
Subjects: LCSH: Investments, Foreign—Law and legislation—European Union countries. | European Union countries—Foreign economic relations. | Investments, Foreign (International law)
Classification: LCC KJE6433 .B47 2021 (print) | LCC KJE6433 (ebook) | DDC 346.24/092—dc23
LC record available at https://lccn.loc.gov/2020026954
LC ebook record available at https://lccn.loc.gov/2020026955

ISBN: 978-0-367-61063-0 (hbk)
ISBN: 978-1-003-10308-0 (ebk)

Typeset in Times New Roman
by Apex CoVantage.LLC

To my parents

Contents

Figures

Acknowledgments

This manuscript was developed from my PhD project within the interdisciplinary Berlin–Potsdam research group "The International Rule of Law – Rise or Decline?"

I am very grateful to everyone involved in my PhD journey. First of all, I would like to thank my supervisor Professor Andreas Zimmermann for the stimulating discussions and for the academic freedom and confidence he endowed me with.

I would also like to thank Professor Meik Thöne for the thorough preparation of the second opinion on my dissertation.

Many people within the research group have contributed in one way or another. I want to thank all of them for this remarkable experience which profoundly enriched my perspective on public international law and allowed me to participate in compelling and confronting conversations about law and politics in the international sphere. I am particularly grateful to Alicia Köppen and Simon Blätgen; their friendship, support and encouragement has been priceless.

This book would not have been possible without the support of many friends and family members. Among them I want to express special thanks to Charlotte Matthews and Till Hesse for their reliable and humorous support in the preparation of the publication, especially regarding linguistic and technical challenges. Furthermore, I wholeheartedly thank my brother Leander Berger for being one of my fiercest but always constructive critics. Thanks to Heide-Rose and Gavriel Berger for their encouragement and all the intellectually inspiring exchanges over the years.

I want to express my deepest appreciation to Juliane Kotzur for her invaluable, unwavering support and kindness during this journey. Grand Merci!

Most of all I thank my parents, Rose-Marie Soulard-Berger and Hanns-Michael Berger, to whom I dedicate this book.

Julien Berger
Berlin, May 2020

Abbreviations

BGH	Bundesgerichtshof (German Federal Supreme Court)
BIT	Bilateral Investment Treaty
BLEU	Belgium-Luxembourg Economic Union
BVerfG	Bundesverfassungsgericht (German Constitutional Court)
CETA	Comprehensive Economic and Trade Agreement
DTA	Double Taxation Agreement
ECHR	European Convention on Human Rights
ECJ	European Court of Justice
ECT	Energy Charter Treaty
ECtHR	European Court of Human Rights
EFC	Economic and Financial Committee
EU	European Union
EU 15	The 15 Member States that joined the EU before 2004
EU Charter	Charter of Fundamental Rights of the European Union
FDI	Foreign Direct Investment
FET	Fair and Equitable Treatment
FTA	Free Trade Agreement
GATT	General Agreement on Tariffs and Trade
ICC	International Chamber of Commerce
ICCPR	International Covenant on Civil and Political Rights
ICJ	International Court of Justice
ICSID	International Centre for Settlement of Investment Disputes
ICSID Convention	Convention on the Settlement of Investment Disputes between States and Nationals of other States
IIA	International Investment Agreement
ILC	International Law Commission
ILM	International Legal Materials
IO	International Organization
ISDS	Investor-State Dispute Settlement
MFN	Most-favoured Nation
MIC	Multilateral Investment Court
MNEs	Multinational Enterprises
MPEPIL	Max Planck Encyclopaedia of Public International Law

MPILux	Max Planck Institute Luxembourg for International, European and Regulatory Procedural Law
Multilateral Agreement for the Termination of intra-EU BITs	Agreement for the Termination of Bilateral Investment Treaties between the Member States of the European Union, signed on May 5, 2020, by 23 EU Member States
New York Convention	1958 New York Convention on the Recognition and Enforcement of Foreign Arbitral Awards
OECD	Organization for Economic Cooperation and Development
OLG	Oberlandesgericht (Higher Regional Court)
PCA	Permanent Court of Arbitration
PCIJ	Permanent Court of International Justice
REIO	Regional Economic Integration Organization
SCC	Stockholm Chamber of Commerce
TEU	Treaty on European Union
TFEU	Treaty on the Functioning of the European Union
TTIP	Transatlantic Trade and Investment Partnership
UN	United Nations
UNCITRAL	United Nations Commission on International Trade Law
UNCITRAL Model Law	UNCITRAL Model Law on International Commercial Arbitration
UNCLOS	United Nations Convention on the Law of the Sea
UNCTAD	United Nations Conference on Trade and Development
UNTS	United Nations Treaty Series
VCLT	Vienna Convention on the Law of Treaties
VCLT II	Vienna Convention on the Law of Treaties between States and International Organizations or between International Organizations
WTO	World Trade Organization
ZPO	Zivilprozessordnung (German Code of Civil Procedure)

Introduction

The flows of international investments are continuously rising and play an important role in today's globalized economy.[1] Investment activities abroad, however, are not a recent phenomenon but have increasingly occurred over the last centuries. Since the early beginnings of international economic exchanges, home States have been interested in protecting their own investors abroad, if necessary, even by the use of armed force.

In order to prevent such 'gunboat diplomacy' and other violent confrontations, many States endeavoured to develop legal means to solve possible disputes arising out of these investment activities. This eventually led to the development of international investment law, which was strongly influenced by European States and today is shaped by a tremendous net of bilateral investment treaties (BITs) stretched across the globe. 1959 marks the year of the signature of the first of these bilateral investment treaties, negotiated between the Federal Republic of Germany and the State of Pakistan. It was followed by many other BITs concluded by European States. In 1965, the International Centre for Settlement of Investment Disputes (ICSID) was created, which provides a procedural framework for the settlement of investor-State disputes and which accelerated the development of what this study understands as 'the international investment protection regime'.[2]

In parallel to the emergence of this mostly BIT-based 'international investment protection regime' after World War II, a similar development took place in the

---

1 While global flows of foreign direct investment (FDI) amounted to US $ 25 billion in 1975, they have reached US $ 1.75 trillion in 2016, cf. UNCTAD, *World Investment Report 2017: Investment and the Digital Economy* (New York, Geneva: United Nations, 2017), at 4. Today at least 82,000 Multinational Enterprises (MNEs) operate worldwide with approximately 810,000 foreign affiliates, collectively employing more than 77 million people abroad and generating roughly eleven per cent of the global GDP, cf. C. W. L. Hill, *International Business: Competing in the Global Marketplace*, 9. ed. (New York: McGraw-Hill Irwin, 2013), at 250 f.

2 There is a general agreement in legal literature and practice that international investment law has evolved to a distinct regime of international law which is more than the sum of its main parts, the predominantly bilateral investment treaties, cf. for a great overview J. W. Salacuse, *The Law of Investment Treaties*, 2. ed. (Oxford: Oxford University Press, 2015), at 1 ff; S. W. Schill, *The Multilateralization of International Investment Law* (Cambridge: Cambridge University Press, 2009).

heart of Western Europe, a region that had been destabilized by wars between neighbouring countries for centuries. On May 9, 1950, the French foreign minister Robert Schuman made a declaration in which he developed the vision of setting up "common foundations for economic developments as a first step in the federation of Europe" in order to "change the destinies" of this war-torn continent.[3] His idea was to render any war between the possible Member States of an integrated economic union to be established "not merely unthinkable, but materially impossible."[4] Schuman envisaged the creation of an integrated economic union enhancing cooperation and interdependencies to prevent further wars among the European neighbours. Inspired and encouraged by this vision, Belgium, France, the Federal Republic of Germany, Italy, Luxembourg and the Netherlands concluded in 1951 the Treaty of Paris, establishing the European Coal and Steel Community, which later merged into the European Economic Community established by the Rome Treaty in 1957. In the following decades, the Schuman plan became a reality. The European Union (EU)[5] became a unique and unprecedented success story of peace, stability and economic development among its Member States.

This development also led to the emergence of what this study understands as the 'European investment protection regime'. It comprises all domestic rules of the Member States and of the EU legal order itself which cover foreign direct investments and their protection. The 1957 Rome Treaty, for instance, already provided for the right to establishment and the guarantee of the free movement of capital, which became a cornerstone of intra-EU foreign investment protection.

Thus, from the end of the 1950s onwards, two parallel legal regimes of investment protection started to evolve at the heart of the European continent, both reflecting an increasing legalization of international economic relations and both pursuing overlapping goals such as the favouring of economic exchange and legal stability.

Whereas the 'international investment protection regime' was based around bilateral investment treaties, the 'European investment protection regime' developed as one of many features of both the institutionalized EU's regional integration process and the Member States' domestic economic policies. Both regimes thereby reached beyond the classical public international law State-to-State cooperation and affected – in the case of the 'international investment protection regime' at least indirectly – the internal regulatory sphere of the States as well as their relationships with individuals and companies.

The present book retraces the development of the relationship between these two investment protection regimes, which attracted more and more States'

---

3 R. Schuman, *The Schuman Declaration – 9 May 1950*. https://europa.eu/european-union/about-eu/ symbols/europe-day/schuman-declaration_en (1 May 2020).

4 Ibid.

5 For the sake of simplicity, this study uses the term European Union in order to refer also to precursor organizations such as the European Economic Community and the European Community. It does not assume that these organizations had the same political, economic and legal nature as today's EU.

participation and increasingly gained importance within Europe. However, while the EU steadily developed throughout the decades, it was only in the 1990s that international investment law and especially investor-State arbitration started to take effect.[6]

With the end of the Cold War and the passage into the 1990s, the legalization and judicialization of international relations accelerated at the global level. This development also affected the global and European investment treaty regime with an unimaginable pace. Thousands of new BITs were concluded and multilateral investment treaties such as the Energy Charter Treaty (ECT) or the North American Free Trade Agreement (NAFTA) emerged. Suddenly, the European continent was covered by a dense net of international investment agreements among EU Member States. A vibrant dispute settlement environment emerged with so far more than 180 investor-State arbitration proceedings initiated by investors from the EU against EU Member States, accounting for approximately 18 per cent of the known treaty-based investor-State arbitration proceedings globally.[7]

But the end of the Cold War did not only influence the development of international investment law. It also brought about fundamental changes for the European Union itself, especially regarding its membership. While the Union counted only 12 Member States before the end of the Cold War, this number has risen to 28 Member States before Brexit.[8]

The post-1990s period can thus be posited as a time of rise of both the EU legal order and the 'European investment protection regime' on the one hand, and the 'international investment protection regime' on the other hand. Their evolution fits perfectly in the global post-1990s developments, which added a 'layer' to international law in general.[9] During that period, some key multilateral treaties were concluded, new institutions such as the World Trade Organization (WTO) were created, 'thicker' human rights standards were recognized and the proliferation of international adjudicative bodies accompanied by an unexpected increase of international adjudication could be observed.

Today, 30 years after the turning point of the end of the Cold War, the world looks different. The EU is experiencing a major political crisis. Multilateralism is increasingly questioned, and many States review their international commitments. At the same time, the EU has emerged as the biggest investor and recipient of foreign direct investments worldwide,[10] due to the great attractiveness of its

---

6 There is only one publicly known treaty-based investor-State arbitration proceeding initiated before the end of the Cold War, *AAPL v Sri Lanka*, ICSID Case No. ARB 87/3.

7 Cf. UNCTAD, *Investment Policy Hub – ISDS*. https://investmentpolicy.unctad.org/investment-dispute-settlement (23 May 2020).

8 For the first time in the EU's history, its number of Member States has declined due to the United Kingdom's withdrawal from the European Union on 1 February 2020, the so-called Brexit.

9 Cf. J. H. H. Weiler, *The Geology of International Law: Governance, Democracy and Legitimacy*, Zeitschrift für ausländisches öffentliches Recht und Völkerrecht 64 (2004), 547–62.

10 Foreign direct investments inflows to the EU amounted to US $ 533 billion in 2016 alone. Regarding FDI outflows, eight of the top 20 home economies in 2016 were EU Member States (including

highly integrated market economy, allowing a company once established in an EU Member State to operate in the entire EU common market with more than 400 million middle-class consumers, and to be able to rely on a skilled labour force and a high degree of political stability.[11]

The major developments within the EU are also reflected on a smaller scale in the conflict of both investment protection regimes in Europe. Notwithstanding their parallel development, both regimes had remained almost totally separated from each other for decades, operating without any major interferences. Their factual separation had many reasons. It was linked among others to the only recent rise of investment arbitration proceedings in Europe, the EU's relative distance towards classical international law and also the European Court of Justice's (ECJ) reluctance to accept preliminary references by arbitral tribunals, deterring the latter from starting a 'judicial dialogue' with the highest court of the EU. As aptly described by Berman,

> European Union law and the law of international arbitration have largely occupied separate worlds. To describe their relationship as one of mutual indifference would scarcely be an overstatement. The past, in which these two bodies of law coexisted, each following its separate and distinctive logic, looks today like something of an age of innocence.[12]

Finally, it was not until 2009 that the Lisbon Treaty redefined the EU's common commercial policy and transferred the area of foreign direct investment from the EU Member States' to the EU's exclusive competence. Even though this transfer of competence only affected extra-EU investments, it created a new dynamic and a greater general attention to this field of transnational economic activities and their legal framework. It is for all these reasons that potential conflicts and collisions between the two investment protection regimes became apparent only in recent years.

The increasing number of investor-State arbitration proceedings initiated against EU Member States and the related number of awards issued at their expense led the EU Commission and some respondent States to try to assert control over

---

the United Kingdom before Brexit). The numbers are similar regard FDI inflows. According to UNCTAD, of the worldwide top 20 host economies in 2017 and 2018, six were EU Member States (including the United Kingdom before Brexit), UNCTAD, *World Investment Report 2019: Special Economic Zones* (New York, Geneva: United Nations, 2019), at 19, 22. European multinational enterprises also play an important role at the global level. 51 out of the 100 most important non-financial MNEs, i.e. MNEs that do not provide financial services such as banks or investment management corporations, are based in EU Member States. UNCTAD, *The World's Top 110 Non-Financial MNEs, Ranked by Foreign Assets 2016: Annex to the World Investment Report 2017.*

11 Notwithstanding this general attractiveness, there is a clear tendency for FDI to flow primarily to the larger EU economies and their important domestic markets, cf. EU Commission, *Towards an FDI Attractiveness Scoreboard: Ref. Ares(2016)2611797*, 6 June 2016, at p. 11.

12 G. A. Bermann, *Navigating EU Law and the Law of International Arbitration*, Arbitration International 28 (2012), 397–445, at 398.

investment protection in Europe. Especially the ambiguous and imprecise standards in BITs and the often investor-friendly approach adopted by arbitral tribunals, pressured them into action. In the Commission's and some Member States' view, the 'outdated' regime of international investment protection treaties within the EU needed to be abolished. Alleging the incompatibility of EU law and international investment law, they started to oppose the jurisdiction of arbitral tribunals and propagated the termination of bilateral investment treaties concluded between EU Member States (intra-EU BITs).

The conflict was further fuelled by the different competing interests of the disputing parties to investor-State arbitration proceedings. One can expect investors to make a continuous effort to discover and exploit the best regulatory regime available to their investment. Investors often engage in regulatory arbitrage which is possible as long as a regulatory system provides for two different regimes applicable to their investments. Within the EU context, in case of conflict, investors thus often tend to rely on international law applied by a neutral body of international adjudication, i.e. an arbitral tribunal, instead of choosing domestic law and domestic adjudication. Host States on the other hand, tend to favour the application of their own domestic law, applied by a domestic court instead of a supranational tribunal controlling the State's compliance with its international obligations. The EU institutions, finally, are driven by the goal to preserve the institutional functioning and the primacy and autonomy of the EU legal order within the Member States.

The collision of the two regimes has developed to a real conflict – at least from an EU legal perspective. It reached its temporary peak with the ECJ's *Achmea* judgment rendered on March 6, 2018,[13] in which the court found the investor-State arbitration provision contained in an intra-EU BITs to be incompatible with the EU legal order. As this study will show, the *Achmea* judgment, however, cannot bring the conflict to an end and only provides limited answers to the open questions of the interrelationship of both legal regimes. Without timely political responses, the conflict might even be intensified. It could reach a new level if, for example, the *Vattenfall v Germany* proceeding[14] is decided in favour of the claimant, which is calling for damages of over € 4 billion as a consequence of Germany's decision to phase out nuclear energy. In that case, the German State might find itself in the dilemma to face the international legal obligation to comply with and to enforce the award even if this enforcement is incompatible with fundamental principles of EU law, which could create an opposite obligation.[15]

As a first political reaction to the ECJ's *Achmea* decision, the EU Member States have issued three slightly differing declarations on the legal consequences

---

13 ECJ, *Achmea*. C-284/16. Judgment, 6 March 2018, ECLI:EU:C:2018:158.
14 ICSID, *Vattenfall v Germany*. Case No. Arb/12/12.
15 See also J. Berger, *Die Bundesrepublik Deutschland – Internationaler Investitionsschutz und das Vattenfall-Verfahren*, Europäische Zeitschrift für Wirtschaftsrecht 31 (2020), 229–33.

of that judgment and announced to terminate all intra-EU BITs.[16] These declarations, however, also reflect the continuing disagreement among Member States, especially regarding *Achmea's* effects on and the future of the Energy Charter Treaty in intra-EU investor-State relations. In May 2020, 23 of the remaining 27 Member States have finally signed a Multilateral Agreement for the Termination of intra-EU BITs, which, however, does not address the question of the Energy Charter Treaty.

Against this backdrop, the present book analyses the development of international investment protection in Europe. The reluctance of some European actors to accept the jurisdiction of investor-State arbitration tribunals stands paradigmatically for an increasing backlash against investor-State arbitration but also international adjudicatory bodies in general. It can be understood as a sign for the decline of this form of judicialization of the international order through the multiplication and expansive practice of such bodies since the 1990s. The United Kingdom's withdrawal from the European Union, Brexit, further complicates the situation and raises many new questions.

The book also assesses whether the 'international investment protection regime' as it stands, continues to represent the most appropriate legal framework for the protection of intra-European investment flows. This does explicitly not imply any normative preunderstanding of whether the 'international investment protection regime' is inherently 'good' or needs to be preserved the way it is right now. The question is rather how the competing interests of stakeholders of foreign direct investments, namely investors, home States and host States, can be reconciled to the benefit of all.

This also raises the more general question of the interrelationship of EU law and international law and the role and self-perception of the EU within the international legal order. The eventual termination of all intra-EU BITs and the open future of the Energy Charter Treaty and its applicability to intra-EU investor-State relations further raise the question of the role of the single EU Member States in the international legal order in times of an increasing harmonization at the regional level led by the European Union.

With regard to intra-European investment flows, this also implies the question whether regulation and norm setting should rather take place within the realm of the European Union, i.e. in a regional and multilateral way, or whether international law approaches outside the EU framework – be they bilateral or multilateral – are more promising and expedient. In any way, the decline of the 'international investment protection regime' within Europe could lead to a rise of a more nuanced, balanced and predictable system of EU investor protection if the

---

16 Representatives of 22 EU Member States, *Declaration on the Legal Consequences of the Judgment of the ECJ in Achmea and on Investment Protection in the EU,* 15 January 2019; Representatives of Finland, Luxembourg, Malta, Slovenia and Sweden, *Declaration on the Enforcement of the Judgement of the ECJ in Achmea and on Investment Protection in the EU,* 16 January 2019; Representative of Hungary, *Declaration on the Legal Consequences of the Judgment of the ECJ in Achmea and on Investment Protection in the EU,* 16 January 2019.

EU succeeds in asserting control over the general framework of investor protection in Europe.

By addressing these issues, the book also aims at tackling the practical problem of legal insecurity arising out of the open questions surrounding the relationship between EU law and international investment law, which affect both EU Member States and EU investors. The clash of both regimes has noticeable practical implications. As the great majority of intra-EU investor-State arbitration proceedings have been initiated within the last four years, many disputes are still pending. Some investors currently try to enforce arbitral awards, which are – from an EU perspective – violating EU law, before domestic courts in the EU but also before courts outside the EU which are not bound by EU law.

Arbitral tribunals are unable to deliver a coherent and foreseeable jurisprudence due to their ad hoc character and due to the lack of a *stare decisis* principle in international arbitration. The lack of predictability and legal certainty make it even more necessary to comprehensively analyse the legal interaction and conflict between both investment protection regimes in order to point out possible solutions to strengthen the international rule of law and the trust into the European legal system. This is even more so as the *Achmea* decision might not only affect intra-EU investment protection but also international investment law at the global level. More than half of the BITs worldwide have at least one EU Member State as a party and the EU Commission is currently negotiating a great number of free trade agreements with other partner countries, which might be influenced by its internal developments regarding investment protection.

References

Berger, Julien, *Die Bundesrepublik Deutschland – Internationaler Investitionsschutz und das Vattenfall-Verfahren*, Europäische Zeitschrift für Wirtschaftsrecht 31 (2020), 229–33.

Bermann, George A., *Navigating EU Law and the Law of International Arbitration*, Arbitration International 28 (2012), 397–445.

Salacuse, Jeswald W., *The Law of Investment Treaties*, The Oxford International Law Library, 2. ed. (Oxford: Oxford University Press, 2015).

Schill, Stephan W., *The Multilateralization of International Investment Law*, International Trade and Economic Law (Cambridge: Cambridge University Press, 2009).

UNCTAD, *World Investment Report 2017: Investment and the Digital Economy*, United Nations Publication (New York, Geneva: United Nations, 2017).

UNCTAD, *World Investment Report 2019: Special Economic Zones*, United Nations Publication (New York, Geneva: United Nations, 2019).

Weiler, Joseph H. H., *The Geology of International Law*: *Governance, Democracy and Legitimacy*, Zeitschrift für ausländisches öffentliches Recht und Völkerrecht 64 (2004), 547–62.

I Setting the stage

To effectively assess the relationship between the law of the European Union (EU law) and international investment law applicable to intra-European investments, the present chapter will illuminate the relevant legal sources and instruments as well as their development over time. It starts with an introduction to the phenomenon of foreign direct investment (FDI) in the EU (I.), followed by an analysis of the development of general international investment law from a European perspective (II.), before presenting the current framework of intra-EU investor protection and the challenges it faces (III.).

I European foreign direct investment

In order to profit from the respective comparative advantages of other national economies, namely the reduction of production costs, the increase of foreign demand for a company's products and the entry into new markets, many companies start business activities abroad.[1] This is also the case within the EU, where intra-EU FDI is steadily gaining importance.[2] Intra-EU FDI has significantly increased with the intensified integration of the European common market and the shift from centrally planned towards free market economies and democratic forms of government in Central and Eastern Europe.[3] The post-socialist and post-communist countries offered huge unsaturated markets with highly skilled but cheap labour force, natural resources and privatization opportunities. In the 1990s, many

---

1 For an extended overview, see J. Bonnitcha, L. S. Poulsen and M. Waibel, *The Political Economy of the Investment Treaty Regime* (Oxford: Oxford University Press, 2017), at 34 ff; H.-C. Moon, *Foreign Direct Investment: A Global Perspective* (Hackensack, NJ: World Scientific, 2016), at 25 ff.

2 In the period between 2003 and 2015, EU companies carried out approximately 76,000 intra-EU FDI activities of a total value of € 3,800 billion, cf. ESPON, *The World in Europe, Global FDI Flows Towards Europe: Intra-European FDI – Main Report,* March 2018, at 2 ff.

3 Cf. C. W. L. Hill, *International Business: Competing in the Global Marketplace*, 9. ed. (New York: McGraw-Hill Irwin, 2013), at 250 f; R. Gilpin, *Global Political Economy: Understanding the International Economic Order* (Princeton: Princeton University Press, 2001), at 278.

Western European States concentrated their FDI in Eastern Europe.[4] Today, however, there is a clear tendency for intra-EU FDI to flow both from and in the direction of the EU 15, i.e. the States that joined the EU until 2004, and among them to be mostly concentrated in the larger Member States.[5]

II Development of international investment law – a European story

As long as companies and individuals have undertaken business operations abroad, the host States in which these operations took place as well as the home States of the business operators have grappled with the treatment of the foreigners and their property.[6] Elihu Root got to the heart of this more than 100 years ago in his timeless and still topical finding that

> The great accumulation of capital in the money centers of the world, far in excess of the opportunities for home investment, has led to a great increase of international investment extending over the entire surface of the earth [...]. All these forms of peaceful interpenetration among the nations of the earth naturally contribute their instances of citizens justly or unjustly dissatisfied with the treatment they receive in foreign countries.[7]

Similar observations by many others led to the development of international investment law, which today has become one of the most dynamic fields of international law.

The following section provides an overview of the historical development of this area of international law, especially focusing on its evolution from a European perspective. Five stages of development are distinguished: the early beginnings

---

4 In the period between 1989 and 2003 the cumulative total of FDI for Eastern Europe as a whole reached $ 117 billion, cf. T. Judt, *Postwar: A History of Europe Since 1945* (London: Vintage, 2010), at 722. See also, R. Gilpin, *Global Political Economy: Understanding the International Economic Order* (Princeton: Princeton University Press, 2001), p. 293; J. Karl, *The Promotion and Protection of German Foreign Investment Abroad*, ICSID Review 11 (1996), 1–36, at 3 f; E. Synowiec and R. Woreta, *Poland's Transition to a Market Economy* in B. Lippert and P. Becker (eds.), *Towards EU-membership: Transformation and Integration in Poland and the Czech Republic* (Bonn: Europa-Union-Verl., 1998), pp. 83–107, at 92 f; P. Becker, *The Joint Venture Between Volkswagen and Skoda* in B. Lippert and P. Becker (eds.), *Towards EU-membership: Transformation and Integration in Poland and the Czech Republic* (Bonn: Europa-Union-Verl., 1998), pp. 293–332.
5 Cf. ESPON, *The World in Europe, Global FDI Flows Towards Europe*, March 2018, 7 ff.
6 Francisco de Vitoria (1492–1546) and Hugo Grotius (1583–1645) already argued for the protection of foreigners, cf. S. Hobe, *The Development of the Law of Aliens and the Emergence of General Principles of Protection Under Public International Law* in M. Bungenberg, et al. (eds.), *International Investment Law: A Handbook* (Baden-Baden: Nomos, 2015), pp. 6–22, at 7 f.
7 E. Root, *The Basis of Protection to Citizens Residing Abroad*, American Journal of International Law 4 (1910), 517–28, at 518 f.

in the 19th century and the first half of the 20th century (1.), the period following World War II (2.), the emergence of investor-State arbitration provisions in the 1970s and 1980s (3.), the proliferation of treaties and investor-State dispute settlement (ISDS) proceedings in the 1990s (4.) and the most current developments and critical questioning of international investment law (5.).

1 19th century and the first half of the 20th century

Modern international investment law did not "arise suddenly and miraculously the way Athena sprang from the head of Zeus"[8] but was inspired by the economic interests of different States reflected in customary international law and already existing international trade treaties that provided some degree of protection to foreigners, especially the bilateral 'Treaties of Friendship, Commerce and Navigation'. Those had been concluded between industrialized States from the late 18th century onwards, the first of them in 1796 between France and the USA.[9]

Nevertheless, it remained a contentious issue for a long time whether aliens should be accorded protection against arbitrary measures of host States by rules of international law or whether they should only rely on the respective domestic laws.

In the late 19th and early 20th centuries, different positions developed, often reflecting both the dichotomy between traditionally capital-exporting States from the northern hemisphere and capital-importing States of the Global South, as well as the colonial and imperialistic context of that time: The turn of the century had been marked by the so-called gunboat diplomacy.[10] Home States had broadened their diplomatic approaches by relying on the threat or the use of force to protect the interests of their nationals abroad. An early appalling example of this practice is the so-called 1838 Pastry War between France and Mexico. As response to the looting of a French pastry shop in Mexico City the French government blocked, bombed and seized Mexican ports and cities until a full compensation was paid.[11] Another example is the naval blockade

---

8　J. W. Salacuse, *The law of investment treaties*, 2. ed. (Oxford, 2015), at 46.

9　Many of these treaties inter alia provided foreign companies with legal standing before domestic courts and guaranteed access to the territory of the other State party. They did not, however, provide for any form of dispute settlement, let alone investor-State arbitration. Cf. C. Brown, *The Evolution of the Regime of International Investment Agreements* in M. Bungenberg, et al. (eds.), *International Investment Law: A Handbook* (Baden-Baden: Nomos, 2015), pp. 153–85, at p. 157; H. P. Connell, *United States Protection of Private Foreign Investment through Treaties of Friendship, Commerce and Navigation,* Archiv des Völkerrechts 9 (1961), 256–77, at 260 ff.

10　For an extended overview, see O. T. Johnson Jr. and J. Gimblett, *From Gunboats to BITs* in K. P. Sauvant (ed.), *Yearbook on International Investment Law & Policy 2010–2011* (New York: Oxford University Press, 2012), pp. 649–92.

11　On the 'Pastry War' with further references, L. S. Poulsen, *Politics of Investment Treaty Arbitration: Forth* in T. Schultz and F. Ortino (eds.), *Oxford Handbook of International Arbitration*, 2018. https://papers.ssrn.com/sol3/papers.cfm?abstract_id=2955166 (1 May 2020), at 4 f.

imposed against Venezuela by Germany, Italy and the United Kingdom in 1902 to enforce claims relating to State-issued bonds.[12]

One reaction to this practice was the conclusion of the 1907 Hague Convention on the Limitation of Employment of Force for Recovery of Contract Debts, also known as the Drago-Porter Convention. In this Convention the Contracting Parties agreed "not to have recourse to armed force for the recovery of contract debts claimed from the Government of one country by the Government of another country as being due to its nationals," unless the "debtor State refuses or neglects to reply to an offer of arbitration, or, after accepting the offer, prevents any compromis from being agreed on, or, after the arbitration, fails to submit to the award."[13] In other words, "honest debtors should be protected from military intervention, honest creditors from feigned insolvency" and recourse to force became the ultima ratio, conditioned by prior arbitration.[14]

Another response to the 'gunboat diplomacy' and related policies – followed mostly by Latin American States – was the Calvo-Doctrine,[15] according to which foreigners had to be granted a purely 'national treatment' that could only be invoked before domestic courts. In other words, foreigners should not be treated in a different or better way than the host State's nationals. The Calvo Doctrine excluded the right to diplomatic protection of the investor's home State as well as an investor's potential access to international courts or tribunals.[16] In a situation in which a host State's national would have no right to compensation, so would neither the foreigner.

But even though the idea of the Calvo-Doctrine was embodied in Latin American constitutions, different statutes and international treaties between Latin American States,[17] the doctrine never prevailed on the global level.

---

12 Cf. S. Hobe, *The Development of the Law of Aliens and the Emergence of General Principles of Protection Under Public International Law* in M. Bungenberg, et al. (eds.), *International Investment Law: A Handbook* (Baden-Baden: Nomos, 2015), p. 8.

13 Cf. Art. 1 of the Hague Convention (II), *Convention Respecting the Limitation of the Employment of Force for the Recovery of Contract Debts* – 36 Stat. 2241; Treaty Series 537, 18 October 1907.

14 A. Eyffinger, *A Highly Critical Moment: Role and Record of the 1907 Hague Peace Conference*, Netherlands International Law Review 54 (2007), 197–228, at 223.

15 In 1896 the Argentine jurisconsult Carlos Calvo (1826–1906) had published his thoughts on the matter, C. M. Calvo, *Le Droit International: Théorique et Pratique – Tome VI Supplément Général*, 5. ed. (Paris: A. Rousseau, 1896).

16 Cf. C. Brown, *The Evolution of the Regime of International Investment Agreements* in M. Bungenberg, et al. (eds.), *International Investment Law: A Handbook* (Baden-Baden: Nomos, 2015), at 158 f; S. Hobe, *The Development of the Law of Aliens and the Emergence of General Principles of Protection Under Public International Law* in M. Bungenberg, et al. (eds.), *International Investment Law: A Handbook* (Baden-Baden: Nomos, 2015), at 9 f; I. F. I. Shihata, *Towards a Greater Depoliticization of Investment Disputes: The Roles of ICSID and MIGA,* ICSID Review 1 (1986), 1–25, at 1 ff.

17 Cf. I. F. I. Shihata, *Towards a Greater Depoliticization of Investment Disputes,* ICSID Review 1 (1986), at 2 f; J. W. Salacuse, *The Law of Investment Treaties* (Oxford: Oxford University Press, 2015), at 75 ff; N. Blackaby, C. Partasides, A. Redfern and M. Hunter, *Redfern and Hunter on International Arbitration*, 6. ed. (New York, London: Oxford University Press, 2015), at para. 8.02 f.

On the other hand, the major capital-exporting, mostly European, States considered that aliens and their property had to be treated in accordance with an 'international minimum standard' set by customary international law and independent from the host State's domestic legal systems.[18] This approach gained new importance after the 1917 Russian Revolution during which all private property had been abolished and foreign enterprises had been expropriated without any compensation.[19] In light of these developments, international courts and tribunals as well as the US–Mexico General Claims Commission affirmed the existence of an 'international minimum standard' as well as the home State's right to diplomatic protection and rejected the ideas of the Calvo Doctrine.[20]

2 After 1945 – the early beginnings of international investment law

a) Resumption of disagreement

After World War II, the interest of the capital-exporting States in guaranteeing a high level of protection for their investors abroad remained unaltered, especially

---

18 Cf. S. Hobe, *The Development of the Law of Aliens and the Emergence of General Principles of Protection Under Public International Law* in M. Bungenberg, et al. (eds.), *International Investment Law: A Handbook* (Baden-Baden: Nomos, 2015), at 9 f; R. Dolzer and C. Schreuer, *Principles of International Investment Law*, 2. ed. (Oxford: Oxford University Press, 2012), at 3. See famously also, E. Root, *The Basis of Protection to Citizens Residing Abroad,* American Journal of International Law 4 (1910), at 521 f.

19 Cf. H. Dickerson, *Minimum Standards,* (October 2010) in *MPEPIL (Online-Edition)* (Oxford: Oxford University Press); S. Hobe, *The Development of the Law of Aliens and the Emergence of General Principles of Protection Under Public International Law* in M. Bungenberg, et al. (eds.), *International Investment Law: A Handbook* (Baden-Baden: Nomos, 2015), at 9 f; A. F. Lowenfeld, *International Economic Law*, 2. ed. (Oxford: Oxford University Press, 2009), at 470 f.

20 See especially the Permanent Court of Arbitration (PCA) in PCA, *Norwegian Shipowners' Claims.* Award, 13 October 1922, UN Reports of International Arbitral Awards Volume I 307, p. 334. The Permanent Court of International Justice (PCIJ) in PCIJ, *The Mavrommatis Palestine Concessions.* Series A No 2. Judgment, 30 August 1924, guaranteeing the State's right to diplomatic protection; in PCIJ, *German interests in Polish Upper Silesia.* No. 7. Judgment, 25 May 1926, Collection of Judgments Series A, p. 22, confirming that vested rights of foreigners have to be recognized and in PCIJ, *Factory at Chorzów.* No. 9. Judgment (Jurisdiction), 26 July 1927, Collection of Judgments Series A, p. 47, requiring compensation for an illegal seizure of property. See finally, the US–Mexico General Claims Commission affirming the existence of a 'minimum standard' in US–Mexico General Claims Commission, *Neer*, 15 October 1926, UN Reports of International Arbitral Awards Volume IV, para. 4; US–Mexico General Claims Commission, *George W. Hopkins*, 31 March 1926, American Journal of International Law 21 (1927) 160, para. 16; US–Mexico General Claims Commission, *Walter H. Faulkner*, 2 November 1926, American Journal of International Law 21 (1927) 349, para. 10; US–Mexico General Claims Commission, *William T. Way*, 18 October 1928, American Journal of International Law 23 (1929) 466, p. 476. See also S. Hobe, *The Development of the Law of Aliens and the Emergence of General Principles of Protection Under Public International Law* in M. Bungenberg, et al. (eds.), *International Investment Law: A Handbook* (Baden-Baden: Nomos, 2015), at 9 f; A. F. Lowenfeld, *International Economic Law* (Oxford: Oxford University Press, 2009), at 473 ff.

regarding the political risk of the investments, i.e. 'illegitimate' interferences of the respective host States in investment activities.

This position was further enhanced by the adoption of socialist and communist economic policies in many countries and the wave of expropriations occurring in the quarter-century following World War II – especially in the former colonies and the newly emerging communist States in Central and Eastern Europe – most of the time not specifically directed against foreigners but against private property in general.[21] Even though these expropriations were in most instances accompanied by compensation, Western States wanted to balance the risks of foreign investments through a specific legal regime. So, several – unsuccessful – attempts were undertaken to draft a multilateral treaty on investment protection.[22] The only multilateral attempt that had success was the 1965 Convention on the Settlement of Investment Disputes between States and Nationals of other States (ICSID Convention),[23] which established an institutional mechanism for investor-State arbitration but did not create any substantive standards of protection.[24] It was adopted by the large majority of Western European States in the 1960s. The great majority of Eastern European States only joined from the 1990s onwards.[25]

The division between 'capital-exporting' and 'capital-importing' States reached its peak with the attempt to reshape the international economic relations by the

---

21 Cf. A. Newcombe and L. Paradell, *Law and Practice of Investment Treaties: Standards of Treatment* (Alphen aan den Rijn: Kluwer Law International, 2009), at 18 f; A. Reinisch, *Expropriation* in P. Muchlinski, et al. (eds.), *The Oxford Handbook of International Investment Law* (Oxford: Oxford University Press, 2008), pp. 407–58, at p. 408. For a detailed account of nationalizations in post war Eastern Europe, cf. G. White, *Nationalisation of Foreign Property* (London: Stevens & Sons Limited, 1961), at 121 ff. Another famous example is the nationalization of the Suez Canal Company by Egypt in 1956 leading to the Suez Crisis, cf. A. F. Lowenfeld, *International Economic Law* (Oxford: Oxford University Press, 2009), at 483 ff.

22 Inter alia the 1957 International Convention for the Mutual Protection of Private Property Rights in Foreign Countries; the 1959 Abs-Shawcross Draft Convention on Investments Abroad; the 1961 Harvard Convention on the International Responsibility of States for Injuries to Aliens; the 1962 OECD Draft Convention on the Protection of Foreign Property. See C. Brown, *The Evolution of the Regime of International Investment Agreements* in M. Bungenberg, et al. (eds.), *International Investment Law: A Handbook* (Baden-Baden: Nomos, 2015), pp. 161–75; R. Dolzer and C. Schreuer, *Principles of International Investment Law* (Oxford: Oxford University Press, 2012), at 8 f.

23 *Convention on the Settlement of Investment Disputes Between States and Nationals of Other States,* UNTS 575, 18 March 1965, 159.

24 The drafters of the Convention primarily thought of arbitration clauses in investor-State contracts. The possibility of treaty-based investor-State arbitration, however, was anticipated in the *travaux préparatoires* of the Convention, cf. N. Blackaby, C. Partasides, A. Redfern and M. Hunter, *Redfern and Hunter on International Arbitration* (New York, London: Oxford University Press, 2015), para. 8.08.

25 There are a few exceptions to this rule: the ICSID Convention entered into force in Portugal only in 1984 and in Spain in 1994. Cyprus joined the Convention in 1966 and Romania in 1975. Until the end of 1989, the ICSID Convention had entered into force in 89 States. Today 154 States have ratified the ICSID Convention. Cf. ICSID, *Database of ICSID Member States*. https://icsid.worldbank.org/en/Pages/about/Database-of-Member-States.aspx (1 May 2020).

adoption of the 1974 Declaration on the Establishment of a New International Economic Order and the 1974 Charter of Economic Rights and Duties of States,[26] inter alia limiting the compensation requirements in cases of expropriation to domestic legal rules.[27] In contrast to the 1962 Resolution on the Permanent Sovereignty over National Resources,[28] which recognized the existence of an international law standard of compensation for expropriation, the 1974 Charter of Economic Rights and Duties of States restated the idea of the Calvo-Doctrine, providing in Art. 2 (2) lit. c) that each State has the right

> to nationalize, expropriate or transfer ownership of foreign property, in which case appropriate compensation should be paid by the State adopting such measures, taking into account its relevant laws and regulations and all circumstances that the State considers pertinent. In any case where the question of compensation gives rise to a controversy, it shall be settled under the domestic law of the nationalizing State and by its tribunals, unless it is freely and mutually agreed by all States concerned that other peaceful means be sought on the basis of the sovereign equality of States and in accordance with the principle of free choice of means.

The Charter was adopted 120 votes to six, with ten abstentions. The voting behaviour of the current EU Member States or their predecessors was diverse: 14 States voted in favour of the Charter, among them four Western European States.[29] Six Western European States abstained[30] and five Western European States voted against the Charter.[31]

Due to the major differences among States towards FDI, a common global attempt to codify the protection of foreign investments was doomed to failure.

---

26 General Assembly, *Resolution 3201 (S-VI) – Declaration on the Establishment of a New International Economic Order* – UN Doc A/Res/S-6/3201, 1 May 1974; General Assembly, *Resolution 3281(XXIX) – Charter of Economic Rights and Duties of States,* International Legal Materials, 12 December 1974, 251–64.

27 Cf. K. Miles, *The Origins of International Investment Law: Empire, Environment, and the Safeguarding of Capital* (Cambridge: Cambridge University Press, 2013), at 93 ff.

28 General Assembly, *Resolution 1803 (XVII) – Declaration on Permanent Sovereignty over Natural Resources* – UN Doc A/5217, 15, 14 December 1962.

29 Bulgaria, Cyprus, Czechoslovakia (its two successor States the Czech Republic and Slovakia are EU Member States), Finland, the German Democratic Republic, Greece, Hungary, Malta, Poland, Portugal, Romania, Sweden, the Union of Soviet Socialist Republics (three of these Republics have meanwhile acceded to the European Union: Estonia, Latvia and Lithuania) and Yugoslavia (two former Yugoslavian Republics, Slovenia and Croatia, have acceded to the EU), cf. General Assembly, 12 December 1974, *Resolution 3281(XXIX) – Charter of Economic Rights and Duties of States,* International Legal Materials, 1974, p. 265. In 1974, Portugal and Greece found themselves in the process of democratic transition from their former military regime and had thus not yet become 'typical' Western European States, cf. T. Judt, *Postwar: A History of Europe Since 1945* (London: Vintage, 2010), at 504 ff.

30 Austria, France, Ireland, Italy, the Netherlands and Spain.

31 Belgium, Denmark, the German Federal Republic, Luxembourg and the United Kingdom.

Hence, while many areas of international law, especially in international economic law (e.g. trade, with the General Agreement on Tariffs and Trade (GATT),[32] or currency and development-related issues with the International Monetary Fund and the World Bank) developed in a multilateral way, the 'international investment protection regime' took – similarly to international tax law – a different development and is today mainly based on bilateral or plurilateral international investment agreements (hereinafter IIAs), mainly in the form of bilateral investment treaties (hereinafter BITs) without any central authority to ensure its unity and consistency.

b) Advent of bilateral investment treaties

BITs are specialized reciprocal treaties. They contain substantive standards of protection for the respective treaty parties' investors and generally provide for a dispute resolution mechanism. BITs address the so-called dynamic or time inconsistency problem. Before making an investment abroad, investors are in an advantageous position over a potential host State, which generally seeks to attract foreign investments. Investors assess a host State's investment climate based on criteria such as the economic situation, political stability and legal security. Once the investment has been made, however, investors may face considerable legal uncertainty as they become dependent upon the host State's actions not to renege on prior commitments or to change its own legal system.[33] This is especially so as most FDIs have a long-term focus which makes it difficult to swiftly recover the capital of the investment once the investment climate changes. In order to attract foreign investors, most States are thus interested in guaranteeing a stable economic and regulatory environment and to signal their trustworthiness to potential investors. Before the creation of BITs, however, States could not really commit to foreign investors, as they could not credibly bind themselves vis-à-vis individuals or companies falling under their jurisdiction. Thus, the reputation and past behaviour of a potential host State was always of major relevance for every decision to investment abroad. In order to enhance this reputation and to strengthen legal certainty for foreign investors and thus eventually attract FDI flows, many States started negotiating BITs.[34]

---

32 *General Agreement on Tariffs and Trade, Annex 1A, Agreement Establishing the World Trade Organization* – 33 ILM 28.

33 Cf. A. T. Guzman, *Why LDCs Sign Treaties That Hurt Them: Explaining the Popularity of Bilteral Investment Treaties*, Virginia Journal of International Law 38 (1997), 639–88, at 658 ff; L. S. Poulsen, *Politics of Investment Treaty Arbitration: Forth* in T. Schultz and F. Ortino (eds.), *Oxford Handbook of International Arbitration*, 2018. https://papers.ssrn.com/sol3/papers.cfm?abstract_id=2955166 (1 May 2020), at 9 f.

34 Cf. J. R. Basedow, *The EU in the Global Investment Regime: Commission Entrepreneurship, Incremental Institutional Change and Business Lethargy* (London: Routledge, 2018), at 55; Z. Elkins, A. T. Guzman and B. A. Simmons, *Competing for Capital: The Diffusion of Bilateral Investment Treaties, 1960–2000*, International Organization 60 (2006), 811–46, at 278 f.

The first BIT was signed in 1959 between the Federal Republic of Germany and Pakistan.[35] Ever since, Germany continued to negotiate similar treaties, mostly with developing countries, and is a world leader in numbers, with 127 BITs in force at the time of writing.[36] The fact that the Federal Republic of Germany became the forerunner in international investment law is understood to be linked to its lack of international influence and political and military power after World War II, which made the conclusion of BITs the most effective way to protect German investments abroad.[37] Following West Germany's example, some other Western European States set up BIT programs in the subsequent years. But the total number of BITs remained modest, with worldwide 57 treaties in force at the end of the 1960s.[38] These early BITs were – apart from two exceptions – exclusively negotiated between highly developed, capital-exporting European States on the one hand and developing countries on the other hand.[39] The vast majority of Southern, Central and Eastern European Member States started to conclude BITs only in the end of the 1980s and the beginning of the 1990s.[40] The German Democratic Republic never concluded any BITs or multilateral investment agreements. Hence, no questions of State succession to investment treaties arose in the context of the 1990 German reunification.[41] Today, most BITs have at least one

---

35 *Treaty Between the Federal Republic of Germany and Pakistan for the Promotion and Protection of Investments* – 457 UNTS 23. It was signed on 25 November 1959 and entered into force on 28 April 1962.

36 Cf. UNCTAD, *Investment Policy Hub – IIAs.* https://investmentpolicy.unctad.org/international-investment-agreements (1 May 2020).

37 Cf. M. Bungenberg, *A History of Investment Arbitration and Investor-State Dispute Settlement in Germany* in A. de Mestral (ed.), *Second Thoughts: Investor State Arbitration Between Developed Democracies* (Montreal: McGill-Queen's University Press, 2017), pp. 259–83, at 260 f. See also J. Karl, *The Promotion and Protection of German Foreign Investment Abroad,* ICSID Review 11 (1996). Especially emphasizing on the development goals allegedly pursued by the Federal Republic of Germany through its BIT program, J. Alenfeld, *Die Investitionsförderungsverträge der Bundesrepublik Deutschland* (Frankfurt am Main: Athenäum, 1971), at 19 ff.

38 Cf. UNCTAD, *Investment Policy Hub – IIAs.* https://investmentpolicy.unctad.org/international-investment-agreements (1 May 2020). Japan and the United States for instance chose to adapt their existing Treaties on Friendship and Navigation to accommodate investments carried out by their nationals, instead of setting up an own BIT program, cf. J. Karl, *The Promotion and Protection of German Foreign Investment Abroad,* ICSID Review 11 (1996), at 5 f.

39 The two exceptions were the 1964 Iraq–Kuwait BIT and the 1966 Egypt–Kuwait BIT. The most active countries regarding the conclusion of BITs until the end of the 1960s were the Federal Republic of Germany with 26 BITs and Switzerland with 16 BITs.

40 There are, however, two exceptions. Malta started concluding BITs from the 1960s onwards. Romania concluded its first BIT with the United Kingdom in 1976.

41 After the German reunification the BITs that had been concluded by the Federal Republic of Germany were routinely applied by the reunified German State. Germany's ICSID membership was automatically extended to the reunified German State. In great detail, C. J. Tams, *State Succession to Investment Treaties: Mapping the Issues,* ICSID Review 31 (2016), 314–43, at 341; P. Dumberry, *A Guide to State Succession in International Investment Law* (Cheltenham, Northampton: Edward Elgar, 2018), at 106 f. On the effects of the German reunification on international treaties of the two German States, see A. Zimmermann, *Staatennachfolge in völkerrechtliche Verträge: Zugleich ein Beitrag zu den Möglichkeiten und Grenzen völkerrechtlicher Kodifikation* (Berlin: Springer, 2000), at 245 ff; D. Papenfuß, *The Fate of the International Treaties of the GDR Within the Framework of German Unification,* American Journal of International Law 92 (1998), 469–88.

EU Member State as Contracting Party and every EU Member State apart from Ireland is party to at least one BIT.

Before the emergence of BITs providing for investor-State dispute settlement, it was not possible for an investor to bring a claim against a State outside of that State's domestic jurisdiction. Still today, the courts of an investor's home State have generally no jurisdiction over investments taking place in another State and are also limited by the rule of State immunity, which hinders them to prosecute a foreign State according to the principle of *par in parem non habet imperium*.[42] Outside international investment law and apart from some human rights treaty regimes, the only available legal means for investors, in case a State infringes an international legal obligation regarding their treatment, is thus to exhaust all available local remedies and then potentially request diplomatic protection by their home State.[43] The effectiveness of diplomatic protection, however, highly depends on the influence of the home State and its willingness to protect its nationals. Because a State that takes up a case of one of its nationals and resorts to diplomatic protection on that national's behalf, "is in reality asserting its own rights – its right to ensure in the person of its subjects, respect for the rules of international law."[44] Thus, while any State can espouse a claim of its nationals under international law, it has complete discretion in deciding whether to do so and in what form. The home State can discontinue the diplomatic protection at any time. In other words, an individual has no right to diplomatic protection under international law; it is an inherent right of the States only.[45]

The early BITs created new international legal obligations regarding the treatment of foreign investors, which could potentially be invoked through diplomatic protection. Until the very end of the 1960s, however, BITs provided for State-to-State dispute resolution only; either through the establishment of arbitral tribunals or the submission of a dispute to the International Court of Justice (ICJ).[46]

3 Emergence of investor-State arbitration

Inter-State relations are generally complex and cover a wide range of topics, which may render a State reluctant to pursue its nationals' claims through diplomatic protection. Therefore, another possibility to solve investment-related disputes between foreign investors and host States was desired, which at the same time could increase the likeliness to attract and promote FDI. Such a way

---

42 R. Dolzer and C. Schreuer, *Principles of International Investment Law* (Oxford: Oxford University Press, 2012), at 235 f; H. Bubrowski, *Internationale Investitionsschiedsverfahren und nationale Gerichte* (Tübingen: Mohr Siebeck, 2013), at 31 ff.

43 Cf. J. Crawford, *Brownlie's Principles of Public International Law*, 8. ed. (Oxford: Oxford University Press, 2012), at 610 ff., 701 ff; M. N. Shaw, *International Law*, 6. ed. (Cambridge: Cambridge University Press, 2008), at 808 ff.

44 PCIJ, *The Mavrommatis Palestine Concessions*. Series A No 2. Judgment, 30 August 1924, p. 12.

45 Cf. ICJ, *Barcelona Traction*. Judgment, 5 February 1970, ICJ Reports 1970, para. 79.

46 For an extensive overview on BIT-based State to State arbitration, cf. A. Roberts, *State-to-State Investment Treaty Arbitration: A Hybrid Theory of Interdependent Rights and Shared Interpretive Authority,* Harvard International Law Journal 55 (2014), 1–70.

presented itself in the form of 'depoliticized' investor-State dispute settlement, which allowed investors to bring their own claims against the host State without the need to rely on diplomatic protection. The idea was to move investor-State disputes from the political inter-State arena to the judicial investment arbitration arena.[47] Disputes should no longer be decided depending on the balance of power of home and host States but by independent arbitrators bound by the law chosen by these States before the occurrence of a specific dispute. The idea was not only to avoid diplomatic protection proceedings between the respective States but also to avoid domestic proceedings, as domestic courts were often perceived as standing in the 'camp' of the respondent State or as not being capable to provide effective remedies to foreign investors.[48]

Thus, from the end of the 1960s onwards, investor-State arbitration provisions were introduced into BITs. The first such treaty was the 1968 Netherlands–Indonesia BIT.[49] But for two decades investor-State dispute settlement provisions remained rather the exception than the rule and it was only in the 1980s that unqualified State consent to investor-State arbitration was commonly introduced in BITs. Ever since, most BITs contain a general and standing offer to arbitration, which an investor, national of the other State party, can implicitly accept by initiating an arbitration proceeding.

Furthermore, most investor-State arbitration provisions do not require the exhaustion of local remedies but allow investors to 'circumvent' the domestic courts of the host States and to directly bring a claim against the host State of the investment before an international forum. Hence, investor-State arbitration offers an extremely effective dispute settlement mechanism that disconnects the investors from their home States for the enforcement of their rights. It creates a balance between the territorial sovereignty of the host State and the personal sovereignty of the investor's home State. The latter renounces the right to diplomatic

---

47 I. F. I. Shihata, *Towards a Greater Depoliticization of Investment Disputes,* ICSID Review 1 (1986), at 24 f; A. F. Lowenfeld, *Separate Opinion: Corn Products International v United Mexican States, ICSID Case No. ARB (AF)/04/1,* 18 August 2009, at paras. 1 ff.

48 In some countries the domestic judiciary is insufficiently equipped and funded and the judges not well trained and badly payed. This can, in certain cases, lead to a corrupt or partially acting judiciary and prevent a fair proceeding from taking place, especially if large investments are affected and the government tries to influence a judicial decision, cf. H. Bubrowski, *Internationale Investitionsschiedsverfahren und nationale Gerichte* (Tübingen: Mohr Siebeck, 2013), p. 32; R. Dolzer and C. Schreuer, *Principles of International Investment Law* (Oxford: Oxford University Press, 2012), at 23, 235 f; S. W. Schill, *Private Enforcement of International Investment Law* in M. Waibel, et al. (eds.), *The Backlash Against Investment Arbitration: Perceptions and Reality* (Alphen aan den Rijn: Wolters Kluwer, 2010), pp. 29–50, at 33 f. Illustrating the fact that discrimination before domestic courts might also occur in highly developed capital exporting States: C. Dugan, D. Wallace, N. D. Rubins and B. Sabahi, *Investor-State Arbitration* (New York: Oxford University Press, 2008), at 13; S. M. Schwebel, *In Defense of Bilateral Investment Treaties,* Arbitration International 31 (2015), 181–92, at 191.

49 Art. 11 of the BIT referred to the ICSID Convention but required a qualified State's consent. The 1969 Italy–Chad BIT was the first BIT with an unqualified State consent to investor-State arbitration (Art. 7 BIT).

protection, whereas the former allows investors to directly bring a claim against the State at their own discretion. This is a unique feature of investor-State arbitration compared to most other international law regimes. A comparable remedy can only be found in human rights treaties, such as the European Convention of Human Rights (ECHR).

4 Development in the 1990s

After the proliferation of investor-State dispute settlement clauses in the 70s and 80s, international investment law took another important evolutive step in the 1990s, inter alia due to the end of the Cold War, the collapse of the Soviet Union and the emergence of Central and Eastern European States as market economies. Many States, especially the former communist Eastern European States – that had opposed the international economic system[50] and the idea of the 'international minimum standard' for decades – started to conclude IIAs with traditionally capital exporting-States but also among each other and joined the ICSID Convention. The classical dichotomy within the international investment regime between capital-exporting and capital-importing States became increasingly blurred and the number of BITs went from some hundreds to more than 2900 among more than 100 States.[51] Although this number seems impressive at first glance, it represents only 12,5 per cent of the possible number of BITs that could have been concluded among the 193 Member States of the United Nations.[52]

In parallel to this unexpected proliferation of BITs, two important substantive multilateral investment agreements were concluded: the 1992 North American Free Trade Agreement and the 1994 Energy Charter Treaty, which both allowed for the first-time investor-State arbitration proceedings among Western industrialized States. It was also only in the 1990s that investor-State arbitration became relevant. The first known investment arbitration award based on an IIA was rendered in June 1990.[53] Since then, case numbers have increased in a previously unimaginable way: Investors from 80 countries have initiated more than 1000 treaty-based investment arbitration proceedings and 120 States have found themselves being respondent in treaty-based ISDS proceedings.[54]

---

50 Some Southern and Eastern European States had, however, already joined the GATT before the end of the Cold War: Cyprus (1963), Hungary (1973), Malta (1964), Poland (1967) and Romania (1971).
51 UNCTAD, *World Investment Report 2019: Special Economic Zones* (New York, Geneva: United Nations, 2019), at 99.
52 The number of possible BITs among the UN Member States is 18,528. Number of possible BITs $= \frac{(n^2 - n)}{2}$. With n being the number of States.
53 ICSID, *AAPL v Sri Lanka*. Case No. ARB/87/3. Final Award, 27 June 1990.
54 Cf. UNCTAD, *Investment Policy Hub – ISDS*. https://investmentpolicy.unctad.org/investment-dispute-settlement (23 May 2020).

5 Recent developments and global backlash

States continue to conclude IIAs. Even though a global agreement on investment protection is not in sight, there is a new tendency towards so-called mega-regional free trade agreements, such as CETA between the EU and Canada[55] and the TTIP negotiations put on hold between the EU and the United States of America. Like BITs, these treaties pursue the goal to foster economic exchange and to protect investments through specific investment protection chapters but mostly to 'shape the rules of globalization'.[56]

Regarding the sheer number of treaties and ISDS proceedings that have emerged, the 'international investment protection regime' can be described as a success story of the second half of the 20th century. This is also true regarding its effect of an increasing juridification and depoliticization of the relationship between foreign investors and host States and the contribution of international investment law to the development of public international law, strengthening the rights of the individual against the State.[57]

Nevertheless, during the last years international investment law has been confronted with unexpected criticism and scepticism, especially regarding investor-State arbitration, a development often described as global backlash.[58] Its main reasons have been aptly summarized by Advocate General Bot in his Opinion on the compatibility of CETA investor-State dispute settlement provisions with EU law:

> investment arbitration in its traditional form is the subject of criticism, in particular as regards the lack of legitimacy and of guarantees that the arbitrators are independent, the lack of consistency and foreseeability of the awards, the inability to review the award made, the risk of 'regulatory chill' and the high costs of the proceedings.[59]

The backlash cannot be assessed in isolation from the growing critical view on the globalization and especially the behaviour of multinational enterprises. Due

---

55 CETA was signed on 30 October 2016 and provisionally entered into force on 21 September 2017. Based on Art. 218 (11) TFEU Belgium requested an ECJ opinion on the compatibility of the investor-State dispute settlement provisions in CETA with the EU Treaties. The ECJ has found these provisions to be compatible with EU law, ECJ, *CETA*. 1/17. Opinion, 30 April 2019, ECLI:EU:C:2019:341.

56 Cf. C. Malmström, *Shaping Globalisation Through EU Trade Policy*, 9 November 2016. http:// trade.ec.europa.eu/doclib/docs/2016/november/tradoc_155082.pdf (2 May 2020). See also the position of the then German economics minister, cited in M. Bendeich, *Germany's Top Court Hears Challenge to EU-Canada Trade Deal*, Reuters, 12 October 2016. www.reuters.com/arti cle/us-eu-trade-canada-germany/germanys-top-court-hears-challenge-to-eu-canada-trade-deal-idUSKCN12C12C (2 May 2020).

57 Cf. S. M. Schwebel, *In Defense of Bilateral Investment Treaties*, Arbitration International 31 (2015), 186.

58 A designation especially influenced by M. Waibel, et al. (eds.), *The Backlash Against Investment Arbitration: Perceptions and Reality* (Alphen aan den Rijn: Wolters Kluwer, 2010).

59 ECJ, *CETA-Opinion*. 1/17. Opinion of Advocate General Bot, 29 January 2019, ECLI:EU:C:2019:72, para. 15.

to alleged or at least perceived economic imperatives such as continuous growth, fragmentation of production processes or the dynamics of global markets, multinational enterprises (MNEs) increasingly engage in mergers and acquisitions, tax avoidance and even tax evasion strategies, often involving offshore financial centres.[60] These methods have come into the public focus through investigative journalism in cases such as the 2016 *Panama Papers* and the 2017 *Paradise Papers*.[61] Against this backdrop, it is not surprising that more and more States complain about multinational investors abusing their corporate nationality through mailbox-companies, corporate restructuring or 'round-tripping investments' to fall under a specific treaty regime through an entity established in another Contracting Party. According to UNCTAD "for more than 40 per cent of foreign affiliates worldwide, investor nationality is not what it seems."[62] The impact of these practices is that the effective coverage of many IIAs has become much larger than initially intended by the State parties, both due to the increasing complexity of ownership structures and the very broad definitions of 'investor' contained in most treaties.[63]

A new dichotomy has emerged. It is no longer developed and capital-exporting States *versus* developing and capital-importing States but rather States *versus* investors and sometimes also *versus* investor-State tribunals. This is especially linked to the widespread perception that ISDS tribunals are generally deciding in favour of investors,[64] thereby constraining the States' 'right to regulate'[65] and undermining their sovereignty. However, whereas some States – such as Venezuela or Ecuador – have terminated their IIAs or withdrawn from institutional

---

60 Cf. UNCTAD, *World Investment Report 2016: Investor Nationality: Policy Challenges* (New York, Geneva: United Nations, 2016), at 124.

61 Cf. Süddeutsche Zeitung, *Panama Papers*, 2016. https://panamapapers.sueddeutsche.de/en/ (2 May 2020); International Consortium of Investigative Journalists, *The Panama Papers*, 2016. www.icij.org/investigations/panama-papers/ (2 May 2020); The Guardian, *Paradise Papers*, 2017. www.theguardian.com/news/series/paradise-papers (2 May 2020).

62 UNCTAD, *World Investment Report 2016* (New York, Geneva: United Nations, 2016), at 182 ff. In about 75 per cent of cases brought by Dutch investors, the ultimate owners of the claiming corporation are not Dutch and do not engage in substantial business activities in the Netherlands, UNCTAD, *Treaty-Based ISDS Cases Brought Under Dutch IIAs,* 2015. https://investmentpolicy. unctad.org/publications/135/treaty-based-isds-cases-brought-under-dutch-iias-an-overview (2 May 2020), at 1, 15. See also L. F. Reed and J. E. Davis, *Who Is a Protected Investor?* in M. Bungenberg, et al. (eds.), *International Investment Law: A Handbook* (Baden-Baden: Nomos, 2015), pp. 614–37, at 614 f; M. Perkams, *Protection for Legal Persons* in M. Bungenberg, et al. (eds.), *International Investment Law: A Handbook* (Baden-Baden: Nomos, 2015), pp. 638–52, at 644 ff. On this issue and the problem of forum and treaty shopping, see in depth Chapter IV: VII. 2. of this study.

63 Cf. UNCTAD, *World Investment Report 2016* (New York, Geneva: United Nations, 2016), at 185 f. See also Chapter II: II. 1.

64 The official numbers, however, show a different picture: As of 2 May 2020, a total of 674 publicly known investor-State arbitration proceedings have been concluded, 246 or 36.5 per cent of which have been decided in favour of the respondent State and 198 or 29,4 per cent decided in favour of the investor, UNCTAD, *Investment Policy Hub – ISDS.* https://investmentpolicy.unctad.org/ investment-dispute-settlement (23 May 2020).

65 For an extensive overview, see A. Titi, *The right to regulate in international investment law* (Baden-Baden: Nomos, 2014).

mechanisms such as the ICSID Convention,[66] most States maintain their IIAs and do not reject the international investment regime as a whole.[67]

The possibility of highly developed 'Western States' becoming respondents to ISDS proceedings was not anticipated or at least repressed by many State actors. Thus, the recent appearance of high-profile investment arbitration cases directed against some of those[68] has further fuelled the criticism and put the issue on the public agenda. Especially during the TTIP and CETA negotiations the question was raised whether international treaties negotiated among stable and rule of law-abiding States should include ISDS mechanisms and if so, how these should be drafted.[69] Faced with substantive criticism, the EU Commission launched a public consultation on the modalities for Investment Protection and ISDS in TTIP in 2014. It received a total of nearly 150,000 responses by participants from all then 28 EU Member States. The outcome was widespread opposition to ISDS and the TTIP itself. ISDS was described as a threat to democracy and public finance and perceived as unnecessary for investor-State relations between the EU and the US, in view of the strength of the respective judicial systems.[70] In response, the European Parliament suggested to replace the classical ISDS system with a system of standing courts with publicly appointed judges and an appellate mechanism ensuring the consistency of judicial decisions.[71] The EU Commission suggested the creation of a Permanent International Investment

66 Cf. T. Brower, *The Tide of Times? A Sectoral Approach to Latin America's Resistance to the Investor-State Arbitration System,* Virginia Journal of International Law 56 (2016), 183–209; C. Peinhardt and R. L. Wellhausen, *Withdrawing from Investment Treaties but Protecting Investment,* Global Policy 7 (2016), 571–76; UNCTAD, *Denunciation of the ICSID Convention and BITs: Impact on Investor-State Claims,* IIA Issue Notes (2010). While withdrawing from the ICSID Convention, Ecuador has led efforts within the Union of South American nations to create a regional arbitration center as an alternative to ICSID, cf. J. Ketcheson, *Investment Arbitration* in S. Hindelang and M. Krajewski (eds.), *Shifting Paradigms in International Investment Law: More Balanced, Less Isolated, Increasingly Diversified* (Oxford: Oxford University Press, 2016), pp. 97–127, at 109 f.

67 There is, however, a tendency to introduce more precise standards in new IIAs, cf. the 2016 Morocco–Nigeria BIT providing for investor obligations.

68 For instance, ICSID, *Grand River Enterprises v USA.* Award, 12 January 2011; ICSID, *Lone Pine Resources v Canada.* Case No. UNCT/15/2; PCA, *Philip Morris Asia v Australia.* Case No. 2012–12. Award on Jurisdiction and Admissibility, 17 December 2015; ICSID, *Vattenfall v Germany.* Case No. Arb/12/12.

69 Cf. A. de Mestral, *Investor State Arbitration Between Developed Democratic Countries* in A. de Mestral (ed.), *Second Thoughts: Investor State Arbitration Between Developed Democracies* (Montreal: McGill-Queen's University Press, 2017), pp. 9–56.

70 EU Commission, *Report – Online Public Consultation on Investment Protection and Investor-State Dispute Settlement in the TTIP,* 13 January 2015. http://trade.ec.europa.eu/doclib/docs/2015/january/tradoc_153044.pdf (2 May 2020), at p. 14. ISDS was also denounced in the context of the CETA signature by the Belgian region of Wallonia in October 2016 for being anti-democratic and endangering the State's regulatory powers.

71 European Parliament, *Negotiations for the TTIP: European Parliament resolution of 8 July 2015 containing the European Parliament's recommendations to the EU Commission on the negotiations for the TTIP (2014/2228(INI)),* 8 July 2015, at 15 f.

Court or 'Investment Court System' to replace the traditional investor-State arbitration.[72] This approach is also reflected in CETA.[73]

III International investment law within the EU – unexpected difficulties

The global developments in the field of foreign investor protection have not stopped at the European borders. As shown previously, many current EU Member States took the lead in the development of this branch of international law.

The European Union, however, is a unique case: This union of States is the result of an ongoing integration process that started in 1951 with the European Coal and Steel Community and continued with the 1957 Rome Treaty. Since then, its institutional framework has changed several times and many new States have acceded to the Union. After the withdrawal of the United Kingdom, the EU counts 27 Member States, which, for the purposes of the present study, can be categorized in two groups. The first one contains the EU 15, which are the founding Member States of the EU and all those which acceded in the first four accession rounds, including the United Kingdom.[74] The second group consists of the Member States, which acceded to the Union after 2004. It comprises 11 former communist Central and Eastern European States that had been part of the Soviet bloc or even the Soviet Union itself, as well as the two Mediterranean island States Cyprus and Malta.[75]

Within the European legal framework, the EU has been competent for the 'common commercial policy' since the 1957 Rome Treaty and had the competence regarding the pre-establishment phase and the market access of foreign investors, while the Member States kept the competence to conclude post-establishment investment protection treaties.[76] In 1993, with the entry into force of the Maastricht

---

72 Council of the EU, *Negotiating directives for a Convention establishing a multilateral court for the settlement of investment disputes: 12981/17 ADD 1 DCL 1*, 20 March 2018. See also, European Economic and Social Committee, *Opinon on investor protection and investor to state dispute settlement in EU trade and investment agreements with third countries: 2015/C 332/06)*.

73 Section F of Chapter 8 CETA. See also ECJ, *CETA-Opinion*. 1/17. Opinion of Advocate General Bot, 29 January 2019, paras. 7, 24 ff.

74 These are Austria, Belgium, Denmark, Finland, France, Germany, Greece, Ireland, Italy, Luxembourg, Netherlands, Portugal, Spain, Sweden and the United Kingdom.

75 These 13 States are Bulgaria, Croatia, Cyprus, Czech Republic, Estonia, Hungary, Latvia, Lithuania, Malta, Poland, Romania, Slovakia, Slovenia. On the categorization of 'former communist' States, cf. T. Judt, *Postwar: A History of Europe Since 1945* (London: Vintage, 2010), p. 720. States like Bulgaria, Czechoslovakia, Hungary, Poland and Romania were not part of the Soviet Union itself but had acceded as soon as 1949 to the Council for Mutual Economic Assistance aiming to unite the economies of the socialist States, cf. G. Csuka, *The Competitiveness of Central and Eastern European Countries* in G. Gorzelak, et al. (eds.), *Regional Development in Central and Eastern Europe: Development Processes and Policy Challenges* (London: Routledge, 2010), pp. 19–33, at 22 f.

76 See M. Hahn, *EU Rules and Obligations Related to Investment* in M. Bungenberg, et al. (eds.), *International Investment Law: A Handbook* (Baden-Baden: Nomos, 2015), pp. 671–84. See also

Treaty, the EU also obtained a shared competence under the chapter on capital movements to negotiate on international investment liberalization.[77] Based on this division of competences the EU Member States concluded a dense network of more than 1000 extra-EU BITs to support and protect their investors abroad, while the EU itself concluded Free Trade Agreements (hereinafter FTAs) covering the market access to the EU.

With the entry into force of the Lisbon Treaty in 2009, the EU Member States have transferred the exclusive competence on post-establishment protection to the EU pursuant to Art. 207 TFEU and are no longer competent to conclude extra-EU BITs. The EU's competence, however, is shared with the EU Member States regarding provisions on investor-State dispute settlement.[78] Based on Art. 207 TFEU the EU has become a central player in the global investment regime and is currently negotiating investment agreements and FTAs containing investment chapters with several countries.[79] Intra-EU BITs, however, do not fall under the provision of Art. 207 TFEU, which is located within the chapter on EU external relations and has no implication whatsoever on intra-European investment activities.

Thus, the rights of investors operating within the geographic scope of the EU, i.e. investment by an investor from one EU Member State in the territory of another EU Member State (intra-EU investments), do not fall under the exclusive competence of the EU. The rights of intra-EU investors are not codified in one treaty, but in the domestic laws of the respective Member States, intra-EU BITs (1.), the Energy Charter Treaty (2.), primary and secondary EU law including the Charter of Fundamental Rights of the EU (3.), as well as the European Convention on Human Rights (4.). Following their assessment, the evolution of intra-EU ISDS proceedings will be presented (5.), before concluding this chapter with the EU's recently started attempts to assert control over investment protection within Europe (6.).

1 Intra-EU BITs

One hundred and eighty-four out of 325 possible intra-EU BITs (post-Brexit) were in force in March 2018 before the European Court of Justice rendered its

---

C. Titi, *International Investment Law and the European Union: Towards a New Generation of International Investment Agreements*, European Journal of International Law 26 (2015), 639–61, at 642 f.

77 Cf. J. R. Basedow, *The EU in the Global Investment Regime: Commission Entrepreneurship, Incremental Institutional Change and Business Lethargy* (London: Routledge, 2018), p. 37.

78 See ECJ, *EU – Singapore FTA.* 2/15. Opinion, 16 May 2017, ECLI:EU:C:2017:376; ECJ, *CETA-Opinion.* 1/17. Opinion of Advocate General Bot, 29 January 2019, para. 47, see also J. R. Basedow, *The EU in the Global Investment Regime: Commission Entrepreneurship, Incremental Institutional Change and Business Lethargy* (London: Routledge, 2018), at 74 ff.

79 For an overview on EU FTAs, see European Commission, *Overview of FTA and Other Trade Negotiations.* https://trade.ec.europa.eu/doclib/docs/2006/december/tradoc_118238.pdf (2 May 2020).

Achmea judgment.[80] The 12 BITs the United Kingdom had concluded with other EU Member States turned into extra-EU BITs with Brexit taking effect on February 1, 2020. Apart from two exceptions,[81] intra-EU BITs have either been concluded between States of the first group of 'old Western European' States, or EU 15, and the second group (in total 130 BITs) or between States within the second group of Southern and Eastern European Member States (54 BITs). Notwithstanding Brexit, the former 12 British intra-EU BITs are analysed in the following, as they constituted an integral part of the net of intra-EU BITs and contributed to the conflict between the EU legal order and international investment law.

No intra-EU BIT has ever been concluded between two current Member States of the EU. Every single treaty was either concluded by 'two non-EU Member States' who later became EU Member States or by one 'already EU Member State' and a 'not-yet EU Member State'. But some intra-EU BITs entered into force closely before the accession of 'not-yet EU Member States' to the EU.[82] Thus, intra-EU BITs are an accession phenomenon as they only turn into intra-EU treaties in the moment of the admission of a new Member State.

In light of the ECJ's *Achmea* judgment,[83] the Member States' political declarations on its effects[84] and the Multilateral Agreement for the Termination of

---

80 The formula to calculate this number is: Number of possible intra-EU BITs $= \frac{(n^2 - n)}{2}$. With n being the number of Member States.

    As Belgium and Luxembourg have always conclude joined BITs within the *Belgium Luxembourg Economic Union* (BLEU) as one entity, there are – post Brexit – 26 State entities within the EU possibly concluding intra-EU BITs, which leads to the result of 325 possible treaties.

    The reader should note that the ten BITs, which Czechoslovakia concluded with Western European States are counted as 18 treaties, as both the Czech Republic and Slovakia succeeded to the rights and obligations of Czechoslovakian treaties concluded with other European States as of 1 January 1993. In great detail, C. J. Tams, *State Succession to Investment Treaties,* ICSID Review 31 (2016), at 330 f; P. Dumberry, *A Guide to State Succession in International Investment Law* (Cheltenham, Northampton: Edward Elgar, 2018), paras. 3.10 ff., 6.05 ff. See also M. Craven, *The Decolonization of International Law: State Succession and the Law of Treaties* (Oxford: Oxford University Press, 2007), at 236 f., 241 f; A. Aust, *Modern Treaty Law and Practice*, 3. ed. (Cambridge: Cambridge University Press, 2013), at 332 f. In difference to the BITs however, a succession to Czechoslovakia's ICSID membership was precluded so that both the Czech Republic and Slovakia had to join the ICSID Convention as new parties in 1993 and 1994 respectively, cf. C. J. Tams, *State Succession to Investment Treaties,* ICSID Review 31 (2016), 323.

81 The Federal Republic of Germany concluded a BIT with Greece which entered into force in 1963 and one with Portugal that entered into force in 1982.

82 The 2005 Bulgaria–Lithuania BIT is especially remarkable. It was signed in 2005, after Lithuania's accession to the EU and one year after the termination of the accession talks with Bulgaria and entered into force in 2006, i.e. one year before Bulgaria's accession to the EU.

83 ECJ, *Achmea.* C-284/16. Judgment, 6 March 2018, ECLI:EU:C:2018:158.

84 Representatives of 22 EU Member States, *Declaration on the Legal Consequences of the Judgment of the ECJ in Achmea and on Investment Protection in the EU,* 15 January 2019; Representatives of Finland, Luxembourg, Malta, Slovenia and Sweden, *Declaration on the Enforcement of the Judgement of the ECJ in Achmea and on Investment Protection in the EU,* 16 January 2019; Representative of Hungary, *Declaration on the Legal Consequences of the Judgment of the ECJ in Achmea and on Investment Protection in the EU,* 16 January 2019.

intra-EU BITs signed by 23 Member States in May 2020,[85] it is more than unlikely that current EU Member States will break with tradition and start to conclude new BITs among each other. Nonetheless, up to 140 further intra-EU BITs could emerge through the accession of new States to the EU, if they are not terminated prior to the new Member States' accession.[86]

The following section will provide an overview on the different generations of intra-EU BITs, including intra-EU BITs concluded by the United Kingdom – as these were part of the intra-EU BITs until Brexit.

From the vantage point of the present, the first intra-EU BIT was the one between the Federal Republic of Germany and Greece, which was signed in 1961 and entered into force two years later. In the ensuing 25 years, until 1986, only seven further BITs were concluded between States that are currently members of the EU, five of them with Malta as a party.[87] These eight BITs are described as 'first generation' intra-EU BITs. They do not contain any investor-State arbitration provision and apart from the 1974 Federal Republic of Germany–Malta, as well as the 1980 Federal Republic of Germany–Portugal BIT, which provide for State-to-State arbitration in case a dispute cannot be settled through diplomatic means, do not provide for any dispute settlement procedure at all.

From 1986 onwards, intra-EU BITs started to include ISDS provisions. However, the great majority of the treaties did not provide for comprehensive ISDS for every dispute arising out of a BIT but limited the scope of application to some specific substantive breaches (mostly expropriation only).[88] These treaties are described as 'second generation' intra-EU BITs.

The majority of intra-EU BITs, however, can be categorized in the 'third generation'. These treaties contain classical ISDS provisions that are not limited to specific substantive protection clauses but can be invoked in the case of any violation of a substantive standard provided for in the BIT.[89]

85 Agreement for the Termination of Bilateral Investment Treaties between the Member States of the European Union, signed on 5 May 2020 by 23 Member States.

86 Seven States have prospects of EU accession: Albania, Bosnia and Herzegovina, Kosovo, Montenegro, North Macedonia, Serbia and Turkey. Currently 21 BITs are in force between Albania and EU Member States as well as four BITs between Albania and other accession candidates. Bosnia and Herzegovina has concluded 18 BITs with EU Member States and four with candidate States; North Macedonia has concluded 19 and five BITs respectively; Montenegro 16 and three respectively; Kosovo has not concluded any BIT; Serbia has concluded 22 BITs with EU Member States and five BITs with accession candidates and Turkey 23 and five BITs respectively. Iceland has concluded two BITs with EU Member States. However, Iceland's application status is currently frozen after the withdrawal of its EU accession application.

87 1967 Italy–Malta BIT; 1974 Federal Republic of Germany–Malta BIT; 1976 France–Malta BIT; 1980 Denmark–Romania BIT; 1980 Federal Republic of Germany–Portugal BIT; 1984 Bulgaria–Malta BIT and 1984 Netherlands–Malta BIT.

88 See for example: Art. 11 of the 1986 Federal Republic of Germany–Hungary BIT; Art. 8 of the 1987 UK–Poland BIT or Art. 8 of the 1988 Belgium Luxembourg Economic Union–Bulgaria BIT.

89 The very first intra-EU 'third generation' treaty, offering unrestricted access to international arbitration for foreign investors, was the 1986 UK–Malta BIT.

In the 1990s, 149 new intra-EU BITs have been concluded. This impressive proliferation was especially linked to the collapse of the Soviet Bloc and the transformation of most Central and Eastern European economies from a centrally planned and State-driven economic model, dominated by large State corporations, to market economies. A new legal framework was needed to safeguard the functioning of these recently established economies. This comprised the aspired integration into the then European Community, the accession to the Council of Europe and other international organizations such as the WTO, the North Atlantic Treaty Organization (NATO) and the Organization for Economic Cooperation and Development (OECD), the adoption of domestic laws to promote a market-oriented economy and to attract and protect investors, as well as the conclusion of IIAs.[90]

Due to a lack of capital, technology and expertise in these States, foreign direct investments were desired. They were understood as being crucial for the transformation and restructuring of the Central and Eastern European economy, thus creating new business opportunities for Western European investors. Against this backdrop, the European Union promoted to conclusion of so-called Europe Agreements with the accession candidates, in order to initiate the steps necessary to prepare an application for EU membership, inter alia by fostering the accession candidates' economic development and to complement their transition to the market economy.[91] Within these agreements, the EU encouraged the conclusion of BITs between its Member States and the former communist accession candidates, establishing an association between the EU and its Member States on the one hand and the accession candidates Hungary,[92] Poland,[93] Romania,[94] Bulgaria,[95] Slovakia,[96] the Czech Republic,[97] Latvia,[98] Lithuania,[99] Estonia,[100] Slovenia[101]

---

90 Cf. B. Lippert, *From Pre-Accession to EU-Membership* in B. Lippert and P. Becker (eds.), *Towards EU-membership: Transformation and integration in Poland and the Czech Republic* (Bonn: Europa-Union-Verl., 1998), pp. 17–62, at 23 ff. See also G. Csuka, *The Competitiveness of Central and Eastern European Countries* in G. Gorzelak, et al. (eds.), *Regional Development in Central and Eastern Europe* (London: Routledge, 2010).

91 Cf. F. Hoffmeister, *General Principles of the Europe Agreements and the Association Agreements with Cyprus, Malta and Turkey* in A. Ott and K. Inglis (eds.), *Handbook on European Enlargement: A Commentary on the Enlargement Process* (The Hague: TMC Asser Press, 2002), pp. 349–66; B. Lippert, *From Pre-Accession to EU-Membership* in B. Lippert and P. Becker (eds.), *Towards EU-membership* (Bonn: Europa-Union-Verl., 1998), at 23 ff.

92 Art. 72 (2) of the Europe Agreement with Hungary of 31 December 1993, OJ 1993 L 347/2 ff.

93 Art. 73 (2) of the Europe Agreement with Poland of 31 December 1993, OJ 1993 L 348/2 ff.

94 Art. 74 (2) of the Europe Agreement with Romania, of 31 December 1994, OJ 1994 L 357/2 ff.

95 Art. 74 (2) of the Europe Agreement with Bulgaria, of 31 December 1994, OJ 1994 L 358/2 ff.

96 Art. 74 (2) of the Europe Agreement with Slovakia of 31 December 1994, OJ 1994 L 359/2 ff.

97 Art. 74 (2) of the Europe Agreement with the Czech Republic of 31 December 1994, OJ 1994 L 360/2 ff.

98 Art. 74 (2) of the Europe Agreement with Latvia of 2 February 1998, OJ 1998 L 26/3 ff.

99 Art. 74 (2) of the Europe Agreement with Lithuania of 20 February 1998, OJ 1998 L 51/3 ff.

100 Art. 73 (2) of the Europe Agreement with Estonia of 9 March 1998, OJ 1998 L 68/3 ff.

101 Art. 75 (2) of the Europe Agreement with Slovenia of 26 February 1999, OJ 1999 L 51/3 ff.

and Croatia[102] on the other. A typical BIT promoting clause can be found in the 1998 Europe Agreement with Estonia. Its Art. 73 entitled Investment Promotion and Protection reads

> (1) Cooperation shall aim at maintaining and, if necessary, improving a legal framework and a favourable climate for private investment and its protection, both domestic and foreign, which is essential to economic and industrial reconstruction and development in Estonia. The cooperation shall also aim to encourage and promote foreign investment and privatisation in Estonia.
>
> (2) The particular aims of cooperation shall be:
>
> – [...] the conclusion, where appropriate, with Member States of bilateral agreements for the promotion and protection of investment.

In the years that followed the Europe Agreements, many BITs were concluded which have become intra-EU BITs in the meanwhile. These treaties, however, have played no role in the actual accession process. The accession treaties[103] did not address the question of BITs at all. The latter remained in force and unquestioned after the accession. This is a strong indication that the EU Commission and the Member States did not anticipate the possible incompatibility of such BITs and their ISDS clauses with EU law at the time of accession but only realized it when the number of ISDS proceedings started to increase. Another indication in that regard is that the 2005 Europe Agreement with Croatia – which acceded to the EU on July 1, 2013 – also propagated the conclusion of BITs, although the agreement was concluded after the accession of eight other Central and Eastern European States to the EU and thus, after the emergence of an important number of intra-EU investor-State arbitration proceedings.

The distribution of intra-EU BITs among EU Member States was rather uneven before the *Achmea* judgment in March 2018:[104] While nine Central and Eastern European States were party to more than 20 intra-EU BITs in force respectively, Ireland and Italy had terminated all their intra-EU BITs, and Cyprus was only party to eight intra-EU BITs. With 26 intra-EU BITs, the Czech Republic had concluded a BIT with every other EU Member State (one being with the Belgium-Luxembourg Economic Union) and the UK. Seven of them, however, had already been terminated. Bulgaria and Poland with respectively 23 BITs had the most intra-EU BITs in force. The EU 15 group was led by Belgium and Luxembourg

---

102 Art. 85 (2) of the Europe Agreement with Croatia of 28 January 2005, OJ 2005 L 26/3 ff.

103 Cf. *Accession Treaty Between the EU and Its Member States and the Czech Republic, the Republic of Estonia, the Republic of Cyprus, the Republic of Latvia, the Republic of Lithuania, the Republic of Hungary, the Republic of Malta, the Republic of Poland, the Republic of Slovenia and the Slovak Republic,* Official Journal of the European Union 46, 2003, 3 ff; *Accession Treaty Between the EU and Its Member States and the Republic of Bulgaria and Romania,* Official Journal of the European Union 48, 2005, 3 ff; *Accession Treaty Between the EU and Croatia,* Official Journal of the European Union 55, 24 April 2012, 10 ff.

104 Figure 1.1 and Figure 1.2.

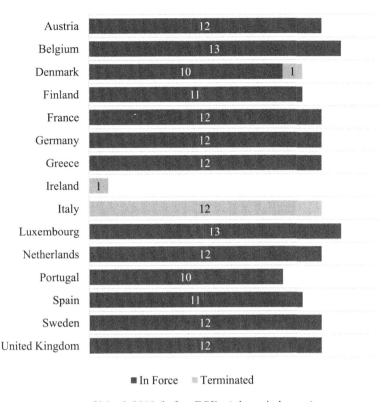

as of March 2018 (before ECJ's *Achmea* judgment)

Figure 1.1 Intra-EU BITs – EU 15 Member States

with 13 intra-EU BITs concluded under the umbrella of the Belgium Luxembourg Economic Union.

2 Energy Charter Treaty

The Energy Charter Treaty (ECT) is another IIA of great importance for intra-EU investments. It is the first multilateral treaty in the energy sector covering trade and environmental aspects of energy, transit and investment protection.[105] The particularity of energy investments is that they are mostly large, long-term projects that need a long period for the recovery of the investment and involve a

---

105 The part on investment protection was highly influenced by existing BITs and especially the UK Model BIT, cf. with further references, T. Roe and M. Happold, *Settlement of Investment Disputes Under the Energy Charter Treaty* (Cambridge: Cambridge University Press, 2011), at 15.

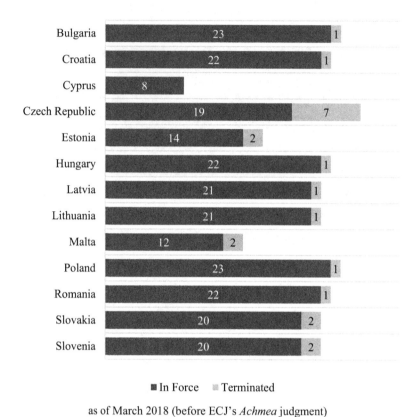

■ In Force ▨ Terminated

as of March 2018 (before ECJ's *Achmea* judgment)

Figure 1.2 Intra-EU BITs – Member States that acceded from 2004 onwards

considerable degree of public or national interests, often characterized by a significant influence of the State, which also creates the (political) risk of later interference in the project.[106]

The leading idea behind the drafting of the ECT was to enhance the East-West cooperation and to attract FDI in the energy sector of Eastern European States from Western European investors, thereby assuring the energy supply for the Western European States and improving the EU's energy security as half of its energy came from outside its borders.[107] The ECT was inspired by its forerunner, the legally non-binding European Energy Charter adopted in 1991, which aimed at improved security and efficiency of energy supply and production and

---

106 P. D. Cameron, *International Energy Investment Law: The pursuit of stability* (Oxford, New York: Oxford University Press, 2010), at xlvii.
107 See J. R. Basedow, *The EU in the Global Investment Regime: Commission Entrepreneurship, Incremental Institutional Change and Business Lethargy* (London: Routledge, 2018), at 114 ff.

the promotion of an efficient energy market based inter alia on the principle of non-discrimination. Its signatories committed themselves to work together to supplement the European Energy Charter with a treaty setting out general rules on energy trade and cooperation. This led to the adoption of the ECT, which entered into force on April 16, 1998. Due to the United States' influence and its concerns about a possible monopolization of the access to the former Soviet Union's energy sector, this originally European project had become one with a potential global reach, even though limited to the energy sector.[108] The United States, however, never became a Contracting Party to the ECT, which is today the most ratified IIA with 48 Contracting Parties, comprising also several non-European States such as Afghanistan, Mongolia and Japan.[109] The European Union and Euratom as well as all EU Member States, apart from Italy, which withdrew from the treaty in 2014,[110] are Contracting Parties to the ECT. Thus, regarding intra-EU relations only, the ECT can be described as an intra-EU multilateral investment treaty, even though it is at the same time an extra-EU treaty regarding non-EU Member States.

The ECT's importance is also reflected in its investor-State arbitration mechanism, which is steadily gaining importance: Since it was invoked for the first time in an ISDS proceeding in 2001,[111] more than 120 proceedings have been initiated on the basis of the ECT.[112]

3 EU investor protection

Within the EU every investment from abroad is subject to the free movement of capital codified in Arts. 63 ff. TFEU, which prohibits all restrictions on the transfer of capital between Member States. If an investment leads to an establishment in the EU, which is understood as an independent, economic activity, including the foundation of a company and the management of already established companies, the freedom of establishment, Art. 49 TFEU, is also applicable. The fundamental freedoms, however, do not protect investments *per se* but guarantee that the movement of capital and the establishment of economic entities by EU nationals in other Member States is kept free from restrictions.

Apart from the TFEU, the Charter of Fundamental Rights of the European Union plays an important role in investment protection. It contains some human rights guarantees applicable to investors, such as the freedom to conduct a business (Art. 16 EU Charter) and the right to property (Art. 17 EU Charter), which

---

108 Cf. T. Roe and M. Happold, *Settlement of Investment Disputes Under the ECT* (Cambridge: Cambridge University Press, 2011), p. 9.
109 Many important energy-producing countries such as Canada, China, Nigeria and the USA are observers to the Energy Charter Conference, cf. Energy Charter Treaty, *Signatories and Contracting Parties*. https://energycharter.org/process/energy-charter-treaty-1994/energy-charter-treaty/signatories-contracting-parties/ (2 May 2020).
110 Italy's withdrawal from the ECT took effect in January 2016.
111 ICSID, *AES Summit Generation v Hungary (I)*. Case No. ARB/01/4.
112 Cf. *List of All Investment Dispute Settlement Cases under the ECT.* https://energycharter.org/what-we-do/dispute-settlement/all-investment-dispute-settlement-cases/ (2 May 2020).

might be invoked both to protect private economic interests affected by a State's acts, as well as to restrict such economic interests, in order to give effect to a conflicting fundamental right.

4 European Convention on Human Rights

Foreign investments within Europe are also protected by the European Convention on Human Rights and the European Court of Human Rights to which every EU Member State is a party.

Regarding the substantive protection, especially the right to a fair trial (Art. 6 ECHR), the right to an effective remedy (Art. 13 ECHR) and the protection of property (Art. 1 of the first Protocol to the ECHR) can be invoked by foreign investors against host States. The latter protects natural and legal persons, independent of their seat, against direct and indirect expropriations that are not in the public interests, not based on a legal foundation or are in violation of international law obligations such as the principle of proportionality, the obligation to provide for a prompt and adequate compensation and the prohibition of discriminatory treatment.[113]

The ECHR also provides for a State-to-State dispute settlement mechanism (Art. 33 ECHR), an individual application mechanism (Art. 34 ECHR) and the provision on the binding force and execution of judgments (Art. 46 ECHR). The individual application to the ECtHR, however, requires the exhaustion of local remedies (Art. 35 ECHR). Furthermore, remedies available to individual claimants are not as effectively enforceable and only allow for 'just satisfaction to the injured parties', namely financial compensation, under very narrow conditions (Art. 41 ECHR).[114] Nonetheless, the ECtHR has been suggested on several occasions as an alternative forum for investment disputes.[115]

---

113 See C. Grabenwarter, *European Convention on Human Rights: Commentary* (München: C. H. Beck, 2014), at 367 ff; B. Rainey, E. Wicks and C. Ovey, *The European Convention on Human Rights: Jacobs, White and Ovey*, 7. ed. (Oxford: Oxford University Press, 2017), at 547 ff.

114 Cf. for a great overview, B. Rainey, E. Wicks and C. Ovey, *The European Convention on Human Rights: Jacobs, White and Ovey* (Oxford: Oxford University Press, 2017), at 51 f; W. A. Schabas, *The European Convention on Human Rights: A Commentary* (Oxford: Oxford University Press, 2015), at 830 ff. The ECtHR has a wide discretion regarding the assessment whether monetary compensation is 'necessary' to be awarded to a claimant. It found so, for example in the investor-State dispute in *Yukos v Russia*, in which Russia was ordered to pay € 1,900,000,000 to the shareholders of Yukos, ECtHR, *Yukos v Russia*. Application no. 14902/04. Judgment, 31 July 2014.

115 See for example, C. Tomuschat, *The European Court of Human Rights an Investment Protection* in C. Binder, et al. (eds.), *International Investment Law for the 21st Century: Essays in Honour of Christoph Schreuer* (Oxford: Oxford University Press, 2009), pp. 636–56; C. Pfaff, *Investitionsschutz durch regionalen menschenrechtlichen Eigentumsschutz am Beispiel der Europäischen Menschenrechtskonvention (EMRK)* in C. Knahr and A. Reinisch (eds.), *Aktuelle Probleme und Entwicklungen im internationalen Investitionsrecht* (Stuttgart: Boorberg, 2008), pp. 163–92. See also with a detailed analysis of the investment-related cases before the ECtHR, E. Decaux and M. Kucera, *La Jurisprudence de la Cour Européenne des Droits de l'Homme en Matière de Protection des Investissements* in C. Leben (ed.), *Droit international des investissements et de l'arbitrage transnational* (Paris: Editions Pedone, 2015), pp. 501–29.

5 Intra-EU investor-state arbitration

Running parallel to the development of intra-EU IIAs, however a bit delayed, was the emergence of investor-State arbitration proceedings within the EU. Although some EU Member States have faced investment arbitration claims brought by non-EU investors, as of May 23, 2020, of all publicly known 250 treaty-based investor-State arbitration proceedings involving an EU Member State as respondent, 190, or 76 per cent, were initiated by EU investors and are thus intra-European investor-State arbitration proceedings.[116] These proceedings will be categorized into three different types of investor-State disputes within the EU – pre-accession cases, transition cases and intra-EU cases:

- **Pre-accession cases**
  Investor-State arbitration proceedings initiated before both State parties to the IIA have acceded to the EU and which have been terminated through an award, settlement or discontinuation before the date of accession of the second State to the EU.
- **Transition cases**
  Investor-State arbitration proceedings initiated before both State parties to the IIA have become an EU Member States but only terminated or still pending after the second State has become an EU Member State.
- **Intra-EU cases**
  Investor-State arbitration proceedings initiated after both State parties to the treaty have become an EU Member State. These cases represent the great majority and form the core of the present study. This differentiation of ISDS proceedings, is based solely on procedural considerations. Therefore, cases initiated after the accession of both treaty parties to the EU are counted as intra-EU cases even if a dispute concerns pre-accession factual matters.[117]

1992 marks the year of the first ISDS proceeding initiated in the EU's current geographical scope. It was the 'pre-accession case' *Saar Papier v Poland*,[118] based on the 1989 Federal Republic of Germany–Poland BIT. The final award was rendered in 1995, nine years before Poland's accession to the EU, but 32 years after the entry into force of the first intra-EU BIT concluded between the Federal Republic of Germany and Greece.

---

116 Cf. UNCTAD, *Investment Policy Hub – ISDS*. https://investmentpolicy.unctad.org/investment-dispute-settlement (23 May 2020).

117 The decisive date in this regard, is the date of accession. Thus, a case such as ICSID, *Riet v Croatia*. Case No. ARB/13/12. Award, 2 November 2016, based on the 2001 BLEU–Croatia BIT and was initiated on 21 June 2013, is not count treated as an intra-EU case, as Croatia only officially acceded to the EU on 1 July 2013. The same is also true for ICSID, *OKO Pankki Oyj v Estonia*. Case No. ARB/04/6. Award, 19 November 2007, based on the 1992 Estonia–Germany and the 1992 Estonia -Finland BIT, which was registered on 20 February 2004, as Estonia acceded to the EU only on 1 May 2004.

118 Ad Hoc Arbitration, *Saar Papier v Poland*. Final Award, 16 October 1995.

In other words, within the first three decades of the existence of BITs between current EU Member States these treaties have played almost no role, as neither investor-State nor State-to-State disputes based on them were initiated. This, however, is also linked to the fact that before 1986 no intra-EU BIT provided for investor-State arbitration.[119] The first intra-EU proceedings based on the ECT were only initiated in 2001.[120]

Until the end of 2014 only 17 ISDS proceedings had been initiated between investors from current EU Member States as claimants and other current EU Member States as respondents, compared to 158 proceedings initiated between 2005 and the end of 2018.[121]

The first intra-EU ISDS proceeding was the case *Eastern Sugar v Czech Republic*,[122] which was initiated in 2004 and already raised the question on the validity of intra-EU BITs and their compatibility with EU law.[123] Until 2014, the great majority of intra-EU ISDS proceedings was based on intra-EU BITs. Ever since, most cases have been based on the ECT. This makes the ECT the most often invoked intra-EU IIA as of the time of writing, with more than 70 intra-EU ISDS proceedings based on the ECT.[124]

As of May 23, 2020, of the 161 known intra-EU ISDS proceedings, 27 have been decided in favour of the investor, 44 have been decided in favour of the respondent State, three cases have been decided in favour of neither party as liability has been found but no damages have been awarded, 19 cases have been settled or discontinued,[125] 67 are pending and for one case the data is not available.

Every EU Member State is or at least has been involved as a treaty party in the international investment law regime.[126] The participation in investor-State arbitration proceedings, however, differs to a high degree among the different

---

119 The two first (intra-EU) BITs providing for ISDS were the Malta–UK BIT, which was signed and entered into force on 4 October 1986, and the Bulgaria–Federal Republic of Germany BIT, which was signed earlier, on 12 April 1986, but only entered into force on 10 March 1988.

120 ICSID, *AES Summit Generation v Hungary (I)*. Case No. ARB/01/4 and SCC Arbitration, *Nykomb Synergetics v Latvia*. Arbitration No. 118/2001.

121 As the proceedings are generally confidential and some arbitration institutions do not publish information on every proceeding administered by them and some cases are pure ad hoc cases without an administering institution, the real figure may be much higher.

122 SCC Arbitration, *Eastern Sugar B.V. v Czech Republic*. SCC No. 088/2004. Partial Award, 27 March 2007.

123 The objections raised by the Czech Republic were eventually all rejected by the arbitral tribunal, which decided the case in favour of the investor, cf. ibid., para. 181, 368.

124 UNCTAD, *Investment Policy Hub – ISDS*. https://investmentpolicy.unctad.org/investment-dispute-settlement (23 May 2020).

125 The present study counts a case as settled if there is public information that the parties reached an agreement and withdrew the case before a final ruling or if the ruling itself contains a settlement by the parties. If the parties reach a settlement during proceedings, they generally revoke the mandate of the arbitral tribunal thereby terminating the jurisdiction and the powers conferred to the arbitral tribunal.

126 Ireland and Italy, however, have terminated all their intra-EU BITs and Italy has withdrawn from the ECT.

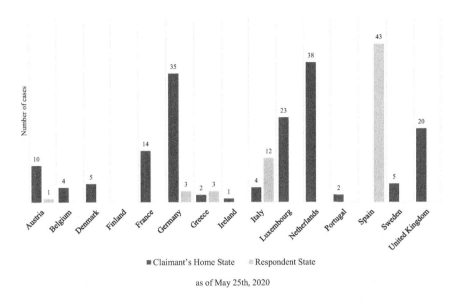

as of May 25th, 2020

Figure 1.3 EU 15 Member States' involvement in intra-EU ISDS proceedings

countries.[127] Although several EU Member States have faced a massive caseload initiated by foreign investors, ten EU Member States as well as the United Kingdom have so far never been respondent to an intra-EU investor-State arbitration proceeding. Of the 161 known intra-EU ISDS cases, 20 were litigated between investors and States from the countries that acceded to the EU since 2004, i.e. disputes among investors from the South-Eastern and Central European Member States and other South-Eastern and Central European Member States. Fifty-seven disputes arose among EU 15 investors and EU 15 Member States. Seventy-nine cases were initiated by EU 15 investors against the post-2004 accession States. And five cases were initiated by post-2004 accession State investors against EU 15 Member States.

By far the most cases have been initiated by Dutch and German investors, while investors from the newer EU Member States have only seldomly initiated intra-EU investor-State arbitration proceedings.[128] Regarding the State involvement, the Central and Eastern European States of the 'second group' have mostly been the respondents in intra-EU proceedings. They have so far been sued at least 99 times, in contrast to 62 cases brought against EU 15 States. The two EU Member States which found themselves the most in the respondent's position are the

127 Figure 1.3 and Figure 1.4.
128 As there can be several claimants in one ISDS proceeding against a host State the numbers of claimants are significantly higher than those of respondents.

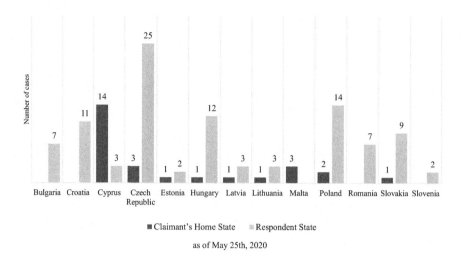

Figure 1.4 Member States' (post 2003 accession) involvement in intra-EU ISDS proceedings

Czech Republic, which has been the respondent in at least 25 proceedings, and Spain, which was sued in total 43 times by intra-EU investors. The Spanish cases were all based on the ECT and, apart from one exception,[129] all initiated by EU 15 investors. Thus, all in all, the intra-EU IIA regime is mainly used by investors stemming from EU 15 States. While IIAs are based on the principle of reciprocity, it is remarkable that so far only five cases against EU 15 States have been initiated before investor-State arbitration tribunals by investors stemming from the South-Eastern EU Member States.[130]

6 *The EU's attempts to assert control over intra-EU investor protection*

In light of the steadily growing number of intra-EU investor-State arbitration proceedings, several EU Member States as well as the EU Commission have increasingly questioned the validity of intra-EU IIAs but also their applicability and especially their benefit within an integrated economic union like the EU. The

129 The case ICSID, *OperaFund Eco-Invest v Spain*. Case No. ARB/15/36, was initiated by an investor from Malta.
130 ICSID, *Bank of Cyprus v Greece*. Case No. ARB/17/4, initiated by a Cypriot investor; ICSID, *OperaFund Eco-Invest v Spain*. Case No. ARB/15/36, initiated by Maltese and Swiss investors; ICSID, *Belegging-Maatschappij "Far East" v Austria*. Case No. ARB/15/32, initiated by a Maltese investor; ICSID, *Cyprus Popular Bank v Greece*. Case No. ARB/14/16, initiated by a Cypriot investor and ICSID, *Poštová Banka v Greece*. ICSID Case No. ARB/13/8. Award, 9 April 2015, initiated by Cypriot and Slovak investors.

questions of the compatibility of intra-EU BITs with EU law became relevant only in 2004 with the accession of ten new Member States to the EU, turning the previously concluded extra-EU BITs into intra-EU BITs. From that moment onwards, both EU law and international investment law were in risk of colliding with each other.

A first evidence of critical percipience of intra-EU BITs can be found in the Economic and Financial Committee's (EFC)[131] Annual Report 2006 in which it is claimed that parts of the BITs content had been superseded by EU law and that the Member States were invited to review the need for such agreements.[132] From that point on, every single EFC Report addressed the issue: In 2008 the EFC reported that the EU Commission had requested Member States to terminate their BITs.[133] In 2012, the Commission organized expert group meetings to work on a possible mechanism for investment protection within the EU.[134] In 2015, the EU Commissioner for Financial Services explained that intra-EU BITs were "outdated" and "no longer necessary in a single market of 28 Member States".[135]

The EU Commission questioned whether there was a need for the 'international investment protection regime' within the scope of application of EU law, as the latter allegedly offered a comparably high degree of protection.[136] Together with some Member States also opposing intra-EU IIAs, the Commission followed two lines of argument to reject the arbitral tribunals' jurisdiction, which it raised as *amicus curiae* in at least 20 intra-EU investor-State arbitration proceedings:[137]

---

131 The Economic and Financial Committee is an advisory body of the EU, which by virtue of Art. 134 TFEU is set up to "promote coordination of the policies of Member States to the full extent needed for the functioning of the internal market." It provides opinions at the request of the Council of the EU or the EU Commission. The Committee is composed of senior officials appointed by the EU Member States, the European Central Bank and the EU Commission.

132 *2006 Annual EFC Report on the Movement of Capital and the Freedom of Payments,* 15 November 2006, at para. 16. Apparently, the EU Commission already addressed the potential incompatibility of pre-accession BITs turning into intra-EU BITs with EU law in 1998. This was at least alleged in a letter by the EU Commission's Internal Market and Services Unit addressed to the Czech Deputy Minister of Finance in 2006, cited in, SCC Arbitration, *Eastern Sugar B.V. v Czech Republic.* SCC No. 088/2004. Partial Award, 27 March 2007, para. 119.

133 *2008 Annual EFC Report on the Movement of Capital and the Freedom of Payments,* 21 November 2008, at paras. 16 ff.

134 *2012 EFC Report on the Movement of Capital and the Freedom of Payments,* 23 November 2012, at paras. 15 ff.

135 Jonathan Hill, EU Commissioner for Financial Services, quoted in EU Commission, *Commission Asks Member States to Terminate Their Intra-EU Bilateral Investment Treaties.* http://europa.eu/rapid/press-release_IP-15-5198_en.htm (2 May 2020).

136 On similarities and differences of investor protection under EU law and international investment law, see in great detail Chapter II.

137 Cf. ICSID, *Electrabel v Hungary.* Case No. ARB/07/19. Decision on Jurisdiction, Applicable Law and Liability, 30 November 2012; ICSID, *AES Summit & AES-Tisza Erömü v Hungary.* ICSID Case No. ARB/07/22. Award, 23 September 2010; ICSID, *Ioan Micula, Viorel Micula and others v Romania.* Case No. ARB/05/20. Award, 11 December 2013; PCA, *Achmea (formerly known as "Eureko") v Slowakia.* Case No. 2008–13. Final Award, 7 December 2012; PCA, *European American Investment Bank v Slovakia.* Case No. 2010–17. Second Award on

The first was the invalidity of intra-EU BITs pursuant to the *lex posterior* rule, codified in Art. 59 Vienna Convention on the Law of the Treaties (VCLT), which was allegedly applicable to intra-EU BITs due to the Member States later accession to the EU Treaties after the conclusion of intra-EU IIAs. The other line of argument considered the intra-EU IIAs' alleged incompatibility with EU law.[138]

In most intra-EU investor-State proceedings, however, the potential conflict between EU law and international investment law was neither mentioned by any party to the dispute nor by the EU Commission as *amicus curiae*.

The issue of the BIT's applicability remained highly controversial among EU Member States. While Italy and the Czech Republic openly positioned themselves against intra-EU BITs and started to terminate their intra-EU IIAs,[139] other Member States took ambiguous positions while awaiting a decision of the ECJ on the matter. For a long time, however, most Member States,[140] just like the investor-State arbitration tribunals,[141] rejected the position of the EU Commission and considered intra-EU BITs to be indispensable to secure legal certainty until an adequate alternative mechanism had been found. Accordingly, several Member States published a 'non-paper' in 2016 according to which,

> the dismantling of intra-EU BITs will be perceived by investors, banks and creditors alike as an overall decrease in the legal protection for EU investors

---

Jurisdiction, 4 June 2014; PCA, *U.S. Steel Global v Slovakia*. Case No. 2013–6; ICSID, *Blusun v Italy*. ICSID Case No. ARB/14/3. Award, 27 December 2016; ICSID, *Masdar Solar v Spain*. Case No. ARB/14/1. Award, 16 May 2018; ICSID, *Vattenfall v Germany*. Case No. ARB/12/12. Decision on the Achmea Issue, 31 August 2018; SCC Arbitration, *Novenergia II v Spain*. Arbitration 2015/063. Final Arbitral Award, 15 February 2018; SCC Arbitration, *Foresight Luxembourg Solar v Spain*. V (2015/150). Final Award, 14 November 2018; ICSID, *Antin v Spain*. Case No. ARB/13/31. Award, 15 June 2018; SCC Arbitration, *Greentech Energy Systems v Italy*. V (2015/095). Final Award, 23 December 2018. Furthermore, the EU Commission submitted *amicus curiae* briefs in seven proceedings brought against the Czech Republic, cf. EU Commission, *Decision C(2014) 3457 final*, 28 May 2014. For a detailed analysis of the EU's *amicus curiae* activities in investor-State arbitration proceedings, see F. Dias Simões, *A Guardian and a Friend? The European Commission's Participation in Investment Arbitration*, Michigan State International Law Review 25 (2017), 233–303; O. Gerlich, *More Than a Friend?* in G. Adinolfi, et al. (eds.), *International Economic Law: Contemporary Issues* (Cham, Torino: Springer, 2017), pp. 253–69.

138 On these arguments, see in detail Chapter III: II. and Chapter III: III.

139 Italy announced its withdrawal from the ECT on 31 December 2014 and terminated all its intra-EU BITs between 2008 and 2013. The Czech Republic also terminated six intra-EU BITs between 2004 and 2011.

140 Cf. *2008 Annual EFC Report on the Movement of Capital and the Freedom of Payments*, 21 November 2008, para. 17: "Most Member States did not share the Commission's concern in respect of arbitration risks and discriminatory treatment of investors and a clear majority of Member States preferred to maintain the existing agreements." See also *2013 Annual EFC Report on the Movement of Capital and the Freedom of Payments*, 28 November 2013, at para. 18; *2016 Annual EFC Report on the Movement of Capital and the Freedom of Payments*, 14 March 2017, at page 15.

141 For a comprehensive analysis of the arbitral practice on this question, see Chapter III.

and create a competitive advantage for foreign investors who can rely on clearly defined and uniform protection standards under the forthcoming EU agreements or on Member States' [extra-EU] BITs.[142]

Notwithstanding this position, the EU Commission continued its attempts to abolish the intra-EU BIT network. As it had explained in its *amicus curiae* brief in 2010 in the *Eureko* proceeding, which was later renamed *Achmea*, "eventually, all intra-EU BITs" would "have to be terminated", at best through a concerted approach of all Member States. However, if the Member States were unable to terminate the BITs, the Commission could not "exclude having resort to infringement proceedings".[143] In June 2015, the EU Commission then initiated infringement procedures against Austria, the Netherlands, Romania, Slovakia and Sweden and requested them to terminate their intra-EU BITs.[144]

These infringement proceedings, however, have been superseded by recent events. On March 6, 2018, the European Court of Justice rendered its decision in *Achmea* and found intra-EU investor-State arbitration provisions to be incompatible with the EU Treaties.[145] In reaction, the EU Member States issued three declarations on the legal consequences of this judgment in January 2019, inter alia announcing the termination of all intra-EU BITs.[146] In the meantime, 23 of the remaining 27 EU Member States have signed the Agreement for the Termination of Bilateral Investment Treaties between the Member States of the European Union. Austria, Ireland, Finland and Sweden, however, abstained. Also, the applicability of the Energy Charter Treaty in intra-EU investment relations continues to be highly disputed.

References

Alenfeld, Justus, *Die Investitionsförderungsverträge der Bundesrepublik Deutschland* (Frankfurt am Main: Athenäum, 1971).

---

142 Austria, Finland, France, Germany and the Netherlands, *Non-Paper on Intra-EU Investment Treaties,* 7 April 2016. www.bmwi.de/Redaktion/DE/Downloads/I/intra-eu-investment-treaties. pdf?__blob=publicationFile&v=4 (23 May 2020), at para. 6.

143 Position of the EU Commission as stated in PCA, *Eureko v Slovakia*. Case No. 2008–13. Award on Jurisdiction, Arbitrability and Suspension, 26 October 2010, para. 182. At that stage of the proceeding the claimant was still named 'Eureko'. It changed its name to 'Achmea' after a merger in 2011.

144 Cf. EU Commission, *Commission Asks Member States to Terminate Their Intra-EU Bilateral Investment Treaties*. http://europa.eu/rapid/press-release_IP-15-5198_en.htm (2 May 2020), p. 8.

145 ECJ, *Achmea*. C-284/16. Judgment, 6 March 2018, para. 62.

146 Representatives of 22 EU Member States, *Declaration on the Legal Consequences of the Judgment of the ECJ in Achmea and on Investment Protection in the EU*, 15 January 2019; Representatives of Finland, Luxembourg, Malta, Slovenia and Sweden, *Declaration on the Enforcement of the Judgement of the ECJ in Achmea and on Investment Protection in the EU*, 16 January 2019; Representative of Hungary, *Declaration on the Legal Consequences of the Judgment of the ECJ in Achmea and on Investment Protection in the EU*, 16 January 2019.

Aust, Anthony, *Modern Treaty Law and Practice*, 3. ed. (Cambridge: Cambridge University Press, 2013).

Basedow, Johann R., *The EU in the Global Investment Regime: Commission Entrepreneurship, Incremental Institutional Change and Business Lethargy* (London: Routledge, 2018).

Becker, Peter, *The Joint Venture Between Volkswagen and Skoda* in B. Lippert and P. Becker (eds.), *Towards EU-membership: Transformation and Integration in Poland and the Czech Republic* (Bonn: Europa-Union-Verl., 1998), 293–332.

Blackaby, Nigel, Partasides, Constantine, Redfern, Alan and Hunter, Martin, *Redfern and Hunter on International Arbitration*, 6. ed. (New York, London: Oxford University Press, 2015).

Bonnitcha, Jonathan, Poulsen, Lauge S. and Waibel, Michael, *The Political Economy of the Investment Treaty Regime* (Oxford: Oxford University Press, 2017).

Brower, Tom, *The Tide of Times? A Sectoral Approach to Latin America's Resistance to the Investor-State Arbitration System*, Virginia Journal of International Law 56 (2016), 183–209.

Brown, Chester, *The Evolution of the Regime of International Investment Agreements* in M. Bungenberg, et al. (eds.), *International Investment Law: A Handbook* (Baden-Baden: Nomos, 2015), pp. 153–85.

Bubrowski, Helene, *Internationale Investitionsschiedsverfahren und nationale Gerichte*, Jus Internationale et Europaeum – Band 79 (Tübingen: Mohr Siebeck, 2013).

Bungenberg, Marc, *A History of Investment Arbitration and Investor-State Dispute Settlement in Germany* in A. de Mestral (ed.), *Second Thoughts: Investor State Arbitration Between Developed Democracies* (Montreal: McGill-Queen's University Press, 2017), pp. 259–83.

Calvo, Carlos M., *Le Droit International: Théorique et Pratique – Tome VI Supplément Général*, 5. ed. (Paris: A. Rousseau, 1896).

Cameron, Peter D., *International Energy Investment Law: The Pursuit of Stability* (Oxford, New York: Oxford University Press, 2010).

Connell, H. P., *United States Protection of Private Foreign Investment through Treaties of Friendship, Commerce and Navigation*, Archiv des Völkerrechts 9 (1961), 256–77.

Craven, Matthew, *The Decolonization of International Law: State Succession and the Law of Treaties* (Oxford: Oxford University Press, 2007).

Crawford, James, *Brownlie's Principles of Public International Law*, 8. ed. (Oxford: Oxford University Press, 2012).

Csuka, Gyöngyi, *The Competitiveness of Central and Eastern European Countries* in G. Gorzelak, et al. (eds.), *Regional Development in Central and Eastern Europe: Development Processes and Policy Challenges* (London: Routledge, 2010), pp. 19–33.

Decaux, Emmanuel and Kucera, Michal, *La Jurisprudence de la Cour Européenne des Droits de l'Homme en Matière de Protection des Investissements* in C. Leben (ed.), *Droit international des investissements et de l'arbitrage transnational* (Paris: Editions Pedone, 2015), pp. 501–29.

Dias Simões, Fernando, *A Guardian and a Friend? The European Commission's Participation in Investment Arbitration*, Michigan State International Law Review 25 (2017), 233–303.

Dickerson, Hollin, *Minimum Standards*, (October 2010) in *MPEPIL (Online-Edition)* (Oxford: Oxford University Press).

Dolzer, Rudolf and Schreuer, Christoph, *Principles of International Investment Law*, 2. ed. (Oxford: Oxford University Press, 2012).

Dugan, Christopher, Wallace, Don, Rubins, Noah D. and Sabahi, Borzu, *Investor-State Arbitration* (New York: Oxford University Press, 2008).

Dumberry, Patrick, *A Guide to State Succession in International Investment Law*, Elgar International Investment Law (Cheltenham, Northampton: Edward Elgar, 2018).

Elkins, Zachary, Guzman, Adrew T. and Simmons, Beth A., *Competing for Capital: The Diffusion of Bilateral Investment Treaties, 1960–2000*, International Organization 60 (2006), 811–46.

Eyffinger, Arthur, *A Highly Critical Moment: Role and Record of the 1907 Hague Peace Conference*, Netherlands International Law Review 54 (2007), 197–228.

Gerlich, Olga, *More Than a Friend?* in G. Adinolfi, et al. (eds.), *International Economic Law: Contemporary Issues* (Cham, Torino: Springer, 2017), pp. 253–69.

Gilpin, Robert, *Global Political Economy: Understanding the International Economic Order*, Princeton Paperbacks (Princeton: Princeton University Press, 2001).

Grabenwarter, Christoph, *European Convention on Human Rights: Commentary* (München: C.H. Beck, 2014).

Guzman, Adrew T., *Why LDCs Sign Treaties That Hurt Them: Explaining the Popularity of Bilteral Investment Treaties*, Virginia Journal of International Law 38 (1997), 639–88.

Hahn, Michael, *EU Rules and Obligations Related to Investment* in M. Bungenberg, et al. (eds.), *International Investment Law: A Handbook* (Baden-Baden: Nomos, 2015), pp. 671–84.

Hill, Charles W. L., *International Business: Competing in the Global Marketplace*, 9. ed. (New York: McGraw-Hill Irwin, 2013).

Hobe, Stephan, *The Development of the Law of Aliens and the Emergence of General Principles of Protection Under Public International Law* in M. Bungenberg, et al. (eds.), *International Investment Law: A Handbook* (Baden-Baden: Nomos, 2015), pp. 6–22.

Hoffmeister, Frank, *General Principles of the Europe Agreements and the Association Agreements with Cyprus, Malta and Turkey* in A. Ott and K. Inglis (eds.), *Handbook on European Enlargement: A Commentary on the Enlargement Process* (The Hague: TMC Asser Press, 2002), pp. 349–66.

Johnson Jr., O. T. and Gimblett, J., *From Gunboats to BITs* in K. P. Sauvant (ed.), *Yearbook on International Investment Law & Policy 2010–2011* (New York: Oxford University Press, 2012), pp. 649–92.

Judt, Tony, *Postwar: A History of Europe Since 1945* (London: Vintage, 2010).

Karl, Joachim, *The Promotion and Protection of German Foreign Investment Abroad*, ICSID Review 11 (1996), 1–36.

Ketcheson, Jonathan, *Investment Arbitration* in S. Hindelang and M. Krajewski (eds.), *Shifting Paradigms in International Investment Law: More Balanced, Less Isolated, Increasingly Diversified* (Oxford: Oxford University Press, 2016), pp. 97–127.

Lippert, Barbara, *From Pre-Accession to EU-Membership* in B. Lippert and P. Becker (eds.), *Towards EU-membership: Transformation and Integration in Poland and the Czech Republic* (Bonn: Europa-Union-Verl., 1998), pp. 17–62.

Lowenfeld, Andreas F., *International Economic Law*, International Economic Law Series, 2. ed. (Oxford: Oxford University Press, 2009).

Mestral, Armand de, *Investor State Arbitration Between Developed Democratic Countries* in A. de Mestral (ed.), *Second Thoughts: Investor State Arbitration Between Developed Democracies* (Montreal: McGill-Queen's University Press, 2017), pp. 9–56.

Miles, Kate, *The Origins of International Investment Law: Empire, Environment, and the Safeguarding of Capital*, Cambridge Studies in International and Comparative Law (Cambridge: Cambridge University Press, 2013).

Moon, Hwi-Chang, *Foreign Direct Investment: A Global Perspective* (Hackensack, NJ: World Scientific, 2016).

Newcombe, Andrew and Paradell, Lluis, *Law and Practice of Investment Treaties: Standards of Treatment* (Alphen aan den Rijn: Kluwer Law International, 2009).

Papenfuß, Dieter, *The Fate of the International Treaties of the GDR Within the Framework of German Unification*, American Journal of International Law 92 (1998), 469–88.

Peinhardt, Clint and Wellhausen, Rachel L., *Withdrawing from Investment Treaties but Protecting Investment*, Global Policy 7 (2016), 571–76.

Perkams, Markus, *Protection for Legal Persons* in M. Bungenberg, et al. (eds.), *International Investment Law: A Handbook* (Baden-Baden: Nomos, 2015), pp. 638–52.

Pfaff, Christina, *Investitionsschutz durch regionalen menschenrechtlichen Eigentumsschutz am Beispiel der Europäischen Menschenrechtskonvention (EMRK)* in C. Knahr and A. Reinisch (eds.), *Aktuelle Probleme und Entwicklungen im internationalen Investitionsrecht*, Internationale Wirtschaft und Recht (Stuttgart: Boorberg, 2008), pp. 163–92.

Rainey, Bernadette, Wicks, Elizabeth and Ovey, Clare, *The European Convention on Human Rights: Jacobs, White and Ovey*, 7. ed. (Oxford: Oxford University Press, 2017).

Reed, Lucy F. and Davis, Jonathan E., *Who Is a Protected Investor?* in M. Bungenberg, et al. (eds.), *International Investment Law: A Handbook* (Baden-Baden: Nomos, 2015), pp. 614–37.

Reinisch, August, *Expropriation* in P. Muchlinski, et al. (eds.), *The Oxford Handbook of International Investment Law*, Oxford Handbooks in Law (Oxford: Oxford University Press, 2008), pp. 407–58.

Roberts, Anthea, *State-to-State Investment Treaty Arbitration: A Hybrid Theory of Interdependent Rights and Shared Interpretive Authority*, Harvard International Law Journal 55 (2014), 1–70.

Roe, Thomas and Happold, Matthew, *Settlement of Investment Disputes Under the Energy Charter Treaty*, Law Practitioner Series (Cambridge: Cambridge University Press, 2011).

Root, Elihu, *The Basis of Protection to Citizens Residing Abroad*, American Journal of International Law 4 (1910), 517–28.

Salacuse, Jeswald W., *The Law of Investment Treaties*, 2. ed. (Oxford: Oxford University Press, 2015).

Schabas, William A., *The European Convention on Human Rights: A Commentary* (Oxford: Oxford University Press, 2015).

Schill, Stephan W., *Private Enforcement of International Investment Law* in M. Waibel, et al. (eds.), *The Backlash Against Investment Arbitration: Perceptions and Reality* (Alphen aan den Rijn: Wolters Kluwer, 2010), pp. 29–50.

Schwebel, Stephen M., *In Defense of Bilateral Investment Treaties*, Arbitration International 31 (2015), 181–92.

Shaw, Malcolm N., *International Law*, 6. ed. (Cambridge: Cambridge University Press, 2008).

Shihata, Ibrahim F. I., *Towards a Greater Depoliticization of Investment Disputes: The Roles of ICSID and MIGA*, ICSID Review 1 (1986), 1–25.

Synowiec, Ewa and Woreta, Robert, *Poland's Transition to a Market Economy* in B. Lippert and P. Becker (eds.), *Towards EU-membership: Transformation and Integration in Poland and the Czech Republic* (Bonn: Europa-Union-Verl., 1998), pp. 83–107.

Tams, Christian J., *State Succession to Investment Treaties: Mapping the Issues*, ICSID Review 31 (2016), 314–43.

Titi, Aikaterini, *The Right to Regulate in International Investment Law* (Baden-Baden: Nomos, 2014).

Titi, Catharine, *International Investment Law and the European Union*: *Towards a New Generation of International Investment Agreements*, European Journal of International Law 26 (2015), 639–61.

Tomuschat, Christian, *The European Court of Human Rights an Investment Protection* in C. Binder, et al. (eds.), *International Investment Law for the 21st Century: Essays in Honour of Christoph Schreuer* (Oxford: Oxford University Press, 2009), pp. 636–56.

UNCTAD, *Denunciation of the ICSID Convention and BITs*: *Impact on Investor-State Claims*, IIA Issue Notes (2010).

UNCTAD, *World Investment Report 2016: Investor Nationality: Policy Challenges*, United Nations Publication (New York, Geneva: United Nations, 2016).

UNCTAD, *World Investment Report 2019: Special Economic Zones*, United Nations Publication (New York, Geneva: United Nations, 2019).

Waibel, Michael, Kaushal, Asha, Chung, Kyo-Hwa L. and Balchin, Claire (eds.), *The Backlash Against Investment Arbitration: Perceptions and Reality* (Alphen aan den Rijn: Wolters Kluwer, 2010).

White, Gillian, *Nationalisation of Foreign Property* (London: Stevens & Sons Limited, 1961).

Zimmermann, Andreas, *Staatennachfolge in völkerrechtliche Verträge: Zugleich ein Beitrag zu den Möglichkeiten und Grenzen völkerrechtlicher Kodifikation*, Beiträge zum ausländischen öffentlichen Recht und Völkerrecht (Berlin: Springer, 2000).

II Comparison of the investment protection regimes

I Introduction

Investment protection in the broad sense covers market access as well as the protection of already established investments. The EU legal order traditionally has a strong focus on market access. One leading idea behind the process of European integration was the one of peace through economic exchange. It led to the creation of a common market without internal borders and with fundamental freedoms guaranteeing market access for foreign direct investments through the creation of a new company or the acquisition of or mergers with existing ones, as well as the free movement of capital. The fundamental freedoms create binding obligations for Member States regarding the market access for intra-EU investments and are supplemented by a great number of EU secondary laws covering capital markets and investments.[1] These secondary rules, however, do not grant substantive investment protection as provided by IIAs. This is mostly due to the EU's lack of competence in the field of investment protection within the EU.[2] It is thus mostly the domestic law of the Member States which regulates foreign investments within the EU. The actual protection of intra-EU investments may thus significantly differ depending on the respective host State.

International investment law on the other hand, focusses mainly on the protection of already established investments. The great majority of intra-EU IIAs cover the treatment of investors 'post-market-admission' or 'post-market-entry' only and do not provide for specific binding commitments regarding the conditions of market access. The decision on admission of foreign investments is left to a host State's legislation. IIAs often contain 'admission clauses' according to which investors of the other contracting State shall be admitted to the domestic market if

---

1 E.g. Directive 2017/593 of 7 April 2016 (safeguarding of financial instruments and funds); Regulation 912/2014 of 23 July 2014 (financial responsibility in ISDS proceedings based on IIAs to which the EU is a party); Regulation 1219/2012 of 12 December 2012 (transitional arrangements for extra-EU BITs).
2 See Chapter I: III.

their investment is undertaken in accordance with the domestic legal rules.[3] A host State can thus generally assess on a case-by-case basis and unilaterally decide whether a specific investment is suitable for admission and also apply differential treatment to different investments and investors as the IIAs' non-discrimination standards only apply to the 'post-market-admission' of an investment.[4]

Even though every single intra-EU BIT in force at the moment of the *Achmea* judgment is an autonomous and unique treaty between two sovereign States, most of the BITs are based on model treaties and share a highly standardized and recurring treaty language containing very vague legal concepts that are open to various interpretations and often have remarkable commonalities in terms of structure and content.[5] Thus, for the purpose of the present comparison, intra-EU IIAs will mostly be dealt with as a bloc. The particularities of the Energy Charter Treaty, being the sole multilateral intra-EU IIA, will – where necessary – be considered separately.

The analysis starts with the scope of application of EU law and intra-EU IIAs in force at the moment of the *Achmea* judgment (II.), before comparing the substantive standards of protection guaranteed to foreign investors and their investments (III.) as well as the judicial remedies available to them (IV.).

II Scope of application

For foreign investors to be protected, their investment must fall within the scope of application of the respective legal regime.

1 Scope of application of intra-EU IIAs

IIAs generally protect any investment of investors, nationals of a State party to the respective IIA, in the territory of another State Party. In this regard, the ECT constitutes a special case as it has a limited sectoral scope of application, which only covers investments associated with economic activities in the energy sector.

There are many different approaches to what constitutes an 'investment' in international investment law. Some IIAs extend the protection to 'any kind' of investment as long as it has been made in accordance with the laws and regulations of the host State, others rely on 'asset-based' definitions with illustrative or closed lists of what constitutes an investment; sometimes including and

---

3 See for example Art. 2 (1) of the 1996 Croatia–Slovakia BIT: "Each Contracting Party shall protect, in its territory investments by investors of the other Contracting Party and shall admit such investments, in accordance with its laws and regulations."

4 Cf. I. Gómez-Palacio and P. Muchlinski, *Admission and Establishment* in P. Muchlinski, et al. (eds.), *The Oxford Handbook of International Investment Law* (Oxford: Oxford University Press, 2008), pp. 227–57, at p. 241; R. Dolzer and C. Schreuer, *Principles of International Investment Law*, 2. ed. (Oxford: Oxford University Press, 2012), at 89.

5 Cf. W. Alschner and D. Skougarevskiy, *Mapping the Universe of International Investment Agreements,* Journal of International Economic Law (2016), 561–88, at 565 ff.

sometimes excluding so-called portfolio investments. The latter do not involve a substantial management or control of the investor but are rather characterized by the lack of intention of the investor to influence the company's management or control and typically consist of shares of a company.[6] Against this backdrop, there is a trend in recent investment treaties to narrow down the definition of 'investment'.[7] The majority of intra-EU IIAs, however, has an extremely wide understanding of 'investment' comprising every kind of asset owned or controlled directly or indirectly by an investor.[8]

The other decisive criterion for the applicability of an IIA is the 'foreignness' of the investor, which is determined by the investor's nationality. Nationals of the host State are in principle excluded from an IIA's protection. Without a foreign ownership or control there is by definition no FDI, and thus no applicability of IIAs. Some IIAs, such as the ECT, however, extend the protection to natural persons who do not possess the citizenship of a contracting State but are permanent residents in the territory of that State.[9] A Brazilian citizen who is a permanent resident in Romania could thus fall under the protection of the ECT, if he or she operates an investment in another ECT Member State, even though Brazil itself is not a Contracting Party to the ECT.

The nationality of an individual or a company depends on the respective domestic laws.[10] Difficulties arise with regard to legal persons that account for the great majority of FDI activities. A corporation's nationality can be determined on the basis of different criteria, namely the company's incorporation in the domestic legal system of a State,[11] i.e. the creation as a legal person in that legal system, or the fact that its centre of administration, i.e. the seat of the company[12] is located within a specific State.[13] The 'seat', however, is not only limited to the corporate

---

6 A good overview on the different approaches is provided by E. C. Schlemmer, *Investment, Investor, Nationality, and Shareholders* in P. Muchlinski, et al. (eds.), *The Oxford Handbook of International Investment Law* (Oxford: Oxford University Press, 2008), pp. 49–88, at 55 ff; M. Sornarajah, *The International Law on Foreign Investment*, 4. ed. (Cambridge: Cambridge University Press, 2017), at 11; J. W. Head, *Global Business Law: Principles and Practice of International Commerce and Investment*, 3. ed. (Durham: Carolina Academic, 2012), at 337 f.

7 See for example Art. 1 (3) of the 2016 Morocco–Nigeria BIT or Art. 2 (1) of the 2017 Colombia–United Arab Emirates BIT.

8 See for example, Art. 1 of the 1991 Czechoslovakia–Netherlands BIT; Art. 1 of the 1993 Bulgaria–Greece BIT; Art. 1 of the 1999 Malta–Sweden BIT and Art. 1 (6) ECT.

9 Art. 1 (7) (a) ECT.

10 Cf. J. Crawford, *Brownlie's Principles of Public International Law*, 8. ed. (Oxford: Oxford University Press, 2012), at 509 f.; ICJ, *Nottebohm*. Judgment, 6 April 1955, ICJ Reports 4, p. 20.

11 See for example Art. 1 (VII) (a) (ii) ECT or Art. 1 (1) of the 2002 Austria–Malta BIT. Also requiring 'effective economic activities', Art. 1 (3) of the 1997 Greece–Slovenia BIT.

12 See for example Art. 1 (2) of the 1989 Poland–Sweden BIT or Art. 1 (1) of the 1997 BLEU–Lithuania BIT.

13 See also ICJ, *Barcelona Traction*. Judgment, 5 February 1970, ICJ Reports 1970, para. 70; J. Crawford, *Brownlie's Principles of Public International Law* (Oxford: Oxford University Press, 2012), at 527 f.

headquarters but can be interpreted by arbitral tribunals as the seat of any entity in question, thus including intermediate entities of MNEs.[14]

A third approach found in some intra-EU IIAs focusses on the company's control and allows a company to qualify as a foreign investor because of its foreign control.[15] It is sufficient that an intermediate entity of the MNE or a natural person somewhere along the 'ownership chain' has the required nationality for an investment to qualify for the protection guaranteed by the IIA. In other words, an investment can even fall under the IIA's protection if it is operated by a company incorporated in the host State, i.e. a local company being the immediate investor, or operated by a company incorporated in a third State, as long as these companies are controlled by an 'investor' from the home State.[16]

None of these nationality criteria require substantive operative activities within the host State and thus allow for nationality planning, i.e. the strategic decision to incorporate a company or chose a seat in a specific legal system, for example for taxation reasons.[17]

2 Scope of application of EU law

EU law is by its nature interwoven with the domestic law of the Member States. The latter act within the scope of application of EU law, when it imposes specific obligations upon them.[18] In other words, EU law is applicable when any broadly defined link to EU law can be identified. For instance, the implementation or application of EU law by an EU Member State, the exercise of fundamental freedoms by EU citizens, or the case of an EU citizen legally staying in another EU

---

14 Cf. UNCTAD, *World Investment Report 2016: Investor Nationality: Policy Challenges* (New York, Geneva: United Nations, 2016), at 173 f; M. Perkams, *Protection for Legal Persons* in M. Bungenberg, et al. (eds.), *International Investment Law: A Handbook* (Baden-Baden: Nomos, 2015), pp. 638–52, at 644 f.

15 See for example Art. 1 (b) of the 1994 Netherlands–Romania BIT which states:

> The term 'investors' shall comprise with regard to either Contracting Party: (i) natural persons having the citizenship or the nationality of that Contracting Party [...]; (ii) legal persons constituted under the law of that Contracting Party; (iii) legal persons owned or controlled, directly or indirectly, by natural persons as defined in (i) or by legal persons as defined in (ii) above.

   See also Art. 1 (2) of the 1996 France–Croatia BIT, Art. 1 (3) of the 1992 France–Lithuania BIT, or Art. 1 (1) of the 1992 Poland–Lithuania BIT.

16 UNCTAD, *World Investment Report 2016* (New York, Geneva: United Nations, 2016), p. 171; R. Dolzer and C. Schreuer, *Principles of International Investment Law* (Oxford: Oxford University Press, 2012), at 56 ff; M. Perkams, *Protection for Legal Persons* in M. Bungenberg, et al. (eds.), *International Investment Law: A Handbook* (Baden-Baden: Nomos, 2015), at 647 f.

17 On the question of nationality planning see in detail Chapter IV: VI. 2.

18 Cf. ECJ, *Jean-Louis Maurin.* C-144/95. Judgment, 13 June 1996, ECLI:EU:C:1996:235, para. 11 f. Regarding the scope of application of EU Fundamental Rights, ECJ, *Siragusa.* C-206/13. Judgment, 6 March 2014, ECLI:EU:C:2014:126, para. 26 f; ECJ, *Hernandéz.* C-198/13. Judgment, 10 July 2014, ECLI:EU:C:2014:2055, para. 35; ECJ, *Åkerberg Fransson.* C-617/10. Judgment, 26 February 2013, ECLI:EU:C:2013:105, para. 25 f.

Member State. Thus, an intra-European cross-border economic situation such as an intra-EU investment activity will always fall within the formal scope of application of EU law.

Concerning the question of nationality, Art. 20 (1) TFEU provides that "every person holding the nationality of a Member State shall be a citizen of the Union." This citizenship, however, is only additional and does not replace the national citizenship which is determined by the Member States' domestic laws. Regarding legal persons, Art. 54 (1) TFEU provides that companies "formed in accordance with the law of a Member State" and having "their registered office, central administration or principal place of business within the Union" are assimilated to "natural persons who are national of a Member State". This corresponds to the aforementioned incorporation and seat approaches, enumerated in *Barcelona Traction*.[19] The control approach, however, is alien to the EU legal order.

3 Interim conclusion

The general scope of application of EU law is much wider than that of intra-EU IIAs. Notwithstanding, regarding the specific field of intra-EU investment activities, the respective scopes of application are similar, as both EU law and intra-EU IIAs cover cross-border economic activities within the territory of the EU. The most significant difference to the EU's scope of application is that some intra-EU IIAs are applicable to individuals or legal persons that are not nationals of a State party if they are permanent residents in another State party to the IIA. Furthermore, some IIAs are also applicable to companies that are neither incorporated in a home State nor have their seat there, but which are solely controlled by nationals of a State party to the treaty. The determination of the investor's 'nationality' is thus much wider in some intra-EU IIAs than within the EU legal order.

III Substantive protection

Substantive guarantees for foreign investors are at the core of every IIA. They can be classified into three different categories: relative standards of protection, i.e. non-discrimination in relation to nationals or other foreigners (1.), absolute standards of protection guaranteeing a minimum level of protection independent of any domestic treatment (2.) and the protection of contractual undertakings (3.).

1 Relative standards of protection: non-discrimination

The principle of non-discrimination and the equal treatment of comparable situations are core elements of the rule of law and form part of customary international

---

19 ICJ, *Barcelona Traction*. Judgment, 5 February 1970, para. 70.

law.[20] In contrast to absolute standards, which have – once defined – a clear substantive content, non-discrimination clauses contained in IIAs relate to legal relations outside the treaty they are contained in and are thus relative standards of protection.

a) Non-discrimination in international investment law

Within the 'international investment protection regime', non-discrimination provisions protect foreign investors on two levels: First 'internationally' by extending benefits – granted to a third State or its nationals – to another foreign investor through the 'most-favoured nation' treatment (in the following referred to as MFN). Second 'domestically' by granting the same 'national treatment' to foreign investors as to nationals of the host State.

Every single intra-EU IIA provides for the 'most-favoured nation' treatment.[21] Only 77 per cent of the analysed intra-EU BITs, however, do contain a 'national treatment' clause.[22] The MFN standard allows investors to benefit from the advantages that are granted to another State or its nationals in a different treaty concluded with the host State. In other words, the standard requires that investors are treated at least as favourably as any investor of a third State, thereby creating a principle of equality between foreign investors, by aligning itself on the most favourable treatment accorded to one of them.[23] The 'national treatment' on the other hand, protects foreign investors against both formal and factual discrimination based on their nationality.[24] It requires a host State to accord to foreign investors a treatment which is not less favourable than that accorded to its own nationals. To ascertain the violation of the national treatment, a 'like circumstance' or 'like situation' must be determined. It generally suffices if the foreign investor operates in the same business sector as its domestic competitors,[25] and

---

20 Cf. R. Jennings and A. Watts, *Oppenheim's International Law*, 9. ed. (Harlow: Longman, 1992), at 931 f; J. Crawford, *Brownlie's Principles of Public International Law* (Oxford: Oxford University Press, 2012), at 645 f; U. Kriebaum, *Expropriation* in M. Bungenberg, et al. (eds.), *International Investment Law: A Handbook* (Baden-Baden: Nomos, 2015), pp. 959–1030, at p. 1021.

21 A typical clause combining the 'national treatment' and MFN treatment can be found in Art. 10 (7) ECT.

22 A national treatment provision lacks in almost every Swedish, Finish and Belgo-Luxembourgish intra-EU BIT.

23 Cf. J. Cazala, *Les Standards Indirects de Traitement* in C. Leben (ed.), *Droit international des investissements et de l'arbitrage transnational* (Paris: Editions Pedone, 2015), pp. 265–86, at p. 266; C. Rossillion, *The Most Favoured Nation Clause in Case Law of the International Court of Justice*, Journal du Droit International 82 (1955), 76–107, at 107.

24 Formal discrimination is openly linked to the nationality, while factual discrimination disadvantages a foreign investors, while appearing to be neutral, cf. J. Cazala, *Les Standards Indirects de Traitement* in C. Leben (ed.), *Droit international des investissements et de l'arbitrage transnational* (Paris: Editions Pedone, 2015), p. 266; A. Reinisch, *National Treatment* in M. Bungenberg, et al. (eds.), *International Investment Law: A Handbook* (Baden-Baden: Nomos, 2015), pp. 846–69, at p. 848.

25 A. Reinisch, *National Treatment* in M. Bungenberg, et al. (eds.), *International Investment Law: A Handbook* (Baden-Baden: Nomos, 2015), p. 856.

has been treated in a less favourable way. The non-discrimination principle is further reflected in clauses explicitly prohibiting 'arbitrary and discriminatory' treatment. The latter has a broader scope and includes discrimination based on race, age, sex, religion, disability, nationality or political affiliation.[26]

b) Non-discrimination in EU law

The principle of non-discrimination is also one of the corner stones of EU law. It has been described as '*Leitmotiv*' or '*Magna Charta*'[27] of the EU and is emphasized at various points in the EU Treaties and implicitly contained in the fundamental freedoms.[28] This principle is linked to the EU's development history. Preferential treatment for a Member State's own nationals was understood as one of the first obstacles that needed to be overcome for the achievement of the EU's goals, especially the proper functioning of the internal market, but also to bring the peoples of Europe ever closer together.[29]

EU law requires an extensive national treatment of European investors and protects them from discrimination. Judges and public officials must apply the non-discrimination provisions *ex officio*, irrespective of whether a party to the proceedings invokes them. However, in difference to intra-EU IIAs, EU law expressly acknowledges the possibility to restrict fundamental freedoms and the non-discrimination principle in favour of competing public interests and provides for justifications of proportionate discriminatory measures of EU Member States.[30] Furthermore, the 'most-favoured nation' treatment is unknown to the EU legal order. Such a standard is not necessary in a common and integrated market in which the Member States are obliged to guarantee an extensive national treatment to every market participant.[31] In other words, differential treatment of European

---

26 Such a clause is included in over 120 intra-EU BITs, for example Art. 3 (1) of the 1989 Hungary–Spain BIT. Some intra-EU BITs provide this guarantee as a separate substantive investment protection, others combine it with different standards.

27 A. von Bogdandy, *Art. 18 AEUV* in E. Grabitz and M. Hilf (eds.), *Das Recht der Europäischen Union* (München: C. H. Beck, 2018), at para. 1; A. Epiney, *Art. 18 AEUV* in C. Calliess and M. Ruffert (eds.), *EUV/AEUV – Kommentar*, 5. ed. (München: C. H. Beck, 2016), at para. 1.

28 Cf. the Preamble, Arts. 2, 3 (3), 9, 21 (1) TEU, Arts. 8, 10, 18, 19 TFEU as well as Art. 21 (2) EU Charter.

29 Cf. D. Chalmers, G. Davies and G. Monti, *European Union Law*, 3. ed. (Cambridge: Cambridge University Press, 2014), at 668 ff; A. von Bogdandy, *Art. 18 AEUV* in E. Grabitz and M. Hilf (eds.), *Das Recht der Europäischen Union* (München: C. H. Beck, 2018), para. 1.

30 Cf. Arts. 36, 45 (3), 52, 62 and 65 TFEU as well as the ECJ's jurisprudence starting with the famous decision ECJ, *Cassis de Dijon*. Case 120/78. Judgment, 20 February 1979, ECLI:EU:C:1979:42.

31 The idea of a most-favoured nation treatment was at least rejected by the ECJ in the double taxation agreement cases, ECJ, *D.* C-376/03. Judgment, 5 July 2005, ECLI:EU:C:2005:424, para. 61; ECJ, *Test Claimants*. C-374/04. Judgment, 12 December 2006, ECLI:EU:C:2006:773, paras. 90 ff. See also, H. Wehland, *Intra-EU Investment Agreements and Arbitration: Is European Community Law and Obstacle?* International and Comparative Law Quarterly 58 (2009), 297–320, at 315 ff. See also ECJ, *Achmea.* C-284/16. Opinion of Advocate General Wathelet, 19 September 2017, ECLI:EU:C:2017:699, para. 71 f., 201, in which the Advocate General explicitly denies the

investors based on their nationality would in principle be incompatible with EU law unless it is a case of a proportionate discrimination in the public interest, which might be justifiable.[32]

2 Absolute standards of protection

Absolute standards provide for a non-relational substantive protection. They ensure a minimum treatment and basic procedural guarantees, such as the due process principle. The most important absolute standards in IIAs are the protection against expropriation without compensation (a), the fair and equitable treatment standard (b), the protection of physical security (c) and the guarantee of the free transfer of funds (d).

a) Expropriation and compensation

There is no legal entitlement for aliens under international law to become economically active abroad. However, if they do, they face the risk to lose their investment, as the host State's right to expropriate alien property is universally recognized in international law as consistent with a State's territorial sovereignty.[33] At the same time, an individual's possibility to freely dispose of his or her own property is a fundamental condition of any economic activity. Expropriations constitute the widest conceivable interference with individual property. Two different types of expropriation need to be distinguished. Direct expropriations are characterized by a formal administrative or legislative measure depriving by force the property of an individual or the possibility to make use of it.[34] In case of an indirect expropriation, the property remains with the owner. The State measure, however, results in a substantial deprivation of the usability and value of the property for its owner.[35] Every single

---

existence of a most-favoured nation treatment. The ECJ, however, remained silent on this question in its *Achmea* decision, ECJ, *Achmea*. C-284/16. Judgment, 6 March 2018, ECLI:EU:C:2018:158.

32 On the different approach regarding double taxation agreements, cf. Chapter III: III. 3.

33 Cf. G. White, *Nationalisation of Foreign Property* (London: Stevens & Sons Limited, 1961), at 35 ff; H. Dickerson, *Minimum Standards* (October 2010) in *MPEPIL (Online-Edition)* (Oxford: Oxford University Press) at para. 14; R. Dolzer and C. Schreuer, *Principles of International Investment Law* (Oxford: Oxford University Press, 2012), p. 98; S. Hobe, *The Development of the Law of Aliens and the Emergence of General Principles of Protection Under Public International Law* in M. Bungenberg, et al. (eds.), *International Investment Law: A Handbook* (Baden-Baden: Nomos, 2015), pp. 6–22, at 19 f.

34 U. Kriebaum, *Expropriation* in M. Bungenberg, et al. (eds.), *International Investment Law: A Handbook* (Baden-Baden: Nomos, 2015), at 970 f. See also ICSID, *LG&G Energy v Argentina*. Case No. ARB/02/1. Decision on Liability, 3 October 2006, para. 187.

35 U. Kriebaum, *Expropriation* in M. Bungenberg, et al. (eds.), *International Investment Law: A Handbook* (Baden-Baden: Nomos, 2015), p. 971. See also Ad Hoc Arbitration, *CME v Czech Republic*. Partial Award, 13 September 2001, para. 591, 604; Ad Hoc Arbitration, *Eureko v Poland*. Partial Award, 19 August 2005, para. 241, 243; ICSID, *ADC v Hungary*. Case No. ARB/03/16. Award of the Tribunal, 2 October 2006, paras. 423 ff.

intra-EU IIA, but also EU law, regulates the conditions and consequences of lawful expropriations.

International law does not prohibit expropriations *per se*. They can be lawful under certain conditions, which are almost identical throughout the 'international investment protection regime', namely that they have been made in the public interest, in a non-discriminatory way and against the payment of adequate and prompt compensation.[36] These conditions are known as the *Hull* formula, named after the US Secretary of State Cordell Hull who addressed the Mexican government in 1938, positing that "no government is entitled to expropriate private property, for whatever purpose, without provision for prompt, adequate, and effective payment therefore."[37] While more recent IIAs often contain exceptions to indirect expropriation provisions,[38] the great majority of intra-EU BITs continues to guarantee an absolute and categorical protection against expropriation without any balancing of interests or consideration of the State's 'right to regulate'.[39] The arbitrators' role is thus to establish whether an allegedly expropriated asset was protected by the invoked IIA, and whether the State's action amounted to an expropriation. The intention of the State's officials is not decisive. To constitute an indirect expropriation, the economic effects of the measure must reach a certain intensity, deprive the investor of (most of) the benefits of its investment for a significant and not just ephemeral period.[40]

The EU as a legal community based on economic cooperation also guarantees the protection of property rights. In its first judgment regarding the question of

---

36 Cf. Art. 4 of the 1976 France–Malta BIT. From the mid-1980s onwards many intra-EU BITs contained the condition that an expropriation must be taken in accordance with due process of law, e.g. Art 5 of the 1997 Finland–Bulgaria BIT; Art. 5 of the 1996 Romania – Slovenia BIT; Art. 4 of the 1994 Bulgaria–Sweden BIT. See also I. Marboe, *State Responsibility and Comparative State Liability for Administrative and Legislative Harm to Economic Interests* in S. W. Schill (ed.), *International investment law and comparative public law* (Oxford: Oxford University Press, 2010), pp. 377–411, at p. 381; B. Sabahi and N. J. Birch, *Comparative Compensation for Expropriation* in S. W. Schill (ed.), *International Investment Law and Comparative Public Law* (Oxford: Oxford University Press, 2010), pp. 755–85, at p. 756.

37 The letter is reprinted in *Official Documents*, AJIL Supplement, 1938, at p. 193. See also C. Brown, *The Evolution of the Regime of International Investment Agreements* in M. Bungenberg, et al. (eds.), *International Investment Law: A Handbook* (Baden-Baden: Nomos, 2015), pp. 153–85, at 159 f.

38 Cf. with further references, M. Sattorova, *Investor Rights Under EU Law and International Investment Law,* Journal of World Investment & Trade 17 (2016), 895–918, at 905.

39 See for example, Art. 5 (2) of the 1989 France–Bulgaria BIT; Art. 5 of the 1997 Spain–Croatia BIT. See also A. Titi, *The Right to Regulate in International Investment Law* (Baden-Baden: Nomos, 2014).

40 M. W. Reisman and R. D. Sloane, *Indirect Expropriations and Its Valuation in the BIT Generation,* British Yearbook of International Law 74 (2004), 115–50, at 120 ff; U. Kriebaum, *Expropriation* in M. Bungenberg, et al. (eds.), *International Investment Law: A Handbook* (Baden-Baden: Nomos, 2015), at 982, 992 f. See also ICSID, *Spyridon Roussalis v Romania.* Case No. ARB/06/1. Award, 7 December 2011, para. 354.

expropriation, the ECJ recognized the, at the time, unwritten right to property and found that it

> is guaranteed in the community legal order in accordance with the ideas common to the constitutions of the member states, which are also reflected in the First Protocol to the European Convention for the Protection of Human Rights.[41]

The term 'property' under EU law, is narrower than 'asset' or 'investment' used in intra-EU IIAs.[42] Furthermore, the protection under EU law is limited by Art. 345 TFEU according to which the EU Treaties shall in no way prejudice the rules in Member States governing the system of property ownership. Thus, the protection of property is first and foremost determined by domestic law. It remains the Member States' competence to decide about contents and limits of private property and about the conditions and modalities of expropriations. The right to property is limited by the host State's inherent competence to regulate and to expropriate property, which again is limited by the EU right to property.[43] However, in contrast to its Member States, the EU itself lacks the competence to formally expropriate.[44]

But Art. 345 TFEU does not exclude the Member States' obligation to observe the fundamental freedoms and the principle of non-discrimination.[45] It does neither affect the ECJ's competence to determine the content and limits of the right to property contained in Art. 17 (1) EU Charter. This latter corresponds to the fundamental right to property contained in the First Protocol to the ECHR.[46] For the ECJ, however, it is not an absolute right, but must be considered in relation to its social function.[47] Restrictions may thus be imposed on property as long as

---

41 ECJ, *Hauer v Rheinland-Pfalz*. Case 44/79. Judgment, 13 December 1979, ECLI:EU:C:1979:290, para. 17.

42 Property does comprise physical and intellectual property but not assets in the extremely broad understanding of IIAs. Cf. with further references, C. Calliess, *Eigentumsgrundrecht* in D. Ehlers (ed.), *Europäische Grundrechte und Grundfreiheiten*, 4. ed. (Berlin, Boston: De Gruyter, 2014), pp. 707–34, at para. 20 f; C. Calliess, *Art. 17 EU Charta* in C. Calliess and M. Ruffert (eds.), *EUV/AEUV – Kommentar*, 5. ed. (München: C. H. Beck, 2016).

43 M. Perkams, *The Concept of Indirect Expropriation in Comparative Public Law* in S. W. Schill (ed.), *International Investment Law and Comparative Public Law* (Oxford: Oxford University Press, 2010), pp. 107–50, at p. 147.

44 See ECJ, *Daniele Annibaldi*. C-309/96. Judgment, 18 December 1977, ECLI:EU:C:1997:631, para. 23; M. Perkams, *The Concept of Indirect Expropriation in Comparative Public Law* in S. W. Schill (ed.), *International Investment Law and Comparative Public Law* (Oxford: Oxford University Press, 2010), p. 139.

45 ECJ, *Segro and Horvath*. Joined Cases C-52/16 and C-113/16. Judgment, 6 March 2018, ECLI:EU:C:2018:157, para. 51.

46 C. Calliess, *Eigentumsgrundrecht* in D. Ehlers (ed.), *Europäische Grundrechte und Grundfreiheiten* (Berlin, Boston: De Gruyter, 2014), para. 3.

47 Cf. ECJ, *Deutsches Weintor*. C-544/10. Judgment, 6 December 2012, ECLI:EU:C:2012:526, para. 54. Referring to ECJ, *Swedish Match*. C-210/03. Judgment, 14 December 2004, ECLI:EU:C:2004:802, para. 72.

they correspond to the objectives of general interest pursued by the EU and do not constitute a disproportionate, discriminatory or intolerable interference with the fundamental right of Art. 17 EU Charter.[48] In a similar vein, the ECJ generally assigns a very wide margin of appreciation to the national institutions in assessing whether an indirect expropriation was proportionate.[49]

The EU property protection provided for in Art. 17 EU Charter has a more limited scope of application than that of the intra-EU IIAs. The latter cover both direct and indirect expropriations unrestrictedly. Whereas EU law also recognizes indirect expropriations, indirect impairments of the right to property can be justified on public grounds if they are proportionate. Furthermore, indirect expropriations generally do not trigger the State's obligation to compensate, and EU law situates the protection of property within the social function of property rights. On the other hand, most intra-EU IIAs provide for an absolute protection against any form of expropriation, be they direct or indirect, without providing for explicit public policy exceptions. This leaves an important, however also unpredictable, leeway to investor-State arbitration tribunals to decide in favour of investors. As aptly summarized by the arbitral tribunal in *Achmea*, while there are

> overlaps with the right to property secured by Art. 17 of the Charter [...], the provision on expropriation is not obviously co-extensive with it. Both the considerable body of jurisprudence on indirect takings that has emerged in the context of BITs, and also the fact that the BIT protects 'assets' and 'investments' rather than the arguably narrower concepts of 'possessions' and 'property' protected by the Charter, give rise to the possibility of wider protection under the BIT than is enjoyed under EU law.[50]

b) *Fair and equitable treatment*

The fair and equitable treatment standard (FET) is the most frequently invoked substantive standard in investor-State arbitration proceedings and a main element

---

48 ECJ, *Deutsches Weintor*. C-544/10. Judgment, 6 December 2012, para. 54; ECJ, *Metronome Musik*. C-200/96. Judgment, 28 April 1998, ECLI:EU:C:1998:172, para. 21. Citing: ECJ, *Irish Farmers Association*. C-22/94. Judgment, 15 April 1997, ECLI:EU:C:1997:187, para. 27; ECJ, *Booker Aquaculture*. Joined Cases C-20/00 and C-64/00. Judgment, 10 July 2003, ECLI:EU:C:2003:397, para. 68. See also EU Commission, *COM(2010) 343 final: Towards a comprehensive European international investment policy,* 7.7.2010.

49 ECJ, *Hauer v Rheinland-Pfalz*. Case 44/79. Judgment, 13 December 1979, paras. 19 ff; M. Perkams, *The Concept of Indirect Expropriation in Comparative Public Law* in S. W. Schill (ed.), *International Investment Law and Comparative Public Law* (Oxford: Oxford University Press, 2010), at 141 ff.

50 PCA, *Eureko v Slovakia*. Case No. 2008–13. Award on Jurisdiction, Arbitrability and Suspension, 26 October 2010, para. 261.

of the fundamental criticism international investment law is currently facing.[51] All but nine of the analysed intra-EU BITs contain this standard, which typically reads: "each Contracting Party shall ensure fair and equitable treatment of the investments of investors of the other Contracting Party."[52]

Due to its broad and not very instructive wording, the fair and equitable treatment standard has become one of the most important standards of IIAs. Its threshold is considerably lower than that of an expropriation. A violation of the standard is thus far easier to establish. As summarized by an arbitral tribunal, the FET standard

> ensures that even where there is no clear justification for making a finding of expropriation [...], there is still a standard which serves the purpose of justice and can of itself redress damage that is unlawful and that would otherwise pass unattended.[53]

In this light, extensive arbitral practice and legal academic writings have developed a general understanding of the FET, which is posited to protect the rule of law and to reflect fundamental principles such as legality, the transparency of governmental actions, the prohibition of arbitrariness, legal certainty, due process, the stability of legal frameworks, proportionality and the protection of 'legitimate expectations'.[54] It can therefore be invoked against various types of a State's misconduct and serves as a catchall standard of protection. Nonetheless, an investor's expectations regarding his or her investments is always based on an assessment of the business environment and legal regime applicable to it at the time of the investment. Against this backdrop, no investor can reasonably expect the circumstances prevailing at the time of investment to remain totally unchanged. As convincingly pointed out by the *Saluka* tribunal a breach of the FET standard must thus be assessed in light of the high measure of deference that international law generally extends to the right of domestic authorities to regulate matters within their own borders. It requires a weighing of the investor's legitimate and reasonable expectations on the one hand and the host State's legitimate regulatory interests on the other.[55] Thus, expectations are not protected by themselves, but require a 'substantial deprivation' of an underlying acquired right. The mere possibility of a particular outcome of an investment or simply encouraging remarks of a host

---

51 See for example, ICSID, *Suez v Argentina*. Case No. ARB/03/19. Decision on Liability – Separate Opinion of Arbitrator Nikken, 30 July 2010, para. 27.

52 See for example, Art. 3 (1) of the 1999 Bulgaria–Netherlands BIT or in a slightly different wording Art. 3 (1) of the 2002 Austria–Malta BIT.

53 ICSID, *Sempra Energy v Argentina*. Case No. ARB/02/16. Award, 28 September 2007, para. 300.

54 Cf. M. Jacob and S. W. Schill, *Fair and Equitable Treatment* in M. Bungenberg, et al. (eds.), *International Investment Law: A Handbook* (Baden-Baden: Nomos, 2015), pp. 700–63, at 713 ff.

55 PCA, *Saluka Investments v Czech Republic*. Partial Award, 17 March 2006, para. 305 f.

State are insufficient to create protected expectations.[56] There is no guarantee in intra-EU IIAs for the investor that the legal framework of the host State will not change.

The EU legal order, on the other hand, is also based on the rule of law.[57] It gives effect to fundamental legal principles such as the separation of powers, the reservation of the law, due process of law, as well as the protection of fundamental rights and the principle of proportionality.[58] Every act of an EU institution or a Member State – acting within the scope of application of EU law – has to apply the proportionality principle, which requires that a measure has to be appropriate for attaining the legitimate objective pursued and must not go beyond what is necessary to achieve it.[59]

Art. 47 EU Charter provides for the right to an effective remedy with due process and independent courts. Also, legal certainty,[60] the legality of the administration and the protection of legitimate expectations[61] are core principles of EU law that can be invoked in court,[62] and which represent "superior rules of law for the protection of the individual".[63] Any time the EU or its Member States apply EU law they are obliged to give full effect to these principles and therefore have to guarantee considerable protection for individuals against unfair governmental

---

56 Cf. M. Jacob and S. W. Schill, *Fair and Equitable Treatment* in M. Bungenberg, et al. (eds.), *International Investment Law: A Handbook* (Baden-Baden: Nomos, 2015), at 726 f; ICSID, *AES Summit & AES-Tisza Erömü v Hungary*. ICSID Case No. ARB/07/22. Award, 23 September 2010, paras. 9.3.6 ff; ICSID, *Parkerings-Compagniet v Lithuania*. ARB/05/8. Award, 11 September 2007, para. 335. See also G. Abi-Saab, *Separate Opinion on Micula v Romania: ICSID Case No. ARB/05/20*, 5 December 2013, at para. 3 f.

57 Cf. the Preamble and Art. 2 TEU.

58 ECJ, *Schräder Kraftfutter*. Case 265/87. Judgment, 11 July 1989, ECLI:EU:C:1989:303, para. 21. See also ECJ, *Tempelman & van Schaijk*. Joined Cases C-96/03 and C-97/03. Judgment, 10 March 2005, ECLI:EU:C:2005:145, para. 47.

59 Cf. ECJ, *Siragusa*. C-206/13. Judgment, 6 March 2014, para. 34; ECJ, *The Queen on the application of Vodafone*. C-58/08. Judgment, 8 June 2010, ECLI:EU:C:2010:321, para. 51. See also EU Commission, *Protection of intra-EU investment – COM (2018) 547/2: Communication from the Commission to the European Parliament and the Council*, 19 June 2018, at p. 13.

60 Cf. ECJ, *ArcelorMittal*. Joined Cases C-201/09 P and C-216/09 P. Judgment, 29 March 2011, ECLI:EU:C:2009:547, para. 68; ECJ, *Gottfried Heinrich*. C-345/06. Judgment, 10 March 2009, ECLI:EU:C:2009:140, paras. 44 ff; ECJ, *Plantanol*. C-201/08. Judgment, 10 September 2009, ECLI:EU:C:2009:539, para. 43; ECJ, *Belgium v Commission*. C-110/03. Judgment, 14 April 2005, ECLI:EU:C:2005:223, para. 30; ECJ, *Westzucker*. Case 1/73. Judgment, 4 July 1973, ECLI:EU:C:1973:78, para. 13; EU Commission, *Protection of intra-EU investment – COM (2018) 547/2*, 19 June 2018, 14 ff.

61 ECJ, *Plantanol*. C-201/08. Judgment, 10 September 2009, para. 43. See also ECJ, *Mulder*. Case 120/86. Judgment, 28 April 1988, paras. 21 ff; ECJ, *Tomadini*. Case 84/78. Judgment, 16 May 1979, paras. 19 ff; ECJ, *Dürbeck*. Case 112/80. Judgment, 5 May 1981, paras. 47 ff. See also, EU Commission, *Protection of intra-EU investment – COM (2018) 547/2*, 19 June 2018, 14 ff.

62 Cf. ECJ, *Gondrand Frères*. Case 169/80. Judgment, 9 July 1981, ECLI:EU:C:1981:171, para. 17; T. Tridimas, *The General Principles of EU Law*, 2. ed. (Oxford: Oxford University Press, 2006), at 242 ff.

63 T. Tridimas, *The General Principles of EU Law* (Oxford: Oxford University Press, 2006), p. 481.

measures.[64] Finally, the stability of institutions guaranteeing the rule of law, is an accession criterion to the EU.[65]

In sum, there is no single provision in EU law that covers the same range of legal principles as the fair and equitable treatment standard. Nonetheless, its elements, which are highly influenced by rule of law considerations are reflected in the EU Treaties. General principles such as the protection of legitimate expectations, legal certainty or the legality of a State's action can be found in both regimes. However, while it is inherent to the EU legal order to balance conflicting interests and to provide for justification and exceptions, the fair and equitable treatment standard with its open wording grants arbitral tribunals a very wide margin of interpretation and allows them to subsume any potential breach of an IIA under this clause. Thus, the FET standard may – in a wide interpretation – allow for a stronger protection of intra-EU investors than the EU legal order.

c) Protection of physical security

An important condition for investors to start and maintain operations abroad is the level of their own physical security in the host State and of the security of the investment itself. Most IIAs contain 'full security and protection' clauses to protect foreign investors from physical threats.[66] These clauses require host States to adopt all reasonable measures to protect assets and property as well as the investors themselves from threats and attacks by third persons or State entities.[67] In case the threat to the investor's security or its investment can be attributed to the host State, the latter incurs full responsibility. A main difference compared to other substantive standards in international investment law is that 'full protection and security' does not only relate to a host State's decision-making process but is also concerned with a State's failure to protect the investment against its own omissions. In other words, it does not only create an obligation for the host State to refrain from certain acts but especially to become active in protecting foreign investors and their investments against physical threats.[68] Regarding injuries and

---

64 Cf. ECJ, *Dansk Rorindustri*. Joined Cases C-189/02 P, C-202/02 P, C-205/02 P to C-208/02 P and C-213/02 P. Judgment, 28 June 2005, ECLI:EU:C:2005:408, para. 211; ECJ, *Töpfer*. Case 112/77. Judgment, 3 May 1978, para. 19.

65 EU Commission, *Copenhagen Accession Criteria*. https://ec.europa.eu/neighbourhood-enlarge ment/policy/glossary/terms/accession-criteria_en (2 May 2020).

66 For example, Art. 3 (3) of the 1989 Cyprus–Hungary BIT: "each Contracting Party shall accord to [...] investments full security and protection."

67 R. A. Lorz, *Protection and Security* in M. Bungenberg, et al. (eds.), *International Investment Law: A Handbook* (Baden-Baden: Nomos, 2015), pp. 764–89, at 777 ff; ICSID, *AES Summit & AES-Tisza Erömü v Hungary*. ICSID Case No. ARB/07/22. Award, 23 September 2010, para. 13.3.2; PCA, *Saluka Investments v Czech Republic*. Partial Award, 17 March 2006, para. 484.

68 Cf. R. A. Lorz, *Protection and Security* in M. Bungenberg, et al. (eds.), *International Investment Law: A Handbook* (Baden-Baden: Nomos, 2015), at 777 ff.

damages caused by private actors, however, the host State is only obliged to exercise due diligence in preventing such incidents; a strict liability is precluded.[69]

There is no direct equivalent in EU law to the 'full security and protection' clause. But the physical integrity of EU investors is equally protected by the fundamental rights of the EU Charter, namely the right to life codified in Art. 2, the right to the integrity of the person enshrined in Art. 3 and the right to liberty and security enshrined in Art. 6. The investment itself is protected by the 'freedom to conduct a business' in Art. 16 EU Charter and especially the right to property in Art. 17 EU Charter.

EU Member States also face due diligence obligations to prevent violent acts of private actors against foreign investors and their investments. This principle in not explicitly stated in the EU Treaties but was developed by the ECJ in the *Spanish Strawberries* case, in which the Court found that

> the fact that a Member State abstains from taking action or [...] fails to adopt adequate measures to prevent obstacles to the free movement of goods that are created, [...] by actions by private individuals on its territory aimed at products originating in other Member States is just as likely to obstruct intra-Community trade as is a positive act.[70]

Although the protection of investments was not the immediate goal of the Court in this ruling, but rather a means to achieve a well-functioning and unrestricted common market, the decision could nevertheless be invoked to ensure the physical integrity and safety of intra-EU investors and their investments.[71]

d) Free transfer of funds

The possibility to transfer funds without major State interference constitutes a key element of foreign direct investments and a main concern of investors operating abroad. It can highly influence a decision to invest. The transfer of funds ensures the implementation of a project, the payment of business expenses, the possibility

---

69 Cf. J. Crawford, *State Responsibility: The General Part* (Cambridge: Cambridge University Press, 2013), at 226 ff; R. A. Lorz, *Protection and Security* in M. Bungenberg, et al. (eds.), *International Investment Law: A Handbook* (Baden-Baden: Nomos, 2015), at 777 ff; ICSID, *AES Summit & AES-Tisza Erömü v Hungary*. ICSID Case No. ARB/07/22. Award, 23 September 2010, para. 13.3.2; PCA, *Saluka Investments v Czech Republic*. Partial Award, 17 March 2006, para. 484; Ad Hoc Arbitration, *Lauder v Czech Republic*. Final Award, 3 September 2001, para. 308.

70 ECJ, *Spanish Strawberries*. C-265/95. Judgment, 9 December 1997, ECLI:EU:C:1997:595, para. 31. This jurisprudence was further developed in ECJ, *Schmidberger*. C-112/00. Judgment, 12 June 2003, ECLI:EU:C:2003:333.

71 See also M. Sattorova, *Investor Rights Under EU Law and International Investment Law,* Journal of World Investment & Trade 17 (2016), at 912 f. With a different view, ECJ, *Achmea*. C-284/16. Opinion of Advocate General Wathelet, 19 September 2017, para. 212.

to reinvest capital, repatriate profits and to disburse shareholders.[72] Thus, the control of, and the liberty to transfer, capital is of great importance for both the host State and the investor. As there is no general rule in international law on the matter and States hold the sovereign right to decide on the transfer of funds and the question of convertibility,[73] the issue is addressed in IIAs by so-called free transfer clauses, which have evolved to a core element of investment protection and are included in every intra-EU IIA. EU law on the other hand covers the question of free transfer through the fundamental freedom of the free movement of capital.

In difference to most other standards, the wording of free transfer clauses in IIAs varies to a large degree. Many clauses include an exhaustive or illustrative list of the different types of transfers and transferable assets covered.[74] An exemplary clause is contained in Art. 6 (1) of the 2000 Croatia–Denmark BIT:

> Each Contracting Party shall with respect to investments in its territory by investors of the other Contracting Party allow the free transfer into and out of its territory of the initial capital [...] the invested capital [...] interests, dividends, profits and other returns.

Currency control regulations or similar acts that confine the investor's assets might violate the free transfer clause and entitle the investor to compensation.[75] Especially, the older intra-EU BITs do not provide for exceptions to the free transfer. More recent treaties, however, recognize legitimate reasons for States to limit the transfer in the exercise of their monetary sovereignty guaranteed by customary international law, for instance in periods of low foreign exchange, in order to address balance of payment problems, ensure the payment of taxes or to avoid capital flight.[76]

With regard to the EU, the free movement of capital is an important cornerstone for the achievement of a common European market, as the liberalization of capital movement is an economic prerequisite for the production factor capital to be used

72 Cf. C. Kern, *Transfer of Funds* in M. Bungenberg, et al. (eds.), *International Investment Law: A Handbook* (Baden-Baden: Nomos, 2015), pp. 870–86, at p. 871; R. Dolzer and C. Schreuer, *Principles of International Investment Law* (Oxford: Oxford University Press, 2012), at 212 ff.

73 Cf. C. Kern, *Transfer of Funds* in M. Bungenberg, et al. (eds.), *International Investment Law: A Handbook* (Baden-Baden: Nomos, 2015), p. 872.

74 See for instance, Art. 14 (1) ECT, or Art. 6 (1) of the 1997 Greece–Slovenia BIT.

75 Cf. N. Blackaby, C. Partasides, A. Redfern and M. Hunter, *Redfern and Hunter on International Arbitration*, 6. ed. (New York, London: Oxford University Press, 2015), at para. 8.130.

76 See for example, Art. 6 (4) of the 2005 Bulgaria–Lithuania BIT which provides that the States "may maintain equitable, non-discriminatory and good faith application of measures, relating to taxation, protection of rights of creditors, or ensuring compliance with other laws and regulations." On such exceptions, see also C. Kern, *Transfer of Funds* in M. Bungenberg, et al. (eds.), *International Investment Law: A Handbook* (Baden-Baden: Nomos, 2015), p. 872; N. Blackaby, C. Partasides, A. Redfern and M. Hunter, *Redfern and Hunter on International Arbitration* (New York, London: Oxford University Press, 2015), para. 8.131.

where it can generate the highest return, which in the end allows a competition among economic locations. Art. 63 TFEU prohibits restrictions on the movement of capital and payments among Member States and between Member States and third countries. This prohibition is directly applicable and, therefore, leads to the inapplicability of incompatible domestic legislation.[77]

In difference to the older intra-EU IIAs, however, the free movement of capital is not guaranteed without exceptions under EU law. According to Art. 65 (1) TFEU, restrictions can be justified to prevent an unequal tax treatment and infringements of national provisions but can also be justified on grounds of public policy or public security,[78] as well as on the unwritten immanent grounds of "overriding requirements of the general interest", as developed by the ECJ.[79]

Furthermore, by virtue of Art. 66 TFEU, the Council may in exceptional circumstances take safeguard measures regarding third countries. Due to the incompatibility of some extra-EU BITs with this EU law exception, the ECJ found in three cases that the unrestricted and non-restrictable free transfer of funds provided for in these extra-EU BITs conflicted with EU law.[80] The affected Member States were obliged to remove the incompatibilities. These ECJ decisions, however, had no effect on intra-EU BITs as the Council is not competent to take Art. 66 TFEU safeguard measures regarding the free movement of capital within the EU.

Both intra-EU IIAs and EU law protect the free movement of capital. In difference to the EU legal order, however, the older intra-EU IIAs provide for an unrestricted free movement of capital without any possible exception. Any limitation of the possibility to freely transfer assets may thus lead to a violation of the host State's obligation arising out of an intra-EU IIA.

---

77 Cf. ECJ, *Emilio Sanz de Lera*. Joined Cases C-163/94, C-165/94 and C-250/94. Judgment, 14 December 1995, ECLI:EU:C:1995:451, para. 47.

78 These exceptions must be interpreted narrowly and cannot be determined unilaterally by Member States without being subject to control by EU institutions. But, the ECJ grants the national authorities some leeway in their decision making, cf. ECJ, *van Duyn*. Case 41/74. Judgment, 4 December 1974, ECLI:EU:C:1974:133, para. 18; ECJ, *Adoui*. Joined Cases 115 and 116/81. Judgment, 18 May 1982, ECLI:EU:C:1982:183, para. 8; ECJ, *Rutili*. Case 36/75. Judgment, 28 October 1975, ECLI:EU:C:1975:137, para. 26.

79 Cf. ECJ, *Golden Shares (I)*. C-483/99. Judgment, 4 June 2002, ECLI:EU:C:2002:327, para. 45; ECJ, *Golden Shares (II)*. C-543/08. Judgment, 11 November 2010, ECLI:EU:C:2010:669, para. 83. These immanent grounds of justification cover inter alia agriculture, environment protection, national infrastructure, culture, education, taxes and workers.

80 Cf. ECJ, *Commission v Sweden*. C-249/06. Judgment, 3 March 2009, ECLI:EU:C:2009:119; ECJ, *Commission v Austria*. C-205/06. Judgment, 3 March 2009, ECLI:EU:C:2009:118; ECJ, *Commission v Finland*. C-118/07. Judgment, 19 November 2009, ECLI:EU:C:2009:715. See also N. Lavranos, *Review of the C-206/06 and C-249/06 Judgements*, American Journal of International Law 103 (2009), 716–22; P. Craig and G. de Búrca, *EU Law: Text, Cases and Materials*, 6. ed. (Oxford: Oxford University Press, 2015), at 359 ff.

e) Interim findings regarding absolute standards of protection

Absolute standards of protection contained in intra-EU IIAs comprise the protection against unlawful expropriation, the protection of legitimate expectations, legal certainty, physical security and the free transfer of funds. Most of these standards are mirrored in EU law. However, especially regarding the fair and equitable treatment, EU law reflects the legal concepts contained therein without guaranteeing a specific subjective right to investors. Furthermore, in difference to EU law, but also other international treaties such as for example Art. XX GATT, the absolute standards of protection contained in intra-EU IIAs are generally guaranteed without exceptions, and do not allow a State to justify a violation of a protection standard for reasons of public interests such as for example human rights, environmental protection or labour law. In sum, intra-EU IIAs are thus more investor friendly. Against this backdrop, they have aptly been described as containing "some of the last vestiges of international economic law's *laissez-faire* liberalism".[81] It is for these reasons that the European Parliament requested the EU Commission to include in all future Free Trade and Investment Protection agreements "specific clauses laying down the right of the parties to the agreement to regulate, inter alia, in the areas of protection of national security, the environment, public health, worker's and consumer's rights, industrial policy and cultural diversity."[82]

3 Protection of contractual undertakings: umbrella clauses

Finally, another substantive protection of foreign investments, different to the relative and absolute standards, is guaranteed through so-called umbrella clauses. More than 110 intra-EU IIAs contain such a clause, for example Art. 10 (1) ECT:

> Each Contracting Party shall observe any obligations it has entered into with an Investor or an Investment of an Investor of any other Contracting Party.[83]

In the course of an international investment project the host State and the foreign investor often conclude a so-called investor-State contract covering the specific undertaking. Such contract is generally governed by the host State's domestic law and the domestic judiciary is thus competent to decide disputes arising out of that

---

81 C. Titi, *International Investment Law and the European Union: Towards a New Generation of International Investment Agreements*, European Journal of International Law 26 (2015), 639–61, at 647.

82 European Parliament, *Resolution on the future European international investment policy (2010/2203(INI))*, 6 April 2011, at para. 25.

83 Hungary is the only EU Member State that has made a reservation regarding its consent to arbitration with respect to disputes concerning umbrella clauses under the ECT, cf. Art. 26 (III) lit. c) ECT.

contract.[84] In order to guarantee the host States' compliance with their contractual obligations arising out of such investor-State contracts, IIA drafters introduced umbrella clauses in many such treaties. These clauses 'internationalize' contractual claims that would otherwise not fall within the ambit of (public) international law.[85] They create a reciprocal duty among contracting States of an IIA to observe the contractual obligations they have entered into with foreign investors of the other contracting State. Due to the frequent appearance of umbrella clauses in combination with arbitration clauses contained in IIAs, they enable investors to invoke breaches of contractual obligations against the host State before investor-State arbitration tribunals, even in the absence of an actual breach of another substantive standard contained in the IIA.[86] The umbrella clause's precise scope of application and its effects, however, remain highly controversial.[87]

There is no equivalent standard in the EU legal order 'internationalizing' Member States' contractual obligations and allowing individuals direct standing before a European court or tribunal against a Member State on the basis of a purely contractual breach.[88] In this regard, EU law resembles customary international law for which the simple breach by a State of a contract with an individual does not *per se* amount to a breach of international law.[89] Rather, a denial of justice, a confiscation of contractual rights or an arbitrary termination is necessary to trigger a State's international responsibility.[90] The situation might be different if the act leading to the contractual breach also restricts the economic freedoms or the EU Charter in an unjustified manner. However, even in that case the violation of a contractual

---

84 Cf. A. von Walter, *State Contracts and the Relevance of Investment Contract Arbitration* in M. Bungenberg, et al. (eds.), *International Investment Law: A Handbook* (Baden-Baden: Nomos, 2015), pp. 80–92.

85 P. Weil, *Problèmes Relatifs aux Contrats Passés Entre un État et un Particulier* in Académie de Droit International (ed.), *Recueil des Cours: Collected Courses of the Hague Academy of International Law 1969 (III)* (Leiden: Brill, 1969), pp. 95–240, at 157 ff.

86 Cf. A. Sinclair, *Umbrella Clauses* in M. Bungenberg, et al. (eds.), *International Investment Law: A Handbook* (Baden-Baden: Nomos, 2015), pp. 887–958, at 888 ff; M. Sattorova, *Investor Rights Under EU Law and International Investment Law*, Journal of World Investment & Trade 17 (2016), at 907 f.

87 See for example ICSID, *SGS v Philippines*. Case No. ARB/02/6. Decision of the Tribunal on Objections to Jurisdiction, 29 January 2004; ICSID, *SGS v Pakistan*. Case No. ARB/01/13. Decision of the Tribunal on Objections to Jurisdiction, 6 August 2003 See also A. Sinclair, *Umbrella Clauses* in M. Bungenberg, et al. (eds.), *International Investment Law: A Handbook* (Baden-Baden: Nomos, 2015), at 887 ff. and 906; T. Roe and M. Happold, *Settlement of Investment Disputes Under the Energy Charter Treaty* (Cambridge: Cambridge University Press, 2011), at 123 ff.

88 See also ECJ, *Achmea*. C-284/16. Opinion of Advocate General Wathelet, 19 September 2017, para. 202.

89 Cf. para. 6 of the Commentary to Art. 4 of the ILC, *Draft Articles on Responsibility of States for Internationally Wrongful Acts, with Commentaries*, 2001.

90 Cf. G. Fitzmaurice, *Hersch Lauterpacht – The Scholar as a Judge: Part I*, British Yearbook of International Law 37 (1961), 1–71, at 64 f; M. Sattorova, *Investor Rights Under EU Law and International Investment Law*, Journal of World Investment & Trade 17 (2016), 908; A. Reinisch, *Expropriation* in P. Muchlinski, et al. (eds.), *The Oxford Handbook of International Investment Law* (Oxford: Oxford University Press, 2008), pp. 407–58, at 418 ff.

obligation does not *per se* trigger the Member State's responsibility under EU law. This is also confirmed by the ECJ's jurisprudence which is rather reluctant regarding the protection of contractually acquired rights under the right to property enshrined in Art. 17 (1) EU Charter.[91] Nonetheless, within the EU legal order, foreign investors remain entitled to rely on the domestic legal system and to start a civil proceeding before the domestic judiciary of the respective Member State if the latter violates a contractual obligation.

4 Interim findings

EU law and intra-EU IIAs are both based on the rule of law and share common goals such as non-discrimination, the prohibition of arbitrariness, due process, proportionality, the protection of private property and physical integrity. The preceding comparison could not avoid generalizing certain aspects and to treat intra-EU IIAs as a closed group. There are, however, some differences among these treaties, especially concerning the coverage of certain standards of protection.[92] Every analysed intra-EU BIT contains a clause dealing with expropriation, the free transfer of funds and most-favoured nation treatment. Although the fair and equitable treatment standard is provided for in almost every intra-EU BIT, this is not the case for the national treatment and the full protection and security clause and the least for umbrella clauses. The ECT provides for every of these standards.

There are several differences in the depth of the respective protection standards. Also, many protection principles are scattered around the EU Treaties, whereas they are mostly contained in specific clauses in IIAs. Some standards of protection such as the most-favoured nation treatment or umbrella clauses are unknown to the EU legal order and the protection of property remains mostly in the Member States' competence.

However, the main difference between intra-EU IIAs and EU law consists in the existence of a sophisticated regime of exceptions in EU law, which is not provided for in the great majority of intra-EU IIAs. These exceptions allow the judiciary to carefully balance conflicting interests and to take the general interest into consideration, while developing a coherent line of jurisprudence, which is hardly achievable in the 'international investment protection regime' due to the inapplicability of the *stare decisis* principle.

Furthermore, under EU law restrictions of fundamental freedoms and fundamental rights can be justified based on explicit grounds,[93] or based on unwritten principles developed by the ECJ.[94] Art. 52 TFEU, for example, allows States to

---

91 ECJ, *Sky Österreich*. C-283/11. Judgment, 22 January 2013, ECLI:EU:C:2013:28, para. 34; M. Sattorova, *Investor Rights Under EU Law and International Investment Law*, Journal of World Investment & Trade 17 (2016), at 910 f.

92 Figure 2.1.

93 Cf. Arts. 36, 45 (2), 52, 62, 65, 66 TFEU, and Art. 52(1) EU Charter.

94 Especially ECJ, *Cassis de Dijon*. Case 120/78. Judgment, 20 February 1979 and the following jurisprudence.

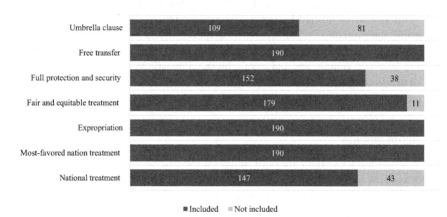

■ Included   ■ Not included

as of March 2018 (before ECJ's *Achmea* judgment)

Figure 2.1 Substantive protection in intra-EU IIAs

impair the right of establishment on the grounds of public policy, public security or public health.[95]

The EU Charter, in turn, contains many different fundamental rights that might be invoked to protect private economic interests affected by a State's acts, as well as to restrict such economic interests, in order to give effect to conflicting fundamental rights. According to its Art. 51 (1) the Charter, however, only applies to EU Member States "when they are implementing Union law". While this provision is interpreted in a broad manner by the ECJ,[96] its actual scope of application remains highly controversial.[97] Nonetheless, one can surmise that intra-EU investments have sufficient close relation to EU law to be treated in accordance with the fundamental rights of the EU Charter, by both EU institutions and the Member State authorities.

While the balancing of conflicting interests by arbitrators in investor-State disputes is not completely precluded by the lack of exceptions or 'interest-balancing' clauses in IIAs, it is less likely that public interests are comprehensively

---

95 ECJ, *Calfa*. C-348/96. Judgment, 19 January 1999, ECLI:EU:C:1999:6.
96 ECJ, *Åkerberg Fransson*. C-617/10. Judgment, 26 February 2013, para. 19, 21. See also ECJ, *Hernandéz*. C-198/13. Judgment, 10 July 2014, para. 34. Different, however, ECJ, *Siragusa*. C-206/13. Judgment, 6 March 2014, paras. 24 ff.
97 Critical towards the ECJ's interpretative approach in particular BVerfG, *Antiterrordatei*. 1 BVR 1215/07. Urteil, 24 April 2014, BVerfGE 133, 277, para. 88; C. Franzius, *Grundrechtsschutz in Europa: Zwischen Selbstbehauptungen und Selbstbeschränkungen der Rechtsordnungen und ihrer Gerichte*, Zeitschrift für ausländisches öffentliches Recht und Völkerrecht 75 (2015), 383–412; C. Latzel, *Die Anwendungsbereiche des Unionsrechts*, Europäische Zeitschrift für Wirtschaftsrecht (2015), 658–64, at 663. See also P. Craig and G. de Búrca, *EU Law: Text, Cases and Materials*, 6. ed. (Oxford: Oxford University Press, 2015), at 409 ff.

considered in investor-State proceedings, if the treaty – the arbitral tribunal bases its jurisdiction upon – does not stipulate to take the State's interests and its 'right to regulate' into account.

In sum, EU law provides for a more sophisticated balance of private and public interests compared to most intra-EU IIAs which totally lack such balance. This leads *per definitionem* to a weaker – but more carefully weighed – substantive protection of foreign investments under the law of the European Union.

IV Procedural protection

The level of investor protection is not only defined by substantive standards guaranteed in different legal instruments, but above all by the remedies accessible to investors in case of an infringement of their substantive rights. In other words, the substantive protection proves its full potential and effectiveness ultimately through the enforcement mechanisms allowing for reparation in case of an infringement.[98]

In principle, foreign investors, operating within a host State's national economy and thus acting within its legal and judicial system, can just like that State's nationals only initiate proceedings against the host State before its domestic courts and potentially request diplomatic protection by their home State after the exhaustion of local remedies.[99] The invocation of substantive rights before any other State's judiciary, be it the home State or a third State is precluded due to the jurisdictional immunities of States and the principle of *par in parem non habet imperium*, i.e. the principle that a State cannot be compelled to appear before or be condemned by courts and tribunals of another State.[100] Nonetheless, a foreign investors can bring a case before an international court or tribunal such as an investor-State arbitration tribunal, in case its jurisdiction has been accepted by the host State. This, however, does not apply to the sophisticated judicial system within the EU.

1 Investor-State dispute settlement in intra-EU IIAs

Most intra-EU BITs as well as the ECT are 'third generation' treaties and provide for a direct and unlimited investor-State dispute settlement mechanism in form of arbitration. The 35 'second generation' BITs, however, provide that only certain disputes arising under a limited number of the BIT's substantive provisions (mostly expropriation) can be referred to arbitration. Under these treaties a breach of another standard such as the fair and equitable treatment or full protection and

---

98 On the "principle of international law that the breach of an engagement involves an obligation to make reparation in an adequate form," see PCIJ, *Factory at Chorzów*. No. 9. Judgment (Jurisdiction), 26 July 1927, *Collection of Judgements Series A*, p. 21 and PCIJ, *Factory at Chorzów*. No. 17. Judgment (Merits), 13 September 1928, *Collection of Judgements Series A*, p. 47.

99 Cf. in greater detail Chapter I: II. 2. b).

100 See M. N. Shaw, *International Law*, 7. ed. (Cambridge: Cambridge University Press, 2014), at 506 f; J. Crawford, *Brownlie's Principles of Public International Law* (Oxford: Oxford University Press, 2012), at 487 ff.

security, cannot be litigated before an international investment arbitration tribunal. The 'first generation' BITs finally, do not provide for ISDS at all. Investors falling under such a treaty can only try to convince their home State to endorse their case through diplomatic action or State-to-State arbitration or bring a case before the domestic courts of the host State.

The following section provides a brief overview on the preconditions and the procedure of investor-State arbitration. It has many similarities with commercial arbitration, however, with the fundamental difference that IIA-based arbitration proceedings rest on international inter-State treaties which are governed by public international law. In the following the different steps of an arbitration proceeding will be presented, namely the arbitration agreement and choice of arbitrators (a), the different possible fora (b), the enforcement of awards (c) and review and annulment possibilities (d).

a) Arbitration agreement and choice of arbitrators

Every sovereign State can freely organize its judicial system and decide on the adjudicative body competent to hear certain claims. Regarding investment related disputes the determination of the forum for dispute settlement is subject to both States parties' autonomy, as no international court or tribunal possesses an 'inherent' compulsory jurisdiction.[101] In other words, it is the States alone that decide if an investor has the right to bring a claim before a domestic court, an international arbitral tribunal, a domestic arbitral tribunal or if the investor may freely choose between different applicable fora.

The consent of the potential home and host States provides the basis for the jurisdiction of investor-State arbitration tribunals. This consent is generally given beforehand by the States parties through an arbitration provision contained in the IIA.[102] The arbitration provision creates a standing offer to arbitrate any investment dispute with any foreign investor of the other State party; an approach often described as 'arbitration without privity'.[103] In other words, the State's consent to arbitrate is not limited to a specific actor or investment undertaking but covers every potential investor stemming from the other State party to the IIA. Any investor falling under the IIA can accept the host State's offer to arbitrate by initiating an arbitral proceeding before the respective forum of arbitration. In most cases the exhaustion of local remedies is no precondition to an ISDS proceeding. Nonetheless, some intra-EU BITs require a temporarily limited interaction with the local administration of justice, also known as 'cooling-off' period, before an investor can initiate an investor-State arbitration proceeding. Thus, investors might have to pursue local remedies and can then – if no settlement has been reached within a

---

101 M. N. Shaw, *International Law* (Cambridge: Cambridge University Press, 2014), at 506 ff.

102 See for example, Art. 26 ECT and Art. 11 of the 1996 Germany–Romania BIT.

103 J. Paulsson, *Arbitration Without Privity*, ICSID Review 10 (1995), 232–57. See also H. E. Kjos, *Applicable Law in Investor-State Arbitration* (Oxford: Oxford University Press, 2013), at 20 f.

certain period – initiate an investor-State arbitration proceeding, generally based on the rules of procedure of their choice.[104] If investors, however, choose to pursue a claim before domestic courts and are eventually unsuccessful, they are likely to be precluded from starting new proceedings before other fora, i.e. to initiate an investor-State arbitration proceeding due to the principle of *res judicata*.[105] In a similar way, many intra-EU IIAs contain so-called fork-in-the-road clauses, which require investors to opt for either a domestic proceeding or international arbitration and impede them to pursue their claim before another forum than the one originally chosen, in case they have been unsuccessful.[106]

In case, an investor chooses arbitration, the arbitral tribunal must be constituted, once the proceedings have been initiated. Most investor-State arbitration tribunals are composed of three arbitrators, one of which is appointed by the respective parties to the dispute. The third arbitrator, who acts in the capacity of president of the tribunal, is generally chosen by the two other arbitrators or the administering institution. There are no strict requirements for the selection of arbitrators. Although some arbitration institutions provide a list of arbitrators, every party to the dispute is generally completely free to choose the respective arbitrator for a specific proceeding.

b) *Different possible fora and rules of procedure*

Typically, an investor is free to choose between an administered arbitration proceeding, conducted by an international arbitration institution, and a non-administered arbitration proceeding on an ad hoc basis,[107] as well as the rules applicable to it. This choice of forum can be based on the practical enforceability of an award,

---

104 See for example Art. 8 (2) of the 1988 Austria–Poland BIT, the 1988 Austria–Hungary BIT and the 1987 BLEU–Malta BIT. The first requires a 'cooling-off' period' of 12 months, the two others an 18 months period before an arbitration proceeding may be initiated. See also A. Aaken van, *Primary and Secondary Remedies in International Investment Law and National State Liability* in S. W. Schill (ed.), *International Investment Law and Comparative Public Law* (Oxford: Oxford University Press, 2010), pp. 721–54, at 739 f.

105 K. Yannaca-Small, *Parallel Proceedings* in P. Muchlinski, et al. (eds.), *The Oxford Handbook of International Investment Law* (Oxford: Oxford University Press, 2008), pp. 1008–48, at 1014 ff; N. Blackaby, C. Partasides, A. Redfern and M. Hunter, *Redfern and Hunter on International Arbitration* (New York, London: Oxford University Press, 2015), para. 9.173.

106 See for example, Art. 26 (3) lit. b) ECT, which limits the State consent to arbitration by providing that the Contracting Parties listed in Annex ID do not give unconditional consent to arbitration if the Investor has previously submitted the dispute to a domestic court or any other previously agreed dispute settlement procedure. Among the States listed in Annex ID are 15 EU Member States. In case of parallel proceedings, the *lis alibi pendens* principle may also be applicable, leading to a stay of one of the proceedings, cf. K. Yannaca-Small, *Parallel Proceedings* in P. Muchlinski, et al. (eds.), *The Oxford Handbook of International Investment Law* (Oxford: Oxford University Press, 2008), at 1021 ff; R. A. Brand, *Forum non conveniens*, (April 2013) in *MPEPIL (Online-Edition)* at para. 3.

107 See also N. Blackaby, C. Partasides, A. Redfern and M. Hunter, *Redfern and Hunter on International Arbitration* (New York, London: Oxford University Press, 2015), paras. 1.143 ff.

or the applicable procedural rules especially regarding the transparency of the proceeding and its costs.

Intra-EU investor-State arbitration proceedings rarely take place on an ad hoc basis but are typically administered by an international arbitration institution which secures the tribunal's functioning. The most important institution in the field of investor-State dispute settlement is the Washington based International Centre for Settlement of Investment Disputes (ICSID), which was created in the early 1960s with the aim to 'depoliticize' investment disputes and to avoid confrontation between home State and host State.[108] Other institutions relied upon for intra-EU ISDS proceedings are the Paris-based International Chamber of Commerce (ICC), the Permanent Court of Arbitration (PCA) in The Hague or the Stockholm Chamber of Commerce (SCC).[109] None of these institutions conducts arbitral proceedings by itself but organizes and supports the respective arbitral tribunal's work.

As of May 23, 2020, of the 161 known intra-EU ISDS proceedings,[110] 12 were pure ad hoc arbitration proceedings, two administered by the ICC, 96 by ICSID, 28 by the PCA and 20 by the SCC. For three cases no data is available.

Besides an administration, arbitral tribunals have to rely on certain rules of procedure, so-called arbitration rules, which are often provided by the administering institutions.[111] A widely used alternative to such institution-related arbitration rules are the 1985 UNCITRAL Arbitration Rules.[112]

The early intra-EU BITs provided for ICSID arbitration only, i.e. for proceedings administered by ICSID and based on the arbitration rules provided for in the ICSID Convention. For the ICSID Convention to be applicable, both States Parties to the IIA must also be parties to the ICSID Convention itself.[113] However, before the end of the Cold War, only two of the current Eastern and Central

---

108 I. F. I. Shihata, *Towards a Greater Depoliticization of Investment Disputes: The Roles of ICSID and MIGA,* ICSID Review 1 (1986), 1–25; R. Dolzer and C. Schreuer, *Principles of International Investment Law* (Oxford: Oxford University Press, 2012), p. 9; A. F. Lowenfeld, *International Economic Law,* 2. ed. (Oxford: Oxford University Press, 2009), at 536 ff.

109 There are many other arbitral institutions, which, however, so far have not played a role in intra-EU ISDS proceedings. For an extensive overview on these institutions, cf. N. Blackaby, C. Partasides, A. Redfern and M. Hunter, *Redfern and Hunter on International Arbitration* (New York, London: Oxford University Press, 2015), at 1.165 ff.

110 For the categorization of pre-accession, transition and intra-EU cases, see Chapter I: III. 5.

111 Out of the 95 intra-EU proceedings administered by ICSID, 94 were based on the ICSID Arbitration rules, and the other on the UNCITRAL arbitration rules. The two ICC proceedings were based on the ICC arbitration rules. Of the 20 proceedings administered by the SCC, 19 were based on the SCC arbitration rules and one on the UNCITRAL arbitration rules. Of the 28 proceedings administered by the PCA, one was based on the SCC arbitration rules and 27 on the UNCITRAL arbitration rules.

112 At least 43 intra-EU ISDS cases were based on these rules, among them 28 cases administered by the PCA, one case administered by the SCC and one case administered by ICSID. Furthermore, every intra-EU ad hoc arbitration proceeding relied on the UNCITRAL arbitration rules.

113 Art. 25 (1) ICSID Convention.

European EU Member States had ratified the ICSID Convention.[114] The other States joined the Convention in the 1990s and early 2000s. As many post-communist countries not being States Parties to the ICSID Convention started to conclude IIAs in the 1990s, the other administering institutions and arbitration rules – originally designed to serve commercial arbitration purposes only – gained importance and were invoked in several disputes. Meanwhile, every EU Member State apart from Poland has become a State party to the ICSID Convention.

The key difference between the ICSID arbitration rules and other arbitration rules, is that the latter require the arbitral tribunals to establish a place of arbitration, i.e. to localize their legal seat and to situate themselves within a national legal system. ICSID arbitration on the other hand is delocalized,[115] which makes domestic judicial control much more limited. In other words, "the place of arbitration in ICSID proceedings is irrelevant for the award's validity and enforcement" as ICSID arbitration is "independent of judicial control in the country where the proceedings take place and the award is rendered".[116] Furthermore, the ICSID Convention is designed to cover investor-State disputes only, while the other rules of arbitration are typical commercial arbitration rules and accordingly have a wider scope of application.[117]

c) Enforcement

Once an arbitral award has been rendered, its enforcement is only necessary if the debtor is not willing to accept the tribunal's decision and to pay the damages awarded to the claimant.[118] Non-compliance with investor-State arbitration awards, has so far rather been the exception than the rule, as non-compliance by the host State might not only affect its economic relations with the investor and its home State but can also create a negative reputation deterring future

---

114 It entered into force in Romania in 1975 and in Hungary in 1987.
115 Ibid., para. 1.888.
116 C. Schreuer, *The ICSID Convention: A Commentary*, 2. ed. (Cambridge: Cambridge University Press, 2009), at Art. 53, para. 22.
117 In difference to other rules of arbitration, Art. 25 (2) lit. a) ICSID Convention requires the claimant to have the nationality of a State party to the Convention. Thus, it is possible that an investor entitled to protection under an IIA might not have the capacity to bring a claim under the ICSID Convention. This could for example be the case for permanent residents in accordance with Art. 1 (7) ECT or dual nationals. Such investors would then have to rely on other arbitration rules than ICSID. See also L. F. Reed and J. E. Davis, *Who Is a Protected Investor?* in M. Bungenberg, et al. (eds.), *International Investment Law: A Handbook* (Baden-Baden: Nomos, 2015), pp. 614–37, at 617 ff.
118 If not precluded by the IIA, primary remedies are equally permissible. The ICSID Convention does not restrict investors to pecuniary damages. Cf. A. Aaken van, *Primary and Secondary Remedies in International Investment Law and National State Liability* in S. W. Schill (ed.), *International Investment Law and Comparative Public Law* (Oxford: Oxford University Press, 2010), p. 734.

investors.[119] Another reason for high compliance is that ISDS awards can effectively be enforced by successful investors outside the respondent State's territory so that the latter's non-compliance might be meaningless in preventing enforcement attempts.

But most importantly, non-compliance with an award constitutes a violation of the host State's international obligation to recognize and enforce an arbitral award. The violation of such an obligation entitles the home State of the investor to exercise diplomatic protection or to refer the dispute to an international court or tribunal in case there is a legal basis for its jurisdiction. In case of an ICSID dispute, the ICJ would be competent to decide such a dispute, if it cannot be settled by negotiation with the host State or the State in which enforcement is sought. No further agreement among these States would be needed as Art. 64 ICSID Convention establishes the ICJ's compulsory jurisdiction in accordance with Art. 36 (1) ICJ Statute.[120]

In any case, recognition and enforcement of an arbitral award are only possible through domestic courts, as the enforcement jurisdiction is strictly territorial.[121] The typical enforcement procedure is a two-stage process, i.e. it is not the award itself which is executed but a decision by a local authority, which confirms or registers the award or declares it enforceable.[122] Only after this decision the actual enforcement can take place, often described as 'execution'.[123] Before starting such a procedure, investors will first have to determine in which State they want to seek enforcement, depending on where the respondent State to the dispute has assets, but also depending on whether the forum State and its judiciary recognize

---

119 S. Kröll, *Enforcement of Awards* in M. Bungenberg, et al. (eds.), *International Investment Law: A Handbook* (Baden-Baden: Nomos, 2015), pp. 1482–504, at p. 1483; H. Bubrowski, *Internationale Investitionsschiedsverfahren und nationale Gerichte* (Tübingen: Mohr Siebeck, 2013), at 278 f.

120 Cf. C. Schreuer, *The ICSID Convention: A Commentary*, 2. ed. (Cambridge: Cambridge University Press, 2009), Art. 64, para. 2.

121 See also Art. III New York Convention and Art. 54 ICSID Convention.

122 The German Code of Civil Procedure (ZPO), for instance, does not provide for direct enforcement of arbitral awards, but requires a formal recognition of the award to convert it into an enforceable title. For domestic arbitral awards, i.e. with the seat of arbitration in Germany, § 1060 ZPO requires a declaration of enforceability. According to § 1061 (1) ZPO the recognition and enforcement of foreign awards, i.e. awards of arbitral tribunals with seats outside the country in which enforcement is sought, is governed by the New York Convention. See also for the enforcement of arbitral awards in France Art. 1487 and Art. 1516 Code de procedure civile. Different regarding domestic awards: § 1 (16) Austrian Exekutionsordnung. Other legal orders, such as the Swedish for example, do not require a formal act of recognition or 'exequatur' for the enforcement, cf. S. Balthasar, *Best Practice in International Arbitration* in S. Balthasar (ed.), *International Commercial Arbitration: International Conventions, Country Reports and Comparative Analysis* (München: C. H. Beck, 2016), pp. 1–43, at 39 f.

123 S. Kröll, *Enforcement of Awards* in M. Bungenberg, et al. (eds.), *International Investment Law: A Handbook* (Baden-Baden: Nomos, 2015), at 1484 f.

and enforce awards rendered at the place of arbitration.[124] The tracing of assets is necessary as international arbitration proceedings usually take place in 'neutral' places, i.e. places to which none of the parties has a connection. Thus, the enforcement of an award generally takes place in a country other than that of the seat of arbitration.[125]

d) Review and annulment

Domestic law defines the limits of arbitration: Arbitral proceedings must comply with rules of due process and may not undermine the *ordre public*.[126] The compliance with these principles is controlled by domestic courts during the review, annulment and enforcement of arbitral awards. The rules applicable to such judicial control, however, highly depend on the question whether – from the point of view of the seized domestic court – the award was rendered by a 'domestic' arbitral tribunal, i.e. a tribunal that had its seat in the country in which enforcement, review or annulment is sought or by a 'foreign' arbitral tribunal or even a 'delocalized' ICSID tribunal. In that sense, a losing party to an investor-State arbitration proceeding has two options to challenge an award: either initiate a review or annulment process before domestic courts at the seat of arbitration or oppose the award's enforcement in any jurisdiction in which the investor seeks to enforce it. The following section will analyse both the available review and annulment mechanisms for non-ICSID and ICSID awards.

NON-ICSID AWARDS

Every award apart from awards rendered under the ICSID Convention can be challenged as a 'domestic' arbitral decision in the domestic courts of the State of the arbitral tribunal's seat according to its applicable laws. An SCC award rendered by a Stockholm-based arbitral tribunal, for example, could be challenged under Swedish domestic law.

A majority of EU Member States has adopted the non-binding 1985 UNCITRAL Model Law on International Commercial Arbitration (UNCITRAL Model Law) and transferred its rules on the recognition, review and enforcement of

---

124 N. Blackaby, C. Partasides, A. Redfern and M. Hunter, *Redfern and Hunter on International Arbitration* (New York, London: Oxford University Press, 2015), paras. 11.25 ff; H. Bubrowski, *Internationale Investitionsschiedsverfahren und nationale Gerichte* (Tübingen: Mohr Siebeck, 2013), at 278 f.

125 Cf. N. Blackaby, C. Partasides, A. Redfern and M. Hunter, *Redfern and Hunter on International Arbitration* (New York, London: Oxford University Press, 2015), para. 11.28; M. L. Moses, *The Principles and Practice of International Commercial Arbitration* (Cambridge: Cambridge University Press, 2017), at 178.

126 See for example, § 1059 German ZPO and Art. 1520 French Code de Procédure Civile.

'domestic' arbitral awards into their domestic laws.[127] The UNCITRAL Model Law allows domestic courts before which enforcement is sought to set aside an arbitral award or to refuse its enforcement in case of formal flaws in the arbitration process, if the subject-matter of the dispute is not capable of settlement by arbitration under the law of the court's State, or if the award is in conflict with the *ordre public* of this State.[128]

The review of 'foreign' arbitral awards is determined by the 1958 New York Convention on the Recognition and Enforcement of Foreign Arbitral Awards (New York Convention), which is applicable in every EU Member State.[129] The New York Convention defines in its Art. 1 'foreign' arbitral awards as "awards that are made in the territory of a State other than the State where the recognition and enforcement are sought". It stipulates the obligation for the ratifying States to recognize foreign arbitral awards as binding and to enforce them in accordance with their rules of procedure.[130] Art. V New York Convention provides for an almost identical and exhaustive list of grounds for non-recognition and non-enforcement of awards as those mentioned in Art. 36 UNCITRAL Model Law. These grounds have been invoked in several intra-EU arbitration award annulment proceedings before domestic courts.[131] A review on the merits, however, is neither provided for in the UNCITRAL Model Law nor in the New York Convention.

The setting aside of an award abolishes its legal effect within the legal order of the overruling court, i.e. the award becomes unenforceable in that State. But an award that has been set aside or annulled can be treated as invalid not only by the courts at the seat of arbitration but also by domestic courts in other countries, as both the UNCITRAL Model Law and the New York Convention stipulate that recognition and enforcement of the award may be refused if "the award has been set aside or suspended by a competent authority of the country in which, or under

---

127 The Model Law has been adopted by 18 EU Member States. Non-signatories are Finland, France, Italy, Latvia, Luxembourg, Netherlands, Portugal, Romania and Sweden. Cf. UNCITRAL, *1985 Model Law on International Commercial Arbitration – Status*. https://uncitral.un.org/en/texts/arbitration/modellaw/commercial_arbitration/status (4 May 2020).

128 Arts. 34 and 36 UNCITRAL Model Law.

129 New York Arbitration Convention, *Ratification Status*. www.newyorkconvention.org/countries (4 May 2020).

130 Art. 1 (3) second sentence New York Convention allows the States parties to make a declaration that they will apply the Convention "only to differences arising out of legal relationships, whether contractual or not, which are considered as commercial under the national law of the State making such declaration." Cyprus, Denmark, Hungary and Romania are the only EU Member States to have made such a declaration.

131 See, for example *Ad Hoc Arbitration, Eureko v Poland. Partial Award, 19 August 2005* invoked before Belgium courts; PCA, *Achmea (formerly known as "Eureko") v Slowakia*. Case No. 2008–13. Final Award, 7 December 2012 invoked in Germany leading to the preliminary reference and the ECJ, *Achmea*. C-284/16. Judgment, 6 March 2018; Ad Hoc Arbitration, *SwemBalt v Latvia*. Decision by the Court of Arbitration, 23 October 2000 invoked before Danish courts or also Ad Hoc Arbitration, *Saar Papier v Poland*. Final Award, 16 October 1995 invoked before Swiss courts.

the law of which the award was made".[132] However, there is no obligation for domestic courts in other jurisdiction to refuse the recognition or the enforcement of an award as the wording is permissive and not mandatory.[133]

As shown previously, the vast majority of intra-EU ISDS proceedings has been administered by the ICSID and was based on the ICSID arbitration rules. The unique characteristic of the ICSID system is, that it provides for 'delocalized' arbitration without a formal seat of arbitration, which precludes the applicability of the *lex loci arbitri*. It creates a quasi-autonomous, self-contained system of review of awards, which are directly enforceable in all ICSID Member States.[134]

While the New York Convention and the UNCITRAL Model Law provide for the possibility of domestic courts to review an arbitral award, Art. 53 ICSID Convention totally excludes domestic courts from the review process. The ICSID Convention even creates an international law obligation for its State Parties to prevent any judicial interference with ICSID awards.[135] However, while the recognition is only subject to the requirements of the ICSID Convention and cannot be refused for reasons of domestic law, the actual execution of awards remains subject to the modalities of the domestic law of the country where execution is sought.[136] Nonetheless, during an enforcement proceeding, a domestic court may solely verify the authenticity of the ICSID award and not re-examine the ICSID tribunal's jurisdiction or the award on its merits.[137]

Thus, the only possibility for a party to the dispute to prevent the enforcement of an award is to initiate an annulment proceeding before an ICSID 'ad hoc Committee' which is totally detached from domestic control, and to make

---

132 Art. V (1) lit. e) New York Convention and with an almost identical wording, Art. 36 (1) lit. a) (v) UNCITRAL Model Law. See also N. Blackaby, C. Partasides, A. Redfern and M. Hunter, *Redfern and Hunter on International Arbitration* (New York, London: Oxford University Press, 2015), paras. 10.06 ff; G. A. Bermann, *Navigating EU Law and the Law of International Arbitration,* Arbitration International 28 (2012), 397–445, at 414.

133 Cf. C. Liebscher, *Article V (1) (e)* in R. Wolff (ed.), *New York Convention – Commentary* (München: C. H. Beck, 2012), pp. 356–80, at 369 f; D. Solomon, *International Commercial Arbitration* in S. Balthasar (ed.), *International Commercial Arbitration: International Conventions, Country Reports and Comparative Analysis* (München: C. H. Beck, 2016), pp. 45–157, at para. 198 ff. See also Chapter IV: IV. 2. a).

134 See R. Dolzer and C. Schreuer, *Principles of International Investment Law* (Oxford: Oxford University Press, 2012), p. 20; C. Schreuer, *The ICSID Convention: A Commentary*, 2. ed. (Cambridge: Cambridge University Press, 2009), Art. 54, para. 81.

135 Cf. C. Schreuer, *The ICSID Convention: A Commentary*, 2. ed. (Cambridge: Cambridge University Press, 2009), Art. 41, para. 22 f.

136 Ibid., Art. 54, para. 47.

137 H. Bubrowski, *Internationale Investitionsschiedsverfahren und nationale Gerichte* (Tübingen: Mohr Siebeck, 2013), at 286 f; C. Schreuer, *The ICSID Convention: A Commentary*, 2. ed. (Cambridge: Cambridge University Press, 2009), Art. 54, para. 42, 81.

an application for a stay of enforcement pursuant to Art. 52 ICSID Convention. In difference to domestic courts, the ICSID 'ad hoc Committee' does not become active *ex officio* but only if requested by a party to the dispute. It examines the award on very limited grounds, partly reflecting the grounds for review contained in the UNCITRAL Model Law and the New York Convention such as exceedance of power by the arbitral tribunal. An incompatibility with an *ordre* public, however, is not a ground for annulment under the ICSID Convention.

2 Remedies before EU courts

In difference to investor-State arbitration, the EU legal order has created a highly sophisticated system of judicial dispute settlement, involving many different types of procedures as well as domestic and EU courts.

In its landmark decision *Les Verts*, the ECJ ruled that the EU is based in particular on

> the rule of law, inasmuch as neither its Member States nor its institutions can avoid a review of the question whether the measures adopted by them are in conformity with the basic constitutional charter, the Treaty.[138]

Any act or omission of both the EU institutions and the Member States which violates EU Law can thus be subject to review by the EU's judiciary that ensures the lawful interpretation and application of EU law.[139] This is also reflected in Art. 19 (1) [2] TEU, which stipulates that "Member States shall provide remedies sufficient to ensure effective legal protection in the fields covered by Union law." As explained by the ECJ in *Associação Sindical dos Juízes Portugueses*, this provision

> entrusts the responsibility for ensuring judicial review in the EU legal order not only to the Court of Justice but also to national courts and tribunals. Consequently, national courts and tribunals, in collaboration with the Court of Justice, fulfil a duty entrusted to them jointly of ensuring that in the interpretation and application of the Treaties the law is observed.[140]

In other words, the judicial system of the EU is characterized by an intense cooperation between domestic and European courts. The domestic courts of the Member States can thus be understood as an extended arm of the European judiciary or

---

138 ECJ, *Parti écologiste 'Les Verts'*. Case 294/83. Judgment, 23 April 1986, ECLI:EU:C:1986:166, para. 23.
139 Cf. K. Lenaerts, I. Maselis and K. Gutman, *EU Procedural Law* (Oxford: Oxford University Press, 2014), at 2.
140 ECJ, *Associação Sindical dos Juízes Portugueses*. C-64/16. Judgment, 27 February 2018, ECLI:EU:C:2018:117, para. 32 f.

even as the 'ordinary courts' of the EU, as cases involving EU law are generally brought before them.[141]

The 'actual' European Union judiciary is the Court of Justice of the European Union which includes the Court of Justice (referred to in this study as ECJ), the General Court and potentially specialized courts.[142] These genuinely European judicial bodies are bound by the principle of conferral provided for in Arts. 5 and 13 (2) TEU. They can only exercise their jurisdiction when it is conferred upon them under the EU Treaties.[143] Most cases involving EU law fall within the Member States domestic courts' residual competences, which are also obliged to apply EU law.[144]

a) *Different procedures before the ECJ*

The ECJ's role is to ensure the correct interpretation and application of EU law. As shown previously, EU law guarantees the fundamental freedoms and the protection of property, the enforcement and control of which according to Art. 17 TEU is mostly the task of the EU Commission. In case of EU law violations, the Commission or a Member State can initiate infringement proceedings against an EU Member State and in case the State is not complying eventually bring the case before the ECJ pursuant to Arts. 258 and 259 TFEU. In such a proceeding, however, the ECJ can according to Art. 260 TFEU only determine whether a Member State has violated an EU obligation but cannot set aside a national act or award any compensation. Nonetheless, it is not only the EU Commission but also to individuals to assert claims under EU law. In the words of the ECJ in its famous 1963 *van Gend en Loos* decision:

> The vigilance of individuals concerned to protect their rights amounts to an effective supervision in addition to the supervision entrusted […] to the diligence of the Commission and of the Member States.[145]

This vigilance, however, is combined with a very limited direct access to the EU courts. Direct access for individuals to EU courts is available by way of action for annulment in accordance with Art. 263 TFEU. It aims at reviewing the legality of legislative acts, of acts of the Council, of the Commission and of the European

---

141 See K. Lenaerts, I. Maselis and K. Gutman, *EU Procedural Law* (Oxford: Oxford University Press, 2014), p. 3; B. W. Wegener, *Art. 267 AEUV* in C. Calliess and M. Ruffert (eds.), *EUV/AEUV – Kommentar*, 5. ed. (München: C. H. Beck, 2016), at para. 1.

142 Art. 19 (1) TEU. The so far only specialized court, the Civil Service Tribunal ceased to exist in 2016.

143 K. Lenaerts, I. Maselis and K. Gutman, *EU Procedural Law* (Oxford: Oxford University Press, 2014), p. 3.

144 Ibid., p. 3; EU Commission, *Protection of intra-EU investment – COM (2018) 547/2*, 19 June 2018, p. 19.

145 ECJ, *Van Gend & Loos*. Case 26/62. Judgment, 5 February 1963, ECLI:EU:C:1963:1, p. 13.

Central Bank, as well as of acts of the European Council and European Parliament intended to produce legal effects vis-à-vis third parties. It does, however, not provide for the review of the legality of acts by the EU Member States. Also, the 'claims for damages procedure' provided for in Art. 268 in conjunction with Art. 340 (2, 3) TFEU is only applicable to disputes relating to compensation for damages caused by the EU or its institutions. Thus, the 'actual' EU courts are not competent to decide on a compensation claim directed against a Member State, a situation that would be comparable to intra-EU investor-State arbitrations.

Notwithstanding, the ECJ found in its *Francovich*[146] and *Brasserie du Pêcheur*[147] decisions that Member States bear liability for the breach of EU law. The Court decided that the effectiveness of EU rules would be impaired if individuals were unable to obtain compensation for infringements of their rights by Member States acting in violation of EU law.[148] According to the ECJ, the Member State's liability for a violation of EU law is 'inherent in the system of the Treaty'.[149] However, the realization of compensation takes place through domestic courts and domestic rules only, which in turn are strengthened by the EU law's 'minimum standards'.[150] Thus, claims for damages based on the violation of EU law by EU Member States must be brought before the domestic courts of the respective Member State, before which individuals can invoke the principles of primacy and direct effect of EU law.[151]

But State liability and the obligation to reparation or compensation under domestic law are generally significantly more limited than under international investment law, which is mostly due to considerations of balancing the public

---

146 ECJ, *Andrea Francovich.* Joined Cases C-6/90 and C-9/90. Judgment, 19 November 1991, ECLI:EU:C:1991:428.

147 ECJ, *Brasserie du Pêcheur.* Joined Cases C-46/93 and C-48/93. Judgment, 5 March 1996, ECLI:EU:C:1996:79.

148 ECJ, *Andrea Francovich.* Joined Cases C-6/90 and C-9/90. Judgment, 19 November 1991, para. 36.

149 Ibid., para. 35.

150 Cf. ECJ, *João Filipe Ferreira.* Case C-160/14. Judgment, 9 September 2015, ECLI:EU:C:2015:565, para. 50. Investors, however, will only be successful if they meet the conditions of the 'Brasserie Test', namely that "the rule of law infringed must be intended to confer rights on individuals; the breach must be sufficiently serious; and there must be a direct causal link between the breach of the obligation resting on the State and the damage sustained by the injured parties." Cf. ECJ, *Brasserie du Pêcheur.* Joined Cases C-46/93 and C-48/93. Judgment, 5 March 1996, para. 51. For a violation to be 'sufficiently serious', a Member State has to have 'manifestly or gravely disregarded' the limits of its discretion, see ibid., para. 55.

151 P. Craig and G. de Búrca, *EU Law: Text, Cases and Materials*, 6. ed. (Oxford: Oxford University Press, 2015), at 261 f; M. Paparinskis, *Investors' Remedies Under EU Law and International Investment Law*, Journal of World Investment & Trade 17 (2016), 919–41, at 925 f. Such proceedings can lead to lengthy itineraries through the judicial stages. The proceeding for damages provided for in the German legal system for example, requires first to take a measure against the administrative act itself, which already might involve up to three instances in administrative courts, before being able to sue for damages in civil courts, with again different stages of appeal. Cf. in greater detail, S. Hindelang, *Repellent Forces: The CJEU and Investor-State Dispute Settlement*, Archiv des Völkerrechts 53 (2015), 68–89, at 78 f.

interests with that of injured persons.[152] In contrast to this sophisticated system within the EU, international investment law takes a binary approach: either there is a breach of the State's duty and thus the obligation to provide full reparation, or there is no breach and no obligation to reparation.[153] Furthermore, the EU legal system and that of the Member States focus primarily on primary legal protection such as the revocation or amendment of administrative acts or even the annulment or inapplicability of laws; secondary, pecuniary damages are generally only subsidiary.[154] Primary remedies are directed against the State act itself with the goal to prevent current and future losses of both the investor and the taxpayer, and to lead to a more stable and predictable legal environment by creating a lawful situation. Secondary remedies on the other hand are actions directed at pecuniary damages only.[155]

Under the domestic law of most EU Member States, the legal review of a State's act or omission is generally separated from the claim for damages and falls under the competences of different judicial instances.[156] This has the effect that "the illegality of the act does not automatically entail a duty to compensate, even less so in full."[157] In German law, for instance, a proprietor is not permitted to accept an interference with his or her property and to bring a legal action for compensation but is required to have the competent administrative court to review the State action's compatibility with the German Constitution.[158]

Finally, a totally different non-judicial possibility for an intra-EU investor to take action against a Member State is to file a complaint with the EU Commission

---

152 Cf. I. Marboe, *State Responsibility and Comparative State Liability for Administrative and Legislative Harm to Economic Interests* in S. W. Schill (ed.), *International Investment Law and Comparative Public Law* (Oxford: Oxford University Press, 2010), p. 409, who compares inter alia the national systems of State liability in France, the UK, Germany, Spain, Italy and Austria.

153 See ibid., p. 409.

154 Cf. A. Aaken van, *Primary and Secondary Remedies in International Investment Law and National State Liability* in S. W. Schill (ed.), *International Investment Law and Comparative Public Law* (Oxford: Oxford University Press, 2010), at 727 ff.

155 Cf. ibid., p. 724; P.-T. Stoll and T. P. Holterhus, *The 'Generalization' of International Investment Law in Constitutional Perspective* in S. Hindelang and M. Krajewski (eds.), *Shifting Paradigms in International Investment Law: More Balanced, Less Isolated, Increasingly Diversified* (Oxford: Oxford University Press, 2016), pp. 339–56, at p. 349.

156 Cf. I. Marboe, *State Responsibility and Comparative State Liability for Administrative and Legislative Harm to Economic Interests* in S. W. Schill (ed.), *International Investment Law and Comparative Public Law* (Oxford: Oxford University Press, 2010), p. 410.

157 Ibid., p. 410. An exception in this regard is France, where the administrative courts are competent to hear both types of claims and illegality leads directly to liability.

158 Cf. M. Perkams, *The Concept of Indirect Expropriation in Comparative Public Law* in S. W. Schill (ed.), *International Investment Law and Comparative Public Law* (Oxford: Oxford University Press, 2010), at 133 ff; J. Wieland, *Art. 14* in H. Dreier (ed.), *Grundgesetz: Kommentar*, 3. ed. (Tübingen: Mohr Siebeck, 2013), at paras. 140 ff; S. Schill, *Investitionsschutz in EU-Freihandelsabkommen: Erosion gesetzgeberischer Gestaltungsmacht?* Zeitschrift für ausländisches öffentliches Recht und Völkerrecht 78 (2018), 33–92, at 79 f. This approach is known in German constitutional law as "Kein dulde und liquidiere," based on the 1981 landmark decision of the German Constitutional Court, BVerfG, *Nassauskiesung*. 1 BvL 77/78, 15 July 1981.

or another Member State (not necessarily the home State), informing it that the host State is breaching EU law.[159] Such complaint may lead to the opening of an infringement procedure according to Art. 258 TFEU. However, the claimant has almost no influence on such a procedure and as it is an ancillary proceeding before the ECJ it cannot result in damages awarded in favour of the investor.[160] Furthermore, as shown previously, the damages of the claimant cannot be redressed through EU channels. Hence, it is not a very powerful tool for investors to claim their rights.

b) Preliminary reference

As claims for damages caused by Member States can only be raised before their respective domestic courts, an involvement of the 'actual' European Courts in intra-EU investor-State disputes is only possible through the preliminary reference procedure provided for in Art. 267 TFEU. This procedure is *the* instrument of cooperation between the ECJ and the domestic courts. It creates the possibility for Member States' courts to raise a question regarding the interpretation of the EU Treaties, or the validity and interpretation of secondary EU legislation. Art. 267 TFEU guarantees the uniform interpretation of EU law, "its consistency, its full effect and its autonomy as well as ultimately, the particular nature of the law established by the Treaties".[161] It is the main source of judicial development of EU law by the ECJ. The *Achmea* decision, for instance, was an answer to the German Federal Supreme Court's (BGH) question on the compatibility of intra-EU BIT ISDS clauses with EU law.[162]

While courts of lower instances may request a preliminary ruling, courts "against whose decisions there is no judicial remedy under national law" are obliged by virtue of Art. 267 (3) TFEU to submit questions concerning EU law raised in a case pending before them to the ECJ. If a domestic court of last instance – like the German BGH – does not comply with the obligation to submit a preliminary question to the ECJ, it is violating the Member State's obligation arising out of Art. 267 TFEU. The Member State could therefore be facing an infringement proceeding. However, so far there has never been an infringement proceeding because of a non-submission; the Commission seems

---

159 K. Lenaerts, I. Maselis and K. Gutman, *EU Procedural Law* (Oxford: Oxford University Press, 2014), para. 5.32. This approach was (unsuccessfully) taken by the claimant in the *Achmea* proceeding before turning to arbitration. See PCA, *Eureko v Slovakia*. Case No. 2008–13. Award on Jurisdiction, Arbitrability and Suspension, 26 October 2010, para. 55 f.

160 K. Lenaerts, I. Maselis and K. Gutman, *EU Procedural Law* (Oxford: Oxford University Press, 2014), paras. 5.69 ff.

161 ECJ, *EU accession to the ECHR*. 2/13. Opinion, 18 December 2014, ECLI:EU:C:2014:2454, para. 176; ECJ, *Achmea*. C-284/16. Judgment, 6 March 2018, para. 37.

162 ECJ, *Achmea*. C-284/16. Judgment, 6 March 2018. Other important preliminary rulings were for instance the famous ECJ, *Van Gend & Loos*. Case 26/62. Judgment, 5 February 1963 and ECJ, *Costa/ENEL*. Case 6/64. Judgment, 15 July 1964, ECLI:EU:C:1964:66.

rather generous regarding the Member States' courts margin of appreciation in this regard.[163] Furthermore, some Member States' legal orders provide that a non-submission of a preliminary question can constitute a violation of the right to a fair trial before a legal judge.[164]

c) Remedies available for intra-EU investors under EU law

Within the EU legal order, affected intra-EU investors have no other option than to bring their claims against a specific Member State's action before its domestic courts.[165] The ECJ has no competence to decide disputes between investors and Member States. Investors must rely on the domestic legal system and domestic procedural law which might be highly influenced by the respective domestic legal culture and tradition.

Nonetheless, the EU legal order does not only require Member States to guarantee access to effective judicial remedies but also the independence of their adjudicative bodies. As recently confirmed by the ECJ in its *Associação Sindical dos Juízes Portugueses* decision, the independence of domestic courts requires that every domestic court,

> exercises its judicial functions wholly autonomously, without being subject to any hierarchical constraint or subordinated to any other body and without taking orders or instructions from any source whatsoever, and that it is thus protected against external interventions or pressure liable to impair the independent judgment of its members and to influence their decisions.[166]

In sum, the EU legal order does not provide for individual remedies before transnational or international courts against Member States and only in very limited way provides for direct remedies before EU courts. Individuals can bring direct legal action before an 'actual' EU court against EU institutions only. There is no equivalent whatsoever to the intra-EU IIA arbitration clauses in EU law. Hence, foreign investors cannot as easily 'circumvent' domestic adjudication as violations of EU law are in principle remedied primarily before domestic courts. The latter have to apply EU law, especially the fundamental

---

163 See B. W. Wegener, *Art. 267 AEUV* in C. Calliess and M. Ruffert (eds.), *EUV/AEUV – Kommentar* (München: C. H. Beck, 2016), para. 35; U. Karpenstein, *Art. 267 AEUV* in E. Grabitz and M. Hilf (eds.), *Das Recht der Europäischen Union* (München: C. H. Beck, 2018), at para. 72.

164 This is the case for instance in the Germany according to Art. 101 (1) second sentence of the German Constitution. See also BVerfG, *Solange II.* 2 BvR 197/83, 22 October 1986, NJW 577, see also for Austria, the decision of Österreichischer Verfassungsgerichtshof (Austrian Constitutional Court) VfGH Österreich. B2300/95, 11 December 1995.

165 On the different remedies available to individuals before domestic courts, see EU Commission, *Protection of intra-EU investment – COM (2018) 547/2*, 19 June 2018, p. 21.

166 ECJ, *Associação Sindical dos Juízes Portugueses.* C-64/16. Judgment, 27 February 2018, para. 44.

freedoms, *ex officio* and to adhere to the preliminary ruling procedure to the ECJ for questions of interpretation of EU law.

3 Interim findings

Although the comparison of the substantive protection of intra-EU investments under EU law and intra-EU IIAs has revealed many similarities, the judicial remedies available to investors under both regimes are fundamentally different. The EU as an integrated union with a long development history is based on totally different underlying assumptions compared to BITs or even the ECT which pursue a limited set of very specific goals. As such, the different judicial protection systems are hardly comparable, especially due to their fundamental structural differences.

In the 'international investment protection regime', investors have many options on how to litigate a dispute. They can rely on the host State's domestic legal system or refer the case to arbitration which can be administered by an institution of their choice and operates according to the rules of arbitration the investor has chosen. An exhaustion of local remedies is generally not required. The outcome of an arbitration proceeding is an award which the investors can – in case the award is in their favour – enforce in almost all States.

The EU legal order on the other hand is more complex and takes a totally different approach: The greatest part of judicial decision making within the EU is done by domestic courts. They are obliged to apply EU law and can be understood as being both domestic and European courts. In cases of doubt regarding the right interpretation of EU law, Member State courts can refer preliminary questions to the ECJ which acts as the guardian of the EU's autonomy and takes care of a uniform and coherent interpretation and application of EU law. Thus, there is no possibility for individuals to 'bypass' the Member States' domestic judiciary and to have direct access to transnational adjudication as provided for in IIAs.

Another fundamental difference is that under international investment law, the State's responsibility for a breach of an IIA obligation is purely determined by international law, which is interpreted and applied by investor-State arbitration tribunals. Under EU law, questions of liability are assessed through domestic rules and domestic courts. Furthermore, secondary remedies are only subsidiary to primary remedies which aim at creating a lawful situation instead of compensating for an unlawful one. This is not the case in ISDS proceedings which virtually always lead to an obligation to compensate the investor in the event his or her case was successful. In other words, the 'international investment protection regime' is governed by the principle of 'accept and liquidate' if a State violates a substantive IIA standards. Foreign investors have to accept State interferences in their investment but can claim compensations.

These differences of primary and secondary remedies also reflect the fundamentally different interests of host States and investors in investment disputes. It may be more attractive for a State to face claims before its own domestic judiciary, especially, to avoid being condemned on the international level, which could deter foreign investors from investing in the country. Furthermore, primary legal protection allows a State to correct possible unlawful acts and to create a clear legal situation, especially in the case of amendment of general rules and laws, and thereby to prevent further legal disputes.

For a foreign investor, however, a proceeding before an international arbitral tribunal can be more tempting, especially to avoid the confrontation with the domestic judicial system and its potential deficiencies as well as possible lengthy itineraries through the judicial stages. Finally, the limited publicness of arbitral proceedings and the specific economic and commercial knowledge of the arbitrators compared to that of 'generalist' domestic judges can influence a decision to rely on investor-State arbitration instead of domestic proceedings.

V Conclusion

EU law never explicitly provided for the protection of (intra-EU) foreign direct investments but aimed at the construction of a common market. Nonetheless, several EU law rules implicitly protect foreign investors, namely the fundamental freedoms, which are all based on the general principle of non-discrimination, the Charter of Fundamental Rights or the Treaties' rule of law principles.

This implicit protection, however, is not as easy to invoke for foreign investors as explicit IIA protection clauses. The EU principles protecting investors are not contained in such broad and unqualified standards as for example the fair and equitable treatment standard but scattered in the treaties. Some IIA provisions such as umbrella clauses are not reflected in EU law at all. But the main difference, is that the tailor-made system of remedies offered to foreign investor through investor-State arbitration has no equivalent in the EU judiciary, which is mostly based on the domestic judiciary.

All in all, EU law and international investment law share many commonalities but have differing goals. Some aspects of investment protection as they are typical for IIAs can be found in EU law. But the law of the European Union has a more comprehensive normativity, seeking to establish an increasingly integrated continent with a common market and social exchanges. EU law covers a broad range of policy areas, seeking to bring them in accordance with each other in order to build a functioning and strong European Union. It is led by the goal to balance public and private interests to the advantage of all stakeholders in the Union.

Intra-EU IIAs on the other hand have a far more specialized and thereby also normatively limited field of application: the attraction of foreign investments and their protection against illicit State behaviour. They do hardly ever envisage the balancing of public interests and individual investor protection. For this reason, it is possible that a Member State is compliant with EU law while violating its obligations arising out of an intra-EU IIA.

Both EU law and international investment law operate with loose legal terms. Within the EU legal order, the latter have generally been concretized by the ECJ's jurisdiction. In international investment law, however, due to the lack of a centralized jurisdiction and because of different wordings they remain open to manifold interpretations as every single arbitral tribunal can potentially interpret the same wording in a different way. The fragmented net of intra-EU IIAs is thus – unlike the EU legal order – not capable to build a coherent and integrated system and can therefore hardly create any legal certainty and predictability, especially due to the decentralized practice of the arbitral tribunals.

While the high level of economic integration within the EU is a crucial aspect for every investor operating in a foreign EU country, the actual investment still takes place in a specific Member State and is governed by the rules and regulations of that State. In other words, even though EU law forms an integral part of the legal orders of its Member States, the domestic legal orders of the respective States remain the legal fundament for all economic activities in the host State, also for intra-EU investments. Disputes between the investor and the host State concerning the investment will be taken to the domestic courts of the respective State. The domestic courts protect foreign property rights especially through the respective national fundamental right of property protection. Thus, the advantages and downsides of the respective EU Member States' domestic legal orders and their administrative practice are of the utmost significance for every intra-EU investor, which makes forum and treaty shopping highly relevant within the EU.

This chapter has revealed the commonalities and differences of intra-EU investor protection under EU law and international investment law. It has become clear that the systems are far from being identical. From an investor's perspective the two regimes might be perceived as being complementary; from a State's perspective as being absolutely incompatible. The presumable clash between both investor protection regimes will be analysed in depth in the following chapter.

In sum, the EU legal order does not grant investor protection in a way comparable to intra-EU IIAs, i.e. independent and detached from the respective host State's legal system as it does not provide direct access to transnational dispute settlement bodies. The EU legal order, however, effectively influences the respective domestic legal orders and has created effective control mechanisms of the States' actions, without the need to allow direct access for individuals to its supranational European courts.

In the end, whether the differences in the level of protection between EU law and intra-EU IIAs can be translated into a deficit of protection by the EU legal order remains rather a political than a legal question. This is reflected by the fact that of possible 325 intra-EU BITs (post-Brexit) only 184 are currently in force and that no BIT has ever been concluded between current EU Member States.

References

Aaken van, Anne, *Primary and Secondary Remedies in International Investment Law and National State Liability* in S. W. Schill (ed.), *International Investment Law and Comparative Public Law* (Oxford: Oxford University Press, 2010), pp. 721–54.

Alschner, Wolfgang and Skougarevskiy, Dmitriy, *Mapping the Universe of International Investment Agreements*, Journal of International Economic Law (2016), 561–88.

Balthasar, Stephan, *Best Practice in International Arbitration* in S. Balthasar (ed.), *International Commercial Arbitration: International Conventions, Country Reports and Comparative Analysis* (München: C.H. Beck, 2016), pp. 1–43.

Bermann, George A., *Navigating EU Law and the Law of International Arbitration*, Arbitration International 28 (2012), 397–445.

Blackaby, Nigel, Partasides, Constantine, Redfern, Alan and Hunter, Martin, *Redfern and Hunter on International Arbitration*, 6. ed. (New York, London: Oxford University Press, 2015).

Brand, Ronald A., *Forum non Conveniens*, (April 2013) in *MPEPIL (Online-Edition)* (Oxford: Oxford University Press).

Brown, Chester, *The Evolution of the Regime of International Investment Agreements* in M. Bungenberg, et al. (eds.), *International Investment Law: A Handbook* (Baden-Baden: Nomos, 2015), pp. 153–85.

Bubrowski, Helene, *Internationale Investitionsschiedsverfahren und nationale Gerichte* (Tübingen: Mohr Siebeck, 2013).

Calliess, Christian, *Eigentumsgrundrecht* in D. Ehlers (ed.), *Europäische Grundrechte und Grundfreiheiten*, 4. ed. (Berlin, Boston: De Gruyter, 2014), pp. 707–34.

Cazala, Julien, *Les Standards Indirects de Traitement* in C. Leben (ed.), *Droit international des investissements et de l'arbitrage transnational* (Paris: Editions Pedone, 2015), pp. 265–86.

Chalmers, Damian, Davies, Gareth and Monti, Giorgio, *European Union Law*, 3. ed. (Cambridge: Cambridge University Press, 2014).

Craig, Paul and Búrca, Gráinne de, *EU Law: Text, Cases and Materials*, 6. ed. (Oxford: Oxford University Press, 2015).

Crawford, James, *Brownlie's Principles of Public International Law*, 8. ed. (Oxford: Oxford University Press, 2012).

Crawford, James, *State Responsibility: The General Part* (Cambridge: Cambridge University Press, 2013).

Dickerson, Hollin, *Minimum Standards*, (October 2010) in *MPEPIL (Online-Edition)* (Oxford: Oxford University Press).

Dolzer, Rudolf and Schreuer, Christoph, *Principles of International Investment Law*, 2. ed. (Oxford: Oxford University Press, 2012).

Fitzmaurice, Gerald, *Hersch Lauterpacht – The Scholar as a Judge*: Part I, British Yearbook of International Law 37 (1961), 1–71.

Franzius, Claudio, *Grundrechtsschutz in Europa*: Zwischen Selbstbehauptungen und Selbstbeschränkungen der Rechtsordnungen und ihrer Gerichte, Zeitschrift für ausländisches öffentliches Recht und Völkerrecht 75 (2015), 383–412.

Gómez-Palacio, Ignacio and Muchlinski, Peter, *Admission and Establishment* in P. Muchlinski, et al. (eds.), *The Oxford Handbook of International Investment Law* (Oxford: Oxford University Press, 2008), pp. 227–57.

Head, John W., *Global Business Law: Principles and Practice of International Commerce and Investment*, 3. ed. (Durham: Carolina Academic, 2012).

Hindelang, Steffen, *Repellent Forces*: The CJEU and Investor-State Dispute Settlement, Archiv des Völkerrechts 53 (2015), 68–89.

Hobe, Stephan, *The Development of the Law of Aliens and the Emergence of General Principles of Protection Under Public International Law* in M. Bungenberg, et al. (eds.), *International Investment Law: A Handbook* (Baden-Baden: Nomos, 2015), pp. 6–22.

Jacob, Marc and Schill, Stephan W., *Fair and Equitable Treatment* in M. Bungenberg, et al. (eds.), *International Investment Law: A Handbook* (Baden-Baden: Nomos, 2015), pp. 700–63.

Jennings, Robert and Watts, Arthur, *Oppenheim's International Law*, 9. ed. (Harlow: Longman, 1992).

Kern, Carsten, *Transfer of Funds* in M. Bungenberg, et al. (eds.), *International Investment Law: A Handbook* (Baden-Baden: Nomos, 2015), pp. 870–86.

Kjos, Hege E., *Applicable Law in Investor-State Arbitration* (Oxford: Oxford University Press, 2013).

Kriebaum, Ursula, *Expropriation* in M. Bungenberg, et al. (eds.), *International Investment Law: A Handbook* (Baden-Baden: Nomos, 2015), pp. 959–1030.

Kröll, Stefan, *Enforcement of Awards* in M. Bungenberg, et al. (eds.), *International Investment Law: A Handbook* (Baden-Baden: Nomos, 2015), pp. 1482–504.

Latzel, Clemens, *Die Anwendungsbereiche des Unionsrechts*, Europäische Zeitschrift für Wirtschaftsrecht (2015), 658–64.

Lavranos, Nikolaos, *Review of the C-206/06 and C-249/06 Judgements*, American Journal of International Law 103 (2009), 716–22.

Lenaerts, Koen, Maselis, Ignace and Gutman, Kathleen, *EU Procedural Law* (Oxford: Oxford University Press, 2014).

Liebscher, Christoph, *Article V (1) (e)* in R. Wolff (ed.), *New York Convention – Commentary* (München: C.H. Beck, 2012), pp. 356–80.

Lorz, Ralph A., *Protection and Security* in M. Bungenberg, et al. (eds.), *International Investment Law: A Handbook* (Baden-Baden: Nomos, 2015), pp. 764–89.

Lowenfeld, Andreas F., *International Economic Law*, 2. ed. (Oxford: Oxford University Press, 2009).

Marboe, Irmgard, *State Responsibility and Comparative State Liability for Administrative and Legislative Harm to Economic Interests* in S. W. Schill (ed.), *International Investment Law and Comparative Public Law* (Oxford: Oxford University Press, 2010), pp. 377–411.

Moses, Margaret L., *The Principles and Practice of International Commercial Arbitration* (Cambridge: Cambridge University Press, 2017).

Paparinskis, Martins, *Investors' Remedies Under EU Law and International Investment Law*, Journal of World Investment & Trade 17 (2016), 919–41.

Paulsson, Jan, *Arbitration Without Privity*, ICSID Review 10 (1995), 232–57.

Perkams, Markus, *The Concept of Indirect Expropriation in Comparative Public Law* in S. W. Schill (ed.), *International Investment Law and Comparative Public Law* (Oxford: Oxford University Press, 2010), pp. 107–50.

Perkams, Markus, *Protection for Legal Persons* in M. Bungenberg, et al. (eds.), *International Investment Law: A Handbook* (Baden-Baden: Nomos, 2015), pp. 638–52.

Reed, Lucy F. and Davis, Jonathan E., *Who Is a Protected Investor?* in M. Bungenberg, et al. (eds.), *International Investment Law: A Handbook* (Baden-Baden: Nomos, 2015), pp. 614–37.

Reinisch, August, *Expropriation* in P. Muchlinski, et al. (eds.), *The Oxford Handbook of International Investment Law* (Oxford: Oxford University Press, 2008), pp. 407–58.

Reinisch, August, *National Treatment* in M. Bungenberg, et al. (eds.), *International Investment Law: A Handbook* (Baden-Baden: Nomos, 2015), pp. 846–69.

Reisman, Michael W. and Sloane, Robert D., *Indirect Expropriations and its Valuation in the BIT Generation*, British Yearbook of International Law 74 (2004), 115–50.

Roe, Thomas and Happold, Matthew, *Settlement of Investment Disputes Under the Energy Charter Treaty*, Law Practitioner Series (Cambridge: Cambridge University Press, 2011).

Rossillion, Claude, *The Most Favoured Nation Clause in Case Law of the International Court of Justice*, Journal du Droit International 82 (1955), 76–107.

Sabahi, Borzu and Birch, Nicholas J., *Comparative Compensation for Expropriation* in S. W. Schill (ed.), *International Investment Law and Comparative Public Law* (Oxford: Oxford University Press, 2010), pp. 755–85.

Sattorova, Mavluda, *Investor Rights Under EU Law and International Investment Law*, Journal of World Investment & Trade 17 (2016), 895–918.

Schill, Stephan, *Investitionsschutz in EU-Freihandelsabkommen: Erosion gesetzgeberischer Gestaltungsmacht?* Zeitschrift für ausländisches öffentliches Recht und Völkerrecht 78 (2018), 33–92.

Schlemmer, Engela C., *Investment, Investor, Nationality, and Shareholders* in P. Muchlinski, et al. (eds.), *The Oxford Handbook of International Investment Law* (Oxford: Oxford University Press, 2008), pp. 49–88.

Schreuer, Christoph, *The ICSID Convention: A Commentary*, 2. ed. (Cambridge: Cambridge University Press, 2009).

Shaw, Malcolm N., *International Law*, 7. ed. (Cambridge: Cambridge University Press, 2014).

Shihata, Ibrahim F. I., *Towards a Greater Depoliticization of Investment Disputes: The Roles of ICSID and MIGA*, ICSID Review 1 (1986), 1–25.

Sinclair, Anthony, *Umbrella Clauses* in M. Bungenberg, et al. (eds.), *International Investment Law: A Handbook* (Baden-Baden: Nomos, 2015), pp. 887–958.

Solomon, Dennis, *International Commercial Arbitration* in S. Balthasar (ed.), *International Commercial Arbitration: International Conventions, Country Reports and Comparative Analysis* (München: C.H. Beck, 2016), pp. 45–157.

Sornarajah, Muthucumaraswamy, *The International Law on Foreign Investment*, 4. ed. (Cambridge: Cambridge University Press, 2017).

Stoll, Peter-Tobias and Holterhus, Till P., *The 'Generalization' of International Investment Law in Constitutional Perspective* in S. Hindelang and M. Krajewski (eds.), *Shifting Paradigms in International Investment Law: More Balanced, Less Isolated, Increasingly Diversified* (Oxford: Oxford University Press, 2016), pp. 339–56.

Titi, Aikaterini, *The Right to Regulate in International Investment Law* (Baden-Baden: Nomos, 2014).

Titi, Catharine, *International Investment Law and the European Union: Towards a New Generation of International Investment Agreements*, European Journal of International Law 26 (2015), 639–61.

Tridimas, Takis, *The General Principles of EU Law*, 2. ed. (Oxford: Oxford University Press, 2006).

UNCTAD, *World Investment Report 2016: Investor Nationality: Policy Challenges*, United Nations Publication (New York, Geneva: United Nations, 2016).

Walter, André von, *State Contracts and the Relevance of Investment Contract Arbitration* in M. Bungenberg, et al. (eds.), *International Investment Law: A Handbook* (Baden-Baden: Nomos, 2015), pp. 80–92.

Wehland, Hanno, *Intra-EU Investment Agreements and Arbitration: Is European Community Law and Obstacle?* International and Comparative Law Quarterly 58 (2009), 297–320.

Weil, Prosper, *Problèmes Relatifs aux Contrats Passés Entre un État et un Particulier* in Académie de Droit International (ed.), *Recueil des Cours: Collected Courses of the Hague Academy of International Law 1969 (III)* (Leiden: Brill, 1969), pp. 95–240.

White, Gillian, *Nationalisation of Foreign Property* (London: Stevens & Sons Limited, 1961).

Yannaca-Small, Katia, *Parallel Proceedings* in P. Muchlinski, et al. (eds.), *The Oxford Handbook of International Investment Law* (Oxford: Oxford University Press, 2008), pp. 1008–48.

III Conflict between intra-EU IIAs and EU law

Intra-EU investor-State arbitration has been contested by the EU Commission and some Member States for several years. Two main arguments were brought forward against the 'international investment protection regime' applicable to intra-EU investments. First, the alleged invalidity of intra-EU BITs as an effect of the *lex posterior* rule because all intra-EU BITs were treaties concluded prior to the Lisbon Treaty and some Member States' accession treaties. Second, the inapplicability of intra-EU IIAs, i.e. the intra-EU BITs and the ECT, due to the primacy of EU law. These arguments have generally been rejected by arbitral tribunals as well as the Advocate General Wathelet in his *Achmea* Opinion. The ECJ, however, has taken a different position in its *Achmea* decision.

If both EU law and international investment law are understood as equally being part of international treaty law, a conflict between them needs to be resolved according to the VCLT rules of conflict, namely its Art. 30 and Art. 59. However, if their relationship is understood as one of international to domestic law, with EU law being part of the domestic law of the Member States, Art. 27 VCLT could be applicable. In that case EU law could not be invoked to justify a violation of an international legal obligation and there would be no actual legal conflict between both regimes at the international level. Finally, if EU law is understood as something outside the classical dichotomy of domestic and international law, the VCLT cannot be readily applied to its relationship with international treaties.

Against this backdrop, the present chapter starts by assessing the position of EU law within the traditional dichotomy between international and domestic law (I.). It then reflects on the question of *lex posterior* and the possible invalidity of intra-EU BITs through new Member States' accession to the EU (II.), before analysing the incompatibility argument, focusing on the *Achmea* judgment and other possible grounds of incompatibility as well as the arbitral practice on the matter (III.). The last part of this chapter assesses the relationship between the multilateral Energy Charter Treaty and EU law with regard to intra-EU investments (IV.), before summarizing the results of the analysis (V.).

I Nature of EU law and its relation to public international law

1 Particularity of EU law

The 'nature' of the EU has been extensively discussed, especially whether the EU is an International Organization (IO) or even a State. In its institutional self-understanding, however, it clearly represents a *new legal order* and an organization *sui generis*. This will quickly be recapitulated in the following.

It is a common understanding that the EU is for a number of reasons not (yet) a State:[1] It lacks 'Kompetenz-Kompetenz', i.e. a State's competence to determine its own competences and cannot exercise public authority in an unlimited way but can only enjoy competences derived from its Member States.[2] There is no European nation to constitute a European State. In difference to a federal State's subdivisions, it is possible for Member States to leave the EU according to Art. 50 TEU.[3] Furthermore, Member States can amend the EU Treaties by virtue of Art. 48 TEU. They remain full subjects of public international law, which is generally not the case for a federal State's subdivisions.[4]

Thus, for many international lawyers the EU continues to constitute an IO, albeit a specific and exceptional one.[5] Indeed, the Union has many commonalities with regional IOs and perfectly fits under Art. 2 lit. a) of the 2011 International Law Commission (ILC) Draft Articles on the Responsibility of International Organizations, which defines an IO as "an organization established by a treaty or other instrument governed by international law and possessing its own international legal personality." The EU also falls under the definition of 'Regional Economic Integration Organization' (REIO) contained in several multilateral treaties

---

1 As explained in ECJ, *EU accession to the ECHR*. 2/13. Opinion, 18 December 2014, ECLI:EU:C:2014:2454, para. 156, "the EU is, under international law, precluded by its very nature from being considered a State."

2 Cf. BVerfG, *Lissabon*. 2 BvE 2/08. Judgment, 30 June 2009, paras. 231 ff. See also T. Lock, *Why the European Union Is Not a State: Some Critical Remarks*, European Constitutional Law Review 5 (2009), 407–20, at 409 f.

3 Cf. D. Thürer and T. Burri, *Self-Determination*, (December 2008) in *MPEPIL (Online-Edition)* (Oxford: Oxford University Press); D. Thürer and T. Burri, *Secession*, (June 2009) in *MPEPIL (Online-Edition)* (Oxford: Oxford University Press).

4 In great detail, W. Rudolf, *Federal States*, (May 2011) in *MPEPIL (Online-Edition)* at para. 16 f. See also J. Crawford, *Brownlie's Principles of Public International Law*, 8. ed. (Oxford: Oxford University Press, 2012), at 116 f.

5 Cf. A. Delgado Casteleiro, *The International Responsibility of the European Union: From Competence to Normative Control* (Cambridge: Cambridge University Press, 2016); B. de Witte, *The European Union as an International Legal Experiment* in G. de Búrca and J. Weiler (eds.), *The Worlds of European Constitutionalism* (Cambridge: Cambridge University Press, 2012), pp. 19–56; M. N. Shaw, *International Law*, 7. ed. (Cambridge: Cambridge University Press, 2014), at 934. See also ICSID, *Electrabel v Hungary*. Case No. ARB/07/19. Decision on Jurisdiction, Applicable Law and Liability, 30 November 2012, para. 4.142.

to which the EU itself is a party.[6] Just like its predecessor organizations, the EU is based on multilateral treaties whose existence are governed by public international law.[7] The Union has a legal personality derived from its Member States.[8] The latter can – just like the EU's institutions – be bound by international agreements concluded by the EU.[9]

Nonetheless, for many observers the EU is 'more' than an IO.[10] The main difference to classical IOs is that the EU treaties allow the organs of the EU not only to create law binding *on* the Member States but also binding *within* the Member States. In other words, the EU's particularity is primarily its direct effect in the domestic legal orders of its Member States and its supremacy vis-à-vis domestic law.[11] While public international law is also incorporated into domestic legal orders through a wilful act of a State, either in the moment of conclusion of a treaty in monist countries or through an act of transformation in dualist countries,[12] the application of international law depends upon the State's will. In difference, EU law, however, is autonomous. Another particularity of the EU legal order is that while it is based on international treaties, their role is inter alia to exclude international law in general from the relationship of the EU's Member States and to replace it with 'internal' EU law, which is also reflected in Art. 344 TFEU. As summarized by the Advocate General in his *Achmea* Opinion, the Member States have "limited, in ever-widening areas, their sovereign rights" in favour of the EU, of which not only themselves but also their nationals are subjects and which is characterized "by its supremacy over the laws of the Member States and also by the direct effect of a range of provisions applicable to their nationals and to the Member States themselves".[13] Thus, from an internal EU and Member States perspective, EU law does neither represent domestic law nor international law *stricto sensu* but creates a sui generis legal order with elements of both.

---

6 See for example, Art. 1 (3) ECT and Art. 2 of the *UN Convention on Biological Diversity* – 1760 U.N.T.S. 69, 1992.

7 See also Art. 54 TEU which provides for a 'entry into force process' based on ratification, which is typical for international treaties.

8 Cf. Art. 47 TEU.

9 Cf. Art. 37 TEU and Art. 216 TFEU.

10 Cf. J. Crawford, *Brownlie's Principles of Public International Law* (Oxford: Oxford University Press, 2012), p. 133.

11 On the direct effect of EU law and its primacy or supremacy over domestic law see in particular the famous decisions in ECJ, *Van Gend & Loos*. Case 26/62. Judgment, 5 February 1963, ECLI:EU:C:1963:1 and ECJ, *Costa/ENEL*. Case 6/64. Judgment, 15 July 1964, ECLI:EU:C:1964:66 as well as the following line of jurisprudence, among others ECJ, *European Patent Court*. 1/09. Opinion, 8 March 2011, ECLI:EU:C:2011:123, para. 65; General Court, *Germany v European Commission*. T-59/09. Judgment, 14 February 2012, ECLI:EU:T:2012:75, para. 63; ECJ, *Kadi*. C-402/05. Opinion of Advocate General Maduro, 16 January 2008, ECLI:EU:C:2008:11, para. 21.

12 See J. Crawford, *Brownlie's Principles of Public International Law* (Oxford: Oxford University Press, 2012), at 48 ff.

13 ECJ, *Achmea*. C-284/16. Opinion of Advocate General Wathelet, 19 September 2017, ECLI:EU:C:2017:699, para. 231.

This sui generis legal order is protected by the ECJ. The latter is not only an international court set up by the European treaties but also the constitutional court and the 'constitutional architect' of the EU. Unlike traditional international courts like the ICJ or the ECtHR it is not only charged with the application, interpretation and validation of a certain treaty regime but also develops general principles and mechanism defining the EU's relationship with its Member States.[14] From a formalistic international law perspective, however, the ECJ remains a regional court that supervises the international agreements it is based upon an which created the regional economic organization, named European Union. In the same vein, the EU's self-understanding does not affect its position within the international legal order and especially of third States in their relation to EU Member States.

2 EU's openness towards international law and international adjudication

In principle EU law is open towards international law. Art. 3 (5) TEU provides that the Union shall contribute to peace, security, sustainable development as well as to the strict observance and the development of international law in its relations with the wider world. This openness is also reflected in the ECJ's jurisprudence emphasizing that international law forms an 'integral part' of the EU legal order that ranks above secondary EU legislation.[15] Nonetheless, especially the *Kadi* decision has shown that in case of conflict, the ECJ might favour its own constitutional principles over international legal obligations.[16]

One way to measure the openness of the EU towards international law, in general, is by assessing its willingness to submit itself to international adjudication outside the EU jurisdiction and to accept it within the scope of application of EU law. The ECJ has repeatedly emphasized that international agreements providing for their own dispute settlement system are in principle compatible with EU law.[17] The Court, however, has at the same time set a high bar for an international court

---

14 Cf. T. Lock, *The European Court of Justice and International Courts* (Oxford: Oxford University Press, 2015), at 75 f.

15 ECJ, *Haegeman*. Case 181/73. Judgment, 30 April 1974, ECLI:EU:C:1974:41, para. 5; ECJ, *Racke*. C-162/96. Judgment, 16 June 1998, ECLI:EU:C:1998:293, para. 41; ECJ, *Air Transport Association of America*. C-366/10. Judgment, 21 December 2011, ECLI:EU:C:2011:864, para. 73, 79. See also K. S. Ziegler, *Beyond Pluralism and Autonomy: Systemic Harmonization as a Paradigm for the Interaction of EU Law and International Law*, Yearbook of European Law 35 (2016), 667–711, at 670.

16 ECJ, *Kadi*. Joined Cases C-402/05 P and C-415/05 P. Judgment, 3 September 2008, ECLI:EU:C:2008:461. See also with further references, H. P. Aust, *Eine völkerrechtsfreundliche Union? Grund und Grenze der Öffnung des Europarechts zum Völkerrecht*, Europarecht 52 (2017), 106–21, at 106 f.

17 ECJ, *European Economic Area*. 1/91. Opinion, 14 December 1991, ECLI:EU:C:1991:490, paras. 40 ff; ECJ, *European Patent Court*. 1/09. Opinion, 8 March 2011, para. 74; ECJ, *EU accession to the ECHR*. 2/13. Opinion, 18 December 2014, para. 182. See also ECJ, *Achmea*. C-284/16. Judgment, 6 March 2018, ECLI:EU:C:2018:158, para. 57.

or tribunal to be acceptable in its own sphere of influence. This is due to several concerns, namely that an international adjudicative body might jeopardize the autonomy and primacy of EU law and the ECJ's monopoly on the final interpretation and application of EU law.[18] Accordingly, the ECJ has developed different conditions international adjudicative bodies have to meet in order to be compatible with the EU legal order:[19] For one, there shall be no personal link between the judges in an international tribunal and the ECJ.[20] Furthermore, the exclusive jurisdiction of the ECJ regarding disputes between EU Member States according to Art. 344 TFEU may not be impaired.[21] An international adjudicatory body must neither interfere with the ECJ's exclusive jurisdiction regarding the validity of secondary EU law and the binding interpretation of EU law and EU fundamental rights need to be safeguarded.[22] Moreover, there shall be no interference with the internal division of competences and responsibilities between the EU and its Member States.[23] Finally, the ECJ has also refused to accept a system under which the Member States transfer a significant amount of cases to an international court or tribunal thereby depriving their own domestic courts of the possibility to refer a preliminary question to the ECJ in breach of their duty of sincere cooperation.[24]

This entire line of jurisprudence can be summarized as the ECJ protecting the autonomy of the EU legal order. The Court thereby has a two-dimensional understanding of autonomy: there is an 'internal dimension' regarding the relationship between EU law and the Member States' domestic law, based on the famous *Costa/ENEL* decision,[25] and an 'external dimension' regarding the relationship between EU law and international law which the Court started to develop in its *Opinion 1/91*.[26] The *Achmea* judgment analysed in this chapter is a continuation

---

18 For a great overview on the ECJ's case law regarding other bodies of international adjudication and their compatibility with EU law, cf. S. Gáspár-Szilágyi, *A Standing Investment Court Under TTIP from the Perspective of the Court of Justice of the European Union,* Journal of World Investment & Trade 17 (2016), 701–42. See also P. Craig and G. de Búrca, *EU Law: Text, Cases and Materials,* 6. ed. (Oxford: Oxford University Press, 2015), at 356 f. and S. Hindelang, *Repellent Forces: The CJEU and Investor-State Dispute Settlement,* Archiv des Völkerrechts 53 (2015), 68–89, at 68.

19 For an overview, cf. Gáspár-Szilágyi, *A Standing Investment Court Under TTIP from the Perspective of the Court of Justice of the European Union,* Journal of World Investment & Trade 17 (2016), at 721 ff.

20 ECJ, *Fund Tribunal.* 1/76. Opinion, 26 April 1977, ECLI:EU:C:1977:63, para. 22; ECJ, *European Economic Area.* 1/91. Opinion, 14 December 1991, paras. 47 ff.

21 ECJ, *MOX Plant.* C-459/03. Judgment, 30 May 2006, paras. 132 ff.

22 ECJ, *Kadi.* Joined Cases C-402/05 P and C-415/05 P. Judgment, 3 September 2008, para. 285.

23 ECJ, *European Economic Area.* 1/91. Opinion, 14 December 1991, paras. 33 ff; ECJ, *EU accession to the ECHR.* 2/13. Opinion, 18 December 2014, para. 201; ECJ, *Kadi.* Joined Cases C-402/05 P and C-415/05 P. Judgment, 3 September 2008, para. 282.

24 ECJ, *European Patent Court.* 1/09. Opinion, 8 March 2011, paras. 68 ff.

25 ECJ, *Costa/ENEL.* Case 6/64. Judgment, 15 July 1964.

26 ECJ, *European Economic Area.* 1/91. Opinion, 14 December 1991. See also T. Lock, *The European Court of Justice and International Courts* (Oxford: Oxford University Press, 2015), at 77 ff; S. Hindelang, *Repellent Forces: The CJEU and Investor-State Dispute Settlement,* Archiv des Völkerrechts 53 (2015), at 71 f.

and a concretization of this line of autonomy jurisprudence, which is reflected at the beginning of the Courts reasoning:

> According to settled case-law [...], an international agreement cannot affect [...] the autonomy of the EU legal system, observance of which is ensured by the Court. [...][27]
>
> The autonomy of EU law with respect both to the law of the Member States and to international law is justified by the essential characteristics of the EU and its law, relating in particular to the constitutional structure of the EU and the very nature of that law. EU law is characterized by the fact that it stems from an independent source of law, the Treaties, by its primacy over the laws of the Member States, and by the direct effect of a whole series of provisions which are applicable to their nationals and to the Member States themselves. Those characteristics have given rise to a structured network of principles, rules and mutually interdependent legal relations binding the EU and its Member States reciprocally and binding its Member States to each other.[28]
>
> In order to ensure that the specific characteristics and the autonomy of the EU legal order are preserved, the Treaties have established a judicial system intended to ensure consistency and uniformity in the interpretation of EU law. In that context, [...] it is for the national courts and tribunals and the Court of Justice to ensure the full application of EU law in all Member States and to ensure judicial protection of the rights of individuals under that law.[29]

3 Interim findings

From an internal EU perspective, EU law constitutes a *sui generis* legal order. Nonetheless, from a formalistic point of view, it remains a very specialized and highly developed form of institutionalized international law within the EU Member States. The direct effect and the primacy of EU law do not alter this fact.

Thus, if an EU Member State invokes EU law, the State does not invoke its domestic law in the sense of Art. 27 VCLT, but a form of international law.[30]

---

27 ECJ, *Achmea*. C-284/16. Judgment, 6 March 2018, para. 32.
28 Ibid., para. 33, see also ECJ, *EU accession to the ECHR*. 2/13. Opinion, 18 December 2014, paras. 165 ff. cited in the *Achmea* decision.
29 ECJ, *Achmea*. C-284/16. Judgment, 6 March 2018, paras. 35 f. See also ECJ, *EU Accession to the ECHR*. 2/13. Opinion, 18 December 2014, para. 174 f.
30 The telos of Art. 27 VCLT is to prevent sovereign States – which can freely design their inner legal order – from abusing their regulatory powers in order to circumvent their international law obligations. States are obliged to adapt their internal legal order to the international legal requirements which they have voluntarily adopted. In other words, Art. 27 VCLT rules out the "most mundane justification for non-compliance, the deviant legal situation within a State," cf. K. Schmalenbach, *Art. 27* in O. Dörr and K. Schmalenbach (eds.), *Vienna Convention on the Law of Treaties: A Commentary*, 2. ed. (Berlin: Springer, 2018), at para. 1. The fact that EU Member States have only limited influence on the EU's legislation reveals that Art. 27 VCLT is not applicable to them regarding EU law.

Hence, the VCLT rules of conflict are applicable to the relationship between EU law and international investment law.

Only from an internal institutional EU perspective, EU law can be understood as something comparable to domestic law, namely 'internal EU law'. By virtue of Art. 27 (2) of the 1986 Vienna Convention on the Law of Treaties between States and International Organizations or between International Organizations (VCLT II), "an international organization party to a treaty may not invoke the rules of the organization as justification for its failure to perform the treaty." Thus, in proceedings in which the EU itself is a respondent – for example in a CETA or ECT proceeding – EU law could not be invoked to justify the EU's failure to perform the treaty.[31]

As will be shown in the following, the opponents of intra-EU IIAs have relied on both international legal arguments mainly based on the VCLT and purely EU law related arguments to convince arbitral tribunals of the inapplicability of these treaties to intra-EU investor-State relations or even to convince the tribunals of the treaties' invalidity.

II Alleged invalidity of intra-EU BITs

The EU Commission and several EU Member States have argued in a number of cases that intra-EU BITs should be considered as terminated in accordance with the *lex posterior* rule codified in Art. 59 VCLT due to the accession of Eastern and Southern Member States to the EU after the BITs' conclusion.[32] In case Art. 59

---

31 Cf. K. Boustany and M. Didat, *Art. 27 of the 1986 Convention* in O. Corten and P. Klein (eds.), *The Vienna Conventions on the Law of Treaties: A Commentary* (Oxford: Oxford University Press, 2011).

32 See for instance the position of the Czech Republic in PCA, *WNC Factoring v Czech Republic.* Case N° 2014–34. Award, 22 February 2017, para. 294 f; SCC Arbitration, *Anglia Auto v Czech Republic.* Case V 2014/181. Final Award, 10 March 2017, paras. 98 ff; SCC Arbitration, *Busta & Busta v Czech Republic.* Case V 2015/014. Final Award, 10 March 2017, paras. 98 ff; SCC Arbitration, *Eastern Sugar B.V. v Czech Republic.* SCC No. 088/2004. Partial Award, 27 March 2007, para. 94; Ad Hoc Arbitration, *Binder v Czech Republic.* Award on Jurisdiction, 6 June 2007, para. 19; ICSID, *A11Y Ltd. v Czech Republic.* Case No. UNCT/15/1. Decision on Jurisdiction, 9 February 2017, para. 152. See also the position of Cyprus as cited in ICSID, *Marfin v Cyprus.* Case No. ARB/13/27. Award, 26 July 2018, para. 583; the position of Poland in SCC Arbitration, *PL Holdings v Poland.* V 2014/163. Partial Award, 28 June 2017, para. 53 and the position of Slovakia in PCA, *European American Investment Bank v Slovakia.* PCA Case No. 2010–17. Award on Jurisdiction, 22 October 2012, para. 56; Ad Hoc Arbitration, *Oostergetel & Laurentius v Slovakia.* Decision on Jurisdiction, 30 April 2010, para. 66.

The EU Commission submitted several *amicus curiae* briefs in this regard, cf. PCA, *European American Investment Bank v Slovakia.* PCA Case No. 2010–17. Award on Jurisdiction, 22 October 2012, para. 61; Ad Hoc Arbitration, *Wirtgen v Czech Republic.* PCA Case No. 2014–03. Final Award, 11 October 2017, para. 241. Remarkably the Czech Republic, which had repeatedly alleged the 'automatic' termination of intra-EU BITs did explicitly not join the EU Commission's argument in that regard in the *Wirtgen* case, cf. Ad Hoc Arbitration, *Wirtgen v Czech Republic.* PCA Case No. 2014–03. Final Award, 11 October 2017, para. 249.

VCLT is applicable to intra-EU BITs, these treaties would have become invalid at the moment of the respective Member State's accession to the EU, and arbitral tribunals based upon them would lack jurisdiction to decide a dispute.

The few arbitral tribunals that had to decide on the matter all rejected the argument.[33] Apart from their concurring legal interpretations, which will be assessed in the following, one reason for their rejection might be a systemic one: an arbitral tribunal rejecting its own jurisdiction based on the invalidity argument, could create an adverse precedent for future intra-EU investor State arbitration proceedings, deterring investors from initiating such cases. Even without the existence of a *stare decisis* doctrine in international investment law, such a refusal could make intra-EU investor-State arbitration an unattractive means of dispute resolution.[34]

1 Applicability of the VCLT's lex posterior rule

Even though the EU legal order has developed an important autonomy and is internally understood as having a *sui generis* character, its foundational treaties as well as the accession treaties to the EU remain typical international agreements and are thus 'treaties' in the sense of Art. 2 VCLT. This is also the case for intra-EU BITs. Furthermore, the VCLT codifies to a large extent existing customary international law, especially with regard to the *lex posterior* rule in its Arts. 59 and Art. 30 (3).[35] It therefore also applies to States that are not party to the Convention itself, such as France and Romania, and to treaties that have been concluded prior to its entry into force in the respective Member States as it is the case with many intra-EU BITs.[36]

---

33 SCC Arbitration, *Eastern Sugar B.V. v Czech Republic.* SCC No. 088/2004. Partial Award, 27 March 2007, para. 172; PCA, *European American Investment Bank v Slovakia.* PCA Case No. 2010–17. Award on Jurisdiction, 22 October 2012, para. 185; Ad Hoc Arbitration, *Binder v Czech Republic.* Award on Jurisdiction, 6 June 2007, para. 40; SCC Arbitration, *Anglia Auto v Czech Republic.* Case V 2014/181. Final Award, 10 March 2017, paras. 115 ff; SCC Arbitration, *Busta & Busta v Czech Republic.* Case V 2015/014. Final Award, 10 March 2017, paras. 115 ff; Ad Hoc Arbitration, *Oostergetel & Laurentius v Slovakia.* Decision on Jurisdiction, 30 April 2010, para. 73 f; SCC Arbitration, *PL Holdings v Poland.* V 2014/163. Partial Award, 28 June 2017, para. 313.

34 See also P. Mariani, *The Future of BITs Between EU Member States* in G. Sacerdoti, et al. (eds.), *General Interests of Host States in International Investment Law* (Cambridge: Cambridge University Press, 2014), pp. 265–86, at p. 284 as well as the claimant's statement in PCA, *Eureko v Slovakia.* Case No. 2008–13. Award on Jurisdiction, Arbitrability and Suspension, 26 October 2010, para. 62.

35 See T. Giegerich, *Art. 59* in O. Dörr and K. Schmalenbach (eds.), *Vienna Convention on the Law of Treaties: A Commentary*, 2. ed. (Berlin: Springer, 2018), at para. 2; K. von der Decken, *Art. 30* in O. Dörr and K. Schmalenbach (eds.), *Vienna Convention on the Law of Treaties: A Commentary*, 2. ed. (Berlin: Springer, 2018), at para. 9; F. Dubuisson, *Art. 59 of the 1969 Convention* in O. Corten and P. Klein (eds.), *The Vienna Conventions on the Law of Treaties: A Commentary* (Oxford: Oxford University Press, 2011), at paras. 6 ff.

36 Malta for instance, only ratified the VCLT in 2012 after the conclusion of all its intra-EU BITs. The same is also true for the Portuguese intra-EU BITs that were all concluded prior to Portugal's ratification of the VCLT in 2004.

2 Preconditions of Art. 59 VCLT

Parties to a treaty have the power to terminate it by any subsequent agreement.[37] If there is a doubt whether a subsequent agreement aimed at the termination of an earlier agreement, Art. 59 VCLT establishes conditions according to which the further co-existence of both treaties or the termination of the earlier can be assessed. In this context, it has been argued that Art. 59 VCLT does not lead to an automatic termination but that an additional notification to the other party according to Art. 65 (1) VCLT is needed to prevent unilateral exits.[38]

To the authors' knowledge no such notification has ever been submitted regarding the possible invalidity of any intra-EU BIT. Nonetheless, it is doubtful whether the lack of such a notification could prevent the automatic termination and invalidity of a treaty according to Art. 59 VCLT. It seems inconsistent to hinge the validity of subsequent agreements, which meet the preconditions of Art. 59 VCLT on such notification. As just seen, Art. 59 VCLT applies to situations in which it is not clear whether a subsequent treatment aimed at the termination of an earlier treaty. According to Art. 59 (1) lit. a) VCLT it suffices for an earlier treaty to be considered terminated if "it appears from the latter treaty" relating to the same-subject matter "that the matter should be governed by that treaty". In other words, Art. 59 VCLT explicitly covers implicit treaty termination through the conclusion of a new treaty. A requirement of a notification pursuant to Art. 65 (1) VCLT would undermine this possibility of implicit termination as it would require an explicit statement regarding a possible termination. Furthermore, Art. 59 VCLT is part of Section 3: Termination and Suspension of the Operation of Treaties, while Art. 65 VCLT stands under the heading of Section 4: Procedure. Thus, in the author's view, relying on a teleological and systematic interpretation, an Art. 65 (1) VCLT notification has only a declaratory effect and is not constitutive for the assessment of a treaty's termination.

The first condition of Art. 59 VCLT is, that all the parties of an earlier treaty must have concluded a later treaty without formally terminating or suspending the earlier one. In the intra-EU investment context, the earlier treaties are the intra-EU BITs. They have all been concluded before the entry into force of the later Lisbon Treaty on December 1, 2009.[39] Every current EU Member State, apart from Croatia, was a State party to the Lisbon Treaty at the time of its conclusion. Also, the

---

37 Art. 54 lit. b) VCLT.
38 A position taken by the arbitral tribunal in PCA, *Eureko v Slovakia.* Case No. 2008–13. Award on Jurisdiction, Arbitrability and Suspension, 26 October 2010, para. 235. See also C. Binder, *A Treaty Law Perspective on Intra-EU BITs,* Journal of World Investment & Trade 17 (2016), 964–83, at 968 f; T. Giegerich, *Art. 59* in O. Dörr and K. Schmalenbach (eds.), *Vienna Convention on the Law of Treaties* (Berlin: Springer, 2018), para. 37; A. Reinisch, *Articles 30 and 59 of the Vienna Convention on the Law of Treaties in Action: The Decisions on Jurisdiction in the Eastern Sugar and Eureko Investment Arbitrations,* Legal Issues of Economic Integration 39 (2012), 157–77, at 163 f.
39 The most recently concluded BIT between Croatia and Lithuania was signed on 15 April 2008 and entered into force on 30 January 2009.

Lisbon Treaty itself constitutes a new multilateral treaty, which had to be ratified by its Contracting Parties in order to enter into force. It thus represents a typical example of a subsequent treaty pursuant to Art. 59 VCLT. Finally, Croatia acceded to the Union on July 1, 2013, and thereby became a State party to this more recent treaty. Croatia's intra-EU BITs thus also meet the prerequisite of Art. 59 VCLT.

Further conditions of Art. 59 VCLT are that the treaties relate to the 'same subject matter' (a), the parties' intention that the matter should be governed by the later treaty (b) or, as an alternative condition, an extensive incompatibility of the earlier and the later treaty (c).

a) 'Same subject matter'

There is no consolidate definition of 'same subject matter' and very little adjudication on this issue, but several authors have developed different approaches to assess this concept. In any case, the 'same subject matter' must be distinguished from questions of incompatibility as referred to in Art. 59 (1) b) VCLT and from the parties' intention regarding the continuity of the preceding treaty. According to the ILC's Report on the Fragmentation of International Law,

> the test of whether two treaties deal with the "same subject matter" is resolved through the assessment of whether the fulfilment of the obligation under one treaty affects the fulfilment of the obligation of another. This "affecting" might then take place either as strictly preventing the fulfilment of the other obligation or undermining its object and purpose in one or another way.[40]

The decisive criterion for the ILC was whether the treaties are so far incompatible that they cannot be applied at the same time. In the author's view, this approach mixes up the 'same subject matter' and the compatibility criterion and rather fits under the prerequisite of incompatibility under Art. 59 (1) lit. b) VCLT. An attempt to define the 'same subject matter', however, is essential to answer the crucial question of the further legal existence of an international treaty.

Some authors apply a strict interpretation and require an identical overall object, as well as a comparable degree of generality and comparability of the two treaties,[41] whereas others find it sufficient if the later treaty takes up the 'same subject matter' as the earlier but also treats other matters.[42] A broad understanding

---

40 ILC, *Fragmentation of International Law: Difficulties Arising from the Diversification and Expansion of International Law*, A/CN.4/L.682, 13 April 2006, at para. 254. See also A. Aust, *Modern Treaty Law and Practice*, 3. ed. (Cambridge: Cambridge University Press, 2013), at 204.
41 See F. Dubuisson, *Art. 59 of the 1969 Convention* in O. Corten and P. Klein (eds.), *The Vienna Conventions on the Law of Treaties* (Oxford: Oxford University Press, 2011), para. 25. See also the position of the claimant as cited in PCA, *European American Investment Bank v Slovakia*. PCA Case No. 2010–17. Award on Jurisdiction, 22 October 2012, para. 160.
42 See T. Giegerich, *Art. 59* in O. Dörr and K. Schmalenbach (eds.), *Vienna Convention on the Law of Treaties* (Berlin: Springer, 2018), para. 11.

was also presented by Slovakia in the *Achmea* arbitration proceeding arguing that intra-EU BITs and EU law relate to the 'same subject matter' "because they cover the same types of investors and investments, serve the same purposes, offer the same standards of protection, and provide for equivalent remedies."[43] The arbitral tribunal in *Achmea*, however, rejected this argument finding that "nothing in Art. 59 [VCLT] requires that the two treaties should be in all respects coextensive; but the latter treaty must have more than a minor incidental overlap with the earlier treaty."[44]

The position of the arbitral tribunal is convincing. The wording of Art. 59 VCLT does not refer to same facts or same situations but to the 'same subject matter'. Many treaties concern fundamentally different subjects (e.g. trade and human rights treaties), but deal with issues arising from the same facts; other treaties might pursue similar goals (such as the protection of the environment) but address totally different factual situations.[45] In such a situation one can hardly argue that these treaties relate to the 'same subject matter'. Rather, the definition provided by the arbitral tribunal in the *European American Investment Bank* case is persuasive:

> the subject matter of a treaty [...] differs both from the concrete situations in which it will be applicable and from its goal [but] is inherent in the treaty itself and refers to the issues with which its provisions deal, i.e. its topic or its substance.[46]

As shown in Chapter II, EU law does not cover the protection of already established investments in a manner identical to intra-EU BITs. EU law has a significantly wider scope of application than intra-EU BITs and regulates the entire EU common market and internal as well as external interaction and cooperation between the EU Member States and their citizens. Intra-EU BITs in contrast cover only the very specific field of intra-EU investment protection. There is an overlap between EU law and intra-EU BITs. Nonetheless, some key elements of the latter namely the investor-State arbitration mechanism, the most-favoured nation treatment or the protection of contractual undertakings through umbrella clauses are not integrated into EU law. The intra-EU BIT's subject-matter can thus be

---

43 Cited in PCA, *Eureko v Slovakia*. Case No. 2008–13. Award on Jurisdiction, Arbitrability and Suspension, 26 October 2010, para. 65.

44 Ibid., para. 242. In a similar way also Ad Hoc Arbitration, *Wirtgen v Czech Republic*. PCA Case No. 2014–03. Final Award, 11 October 2017, para. 253; ICSID, *A11Y Ltd. v Czech Republic*. Case No. UNCT/15/1. Decision on Jurisdiction, 9 February 2017, para. 177 f.

45 Cf. PCA, *European American Investment Bank v Slovakia*. PCA Case No. 2010–17. Award on Jurisdiction, 22 October 2012, para. 169 f; ICSID, *Marfin v Cyprus*. Case No. ARB/13/27. Award, 26 July 2018, para. 587.

46 PCA, *European American Investment Bank v Slovakia*. PCA Case No. 2010–17. Award on Jurisdiction, 22 October 2012, para. 171 f. See also in a similar vein, J. Finke, *Regime-collisions* in C. J. Tams, et al. (eds.), *Research Handbook on the Law of Treaties* (Cheltenham: Edward Elgar, 2014), pp. 415–46, at p. 428.

described as intra-EU foreign direct investments, which is a field in which the EU has no direct jurisdiction.[47] The author agrees with the *European American Investment Bank* tribunal that "to accede to an economic community is simply not the same as to set up a specific investment protection regime providing for investor-State arbitration."[48] In the author's view, intra-EU BITs do not relate to the 'same subject matter' as the EU Treaties, with the effect that Art. 59 VCLT is not applicable to the relationship between those two treaty regimes. Accordingly, the intra-EU BITs have not been terminated by virtue of Art. 59 VCLT.

Nonetheless, even if arguendo one were to take the view that EU law and intra-EU BITs relate to the 'same subject matter', Art. 59 VCLT would not be applicable to intra-EU BITs as its other conditions are neither pertinent. This will be shown in the following. The analysis will thus be continued based on the (refuted) presumption that the successive treaties relate to the 'same subject matter'. In this case Art. 59 (1) VCLT requires either the subjective criterion of the parties' intention or the objective criterion of the incompatibility of the two treaties.

b) Intention

When States knowingly conclude treaties that contain mutually exclusive obligations, they generally address the relationship between these treaties by including so-called conflict clauses.[49] As defined by the ILC, such clauses are provisions

> intended to regulate the relation between the provisions of the treaty and those of another treaty or of any other treaty relating to the matters with which the treaty deals. Sometimes the clause concerns the relation of the treaty to a prior treaty, sometimes its relation to a future treaty and sometimes to any treaty past or future. Whatever the nature of the provision, the clause has necessarily to be taken into account in appreciating the priority of successive treaties relating to the same subject-matter.[50]

Such a 'conflict clause' is enshrined in Art. 30.8 CETA, which explicitly declares the termination of previous BITs between Canada and EU Member States from the date of the entry into force of CETA. No similar provision, however, is contained

---

47 On this, see Chapter I: III.
48 PCA, *European American Investment Bank v Slovakia*. PCA Case No. 2010–17. Award on Jurisdiction, 22 October 2012, para. 184. In the same vein, see also T. Giegerich, *Art. 59* in O. Dörr and K. Schmalenbach (eds.), *Vienna Convention on the Law of Treaties* (Berlin: Springer, 2018), para. 11.
49 Cf. J. Finke, *Regime-collisions* in C. J. Tams, et al. (eds.), *Research Handbook on the Law of Treaties* (Cheltenham: Edward Elgar, 2014), p. 420. See also K. von der Decken, *Art. 30* in O. Dörr and K. Schmalenbach (eds.), *Vienna Convention on the Law of Treaties* (Berlin: Springer, 2018), paras. 16 ff.
50 A. Watts, *The International Law Commission 1949–1998: Volume Two: The Treaties Part II* (New York: Oxford University Press, 1999), at 675.

in any intra-EU BIT. Regarding the relationship between intra-EU BITs and the EU Treaties, the only clause that might come into question is Art. 351 TFEU, which deals with treaties concluded by EU Member States with third States prior to the Member States' accession to the EU. Pursuant to Art. 351 (2) TFEU, an EU Member State might even be obliged to denounce a treaty.[51] This article, however, is, due to its explicit wording, not applicable to treaties *among* EU Member States whether concluded before or after the accession to the EU.[52] Hence, the intention of the parties must be assessed by other means.

When States conclude a new treaty on a subject-matter that is already covered by a previous treaty between them, one might reasonably assume that their intention is to replace the older by the new one.[53] However, without a 'conflict clause' the assessment of the States' intention becomes somewhat difficult. Especially, if there is only an overlap regarding certain provisions, and the two treaties seem only incidentally or accidentally to be in conflict with each other, the presumption of the States' intention to terminate the preceding treaty is questionable.

In that regard it has been argued that the presumption of a later treaty prevailing over a preceding one should only be rebuttable provided there is evidence of the parties' will to maintain the earlier treaty.[54] In other words, that not the parties' intention to terminate but the intention to sustain the preceding treaty must be proven in order to maintain the latter in force. This approach, however, is not convincing as Art. 59 VCLT explicitly provides that the intention of the parties must be that the 'same subject matter' should be governed by the later treaty. Furthermore, this approach would create considerable legal uncertainty.

The Member States' intention is difficult to determine in the present case. There is no explicit statement regarding intra-EU BITs in the Accession Treaties of the Southern and Eastern European Member States or in the Lisbon Treaty itself. Intra-EU investment protection is not mentioned at all. As discussed previously,[55] the *Europe Agreements* preparing the later EU accessions in fact promoted the conclusion of BITs between accession candidates and Member States without considering the treaties' possible future after the candidates' EU accession.

On the other hand, no Member State has amended an intra-EU BIT after the entry into force of the Lisbon Treaty which would reflect its will to keep up the BIT's validity. Hence, the only way to construct the BIT's termination according

---

51 ECJ, *Commission v Portugal*. C-62/98. Judgment, 4 July 2000, ECLI:EU:C:2000:358, para. 49.

52 See also ECJ, *Matteucci*. Case 235/87. Judgment, 27 September 1988, ECLI:EU:C:1988:460, para. 21; ECJ, *Commission v Luxembourg*. C-473/93. Judgment, 2 July 1996, ECLI:EU:C:1996:263, para. 40; ECJ, *Commission v Austria*. C-147/03. Judgment, 7 July 2005, ECLI:EU:C:2005:427, para. 58; ILC, *Fragmentation of International Law*, 13 April 2006, para. 284.

53 See also J. Finke, *Regime-collisions* in C. J. Tams, et al. (eds.), *Research Handbook on the Law of Treaties* (Cheltenham: Edward Elgar, 2014), p. 420.

54 P. Mariani, *The Future of BITs Between EU Member States* in G. Sacerdoti, et al. (eds.), *General Interests of Host States in International Investment Law* (Cambridge: Cambridge University Press, 2014), at 272 f.

55 On this, see Chapter I: III. 1.

to Art. 59 VCLT is a tacit, implicit abrogation, i.e. by virtue of Art. 59 (1) lit. a) VCLT, according to which it must "appear from the later treaty or be otherwise established that the parties intended that the matter should be governed by that treaty."

As seen previously, a great innovation of the Lisbon Treaty was to include a new EU competence on external trade and investment relations. Intra-EU investments, however, were not regulated. Against this backdrop, one could raise the *e contrario* argument that the Member States intended the intra-EU investment regime not to be covered by the more recent Lisbon Treaty. At the time the latter entered into force, 26 intra-EU investor-State arbitration proceedings had already been initiated. However, according to the accessible documents, by then only six of them had already been terminated either through an award or through settlement.[56] The great majority of cases, was only initiated and decided after the Lisbon Treaty's entry into force, which further suggests, that the EU Member States had no intention to implicitly terminate the existing intra-EU BITs through the Lisbon Treaty as their practical relevance and impact was still largely unknown to them.

The conditions of Art. 59 (1) lit. a) VCLT are not met. There was no discernible will of the Member States – neither explicit nor implicit – to terminate the existing intra-EU BITs through the conclusion of the Lisbon Treaty. Thus, even if it is assumed that EU law and intra-EU BITs relate to the 'same subject matter', they would not have been terminated by virtue of Art. 59 (1) lit. a) VCLT.

c) Incompatibility

As there was no apparent intention by the States parties to terminate the intra-EU BITs, the objective criterion of incompatibility needs to be assessed. Art. 59 (1) lit. b) VCLT defines 'incompatibility' as a situation in which two treaties cannot be applied at the same time. This is the case when the Treaty parties cannot comply simultaneously with the obligation arising out of one of the treaties without breaching the other treaty.[57]

Whether provisions of the EU Treaties are conflicting with earlier intra-EU BITs in the way that they are not capable of being applied at the same time, however, depends on the analysis of their relationship from an EU law perspective. In other words, supposed intra-EU BITs cover the 'same subject matter' as the EU

---

56 At the time of the entry into force of the Lisbon treaty, however, 11 pre-accession and 11 transition cases had been filed, most of which had already been decided or settled. On the classification of intra-EU, transition and pre-accession cases, see Chapter I: III. 5.

57 Cf. K. von der Decken, *Art. 30* in O. Dörr and K. Schmalenbach (eds.), *Vienna Convention on the Law of Treaties* (Berlin: Springer, 2018), para. 14; PCA, *European American Investment Bank v Slovakia*. PCA Case No. 2010–17. Award on Jurisdiction, 22 October 2012, para. 216. See also J. Finke, *Regime-collisions* in C. J. Tams, et al. (eds.), *Research Handbook on the Law of Treaties* (Cheltenham: Edward Elgar, 2014), at 416 f; ILC, *Fragmentation of International Law*, 13 April 2006, para. 254.

Treaties at the first place, they might have been terminated if the entire treaties are from an EU point of view incompatible with EU law.

The ECJ found in its *Achmea* decision,[58] that investor-State arbitration provisions contained in intra-EU BITs are incompatible with EU law.[59] From an EU legal perspective, this decision has to be considered by arbitral tribunals when applying and interpreting EU law, as the ECJ is the highest court of the EU legal order and competent to interpret the EU Treaties in a final and binding manner. However, as an investor-State arbitration tribunal is constituted on the basis of a BIT and only competent to interpret the BIT, it could reach a different conclusion regarding the relationship of EU law and intra-EU BITs and potentially ignore the ECJ's *Achmea* judgment, finding that intra-EU investor-State arbitration provisions contained in a BIT are compatible with the EU Treaties.[60]

Notwithstanding possible interpretations of arbitral tribunals, Art. 59 (1) lit. b) VCLT requires an incompatibility preventing the simultaneous application of both treaties. This, however, is not the case regarding the relationship between EU law and intra-EU BITs as will be shown in the next subchapter. Even if an intra-EU BIT arbitration provision is found to be incompatible with EU law, other provisions contained in that specific BIT can still be applied. This is also reflected in the impressive number of intra-EU investor-State arbitration proceedings in which no incompatibility of the BIT was alleged by any party or even the EU Commission.

In sum, neither the condition of Art. 59 (1) lit. b) VCLT is met. There is no 'absolute' incompatibility of intra-EU BITs and the EU Treaties preventing them from being applied at the same time.

d) Interim findings

The allegation of the Commission and of some Member States that EU law has replaced intra-EU BITs has been refuted. The essential element of Art. 59 VCLT, i.e. that both EU law and intra-EU BITs cover the 'same subject matter', is not fulfilled. Furthermore, there is no recognizable intention of the EU Member States to terminate their BITs, neither by acceding to the EU, nor by concluding the Lisbon Treaty. Also, the condition of incompatibility is not met to a degree sufficient to terminate the BITs presumed they would indeed cover the 'same subject matter' as the EU Treaties.

The author thus shares the assessment of most arbitral tribunals that both intra-EU BITs and EU law continue to exist side by side and have not been 'automatically' terminated. The intra-EU BITs have neither been suspended by virtue of

---

58 ECJ, *Achmea*. C-284/16. Judgment, 6 March 2018.
59 See in great detail, Chapter III: III. 1.
60 The question, however, whether an arbitral tribunal has to consider the ECJ's decision at all, will be discussed at a later stage, see Chapter III: III. 6. and Chapter IV: V.

Art. 59 (2) VCLT. In difference to an abrogation such a suspension would only have a temporal effect, allowing the earlier treaty to become operative again after the termination of the later treaty.[61]

The ECJ appears to share this position. While it did not openly treat the question of the BIT's validity in *Achmea*, the Court, just like the German BGH in its preliminary reference implicitly recognized the intra-EU BITs validity by dealing with the content of one of these BITs.[62]

III Incompatibility of intra-EU BITs with EU law

The possible incompatibility of intra-EU BITs and intra-EU investor-State arbitration with EU law has been a highly controversial topic in the last years. While the EU Commission, supported by some Member States and parts of the European legal academia, was convinced of such incompatibility, arbitral practice and large parts of the academic investment law community claimed the opposite, namely the perfectly possible coexistence and complementarity of the two legal regimes. The ECJ's recent *Achmea* decision has provided some answers to this debate. Many questions, however, remain unsolved. After having determined the further validity of intra-EU BITs in the last section, the following part will now analyse the questions of (in)compatibility from both an EU legal perspective and a public international law perspective.

There is no explicit rule in primary EU law that prohibits intra-EU BITs or investor-State arbitration.[63] Nonetheless, starting with its 1988 *Matteucci* decision, the case law of the ECJ has long affirmed that EU law takes precedence over colliding bilateral treaties between Member States concluded before the entry into force of the EU Treaties or before the accession of one of these States to the EU.[64] According to the ECJ, the provisions of a treaty

> concluded after 1 January 1958 by a Member State with another State could not, from the accession of the latter State to the Community, apply in the

---

61 T. Giegerich, *Art. 59* in O. Dörr and K. Schmalenbach (eds.), *Vienna Convention on the Law of Treaties* (Berlin: Springer, 2018), para. 34 f; F. Dubuisson, *Art. 59 of the 1969 Convention* in O. Corten and P. Klein (eds.), *The Vienna Conventions on the Law of Treaties* (Oxford: Oxford University Press, 2011), para. 49.

62 BGH, *Preliminary reference – Achmea*. I ZB 2/15. Beschluss, 3 March 2016, EuZW 13 (2016), 512. Slovakia also withdrew its initial argument that the entire BIT had been terminated through the Slovak's accession to the EU, cf. OLG Frankfurt am Main, *Achmea v Slovakia*. 26 SchH 11/10. Beschluss, 10 May 2012, SchiedsVZ 2013, 119, page. 23.

63 Cf. PCA, *Eureko v Slovakia*. Case No. 2008–13. Award on Jurisdiction, Arbitrability and Suspension, 26 October 2010, para. 274. Regarding intra-EU investor-State arbitration based on the ECT, cf. ICSID, *Charanne v Spain*. Arb. No. 062/2012. Final Award, 21 January 2016, para. 438; ICSID, *Eiser Infrastructure v Spain*. Case No. ARB/13/36. Award, 4 May 2017, para. 204.

64 ECJ, *Matteucci*. Case 235/87. Judgment, 27 September 1988, para. 22. See also ECJ, *Commission v Italy*. Case 10/61. Judgment, 27 February 1962, ECLI:EU:C:1962:2.

relations between those States if they were found to be contrary to the rules of the Treaty.[65]

Thus, from an EU perspective, intra-EU BITs are inapplicable if they collide with the EU Treaties. Several conceivable grounds for the incompatibility of intra-EU BITs have been presented at different occasions. The ECJ's *Achmea* decision rendered on March 6, 2018, discusses some of them. The following part analyses the *Achmea* judgment (1.) and discusses whether it is transferable and applicable to other intra-EU BITs (2.), before assessing other possible grounds of incompatibility of intra-EU BITs with the EU legal order, namely the non-discrimination provision of Art. 18 TFEU (3.), the principle of 'mutual trust' (4.) and questions of State aid (5.). It ends with the public international law perspective on the (in)compatibility of the 'international investment protection regime' within Europe with the law of the European Union (6.).

1 Incompatibility found in Achmea

To start with, the background and proceedings leading to the *Achmea* decision will be briefly presented (a). Then, the different positions regarding the compatibility of intra-EU BIT arbitration clauses with the autonomy of EU law enshrined in Art. 344 and Art. 267 TFEU will be assessed (b), before analysing the actual decision of the ECJ (c).

a) Main proceeding and background to the ECJ's Achmea judgment

The background to the ECJ's *Achmea* decision is an investor-State arbitration proceeding, confronting the Dutch insurance company Eureko, later renamed Achmea,[66] and Slovakia. The proceeding was based on the 1991 Netherlands–Czechoslovakia BIT, which entered into force on January 10, 1992; three months before the division of Czechoslovakia into two new States, the Czech Republic and Slovakia, which both succeeded to the treaty.[67] In 2004, Slovakia acceded to the EU and opened its market to private health insurance providers, both domestic and foreign. Thereupon, the Achmea group established a subsidiary in Slovakia. After a change of government in 2006 the liberalization of the health insurance market was partially revoked, which according to Achmea seriously infringed its

---

65 ECJ, *Exportur.* C-3/91. Judgment, 10 November 1992, ECLI:EU:C:1992:420, para. 8. See also ECJ, *American Bud.* C-478/07. Judgment, 8 September 2009, ECLI:EU:C:2009:521, para. 98; ECJ, *Commission v Germany.* C-546/07. Judgment, 21 January 2010, ECLI:EU:C:2010:25, para. 44; ECJ, *Ravil.* C-469/00. Judgment, 20 May 2003, ECLI:EU:C:2003:295, para. 37.

66 Eureko's name was changed to 'Achmea' after a merger on 18 November 2011. For further details, see PCA, *Achmea (formerly known as "Eureko") v Slowakia.* Case No. 2008–13. Final Award, 7 December 2012, para. 1.

67 On this State succession, see Chapter I: III. 1. footnote 80.

investment and thus constituted a breach of several provisions of the Netherlands–
Czechoslovakia BIT. Achmea – unsuccessfully – filed a complaint with the EU
Commission claiming that the Slovak policies were violating basic principles of
EU law.[68] Subsequently, the company initiated an investor-State arbitration proceeding based on the BIT claiming damages of € 65 million. The PCA was designated to act as registry and Frankfurt am Main in Germany was chosen as the
seat of arbitration.[69]

The Award on Jurisdiction rendered by the tribunal on October 26, 2010,[70]
was challenged by Slovakia before the Higher Regional Court (OLG) Frankfurt
am Main, which rejected the application.[71] On December 7, 2012, the arbitral
tribunal rendered its Final Award finding that Slovakia had violated both the fair
and equitable treatment standard and the free transfer of capital provided for in
the BIT. It thus ordered the respondent State to pay damages of € 22.1 million.[72]
In the following, Slovakia initiated a proceeding to set aside the award. It argued
that the offer to arbitrate contained in the BIT had become inapplicable due to
the countries accession to the EU in 2004 with the effect that the arbitral tribunal
lacked jurisdiction. Again, the OLG was competent to decide the dispute. However, as it could not find any ground of reversal applicable to the case, it once
more rejected Slovakia's claim.[73] The latter thus lodged an appeal before the
German BGH, which in turn decided in March 2016 to stay the proceedings and to
refer following questions regarding the compatibility of the investor-State arbitration clause in the Netherlands–Czechoslovakia BIT to the ECJ:

1   Does Article 344 TFEU preclude the application of a provision in a bilateral
    investment protection agreement between Member States of the European
    Union (a so-called intra-EU BIT) under which an investor of a Contracting
    State, in the event of a dispute concerning investments in the other Contract-
    ing State, may bring proceedings against the latter State before an arbitral
    tribunal where the investment protection agreement was concluded before
    one of the Contracting States acceded to the European Union but the arbitral
    proceedings are not to be brought until after that date?
    If Question 1 is to be answered in the negative:

---

68 See also P. Mariani, *The Future of BITs Between EU Member States* in G. Sacerdoti, et al. (eds.),
    General Interests of Host States in International Investment Law (Cambridge: Cambridge Univer-
    sity Press, 2014), at 276 f.
69 PCA, *Achmea (formerly known as "Eureko") v Slowakia*. Case No. 2008–13. Final Award, 7
    December 2012, para. 15 f.
70 PCA, *Eureko v Slovakia*. Case No. 2008–13. Award on Jurisdiction, Arbitrability and Suspension,
    26 October 2010.
71 OLG Frankfurt am Main, *Achmea v Slovakia*. 26 SchH 11/10. Beschluss, 10 May 2012. A later
    appeal to the BGH against this decision was also dismissed, BGH. III ZB 37/12. Beschluss, 19
    September 2013, SchiedsVZ 2013, 333.
72 PCA, *Achmea (formerly known as "Eureko") v Slowakia*. Case No. 2008–13. Final Award, 7
    December 2012, para. 352.
73 OLG Frankfurt am Main, *Wirksamkeit einer Schiedsklausel*. 26 Sch 3/13. Beschluss, 18 Decem-
    ber 2014, BeckRS 2015, 06323.

2   Does Article 267 TFEU preclude the application of such a provision?
    If Questions 1 and 2 are to be answered in the negative:
3   Does the first paragraph of Article 18 TFEU preclude the application of such a provision under the circumstances described in Question 1?[74]

The importance of these questions and the potentially massive political effects of the answers given by the Luxembourg Court are illustrated by the fact that apart from the EU Commission, 15 Member States lodged written observations or presented oral observations in the proceedings before the ECJ.[75]

b) Autonomy of EU law enshrined in Art. 344 and Art. 267 TFEU

The questions submitted by the German BGH regarding the interpretation of Art. 344 TFEU and Art. 267 TFEU were not unheard of but had already been extensively discussed by legal academia and arbitral tribunals.

The first question the ECJ was supposed to answer was that of the compatibility of intra-EU BIT arbitration clauses with Art. 344 TFEU. This provision obliges Member States not "to submit a dispute concerning the interpretation or application of the Treaties to any method of settlement other than those provided for therein." The wording is clear, insofar as it precludes Member States from agreeing on the jurisdiction of any other court or tribunal regarding disputes that arise between them and concern EU law. The ECJ has the judicial monopoly on cases between Member States, i.e. Art. 344 TFEU gives priority to internal EU dispute procedures.

The principle enshrined in Art. 344 TFEU was included in the European Treaties from the very beginning of European integration so as to avoid conflicts of jurisdictions with other international dispute settlement regimes the Member States had signed up to.[76] As emphasized by the ECJ in the famous *MOX Plant* decision, "the institution and pursuit of proceedings" before an arbitral tribunal "involve a manifest risk that the jurisdictional order laid down in the Treaties and, consequently, the autonomy of the Community legal system may be adversely affected".[77] Hence, according to Art. 344 TFEU, as well as according to their general duty of loyalty codified in Art. 3 (4) TEU, the Member States are obliged to

---

74 ECJ, *Achmea.* C-284/16. Judgment, 6 March 2018, para. 23. See also BGH, *Preliminary reference – Achmea.* I ZB 2/15. Beschluss, 3 March 2016.

75 ECJ, *Achmea.* C-284/16. Opinion of Advocate General Wathelet, 19 September 2017, para. 31 f. The Advocate General categorized these States in two groups, one consisting "essentially of countries of origin of the investors and therefore never or rarely respondents in arbitral proceedings launched by investors" and the other consisting of States which "have all been respondents in a number of arbitral proceedings," the latter being supportive of Slovakia's position, cf. ibid., paras. 34 ff.

76 See already Art. 292 of the Treaty of Rome and Art. 219 European Economic Community. See also T. Lock, *The European Court of Justice and International Courts* (Oxford: Oxford University Press, 2015), at 82 f.

77 ECJ, *MOX Plant.* C-459/03. Judgment, 30 May 2006, para. 154. See also P. Craig and G. de Búrca, *EU Law: Text, Cases and Materials*, 6. ed. (Oxford: Oxford University Press, 2015), p. 357.

have recourse to the EU's judicial system in case of conflict and to respect the ECJ's exclusive jurisdiction protecting the autonomy of the EU legal order and guaranteeing its uniform interpretation and application.[78]

In its *Patent Court Opinion,* the ECJ further found that Art. 344 TFEU does not concern disputes between private parties as the "article merely prohibits Member States from submitting a dispute concerning the interpretation or application of the Treaties."[79] This statement, however, brought no clarity on the question whether also investor-State arbitration in the intra-EU context would fall under the prohibition of Art. 344 TFEU. Many authors, domestic courts and most arbitral tribunals were convinced that the article was, due to its wording, systematic position and telos, not applicable to disputes between individuals and Member States.[80] According to the German BGH, the ECJ's competence was not affected by an intra-EU investor-State arbitration as the European Treaties did not provide for a procedure in which an individual could bring a claim against a Member State directly before the ECJ.[81] Accordingly, the Advocate General found in his extensive *Achmea* Opinion that Art. 344 TFEU would not be applicable to investor-State arbitration, as such disputes would not concern the "interpretation or application of the Treaties", nor undermine the allocation of powers determined by the EU Treaties or affect the autonomy of the EU legal order.[82]

On the other hand, for Slovakia, some other Member States and the EU Commission, Art. 344 TFEU had to be interpreted in a wide way only excluding purely horizontal situations between individuals. It would thus be applicable to "disputes between an individual and a Member State, especially in the light of its wording,

---

78 ECJ, *MOX Plant.* C-459/03. Judgment, 30 May 2006, para. 169. See also ECJ, *EU accession to the ECHR.* 2/13. Opinion, 18 December 2014, para. 202; BGH, *Preliminary reference – Achmea.* I ZB 2/15. Beschluss, 3 March 2016, para. 37.

79 ECJ, *European Patent Court.* 1/09. Opinion, 8 March 2011, para. 63.

80 Cf. BGH, *Preliminary reference – Achmea.* I ZB 2/15. Beschluss, 3 March 2016, para. 26; OLG Frankfurt am Main, *Wirksamkeit einer Schiedsklausel.* 26 Sch 3/13. Beschluss, 18 December 2014, para. 51; ICSID, *Electrabel v Hungary.* Case No. ARB/07/19. Decision on Jurisdiction, Applicable Law and Liability, 30 November 2012, para. 4.151; PCA, *Eureko v Slovakia.* Case No. 2008–13. Award on Jurisdiction, Arbitrability and Suspension, 26 October 2010, para. 276; Ad Hoc Arbitration, *Wirtgen v Czech Republic.* PCA Case No. 2014–03. Final Award, 11 October 2017, para. 258; SCC Arbitration, *PL Holdings v Poland.* V 2014/163. Partial Award, 28 June 2017, para. 314; SCC Arbitration, *Anglia Auto v Czech Republic.* Case V 2014/181. Final Award, 10 March 2017, paras. 126 ff; ICSID, *Blusun v Italy.* ICSID Case No. ARB/14/3. Award, 27 December 2016, para. 289; SCC Arbitration, *Busta & Busta v Czech Republic.* Case V 2015/014. Final Award, 10 March 2017, paras. 126 ff; D. Dittert, *Art. 344 AEUV* in *Europäisches Unionsrecht: Kommentar,* 7. ed. (Baden-Baden: Nomos, 2015), at para. 4; C. Kaddous, *Arbitrage, Union européenne et accords bilatéraux d'investissement,* Swiss Review of International and European Law (2013), 3–8, at 5 f; T. Lock, *The European Court of Justice and International Courts* (Oxford: Oxford University Press, 2015), at 141 f.

81 BGH, *Preliminary reference – Achmea.* I ZB 2/15. Beschluss, 3 March 2016, para. 38.

82 ECJ, *Achmea.* C-284/16. Opinion of Advocate General Wathelet, 19 September 2017, para. 159, 228, 272. For a detailed analysis, see J. Berger, *Intra-EU Investor-State Arbitration – The Uncertainty Continues: Unpacking the Advocate General's Opinion in Case C-284/16 (Achmea),* Zeitschrift für Schiedsverfahren 15 (2017), 282–91.

which unlike Art. 273 TFEU", would not expressly "limit its scope to disputes between Member States".[83] Accordingly, Art. 344 TFEU and the ECJ's case law would prohibit Member States to enter into treaties allowing investors to circumvent the EU's own rules and proceedings for resolving disputes concerning the interpretation or application of EU law.[84]

The second question the ECJ was supposed to answer was that of the compatibility of intra-EU BIT arbitration clauses with Art. 267 TFEU. According to this provision, only courts or tribunals of Member States are entitled to refer cases to the ECJ.[85] The ECJ has precluded (commercial) arbitral tribunals from submitting preliminary references, as they do not have compulsory jurisdiction and because such arbitration proceedings do not provide for sufficient public control, even though it is possible for domestic courts to review the proceedings and awards at least at the stage of enforcement.[86]

Investor-State arbitration tribunals have to decide whether provisions of an IIA their jurisdiction is based upon have been breached. They do not have jurisdiction to rule on breaches of EU law as such. Nonetheless, there might be situations in which an arbitral tribunal has to apply or interpret EU law or at least must take it into consideration while assessing the legality of a Member State's conduct, i.e. its compliance with international obligations. If such an application or interpretation of EU law takes place in a final and binding way, it could possibly circumvent the ECJ's interpretative monopoly and the autonomy of EU law if the investor-State arbitration tribunal was precluded from submitting preliminary references to the ECJ. The ECJ's line of jurisprudence regarding commercial arbitration, however, also applies to investor-State arbitration tribunals, which are precluded from submitting preliminary references to the ECJ.[87] Surprisingly, however, Advocate

---

83 Cf. the position of Slovakia and others as cited in ECJ, *Achmea.* C-284/16. Opinion of Advocate General Wathelet, 19 September 2017, para. 144. See also the position of Slovakia, as cited in OLG Frankfurt am Main, *Wirksamkeit einer Schiedsklausel.* 26 Sch 3/13. Beschluss, 18 December 2014, para. 30 and the position of Spain, as cited in ICSID, *Charanne v Spain.* Arb. No. 062/2012. Final Award, 21 January 2016, para. 442.

84 Position of the EU Commission in PCA, *U.S. Steel v Slovakia.* Case No. 2013–6. Amicus Curiae Brief by the EU Commission, 15 May 2014, para. 44 f. In a similar way, EU Commission, *Observation on jurisdiction regarding the PCA Case No. 2010–17 – European American Investment Bank v Slovakia: L. Romero Requena, Director General EU Commission Legal Service,* 13 October 2011, at 3 f.

85 For greater detail, see Chapter II: IV. 2. b).

86 ECJ, *Nordsee.* Case 102/81. Judgment, 23 March 1982, ECLI:EU:C:1982:107, paras. 7 ff; ECJ, *Eco Swiss.* C-126/97. Judgment, 1 June 1999, ECLI:EU:C:1999:269, paras. 34 ff; ECJ, *Denuit.* C-125/04. Judgment, 27 January 2005, ECLI:EU:C:2005:69, paras. 13 ff.

87 Notwithstanding, the arbitral tribunal in *Eastern Sugar* was requested by the Czech Republic to refer the question of its own jurisdiction to the ECJ. However, due to the ECJ's settled jurisprudence, the arbitral tribunal found this to be a "route not open to arbitral tribunals," SCC Arbitration, *Eastern Sugar B.V. v Czech Republic.* SCC No. 088/2004. Partial Award, 27 March 2007, para. 131. In a similar way, Slovakia unsuccessful requested the tribunal in Oostergetel to ask a domestic court to file a preliminary reference to the ECJ, for the latter to answer EU law related questions of jurisdiction and applicable law, Ad Hoc Arbitration, *Oostergetel & Laurentius v Slovakia.* Decision on Jurisdiction, 30 April 2010, para. 105.

General Wathelet took the position that an arbitral tribunal constituted in accordance with an intra-EU BIT

> is a court or tribunal within the meaning of Art. 267 TFEU, common to two Member States, […] and is therefore permitted to request the Court to give a preliminary ruling.[88]

The Advocate General's Opinion analysed every single precondition developed by the ECJ's jurisprudence for an adjudicatory body to be a court or tribunal of a Member State, in particular the condition that the adjudicatory body is established by law, permanent, independent, with compulsory jurisdiction, an inter partes procedure and applying rules of law.[89] In view of the Advocate General, all these conditions were met in the case at hand.[90]

c) Incompatibility of investor-State arbitration provisions with EU law

In *Achmea*, the Grand Chamber of the ECJ answered the questions referred to it by the BGH in a very short judgment, thereby omitting to treat the question of the compatibility with Art. 18 TFEU, and not considering the Advocate General's Opinion at all.[91]

The Court's decision may be summarized as follows: intra-EU investor-State arbitration tribunals based on an arbitration provision such as the one contained in the Netherlands–Czechoslovakia BIT might interpret and apply EU law as part of the domestic law of the respondent State or as part of international law. Such tribunals, however, are not 'courts or tribunals of the Member States' within the meaning of Art. 267 TFEU, and thus cannot submit preliminary references to the ECJ. The potential review of arbitral awards by Member State courts is also not sufficient. Therefore, an investor-State arbitration clause contained in an intra-EU BIT, such as the one between the Netherlands and Czechoslovakia, is incompatible with the principle of 'mutual trust' and the autonomy of the EU legal order.

This decision is a confirmation of the recent autonomy jurisprudence of the ECJ, namely of *Opinion 2/13* on the EU's accession to the ECHR and *Opinion 1/09* regarding the Patent Court. For the ECJ, EU law is autonomous not only vis-à-vis

---

88 ECJ, *Achmea*. C-284/16. Opinion of Advocate General Wathelet, 19 September 2017, para. 85. See also, K. von Papp, *Clash of "Autonomous Legal Orders": Can EU Member State Courts Bridge the Jurisdictional Divide Between Investment Tribunals and the ECJ?* Common Market Law Review 50 (2013), 1039–81, at 1074 ff.

89 ECJ, *Achmea*. C-284/16. Opinion of Advocate General Wathelet, 19 September 2017, para. 86.

90 Ibid., paras. 90 ff. For a critical analysis, cf. J. Berger, *Intra-EU Investor-State Arbitration – The Uncertainty Continues,* Zeitschrift für Schiedsverfahren 15 (2017), at 284 ff.

91 The only mentioning of the Opinion can be found in ECJ, *Achmea*. C-284/16. Judgment, 6 March 2018, paras. 24 ff. in which the ECJ rejects the request by several Member States – which had expressed their disagreement with the Advocate General's Opinion – to reopen the oral procedure.

Member States law, but also vis-à-vis international law. No international legal obligation can alter core principles of the EU legal order. The application of EU law must remain in the hands of the EU judiciary, which includes national courts but at least since the *Achmea* judgment excludes intra-EU investment tribunals based on an arbitration clause such as the one in the Netherlands–Czechoslovakia BIT. The judgment is analysed in the following, starting with the principles regarding the law applicable to intra-EU investor-State arbitration proceedings in general and the applicable law in the specific *Achmea* case, before assessing the ECJ's conclusions regarding intra-EU investor-State arbitration tribunals.

APPLICABLE LAW IN INTRA-EU INVESTOR-STATE ARBITRATION PROCEEDINGS

For the ECJ, the main problem regarding investor-State arbitration is that an arbitral tribunal may apply EU law without the Court having a chance to control its interpretation and application. To understand this concern, one must comprehend the importance and significance of the laws applicable in international arbitration, i.e. the different legal rules an arbitral tribunal must consider when finding a solution to a dispute pending before it. Different laws apply to different 'elements' or 'stages' of a treaty-based investor-State arbitration proceeding. They will be presented in a chronological way:

Law governing the IIA   The arbitral tribunal bases its jurisdiction on an IIA, which provides for a standing offer to arbitrate. The latter solely has to be accepted by an investor stemming from another State party to the IIA in order to initiate the arbitration proceeding.[92] The IIA itself and the clauses contained therein are governed by public international law.

Lex arbitri   The existence of the arbitral tribunal and the proceedings in itself are governed by the so-called *lex arbitri*. It is the law of the country in which the arbitration takes place, i.e. the law of the tribunal's seat.[93] Hence, the importance of the seat of arbitration, which "is not merely a matter of geography", but the arbitration's "legal centre of gravity", creating the link between the arbitral proceeding and the law of the place where it is actually situated.[94]

The *lex arbitri* determines the internal procedure of the arbitration, i.e. the composition of the arbitral tribunal, its competence to rule on its own jurisdiction, general principles of procedure such the equal treatment of the parties or rules

---

92 On this in further detail, Chapter II: IV. 1. a).

93 See N. Blackaby, C. Partasides, A. Redfern and M. Hunter, *Redfern and Hunter on International Arbitration*, 6. ed. (New York, London: Oxford University Press, 2015), at para. 3.37; C. McLachlan, *Investment Treaty Arbitration* in A. J. van den Berg (ed.), *50 Years of the New York Convention* (Alphen aan den Rijn: Kluwer Law International, 2009), pp. 95–145, at 123 f. See also Art. V (1) a), d), e) New York Convention and Art. 1 (2) of the UNCITRAL Model Law.

94 N. Blackaby, C. Partasides, A. Redfern and M. Hunter, *Redfern and Hunter on International Arbitration* (New York, London: Oxford University Press, 2015), para. 3.56.

on hearings.[95] It also determines external intervention in the arbitral process, i.e. provides sources of arbitral rules to fill lacunae in the party chosen rules of procedure, places mandatory limits on the parties' autonomy, e.g. with regard to the form and validity of the arbitration award, and provides for possible support of the arbitral tribunal by domestic courts.[96] In most EU Member States, the legal rules constituting the *lex arbitri* form part of the Code of Civil Procedure.[97] If the IIA an arbitral tribunal bases its jurisdiction upon does not provide an explicit choice of seat of arbitration, the parties are generally free to choose the seat and can thus also choose the *lex arbitri*. If they cannot agree on the seat, the choice is either made by the arbitral tribunal or by a designated arbitral institution.[98]

International arbitration usually take place in 'neutral' countries, i.e. places with no nexus to either of the parties.[99] The *Achmea* proceeding, for instance, was conducted in Germany, even though Slovakia was the respondent and the claimant was a Dutch company. However, in case of an arbitration proceeding based on the ICSID Convention, the proceeding is 'delocalized', i.e. it has no seat of arbitration in the legal sense. In ICSID proceedings, the *lex arbitri* thus consists of the ICSID Convention and the ICSID arbitration rules.[100] This has the effect that the only point of control outside the ICSID regime is the place where enforcement is sought.[101]

The *lex arbitri* is generally supplemented by more detailed rules of procedure that are often contained in specific treaties such as the UNCITRAL arbitration rules or the ICSID Convention or which are provided by arbitral institutions.[102]

Lex causae   If not expressed otherwise by the parties, an investor-State dispute must be solved on the basis of the law. The law governing the substantive issues

---

95 Ibid., para. 3.46; C. McLachlan, *Investment Treaty Arbitration* in A. J. van den Berg (ed.), *50 Years of the New York Convention* (Alphen aan den Rijn: Kluwer Law International, 2009), p. 124.

96 Cf. N. Blackaby, C. Partasides, A. Redfern and M. Hunter, *Redfern and Hunter on International Arbitration* (New York, London: Oxford University Press, 2015), para. 3.46; C. McLachlan, *Investment Treaty Arbitration* in A. J. van den Berg (ed.), *50 Years of the New York Convention* (Alphen aan den Rijn: Kluwer Law International, 2009), p. 124.

97 Cf. N. Blackaby, C. Partasides, A. Redfern and M. Hunter, *Redfern and Hunter on International Arbitration* (New York, London: Oxford University Press, 2015), para. 3.62.

98 Cf. G. A. Bermann, *International Arbitration and Private International Law* (Leiden: Brill, 2017), at para. 215; N. Blackaby, C. Partasides, A. Redfern and M. Hunter, *Redfern and Hunter on International Arbitration* (New York, London: Oxford University Press, 2015), para. 3.40; See also Art. 18 (1) UNCITRAL Arbitration Rules and Art. 18 (1) ICC Rules.

99 Cf. G. A. Bermann, *International Arbitration and Private International Law* (Leiden: Brill, 2017), para. 214.

100 C. McLachlan, *Investment Treaty Arbitration* in A. J. van den Berg (ed.), *50 Years of the New York Convention* (Alphen aan den Rijn: Kluwer Law International, 2009), p. 123.

101 On this, see Chapter II: IV. 1. d).

102 Cf. N. Blackaby, C. Partasides, A. Redfern and M. Hunter, *Redfern and Hunter on International Arbitration* (New York, London: Oxford University Press, 2015), paras. 3.48 ff.

in dispute, i.e. the law applicable to the merits of the case, is generally described as the 'applicable law' or *lex causae*. It is the law provided for in the respective IIA in a so-called choice of law clause which often also refers to the substantive provisions of the treaty itself.[103] While concluding a treaty, States parties are free to choose the law applicable to the merits of a dispute. Nonetheless, many intra-EU IIAs lack such a designation.[104] In the absence of a choice of law clause the law to be applied by the arbitral tribunal depends on the provisions in the applicable rules of procedure or the choice of law rules set out in the *lex arbitri*, unless the parties have agreed otherwise.[105] A failure to apply the *lex causae* may lead to the annulment of an award.[106]

Law governing recognition and enforcement   Finally, the recognition and the enforcement of the award is governed by the law of the country in which a successful party seeks enforcement and by the applicable international treaties covering these issues such as the New York Convention or the ICSID Convention.[107]

APPLICABLE LAW AND THE INTERPRETATION OF EU LAW IN *ACHMEA*

In its *Achmea* decision, the ECJ focusses on the law governing the substantive issues, i.e. the *lex causae* or the 'applicable law'. The *lex causae* is explicitly provided for in Art. 8 (6) of the Netherlands–Czechoslovakia BIT:

> The arbitral tribunal shall decide on the basis of the law, taking into account in particular though not exclusively:
>
> * the law in force of the Contracting Party concerned;
> * the provisions of this Agreement, and other relevant agreements between the Contracting Parties;
> * the provisions of special agreements relating to the investment;
> * the general principles of international law.

---

103 See for example Art. 26 (VI) ECT: *A tribunal [...] shall decide the issues in dispute in accordance with this Treaty and applicable rules and principles of international law.* Another example is Art. 8 (6) of the 1991 Netherlands–Slovakia BIT which was invoked in the *Achmea* proceeding.

104 See for example, the 1990 Denmark–Poland BIT, the 1991 Greece–Slovakia BIT, the 1993 Lithuania–UK BIT, the 1996 Bulgaria–Croatia BIT, the 1998 France–Slovenia BIT, the 2001 Cyprus–Czech Republic BIT and the 2002 Romania–Sweden BIT.

105 See for example, Art. 42 ICSID Convention. See also O. Spiermann, *Investment Arbitration: Applicable Law* in M. Bungenberg, et al. (eds.), *International Investment Law: A Handbook* (Baden-Baden: Nomos, 2015), pp. 1373–90.

106 Ibid., para. 1373 f.

107 On this in greater detail, see Chapter II: IV. 1.

In its Award on Jurisdiction the *Achmea* tribunal had found that EU law might have an effect on the case as it forms part of the applicable law under the BIT, namely "the law in force of the Contracting Party concerned", "other relevant Agreements between the Contracting Parties" and as part of "the general principles of international law". Hence, the tribunal might need to apply the EU legal principles of supremacy, precedence, direct effect and direct applicability.[108] Furthermore, according to the *Achmea* tribunal,

> Far from being precluded from considering and applying EU law the Tribunal is bound to apply it to the extent that it is part of the applicable law(s). [...] The argument that the ECJ has an "interpretative monopoly" and that the Tribunal therefore cannot consider and apply EU law, is incorrect. The ECJ has no such monopoly. Courts and arbitration tribunals throughout the EU interpret and apply EU law daily. What the ECJ has is a monopoly on the final and authoritative interpretation of EU law: but that is quite different. Moreover, even final courts are not obliged to refer questions of the interpretation of EU law to the ECJ in all cases. The acte clair doctrine is well-established in EU law.[109]

The tribunal stressed, however, that its jurisdiction was confined to disputes concerning violations of the BIT and that it had no jurisdiction to rule on breaches of EU law as such.[110]

This position reflects the tribunal's awareness of possible conflicts regarding the *lex causae*. Nonetheless, the *Achmea* tribunal found that the BIT it based its jurisdiction upon explicitly assigned the task of interpretation to the arbitral tribunal and thus rejected the argument of the BITs collision with EU law. Furthermore, in its view the application of EU law by other courts is a completely natural course of action that does not infringe the ECJ's monopoly on a final interpretation of EU law. Especially as such an interpretation is not binding on the ECJ.

In its *Achmea* judgment, the ECJ took the same position as regarding the possibility of an arbitral tribunal based on the Netherlands–Czechoslovakia BIT, to interpret EU law, explaining that such a tribunal has to take into account in particular

> the law in force of the contracting party concerned and other relevant agreements between the contracting parties. Given the nature and characteristics of EU law [...] that law must be regarded both as forming part of the law in force in every Member State and as deriving from an international agreement

---

108 PCA, *Eureko v Slovakia*. Case No. 2008–13. Award on Jurisdiction, Arbitrability and Suspension, 26 October 2010, para. 279, 289.

109 Ibid., para. 281 f.

110 Ibid., para. 290.

between the Member States. It follows that on that twofold basis the arbitral tribunal referred to in Art. 8 of the BIT may be called on to interpret or indeed to apply EU law, particularly the provisions concerning fundamental freedoms.[111]

The EU Commission had earlier argued in the same direction, finding in its *amicus curiae* brief in *European American Investment Bank* that

> all natural and legal persons, as well as all states [...] involved in the arbitration [...], are subject to and bound by the law of the European Union. All are therefore required to respect the primacy of EU law as well as the autonomy of its judicial system. [...]
>
> The fundamental elements of the EU legal order and its judicial system, as designed by the founding Treaties and developed by the case-law of the Court of Justice of the European Union, form part of the public order of all its Member States and therefore of the law to be applied by the arbitrators.[112]

Although the ECJ agreed on the possibility of an arbitral tribunal to interpret and to apply EU law, it reached a totally different conclusion of the legal effects of this finding as will be shown in the following.

INVESTOR-STATE ARBITRATION TRIBUNALS ARE NOT COURTS OR TRIBUNALS OF THE MEMBER STATES

As just shown, an intra-EU investor-State arbitration tribunal might interpret and apply EU law. This raises the question whether such a tribunal can be understood as being a court or tribunal of a Member State in the sense of Art. 267 TFEU, i.e. whether it could refer preliminary questions to the ECJ and enter a judicial dialogue with the highest court of the EU. The ECJ has a clear stance on this question in its *Achmea* judgment:

> The arbitral tribunal is not part of the judicial system of the Netherlands or Slovakia. Indeed, it is precisely the exceptional nature of the tribunal's jurisdiction compared with that of the courts of those two Member States that is one of the principal reasons for the existence of Art. 8 of the BIT. [Thus] it cannot in any event be classified as a court or tribunal 'of a Member State' within the meaning of Art. 267 TFEU [...], and is not therefore entitled to make a reference to the Court for a preliminary ruling.[113]

---

111 ECJ, *Achmea*. C-284/16. Judgment, 6 March 2018, paras. 40 ff.
112 EU Commission, *Observation on jurisdiction regarding the PCA Case No. 2010–17 – European American Investment Bank v Slovakia*, 13 October 2011, p. 2.
113 ECJ, *Achmea*. C-284/16. Judgment, 6 March 2018, para. 45 f., 49.

In other words, due to its exceptional nature and the lack of links with the judicial system of a Member States, an investor-State arbitration tribunal based on the Netherlands–Czechoslovakia BIT does not fall under Art. 267 TFEU. It is not a court or tribunal of a Member State as understood in the EU legal order.

This position is not surprising. It reflects the understanding of the EU Commission[114] and follows the ECJ's established line of jurisprudence. As shown previously, it is settled case law of the ECJ that (commercial) arbitration tribunals, even if they have their seat in the territory of a Member State and are thus governed by that State's law, do not constitute courts or tribunals of the Member States and are thus not entitled to refer preliminary questions to the ECJ.[115] It is, however, the first time that the ECJ explicitly excluded investor-State arbitration tribunals from Art. 267 TFEU.

Even with investor-State arbitration tribunals not being courts or tribunals of the Member States, the autonomy of EU law could be sufficiently protected if domestic courts could monitor the arbitral tribunals' decision at some stage in the proceeding and had then the possibility to submit a reference for a preliminary ruling to the ECJ.

In the *Achmea* case, the seat of arbitration was Frankfurt am Main. This allowed Slovakia to seek judicial review of the award in accordance with German law before the competent German courts.[116] It was in the course of these proceedings that the German BGH submitted the preliminary question to the ECJ. But in the ECJ's view, this domestic judicial review was not sufficient, as such review is only possible to the extent permitted by national law which is regularly limited to the validity of the arbitration agreement and the consistency with the *ordre public* of the respective State.[117]

Indeed, the ECJ had accepted such limited review regarding commercial arbitration awards within the EU, "provided that the fundamental provisions of EU law can be examined in the course of that review, and, if necessary, be subject of a reference to the Court for a preliminary ruling".[118] According to the ECJ, however, this jurisprudence is not applicable to investor-State arbitration proceedings such as those based on the Netherlands–Czechoslovakia BIT. For the Court such proceedings must be distinguished from commercial arbitration proceedings, as they

> derive from a treaty by which Member States agree to remove from the jurisdiction of their own courts, and hence from the system of judicial remedies

---

114 Cf. EU Commission, *Observation on jurisdiction regarding the PCA Case No. 2010–17 – European American Investment Bank v Slovakia*, 13 October 2011, p. 5.

115 ECJ, *Eco Swiss*. C-126/97. Judgment, 1 June 1999, para. 34; ECJ, *Nordsee*. Case 102/81. Judgment, 23 March 1982, paras. 7 ff; ECJ, *Denuit*. C-125/04. Judgment, 27 January 2005, para. 13. See also G. A. Bermann, *Navigating EU Law and the Law of International Arbitration*, Arbitration International 28 (2012), 397–445, at 405.

116 ECJ, *Achmea*. C-284/16. Judgment, 6 March 2018, para. 52.

117 Cf. ibid., para. 53. For greater detail, see also Chapter II: IV. 1. d).

118 Ibid., para. 54, referring to ECJ, *Eco Swiss*. C-126/97. Judgment, 1 June 1999, para. 35, 36, 40; ECJ, *Mostaza Claro*. C-168/05. Judgment, 26 October 2006, ECLI:EU:C:2006:675, paras. 34 ff.

which the second subparagraph of Art. 19(1) TEU requires them to establish in the fields covered by EU law, disputes which may concern the application or interpretation of EU law. [...]

Consequently, [...] it must be considered that, by concluding the BIT, the Member States parties to it established a mechanism for settling disputes between an investor and a Member State which could prevent those disputes from being resolved in a manner that ensures the full effectiveness of EU law, even though they might concern the interpretation or application of that law.[119]

Just like the Advocate General, the ECJ did not differentiate between applicable rules of arbitration, especially in ICSID or non-ICSID proceedings, localized and 'delocalized' arbitration proceedings, proceedings with a seat in the EU or outside. It did neither differentiate between proceeding in which the enforcement is sought in an EU Member State or in a third State.[120] In his Opinion, the Advocate General had solely focused on the specific details of the *Achmea* dispute.[121] The ECJ in turn treated all possible types of intra-EU investor-State arbitration proceedings jointly and omitted to render a differentiated and well developed answer to the questions regarding intra-EU ISDS proceedings in general. Rather, for the ECJ, the investor-State arbitration clause contained in the Netherlands–Czechoslovakia BIT,

is such as to call into question not only the principle of mutual trust between the Member States but also the preservation of the particular nature of the law established by the Treaties, ensured by the preliminary ruling procedure provided for in Art. 267 TFEU, and is not therefore compatible with the principle of sincere cooperation [...] In those circumstances, Art. 8 of the BIT has an adverse effect on the autonomy of EU law.

Consequently, the answer [...] is that Art. 267 and 344 TFEU must be interpreted as precluding a provision in an international agreement concluded between Member States, such as Article 8 of the BIT, under which an investor from one of those Member States may, in the event of a dispute concerning investments in the other Member State, bring proceedings against the latter Member State before an arbitral tribunal whose jurisdiction that Member State has undertaken to accept.[122]

---

119 ECJ, *Achmea*. C-284/16. Judgment, 6 March 2018, para. 55 f.
120 An argument brought up by the European Commission and discussed by the Advocate General, ECJ, *Achmea*. C-284/16. Opinion of Advocate General Wathelet, 19 September 2017, paras. 251 ff.
121 Ibid., paras. 245 ff. Critical on this aspect of the Advocate General's Opinion, J. Berger, *Intra-EU Investor-State Arbitration – The Uncertainty Continues*, Zeitschrift für Schiedsverfahren 15 (2017), 286.
122 ECJ, *Achmea*. C-284/16. Judgment, 6 March 2018, paras. 58 ff. With a totally different position, ECJ, *Achmea*. C-284/16. Opinion of Advocate General Wathelet, 19 September 2017, para. 237.

In other words, in its view the arbitration provision contained in Art. 8 of the Netherlands–Czechoslovakia BIT was incompatible with Art. 267 and Art. 344 TFEU.

2 Applicability of the Achmea *decision to other intra-EU BITs*

The ECJ's *Achmea* decision explicitly deals with the arbitration clause contained in Art. 8 of the Netherlands–Czechoslovakia BIT. The question is whether this finding is transferable to other intra-EU BITs.

In principle, an Art. 267 TFEU decision of the ECJ has an *inter partes effect*.[123] The court of the main proceeding, i.e. in the present case the German BGH,[124] was bound to apply EU law according to the ECJ's interpretation. Only decisions of the ECJ determining the validity or invalidity of secondary EU law have an immediate *erga omnes* effect.[125] Nevertheless, an ECJ decision that clarifies the interpretation of primary EU norms also affects other courts in so far as they are obliged to apply and interpret the respective norms in light of the ECJ's decision.[126] Thus, if the ECJ establishes that a legal norm is incompatible with EU law and a quasi-identical norm can be found in the legal order of another Member State or a similar BIT, a Member State's court or tribunal is also bound by the ECJ's interpretation. In other words, the transferability of the *Achmea* judgment depends on the similarity of the Netherlands–Czechoslovakia BIT and other intra-EU BITs.

The wordings of intra-EU BITs differ to a large degree. As shown previously,[127] eight of these BITs do not provide for investor-State arbitration at all and are thus not comparable to the one analysed in the *Achmea* judgment. While the other intra-EU BITs contain an investor-State arbitration provision, most do not explicitly state the law applicable to the merits of the case.[128]

In the absence of a choice of law clause, an arbitral tribunal generally relies on the applicable arbitration rules determining the *lex causae*.[129] The most commonly used arbitration rules in intra-EU proceedings are the ICSID Convention and the

---

123 B. W. Wegener, *Art. 267 AEUV* in C. Calliess and M. Ruffert (eds.), *EUV/AEUV – Kommentar*, 5. ed. (München: C. H. Beck, 2016), at para. 49; U. Ehricke, *Art. 267 AEUV* in R. Streinz (ed.), *EUV/AEUV* (München, 2012), at para. 68.

124 Cf. BGH, *Achmea*. I ZB 2/15. Beschluss, 31 October 2018. On the BGH's decision, see in greater detail, Chapter IV: IV. 1.

125 B. W. Wegener, *Art. 267 AEUV* in C. Calliess and M. Ruffert (eds.), *EUV/AEUV – Kommentar* (München: C. H. Beck, 2016), para. 50.

126 U. Karpenstein, *Art. 267 AEUV* in E. Grabitz and M. Hilf (eds.), *Das Recht der Europäischen Union* (München: C. H. Beck, 2018), at para. 104.

127 Cf. Chapter I: III. 1.

128 See for example, the 1990 Denmark–Poland BIT, the 1991 Greece–Slovakia BIT, the 1993 Lithuania–UK BIT, the 1996 Bulgaria–Croatia BIT, the 1998 France–Slovenia BIT, the 2001 Cyprus–Czech Republic BIT and the 2002 Romania–Sweden BIT.

129 Cf. in greater detail Chapter III: III. 1. c).

UNCITRAL Arbitration Rules.[130] The ICSID Convention provides in Art. 42 (1) that in absence of an explicit provision on the applicable laws,

> the Tribunal shall apply the law of the Contracting State party to the dispute (including its rules on the conflict of laws) and such rules of international law as may be applicable.

Art. 33 (1) UNCITRAL Arbitration Rules offers an even greater discretion in such a case:

> the arbitral tribunal shall apply the law determined by the conflict of laws rules which it considers applicable.[131]

The ICSID Convention refers to the domestic law of the respondent State and rules of international law that might be applicable to the case. As shown in the beginning of this chapter, both the law of the respondent State and applicable international law rules to the case might comprise EU law. Thus, even if the BIT does not explicitly refer to the law of the European Union, an arbitral tribunal might interpret EU law in an ICSID arbitration proceeding.

In UNCITRAL and SCC arbitrations, however, the arbitral tribunal has a wide margin of appreciation regarding the applicable law. It could thus be argued that in the case of an intra-EU investor-State arbitration based on a BIT, which does not explicitly state which law to apply to the merits and which is based on UNCITRAL or SCC arbitration rules, the situation would not be comparable to that in *Achmea* and the ECJ's finding of incompatibility of the BIT could not be transferred.

An intra-EU investor-State arbitration tribunal, however, will always have to consider domestic and thus also EU law: Even if a BIT or the arbitration rules refer to international law only or a claim brought under a BIT is international in nature, the existence of an investment in the form of property rights is generally defined by domestic law.[132] Arbitrators might need to apply domestic law to assess whether an actual investment has been made, to whom the rights constituting the investment vest and to find out whether substantive rights of the IIA have been violated, since there are no rules of international law on the substance of an investment.[133]

---

130 Cf. Chapter II: IV. 1. b).
131 The 2017 SCC Arbitration Rules are almost identical. According to their Art. 27 (1) "the Arbitral Tribunal shall apply the law or rules of law which it considers to be most appropriate."
132 Cf. H. E. Kjos, *Applicable Law in Investor-State Arbitration* (Oxford: Oxford University Press, 2013), at 242; C. McLachlan, *Investment Treaty Arbitration* in A. J. van den Berg (ed.), *50 Years of the New York Convention* (Alphen aan den Rijn: Kluwer Law International, 2009), at 114 ff.
133 N. Blackaby, C. Partasides, A. Redfern and M. Hunter, *Redfern and Hunter on International Arbitration* (New York, London: Oxford University Press, 2015), para. 8.70; H. E. Kjos, *Applicable*

In other words, many preliminary questions in an investment dispute are governed by domestic law, especially questions of the nationality of the claimant and of its capacity to bring a claim, but also whether an investment was established in accordance with the domestic rules, the scope of a State organ's authority and whether a representative was empowered to act on behalf of the State.[134] Hence a BIT cannot be interpreted in a vacuum. "It is not a self-contained legal system limited to provide for substantive material rules of direct applicability" but has to be applied within a wider juridical context,[135] which comprises the domestic legal system and thus in the case of EU Member States also the legal order of the EU. As rightly emphasized by the Advocate General, EU law has to be taken into account by an arbitral tribunal in any event, "because that obligation results by default from Art. 31 (3) lit. a) and lit. c) VCLT."[136] It is on this ground that even the ECJ has from time to time applied certain provisions outside the EU Treaties and thereby implicitly extended its jurisdiction to these provisions.[137]

Nonetheless, it remains highly controversial what exact role domestic law has to play. Although it might need to be considered by international courts and tribunals, it generally remains a factual matter and international adjudicatory bodies generally do not interpret the domestic laws as such but only the international instruments they are called to interpret and apply.[138]

Law in Investor-State Arbitration (Oxford: Oxford University Press, 2013), p. 242; M. Sasson, *Substantive Law in Investment Treaty Arbitration: The Unsettled Relationship Between International Law and Municipal Law*, 2. ed. (Alphen aan den Rijn: Wolters Kluwer, 2017), at 244 ff. See also Ad Hoc Arbitration, *Invesmart v Czech Republic*. Award, 26 June 2009, para. 198.

134 Cf. ICJ, *Barcelona Traction*. Judgment, 5 February 1970, ICJ Reports 1970, para. 38. See also O. Spiermann, *Investment Arbitration: Applicable Law* in M. Bungenberg, et al. (eds.), *International Investment Law: A Handbook* (Baden-Baden: Nomos, 2015), p. 1387; H. E. Kjos, *Applicable Law in Investor-State Arbitration* (Oxford: Oxford University Press, 2013), p. 241.

135 Position of Romania, as cited in ICSID, *Ioan Micula, Viorel Micula and others v Romania*. Case No. ARB/05/20. Award, 11 December 2013, para. 304.

136 ECJ, *Achmea*. C-284/16. Opinion of Advocate General Wathelet, 19 September 2017, para. 172. Against this backdrop, many international courts and tribunals outside the international investment law regime, such as the ICJ, the ECtHR, WTO dispute settlement panels and the WTO Appellate Body or the Administrative Tribunal of the International Labour Organization, already had to deal with EU law. On this, see also ICSID, *Electrabel v Hungary*. Case No. ARB/07/19. Decision on Jurisdiction, Applicable Law and Liability, 30 November 2012, para. 4.147.

137 Cf. K. von Papp, *Clash of "Autonomous Legal Orders": Can EU Member State Courts Bridge the Jurisdictional Divide Between Investment Tribunals and the ECJ?* Common Market Law Review 50 (2013), at 1055 ff.

138 See famously PCIJ, *German interests in Polish Upper Silesia*. No. 7. Judgment, 25 May 1926, *Collection of Judgements Series A*, p. 19. See also ECJ, *CETA-Opinion*. 1/17. Opinion of Advocate General Bot, 29 January 2019, ECLI:EU:C:2019:72, para. 134; N. Blackaby, C. Partasides, A. Redfern and M. Hunter, *Redfern and Hunter on International Arbitration* (New York, London: Oxford University Press, 2015), para. 8.70 and the arbitral tribunals in *Busta & Busta, Anglia Auto* and in *AES Summit*, which argue that they are called to interpret and apply the BIT only and not EU law, SCC Arbitration, *Busta & Busta v Czech Republic*. Case V 2015/014. Final Award, 10 March 2017, para. 127; SCC Arbitration, *Anglia Auto v Czech Republic*. Case V 2014/181. Final Award, 10 March 2017, para. 127; ICSID, *AES Summit & AES-Tisza Erömü*

Whether domestic and EU law is treated as a fact or as applicable law depends on the respective interpretation of the competent courts and tribunals. It is, however, not decisive to answer the question whether the *Achmea* decision is transferable to other intra-EU BITs, since in any case in which an arbitral tribunal deals with questions of domestic or EU law, an international adjudicatory body makes a legal interpretation in the wide sense of the term and eventually renders a binding decision based on this interpretation. This is exactly the reason why the ECJ found Art. 8 of the Netherlands–Czechoslovakia BIT to be incompatible with EU law. The *Achmea* decision is thus transferable to every other intra-EU BIT which provides for investor-State arbitration, independent from the law to be applied in the case of disputes regarding the respective intra-EU BIT.[139]

The *Achmea* judgment constitutes a continuation of the ECJ's preceding autonomy jurisprudence. It confirms the decisions in *Opinion 1/09, Opinion 2/13* and *Kadi* by reaffirming that EU law is not only autonomous in relation to the domestic law of the Member States but also in relation to international law. For the ECJ, the sole possibility of the application or interpretation of EU law by an investor-State arbitration tribunal suffices for the incompatibility of the arbitration provision contained in an intra-EU BIT with EU law. The ECJ thereby implicitly rejects the 'harmonious interpretation' approaches[140] that had been suggested to solve the conflict between the two regimes.

There have been many interpretations and critical reviews of the ECJ's judgment. Many of them, however, depart from the actual wording of the decision. It should thus be recalled at this point what the *Achmea* judgment actually says: It states that clauses such as the one in Art. 8 of the Netherlands–Czechoslovakia BIT are inapplicable under EU law, and that tribunals created under such treaties are not 'courts or tribunals of the Member States'. As just shown, this reasoning based on the interpretation of Art. 344 and Art. 267 TFEU is also transferable and applicable to other intra-EU BITs providing for investor-State arbitration due to

---

v Hungary. ICSID Case No. ARB/07/22. Award, 23 September 2010, para. 7.6.12. According to Kjos, domestic law should generally be classified as a factual matter, especially concerning questions of discriminatory State behaviour. In cases regarding expropriation and umbrella clause, however, she emphasizes that "the better perspective is to consider national law as being truly applied to the merits, albeit indirectly as part of the determination of the international claim." Cf. H. E. Kjos, *Applicable Law in Investor-State Arbitration* (Oxford: Oxford University Press, 2013), at 254 f.

139 See also Representatives of 22 EU Member States, *Declaration on the Legal Consequences of the Judgment of the ECJ in Achmea and on Investment Protection in the EU,* 15 January 2019; Representatives of Finland, Luxembourg, Malta, Slovenia and Sweden, *Declaration on the Enforcement of the Judgement of the ECJ in Achmea and on Investment Protection in the EU,* 16 January 2019; Representative of Hungary, *Declaration on the Legal Consequences of the Judgment of the ECJ in Achmea and on Investment Protection in the EU,* 16 January 2019.

140 See for example, ICSID, *Electrabel v Hungary.* Case No. ARB/07/19. Decision on Jurisdiction, Applicable Law and Liability, 30 November 2012, paras. 4.143 ff; C. Tietje and C. Wackernagel, *Enforcement of Intra-EU ICSID Awards: Multilevel Governance, Investment Tribunals and the Lost Opportunity of the Micula Arbitration,* Journal of World Investment & Trade 16 (2015), 205–47, at 241 ff.

their similarity with the Netherlands–Czechoslovakia BIT, even if they do not have a similar wording, especially regarding the applicable law.

What the *Achmea* decision does *not* say, however, is anything regarding the effect of the decision on currently pending intra-EU arbitration proceedings or awards that have already been rendered. It says nothing, neither about the substantive investment protection provisions contained in the BITs and their compatibility with EU law nor anything about the Energy Charter Treaty. The transferability of the decision to the ECT will be discussed further below.[141] The effects of *Achmea* on pending proceedings, already rendered awards and the IIAs themselves will be discussed and analysed in depth in the following chapter.

3 Non-discrimination

In its preliminary reference to the ECJ in *Achmea* the BGH had also asked whether the investor-State arbitration provision contained in the Netherlands–Czechoslovakia BIT was compatible with the non-discrimination principle enshrined in Art. 18 (1) TFEU. However, as the ECJ found an incompatibility of the BIT's arbitration provision with Arts. 344 and 267 TFEU it saw no need to answer this question.[142] This is remarkable, as several Member States and the EU Commission had argued during the proceedings that the substantive provisions of the BIT, as well as its ISDS mechanism, were discriminatory as they afforded a preferential treatment to investors from the Netherlands who had invested in Slovakia, whereas the investors of Member States, which had not concluded a BIT with Slovakia providing for ISDS did not benefit from that treatment.[143]

a) Preconditions for a discrimination

Every intra-EU BIT contains non-discrimination clauses such as the most-favoured nation or national treatment standard. A discrimination, however, could arise out of the fact that only investors of the respective two contracting States fall under the specific BIT's regime. As only a small part of the potential number of intra-EU BITs have been concluded,[144] many investors cannot benefit from the 'additional' BIT protection. This is for instance the case for investors from the EU 15 investing in another EU 15 Member State.

A good example to understand the alleged discriminations, is the case of Germany. The latter has concluded 12 intra-EU BITs, three of which do not provide for ISDS. In other words, investors from nine European States investing in Germany do fall under the protection of a BIT, which provides for investor-State

---

141 See Chapter III: IV. 2.
142 ECJ, *Achmea*. C-284/16. Judgment, 6 March 2018, para. 61.
143 See the positions of several Member States, as reported by the Advocate General in ECJ, *Achmea*. C-284/16. Opinion of Advocate General Wathelet, 19 September 2017, para. 60.
144 Cf. Chapter I: III. 1.

arbitration and can thus invoke possible breaches of the BIT before an arbitral tribunal. The same is true for German investors in nine European countries. However, neither investors from the other remaining 17 Member States investing in Germany, nor German investors investing in these 17 countries are protected by a BIT, or at least do not fall under a BIT that provides for investor-State arbitration. Therefore, the question arises whether these investors are discriminated vis-à-vis the protected investors on ground of their nationality, i.e. whether these arbitration provisions constitute a violation of Art. 18 TFEU.

A discrimination cannot consist of one Member State acting in a different way than another, as the standard of comparison can only be the acts of the same public authority.[145] Hence, if one Member State had concluded BITs providing for ISDS with every other Member State but others would not have done so, this disparity between different Member States would not amount to a discrimination. As no Member State has concluded a BIT with every other Member State, the risk of discriminatory treatment by the host State persists, as it is granting investment protection only to investors stemming from Member States with which it has concluded a BIT. Whether such a differential treatment amounts to a discrimination is highly controversial. For the EU Commission and many Member States intra-EU BIT-based investor-State arbitration amounts to a forbidden discrimination as it provides the possibility of choice of dispute resolution procedures for some investors, giving them an advantage over investors from other Member States.[146] The arbitral tribunal in *Achmea*, as well as the German BGH and the OLG Frankfurt am Main, did not rule out a discrimination but considered its legal effects not to be an exclusion of protection of the investors falling under the specific BIT.[147] Other tribunals and commentators, however, took the position that BIT protection and especially investor-State arbitration can be understood neither as a discrimination nor as a disadvantage of a certain group, but rather as an acquisition of further legal rights for another group.[148] In a similar way, the Advocate General denied in his *Achmea* Opinion

---

145 A. Epiney, *Art. 18 AEUV* in C. Calliess and M. Ruffert (eds.), *EUV/AEUV – Kommentar*, 5. ed. (München: C. H. Beck, 2016), at para. 10.

146 Cf. PCA, *Eureko v Slovakia*. Case No. 2008–13. Award on Jurisdiction, Arbitrability and Suspension, 26 October 2010, para. 183. Position of the Czech Republic, as cited in ICSID, *A11Y Ltd. v Czech Republic*. Case No. UNCT/15/1. Decision on Jurisdiction, 9 February 2017, para. 157 f; Ad Hoc Arbitration, *Binder v Czech Republic*. Award on Jurisdiction, 6 June 2007, para. 18. See also P. Mariani, *The Future of BITs Between EU Member States* in G. Sacerdoti, et al. (eds.), *General Interests of Host States in International Investment Law* (Cambridge: Cambridge University Press, 2014), p. 273; C. I. Nagy, *Central European Perspectives on Investor-State Arbitration* in A. de Mestral (ed.), *Second Thoughts: Investor State Arbitration Between Developed Democracies* (Montreal: McGill-Queen's University Press, 2017), pp. 309–31, at p. 314.

147 PCA, *Eureko v Slovakia*. Case No. 2008–13. Award on Jurisdiction, Arbitrability and Suspension, 26 October 2010, para. 266; BGH, *Preliminary reference – Achmea*. I ZB 2/15. Beschluss, 3 March 2016, paras. 70 ff; OLG Frankfurt am Main, *Achmea v Slovakia*. 26 SchH 11/10. Beschluss, 10 May 2012, p. 125.

148 Cf. Ad Hoc Arbitration, *Binder v Czech Republic*. Award on Jurisdiction, 6 June 2007, para. 65.

any discrimination based on intra-EU BITs due to their comparability to non-discriminatory intra-EU double-taxation agreements (DTAs).[149]

In a line of jurisprudence, the ECJ had found that bilateral DTAs concluded among EU Member States were not violating the principle of non-discrimination but were compatible with EU law. The first case in this regard, *D.*, was based on the refusal of the Dutch authorities to grant a wealth tax allowance to a German citizen, who had invested in real estate in the Netherlands, but was residing in Germany. The German citizen claimed to be discriminated as the tax allowance, he was precluded from, was granted to Belgian citizens that had made similar investments in the Netherlands on the basis of a DTA between the Netherlands and Belgium.[150] The ECJ had to decide whether such a differential treatment of different EU citizens on the basis of a bilateral DTA was lawful under the treaties or whether those

> preclude a Member State from according, pursuant to a bilateral convention for the avoidance of double taxation, only to residents of the other State party to the convention the allowance which it grants to its own residents, without extending the allowance to residents of the other Member States.[151]

For the ECJ, the precondition of a possible discrimination was that both the person falling under a DTA and the one not falling under it could be regarded as being in the same situation. It found, however, that

> It is to be remembered that, in order to avoid the same income and assets being taxed in both the Netherlands and Belgium, [the DTA] allocates powers of taxation between those two Member States and [...] lays down a rule under which natural persons resident in one of those two States are entitled in the other to the personal allowances which are granted by it to its own residents.
>
> The fact that those reciprocal rights and obligations apply only to persons resident in one of the two Contracting Member States is an inherent consequence of bilateral double taxation conventions. It follows that a taxable person resident in Belgium is not in the same situation as a taxable person resident outside Belgium so far as concerns wealth tax on real property situated in the Netherlands.[152]

The ECJ confirmed this decision in *Test Claimants*, restating that it is inherent to bilateral DTAs to provide for rights and obligations which are only applicable to residents in the contracting Member States, with the effect that the situation of residents and non-residents is not the same.[153]

---

149 ECJ, *Achmea*. C-284/16. Opinion of Advocate General Wathelet, 19 September 2017, paras. 65 ff.

150 ECJ, *D.* C-376/03. Judgment, 5 July 2005, ECLI:EU:C:2005:424, paras. 15 ff.

151 Ibid., para. 46.

152 Ibid., paras. 59 ff.

153 ECJ, *Test Claimants*. C-374/04. Judgment, 12 December 2006, ECLI:EU:C:2006:773, para. 91.

According to the Advocate General, these decisions are transferable to intra-EU BITs as they illustrate that "there is no discrimination where a Member State does not afford the nationals of another Member State the treatment which it affords, by convention, to the nationals of a third Member State."[154] For the Advocate General, the analogy between DTAs and intra-EU BITs "is perfect" as in the case of BITs some investors in a specific country benefit from the material protection provided by a BIT while others do not.[155] For him, both DTAs and BITs are international treaties with a scope limited to the natural or legal persons explicitly referred to, namely persons that have the nationality or are constituted under the laws of one Contracting State.[156] Thus,

> the fact that the reciprocal rights and obligations created by the BIT apply only to investors from one of the two Contracting Member States is a consequence inherent in the bilateral nature of BITs. It follows that a non-Netherlands investor is not in the same situation as a Netherlands investor so far as an investment made in Slovakia is concerned.[157]

According to the Advocate General, this is further emphasized by the fact that both DTAs and BITs are "aimed at the same economic activities, both the entry and exit of capital".[158]

It is more than doubtful whether the 'analogy' described by the Advocate General is truly 'perfect' and whether the principle of the ECJ's DTA jurisprudence are transferable to intra-EU BITs. The main difference between intra-EU BITs and DTAs is that the connecting point of the former is the nationality and the connecting point of the latter the residence. Furthermore, as explained by the ECJ, a particularity of the field of double taxation is that under Art. 293 of the Treaty establishing the European Community, which was abolished by the Lisbon Treaty, the Member States should so far as necessary enter into negotiations with each other to secure for the benefit of their nationals the abolition of double taxation within the European Community.[159] Based on that article, an incredible number of bilateral DTAs was concluded among EU Member States.[160] No similar provision regarding investment protection was ever part of the European Treaties.

---

154 ECJ, *Achmea*. C-284/16. Opinion of Advocate General Wathelet, 19 September 2017, para. 71.
155 Ibid., para. 73.
156 Ibid., para. 74.
157 Ibid., para. 75.
158 Ibid., para. 79.
159 Cf. ECJ, *D*. C-376/03. Judgment, 5 July 2005, para. 49. See also P. Mariani, *The Future of BITs Between EU Member States* in G. Sacerdoti, et al. (eds.), *General Interests of Host States in International Investment Law* (Cambridge: Cambridge University Press, 2014), at 274 ff.
160 Cf. EU Commission, *Treaties for the Avoidance of Double Taxation Concluded by Member States*. https://ec.europa.eu/taxation_customs/individuals/personal-taxation/treaties-avoidance-double-taxation-concluded-member-states_en (5 May 2020).

Finally, the approach taken by the Advocate General could lead to a massive abuse. In light of the Advocate General's argument every discrimination based on the nationality could in theory be justified through bilateral treaties with reciprocal rights and obligations only applicable to nationals of the two Contracting Member States as "a consequence inherent in the bilateral nature" of the respective treaty. This would undermine the principle of non-discrimination, which remains one of the corner stones of EU integration.[161]

The present author thus disagrees with the Advocate General and understands intra-EU BITs to be incompatible with Art. 18 TFEU.

b) Consequences of a possible discrimination

Provided that intra-EU BITs are in violation of the principle of non-discrimination, the question remains what legal consequences arise out of that discrimination. Art. 18 TFEU is silent regarding the legal consequences of a violation. It is for that reason that the opponents of intra-EU BITs and intra-EU ISDS have claimed that the former must be abolished, while the supporters of the 'international invest- ment protection regime' have advocated that the consequence of a possible dis- crimination should be the extension of the BITs' guarantees to all investors from EU Member States. This argument refers to the ECJ's position in *D.*, in which the Court found that while the scope of a bilateral DTA is limited to natural or legal persons referred to in it,

> there are situations where the benefits under a bilateral convention may be extended to a resident of a Member State which does not have the status of party to that convention.[162]

The Court took a similar position in *Gottardo* with regard to a bilateral social security convention between Italy and Switzerland, where it found that in the case of such a bilateral convention between a Member State and a third State,

> the fundamental principle of equal treatment requires that that Member State grant nationals of other Member States the same advantages as those which its own nationals enjoy under that convention unless it can provide objective justification for refusing to do so.[163]

These decisions indicate that the preferential treatment of some nationals based on bilateral treaties of EU Member States with third States or other Member States

---

161 On this in greater detail, Chapter II: III. 1. b).

162 ECJ, D. C-376/03. Judgment, 5 July 2005, para. 54 f.

163 ECJ, *Gottardo*. C-55/00. Judgment, 15 January 2002, ECLI:EU:C:2002:16, para. 34. See also concerning a German–Belgian bilateral agreement on study scholarships, ECJ, *Matteucci*. Case 235/87. Judgment, 27 September 1988, para. 16 and the tax related case ECJ, *Saint-Gobain*. C-307/97. Judgment, 21 September 1999, ECLI:EU:C:1999:438, para. 59.

might be understood as a violation of the non-discrimination principle enshrined in Art. 18 TFEU and that the legal consequence of such a discrimination can be to extend the favourable treatment or 'advantages' provided in that treaty to nationals of other Member States.

A similar extension of the 'advantages' offered in intra-EU BITs – especially access to ISDS proceedings – to all EU nationals could avoid their discrimination without limiting the protection of those investors already falling under the BIT. This approach was suggested by several arbitral tribunals,[164] the OLG Frankfurt am Main[165] and the German BGH.[166]

In contrast, the EU Commission rejected the suggestion to 'positively' resolve a discrimination by extending the preferential treatment to all EU investors, as "unacceptable from an institutional EU law perspective".[167]

The approach taken by the German courts and the investor-State arbitration tribunals extending the ECJ's jurisprudence on DTAs and social security conventions to intra-EU BITs is not convincing. In difference to DTAs, intra-EU BITs do not grant 'advantages' which investors can invoke vis-à-vis their home States, as it is the case for example in DTAs, but rather oblige the other State party to treat a foreign investor in a certain way. Furthermore, the suggested extension of guarantees contained in an intra-EU BITs to every other EU citizen, would introduce the most-favoured nation principle through the back door. This principle would not be limited to BITs but would be applicable to every singly bilateral treaty of an EU Member State granting individual rights, which could amount to a massive interference with the Member States' external competences. Against this backdrop, it is highly questionable whether Member States could be obliged to grant a most-favoured nation treatment to investors which originally did not fall under the protection of the respective BIT. And even if the Member States would be obliged to grant the protection standards provided for in an intra-EU BIT to all other European investors, it would still remain highly controversial whether the effect of this most-favoured nation treatment would also encompass investor-State dispute settlement.[168] Even if the substantive protection provided for in an intra-EU BIT was extended to other European investors, it is questionable whether arbitral tribunals would have jurisdiction based on the most-favoured nation treatment in cases

---

164 PCA, *Eureko v Slovakia*. Case No. 2008–13. Award on Jurisdiction, Arbitrability and Suspension, 26 October 2010, para. 267; SCC Arbitration, *Eastern Sugar B.V. v Czech Republic*. SCC No. 088/2004. Partial Award, 27 March 2007, para. 170; PCA, *WNC Factoring v Czech Republic*. Case N° 2014–34. Award, 22 February 2017, para. 309.

165 OLG Frankfurt am Main, *Achmea v Slovakia*. 26 SchH 11/10. Beschluss, 10 May 2012, p. 125.

166 BGH, *Preliminary reference – Achmea*. I ZB 2/15. Beschluss, 3 March 2016, para. 77 f.

167 Position of the EU Commission, as cited in PCA, *Eureko v Slovakia*. Case No. 2008–13. Award on Jurisdiction, Arbitrability and Suspension, 26 October 2010, para. 184.

168 See also A. Reinisch, *Most Favoured Nation Treatment* in M. Bungenberg, et al. (eds.), *International Investment Law: A Handbook* (Baden-Baden: Nomos, 2015), pp. 807–45, at 817 f; ICSID, *A11Y Ltd. v Czech Republic*. Case No. UNCT/15/1. Decision on Jurisdiction, 9 February 2017, paras. 93 ff; ILC, *Most-Favoured-Nation clause: Final Report of the Study Group on the Most-Favoured-Nation clause* (2015), at paras. 93 ff.

in which an investor from a European Member State, which is not an original party to the BIT would initiate a dispute against the host State of the investment. A rejection of the tribunal's jurisdiction, however, would maintain the discriminatory effect, even if the substantive standards were extended to other EU investors.

The consequence of the intra-EU BITs' discriminatory effect can thus not be to extend the substantive and ISDS provisions to other European investors. The effect of the violation of Art. 18 TFEU is rather that the discriminatory provisions contained in the respective intra-EU BITs are inapplicable under EU law.

c) Reverse discrimination

Another question arises in relation to the concept of 'reverse discrimination'. This phenomenon is well known in EU law and is also of relevance with regard to intra-EU BITs, which solely benefit foreign investors. In difference to the latter, domestic investors can only bring claims before national jurisdictions and have no 'additional' procedural remedy to rely on. This 'discrimination' of nationals is highly contested, as the two examples of the Spanish renewable energy cases and the German phasing out of nuclear energy reveal. In both situations, domestic and foreign investors were similarly affected by the legislative changes. However, while the foreign investors were able not only to bring their claims before the domestic courts but also before investor-State arbitration tribunals, the latter path was precluded for the domestic companies, even though the legal arguments raised in the respective proceedings were highly similar and mainly based on the protection of legitimate expectations.[169]

Reverse discrimination, however, is not a question of compatibility with EU law. It does, in principle, not fall under Art. 18 TFEU, even though it might be applicable to nationals in situations in which they have exercised their fundamental freedoms.[170] In other words, the problem of reverse discrimination falls into the

---

169 The German decision of nuclear phase out affected four energy operators, three of them German as well as the Swedish company Vattenfall. Two German companies as well as Vattenfall lodged a constitutional complaint with the German Constitutional Court (BVerfG). Vattenfall – in parallel – also initiated an investor-State arbitration against Germany, administered by the ICSID and based on the Energy Charter Treaty, claiming damages of approximately € 4,7 billion. In its decision the BVerfG found that the most recent amendment of the German Atomic Energy Act leading to the phase out violated the fundamental right to property in Art. 14 of the German Grundgesetz (Basic Law), cf. BVerfG, *Vereinbarkeit der 13. Novelle des AtomG mit dem GG.* 1 BvR 2821/11, 1 BvR 321/12, 1 BvR 1456/12, 6 December 2016, NJW 2017 217. Notwithstanding this decision, Vattenfall continued the proceedings before the ICSID arbitral tribunal, cf. ICSID, *Vattenfall v Germany.* Case No. Arb/12/12. On the Vattenfall arbitration, see J. Berger, *Die Bundesrepublik Deutschland – Internationaler Investitionsschutz und das Vattenfall-Verfahren,* Europäische Zeitschrift für Wirtschaftsrecht 31 (2020), 229–33. On the Spanish renewable energy cases, see C. O. García-Castrillón, *Spain and Investment Arbitration* in A. de Mestral (ed.), *Second Thoughts: Investor State Arbitration Between Developed Democracies* (Montreal: McGill-Queen's University Press, 2017), pp. 285–308.

170 Cf. ECJ, *Government of the French Community, and Walloon Government v Flemish Government.* C-212/06. Judgment, 1 April 2008, ECLI:EU:C:2008:178, para. 33; ECJ, *Tas Hagen.*

area of the domestic legal order of the respective Member States. It is for them to find ways under their domestic legal systems – if politically desired – to provide their own nationals with similar rights and remedies as provided under EU law.

d) Interim findings

Intra-EU BITs are incompatible with the non-discrimination principle codified in Art. 18 TFEU. The legal consequence of this discrimination, however, is not the extenion of the substantive and procedural protection contained in the BITs to other investors, which would lead to the creation of a most-favoured nation principle in EU law, but the inapplicability of the BITs' discriminatory provision from an EU legal perspective. The general disadvantage of domestic investors compared to foreign investors falling under a BIT, however, is not covered by EU law but has to be tackled by the respective domestic legal orders.

4 Mutual trust

The principle of 'mutual trust' is another potential source of incompatibility of intra-EU BITs with EU law. It is not explicitly codified in EU primary law but was developed by the ECJ's case law and is reproduced in different acts of secondary legislation.[171] Its importance is continuously stressed by the EU institutions.[172] 'Mutual trust' requires each Member State, "to consider all the other Member States to be complying with EU law"[173] and is founded on the premise, enshrined in Art. 2 TEU, that all Member States do not only affirm common values, but have accepted the mutual obligation to preserve and protect these values, which comprise common fundamental rights, similar domestic procedural standards and the reciprocal expectation of a legally correct application in the respective Member State.[174] Accordingly, judicial decisions of other Member States' courts and tribunals have to be implemented automatically and expeditiously. The 'mutual trust' is not irrefutable, but Member States have to abstain from mutual control

---

C-192/05. Judgment, 26 October 2006, ECLI:EU:C:2006:676, para. 31. In exceptional circumstances, the ECJ has accepted that EU citizens fall within the scope of EU law, even if they have never made use of their fundamental freedoms of EU law, as long as there is a clear link with another EU Member State, cf. ECJ, *Zhu and Chen.* C-200/02. Judgment, 19 October 2004, ECLI:EU:C:2004:639, para. 19; ECJ, *Schempp.* C-403/03. Judgment, 12 July 2005, ECLI:EU:C:2005:446, paras. 22 ff.

171 For example, the preamble of the Brussels I Regulation: Regulation (EU) No 1215/2012 of the European Parliament and of the Council of 12 December 2012 on jurisdiction and the recognition and enforcement of judgments in civil and commercial matters.

172 In great detail M. Weller, *Mutual Trust: In Search of the Future of European Union Private International Law,* Journal of Private International Law 11 (2015), 64–102, at 65 ff.

173 ECJ, *EU accession to the ECHR.* 2/13. Opinion, 18 December 2014, para. 191.

174 F. Meyer, *Der Grundsatz gegenseitigen Vertrauens: Konzeptualisierung und Zukunftsperspektiven eines neuen Verfassungsprinzips,* Europarecht 52 (2017), 163–86, at 165.

to maintain the trust.[175] Though the ECJ has started to give the concept a more precise content in its recent jurisprudence,[176] it remains an abstract normative goal without any concrete effects.

The argument of the incompatibility of intra-EU BITs with the principle of 'mutual trust' was raised by several EU Member States, respondents in intra-EU investor-State arbitration proceedings,[177] as well as by the ECJ, which in an *obiter dictum* explained in *Achmea* that investor-State arbitration clauses in intra-EU BITs are such as to "call into question" inter alia "the principle of mutual trust between Member States".[178] The court thereby followed the EU Commission's position, which had repeatedly stressed that intra-EU investor-State arbitration was in conflict with the concept of 'mutual trust'. Accordingly, the Commission had found in its written observations in *Achmea* that

> Continued resort to outside dispute settlement mechanisms by EU subjects based on intra-EU BITs [...] reveals mistrust in the courts of EU Member States. This has no place in the current post-enlargement context, which is rooted in mutual trust between Member States and founded on the development of a common favourable investment environment. Mutual trust in the administration of justice in the European Union is one of the principles regarded necessary by the ECJ for the sound operation of the internal market.[179]

The ECJ took up the argument in its *Achmea* judgment and explained that EU law is based

> on the fundamental premiss that each Member State shares with all the other Member States, and recognises that they share with it, a set of common values on which the EU is founded, as stated in Art. 2 TEU. That premiss implies and justifies the existence of mutual trust between the Member States that those values will be recognised, and therefore that the law of the EU that implements them will be respected. It is precisely in that context that the

175 Cf. ibid., 165; A. von Bogdandy and M. Ioannidis, *Das systemische Defizit: Merkmale, Instrumente und Probleme am Beispiel der Rechtsstaatlichkeit und des neuen Rechtsstaatlichkeitsverfahrens,* Zeitschrift für ausländisches öffentliches Recht und Völkerrecht 74 (2014), 283–328, at 319.

176 See especially, ECJ, *EU accession to the ECHR.* 2/13. Opinion, 18 December 2014. See also with further references, F. Meyer, *Der Grundsatz gegenseitigen Vertrauens: Konzeptualisierung und Zukunftsperspektiven eines neuen Verfassungsprinzips,* Europarecht 52 (2017), at 163 f.

177 See for example, the position of the Czech Republic, as referred to in Ad Hoc Arbitration, *Binder v Czech Republic.* Award on Jurisdiction, 6 June 2007, para. 17 and in SCC Arbitration, *Eastern Sugar B.V. v Czech Republic.* SCC No. 088/2004. Partial Award, 27 March 2007, para. 107.

178 ECJ, *Achmea.* C-284/16. Judgment, 6 March 2018, para. 58. See also ECJ, *CETA-Opinion.* 1/17. Opinion of Advocate General Bot, 29 January 2019, para. 105.

179 Position of the European Commission as cited in, PCA, *Eureko v Slovakia.* Case No. 2008–13. Award on Jurisdiction, Arbitrability and Suspension, 26 October 2010, para. 185.

Member States are obliged, [...] to ensure in their respective territories the application of and respect for EU law, and to take for those purposes any appropriate measure, whether general or particular, to ensure fulfilment of the obligations arising out of the Treaties.[180]

Hence, in view of the ECJ and the EU Commission, the existence of BITs providing for a detached dispute settlement, independent from the judiciary of the EU and its Member States can be seen as a sign for the lack of trust or even mistrust among Member States, which prefer to provide their investors with an additional protection regime. This mistrust can be understood as forming the basis for all BITs and as being incompatible with the principle of mutual trust and the principle of loyal cooperation established in Art. 4 TEU.

The Advocate General, however, reached a different conclusion. For him, intra-EU investor-State arbitration proceedings are not incompatible with the principle of 'mutual trust', since they take place "only with the consent of the Member States concerned" and with the investor's "freely expressed choice to use the facility which the Member States offered it".[181] Accordingly, there is no connection between intra-EU BIT arbitration provisions and the principle of 'mutual trust', as such provisions do not imply that the States parties have "any doubts as to whether the other party would comply with EU law", but just provide an alternative forum for investors to bring an action against the home State of an investment.[182] The intra-EU arbitral tribunal in *Eastern Sugar* took a similar position. It found investor-State arbitration not to be contrary to 'mutual trust' in domestic court systems, which it found also emphasized by the fact that the Brussels I Regulation excludes arbitration from its ambit.[183] The intra-EU arbitral tribunal in *Binder* rejected the Commission's argument finding that "such a soft-law principle is not susceptible of abrogating or amending validly undertaken treaty obligations."[184]

This approach is convincing. Intra-EU BITs are not violating primary or secondary EU law on 'mutual trust'. It is not persuasive to argue that intra-EU BITs are inapplicable because of their alleged incompatibility with a non-codified soft-law principle developed by the ECJ's jurisprudence. This is especially so in times of growing scepticism regarding some Member States' compliance with the rule

---

180 ECJ, *Achmea*. C-284/16. Judgment, 6 March 2018, para. 34, quoting ECJ, *EU accession to the ECHR*. 2/13. Opinion, 18 December 2014, para. 168.

181 ECJ, *Achmea*. C-284/16. Opinion of Advocate General Wathelet, 19 September 2017, para. 261.

182 Ibid., para. 263 f.

183 SCC Arbitration, *Eastern Sugar B.V. v Czech Republic*. SCC No. 088/2004. Partial Award, 27 March 2007, para. 171. See para. 26 of the Preamble of the Regulation (EU) No 1215/2012 of the European Parliament and of the Council of 12 December 2012 on jurisdiction and the recognition and enforcement of judgments in civil and commercial matters (Brussels I Regulation). In a similar vein, see also OLG Frankfurt am Main, *Achmea v Slovakia*. 26 SchH 11/10. Beschluss, 10 May 2012, 125.

184 Ad Hoc Arbitration, *Binder v Czech Republic*. Award on Jurisdiction, 6 June 2007, para. 43.

of law and the impartiality of their judicial systems.[185] Thus, even if intra-EU BITs might conflict with the normative goal of 'mutual trust', this does not lead in itself to an incompatibility of the BITs with EU law.

5 State aid

Another possible source of incompatibility of intra-EU BITs with EU law, which has been invoked on several occasions,[186] is so-called State aid. According to Art. 107 TFEU, almost any subsidy or 'State aid' to companies is, "in so far as it affects trade between Member States", incompatible with EU law and can thus be prohibited.[187] The definition of State aid, however, remains highly contentious, especially as once a measure is considered to be a State aid, a Member State has to notify the Commission and wait for its approval.[188] If the EU Commission reaches the conclusion that a State aid is unlawful, it can order its recovery.[189] Such a decision of the EU Commission can create major difficulties regarding conflicting intra-EU investor-State arbitration awards, if the affected investments have been made prior to the host State's accession to the EU. The difficulties do not arise with investments made after the host State's accession to the EU. Questions of State aid are thus of minor importance regarding the possible incompatibility of intra-EU ISDS proceedings and intra-EU BITs with EU law.

The enforcement of an intra-EU investor-State arbitration award does not constitute an illegal State aid in itself but only reflects compliance with an arbitral decision to pay damages for an unlawful State behaviour. However, in cases in which a State measure that violated an IIA obligation consists in the revocation of subsidies constituting illegal State aid under EU law, the enforcement of the award granting damages for that revocation could in itself represent an illegal State aid. Such an award would thus not be enforceable within the EU.[190]

---

185 See Chapter IV: VI. 1.
186 Cf. position of Romania as cited in ICSID, *Ioan Micula, Viorel Micula and others v Romania*. Case No. ARB/05/20. Award, 11 December 2013, para. 310. See also the position of the EU Commission as cited in ICSID, *Electrabel v Hungary*. Case No. ARB/07/19. Decision on Jurisdiction, Applicable Law and Liability, 30 November 2012, paras. 4.104 ff. and in PCA, *U.S. Steel v Slovakia*. Case No. 2013–6. Amicus Curiae Brief by the EU Commission, 15 May 2014.
187 On the State aid regime in EU law, see D. Chalmers, G. Davies and G. Monti, *European Union Law*, 3. ed. (Cambridge: Cambridge University Press, 2014), at 1052 ff.
188 Ibid., p. 1057.
189 See Art. 14 of Council Regulation 659/1999 of 22 March 1999.
190 See the position of the EU Commission, as cited in ICSID, *Electrabel v Hungary*. Case No. ARB/07/19. Decision on Jurisdiction, Applicable Law and Liability, 30 November 2012, para. 4.110. See also C. Tietje and C. Wackernagel, *Enforcement of Intra-EU ICSID Awards: Multilevel Governance, Investment Tribunals and the Lost Opportunity of the Micula Arbitration*, Journal of World Investment & Trade 16 (2015), at 219 ff. In its *amicus curiae* brief before the US Court of Appeal for the 2nd Circuit, the EU Commission referred to a judgment of 26 January 2016, in which the Court of First Instance of Brussels held in Case R.G. 15/7242/A, that the Micula v Romania award was unenforceable in Belgium, United States Court of Appeals for the Second

The most notorious case in this regard, is the 'transition case' *Micula v Romania*.[191] It was initiated in August 2005, two years before Romania's accession to the EU. The claimants had made investments in Romania in reliance on economic incentives instituted by the Romanian government for the development of certain disfavoured regions in Romania, including exemptions from custom duties and the payment of profit tax as well as preferential subsidies from a special State development fund.[192] These advantages were supposed to remain in place until 2009. Romania, however, revoked the incentives in 2004 to bring its laws in compliance with the EU rules on State aid before acceding to the EU. As the claimants experienced significant financial losses, they initiated ICSID proceedings based on the 2002 Sweden–Romania BIT, alleging that its fair and equitable treatment provision had been violated. While the EU Commission submitted an *amicus curiae* brief requesting the tribunal to consider EU State aid law,[193] the arbitral tribunal held in its 2013 award that the fair and equitable treatment standard had been violated and ordered Romania to compensate the claimant.[194] In response, the EU Commission issued a suspension injunction prohibiting Romania from complying with the award, as its execution "would constitute unlawful State aid" under Art. 107 TFEU.[195] Romania thus faced the obligation under Arts. 53 and 54 ICSID Convention to comply with the terms of the award and to enforce it, while EU law at the same time obliged it not to enforce the award, as the payment of damages to the claimant would amount to a new unlawful State aid. In other words, its international legal obligations required from Romania to act in violation of its EU law obligations and vice versa.

Romania unsuccessfully sought for a stay of enforcement of the award and submitted an annulment application which was rejected by the ICSID 'ad hoc Committee' in 2016.[196] Meanwhile the claimants issued proceedings against the EU Commission before the ECJ to overturn the injunction issued by the Commission against Romania,[197] and continued their attempts to enforce the award in different countries, inter alia the UK, Sweden, Belgium and the USA.[198] The EU

Circuit, *Micula v Romania*. 15–3109-cv. Amicus curiae brief of the EU Commission, 4 February 2016, page 11, footnote 7.

191 ICSID, *Ioan Micula, Viorel Micula and others v Romania*. Case No. ARB/05/20. Award, 11 December 2013.

192 ICSID, *Micula v Romania*. Case No. ARB/05/20. Decision on Jurisdiction and Admissibility, 24 September 2008, paras. 28 ff.

193 Position of the EU Commission, as cited in ICSID, *Ioan Micula, Viorel Micula and others v Romania*. Case No. ARB/05/20. Award, 11 December 2013, para. 317.

194 Ibid., para. 1329.

195 EU Commission, *Letter to Romania C(2014) 6848 final: State aid SA.38517(2014/C) (ex 2014/ NN) – Romania: Implementation of Arbitral award Micula v Romania of 11 December 2013*, 1 October 2014, at para. 6.

196 ICSID, *Micula v Romania*. Case No. ARB/05/20. Decision on Annulment, 26 February 2016.

197 Cf. Case T-624/15, Case T-694/15 and Case T-704/15.

198 See in greater detail and with further references on the *Micula* 'saga' and the attempts of the claimants to enforce the award outside Romania C. I. Nagy, *Intra-EU Bilateral Investment*

Commission, again participating as *amicus curiae*, tried to hinder the enforcement in the USA by arguing that it would intrude the EU's sovereign competences and the pending ECJ case. In seeking to resist enforcement of the award in the USA, Romania argued that it had complied with the award in three steps, namely

> by setting off part of the compensation due against taxes owed by one of the ICSID claimants; second, by bailiffs seizing certain funds from Romanian Ministry of Finance accounts; and third, by a direct payment of € 106.5 million into a special treasury account in the claimants' names.[199]

In reaction, the EU Commission announced in December 2018 to refer Romania to the ECJ in accordance with Art. 108 (2) TFEU for failure to implement the Commission's decision to recover the entire illegal State aid granted to the Micula investors.[200] In the meantime, a US court has decided to enforce the award in September 2019.[201]

Although the *Micula* case reflects many interesting legal questions arising out of the accession of a new Member State to the EU, it is only of relevance for disputes concerning investments made prior to the host State's accession to the EU. It does therefore only – if at all – affect 'transition cases'.[202] In intra-EU cases, however, investors will hardly be able to convince an arbitral tribunal of the violation of a BIT's protection standard by arguing that they had legitimate expectations regarding State subsidies granted to them by an EU Member State in violation of the EU's State aid regime.[203] As discussed previously, an investor's investment decision is always based on

> an assessment of the state of the law and the totality of the business environment at the time of the investment as well as on the investor's expectation that the conduct of the host State subsequent to the investment will be fair and equitable.[204]

An investor becoming active within the EU must take the EU State aid law into consideration and can thus not rely on the 'fair and equitable treatment'

Treaties and EU Law After Achmea: "Know Well What Leads You Forward and What Holds You Back," German Law Journal 19 (2018), 981–1015, at 985 f.

199 J. Hepburn, *European Commission refers Romania to European Court over failure to recover Micula compensation*, IA Reporter, 10 December 2018.

200 EU Commission, *State Aid: Commission Refers Romania to Court for Failure to Recover Illegal*, 7 December 2018. http://europa.eu/rapid/press-release_IP-18-6723_en.htm (20 May 2020).

201 D. Charlotin, *US Court Enforces an Intra-EU BIT Award, Waving Aside Achmea-Related Argument, but Stresses That Dispute Centered on Romanian Actions That Pre-Dated Its Accession to EU*, IA Reporter, 15 September 2019.

202 For the categorization of pre-accession, transition and intra-EU cases, see Chapter I: III. 5.

203 See also ICSID, *Electrabel v Hungary*. Case No. ARB/07/19. Decision on Jurisdiction, Applicable Law and Liability, 30 November 2012, para. 4.141.

204 PCA, *Saluka Investments v Czech Republic*. Partial Award, 17 March 2006, para. 143 f. See in greater detail, Chapter II: II. 2. b) bb).

standard in order to maintain State subsidies, which are unlawful under EU law. An arbitral tribunal considering such a State aid case must take this into consideration, especially as State aid rules are fundamental to the EU legal order. A revocation of such aids which are incompatible with EU law will thus generally not violate the legitimate expectations of foreign investors and not amount to an infringement of the fair and equitable treatment standard contained in an intra-EU BIT.

6 Public international law perspective

The previous sections of this chapter have revealed a conflict between intra-EU BITs and the EU Treaties, which from an EU perspective leads to the incompatibility of intra-EU BIT investor-State arbitration provisions with EU law. The following section analyses the relationship of both regimes from a public international law perspective.

As emphasized by the *Electrabel* tribunal, a treaty-based investor-State arbitration tribunal "is placed in a public international law context and not a national or regional context".[205] A purely EU law based interpretation is thus out of question for investor-State arbitration tribunals, which haven taken many different positions on the relevance of EU law for their intra-EU proceedings, but so far have never rejected their own competence to decide a case. In other words, the arbitral practice has not followed the arguments raised by the EU Commission and EU Member States. The dissenting Opinion of arbitrator Marcelo Kohen in the *Adamakopoulos v Cyprus*, is the only publicly known case of an arbitrator upholding the intra-EU jurisdictional objection.[206]

Public international law is generally 'blind' regarding the internal domestic organization of its subjects. It imposes obligations on States but leaves it to the latter how to comply with them. As there is no general hierarchy of norms in public international law, principles such as the primacy of EU law over domestic law cannot be transferred to the relation between EU law and international law.[207] The same is true for the concept of 'autonomy of EU law' which does in principle not affect international law and thus has no effects outside the EU legal order, which is the legal order of a highly integrated regional international organization with – post-Brexit – 27 sovereign Member States, which themselves are subjects of public international law.

While investor-State arbitration tribunals have so far not considered the argument of 'autonomy' of the EU legal order, they might nonetheless have to consider

---

205 ICSID, *Electrabel v Hungary*. Case No. ARB/07/19. Decision on Jurisdiction, Applicable Law and Liability, 30 November 2012, para. 4.112. See also ICSID, *UP and C.D. v Hungary*. Case No. ARB/13/35. Award, 9 October 2018, para. 253.

206 ICSID, *Adamakopoulos v Cyprus*. Case No. ARB/15/49. Statement of Dissent of Prof. Marcelo G. Kohen, 3 February 2020.

207 Cf. C. Binder, *A Treaty Law Perspective on Intra-EU BITs*, Journal of World Investment & Trade 17 (2016), at 966 f.

EU law and the Member States' domestic law and thus cannot totally ignore the EU's autonomy argument.[208]

As already discussed, the relationship between intra-EU BITs and EU law is one of subsequent international treaties. It is governed by Art. 30 VCLT, which is a codification of customary international law and which according to its heading determines the "application of successive treaties relating to the same subject-matter".

Regarding intra-EU BITs, however, the collision norm of Art. 30 (2) VCLT is not applicable. It provides that "when a treaty specifies that it is subject to, or that it is not to be considered as incompatible with, an earlier or later treaty, the provisions of that other treaty prevail." Such subordination clause required by Art. 30 (2) VCLT, however, is contained in none of the intra-EU BITs. The TFEU contains two subordination clauses, namely Art. 350 TFEU, which regulates the relationship between the EU Treaties and the different regional unions between Belgium, Luxembourg and the Netherlands, and Art. 351 TFEU, which covers extra-EU pre-accession treaties.[209] Both, however, are not applicable to the conflict at hand. Nonetheless, the sole fact of their existence reveals that the European Member States were aware of the risk of collision with earlier international agreements when drafting the EU Treaties.

As there is no collision norm dealing with the relationship between intra-EU BITs and EU Law, Art. 30 (3) VCLT could be applicable. While Art. 59 VCLT determines when an entire previous treaty is terminated, Art. 30 (3) VCLT concerns cases in which a subsequent treaty is only partially incompatible with the previous one. Only if a case is not covered by Art. 59 VCLT, i.e. both treaties remain in force and operational, it can be covered by the 'catchall provision' of Art. 30 (3) VCLT. Both articles have common prerequisites and govern the relationship between two successive treaties concluded by the same parties and relating to the 'same subject-matter'. But, in difference to Art. 59 VCLT, Art. 30 (3) VCLT does not require the intention of the States Parties to terminate a specific provision. Another important difference in terms of legal consequences is that Art. 59 VCLT suspends the entire treaty, whereas in case of Art. 30 (3) VCLT the previous treaty remains in force and just some specific provisions of the earlier

---

208 See for example, SCC Arbitration, *Eastern Sugar B.V. v Czech Republic.* SCC No. 088/2004. Partial Award, 27 March 2007, para. 196 according to which "only where international law is silent [...] the Arbitral Tribunal should consider before reaching any decision how non conflicting provisions of [domestic] law might be relevant, and if so, could be taken into account." See also Ad Hoc Arbitration, *Oostergetel & Laurentius v Slovakia.* Final Award, 23 April 2012, para. 140 stating that "the Tribunal will apply, in addition to the BIT, municipal law, as well as general principles of international law. Whenever the BIT is silent on an issue, the Tribunal will resort to either municipal or international law depending on the nature of the issue in question."

209 See also ECJ, *Matteucci.* Case 235/87. Judgment, 27 September 1988, para. 21; ECJ, *Commission v Luxembourg.* C-473/93. Judgment, 2 July 1996, para. 40; ECJ, *Commission v Austria.* C-147/03. Judgment, 7 July 2005, para. 58; ILC, *Fragmentation of International Law,* 13 April 2006, para. 284.

treaty become inapplicable.[210] In other words, Art. 30 (3) VCLT could lead to the inapplicability of the investor-State dispute settlement provisions in intra-EU BITs while the other BIT provisions could remain unaffected.

Art. 30 (3) VCLT has only been invoked in a few intra-EU investor-State arbitration cases to challenge the arbitral tribunal's jurisdiction. In these cases, both the Member States[211] and the EU Commission[212] argued that the respective investor-State arbitration provision contained in the BIT would be inapplicable because of its incompatibility with EU law.[213] The arbitral tribunals, however, rejected the applicability of Art. 30 (3) VCLT and found the BITs to be fully applicable as they did not relate to the 'same-subject matter' as the EU Treaties,[214] and were not incompatible but rather complementary to the EU legal order.[215] The summary of the *European American Investment Bank* tribunal is paradigmatic in that regard:

> The BIT and [EU law] do not have the same subject matter, and as such coexist and are complementary in the international sphere, where they should be

---

210 Cf. K. von der Decken, *Art. 30* in O. Dörr and K. Schmalenbach (eds.), *Vienna Convention on the Law of Treaties* (Berlin: Springer, 2018), para. 35.

211 See the position of Cyprus, as cited in ICSID, *Marfin v Cyprus*. Case No. ARB/13/27. Award, 26 July 2018, para. 583; the position of Greece, as cited in ICSID, *Poštová Banka v Greece*. ICSID Case No. ARB/13/8. Award, 9 April 2015, para. 204; the position of Poland, as cited in SCC Arbitration, *PL Holdings v Poland*. V 2014/163. Partial Award, 28 June 2017, para. 301 f.; the position of the Czech Republic, in SCC Arbitration, *Busta & Busta v Czech Republic*. Case V 2015/014. Final Award, 10 March 2017, para. 119, in SCC Arbitration, *Anglia Auto v Czech Republic*. Case V 2014/181. Final Award, 10 March 2017, para. 119, in PCA, *WNC Factoring v Czech Republic*. Case N° 2014–34. Award, 22 February 2017, para. 295 and in ICSID, *A11Y Ltd. v Czech Republic*. Case No. UNCT/15/1. Decision on Jurisdiction, 9 February 2017, para. 154; the position of Slovakia, as referred to in PCA, *European American Investment Bank v Slovakia*. PCA Case No. 2010–17. Award on Jurisdiction, 22 October 2012, para. 140, in PCA, *Eureko v Slovakia*. Case No. 2008–13. Award on Jurisdiction, Arbitrability and Suspension, 26 October 2010, para. 128 and Ad Hoc Arbitration, *Oostergetel & Laurentius v Slovakia*. Decision on Jurisdiction, 30 April 2010, para. 67.

212 Position of the EU Commission, as reported in Ad Hoc Arbitration, *Wirtgen v Czech Republic*. PCA Case No. 2014–03. Final Award, 11 October 2017, para. 241 and in PCA, *Eureko v Slovakia*. Case No. 2008–13. Award on Jurisdiction, Arbitrability and Suspension, 26 October 2010, paras. 188 ff.

213 Remarkably, in *Wirtgen* the Czech Republic did not join the EU Commission's objection that the applicability of EU law deprives the tribunal of its jurisdiction, cf. Ad Hoc Arbitration, *Wirtgen v Czech Republic*. PCA Case No. 2014–03. Final Award, 11 October 2017, para. 249.

214 On the question of 'same subject-matter' of intra-EU BITs and EU law in general, see Chapter III: II. 2. a).

215 See inter alia: PCA, *Achmea (formerly known as "Eureko") v Slovakia*. Case No. 2008–13. Final Award, 7 December 2012, para. 59, 240 f; Ad Hoc Arbitration, *Oostergetel & Laurentius v Slovakia*. Decision on Jurisdiction, 30 April 2010, para. 104; PCA, *European American Investment Bank v Slovakia*. PCA Case No. 2010–17. Award on Jurisdiction, 22 October 2012, paras. 239 ff; SCC Arbitration, *Busta & Busta v Czech Republic*. Case V 2015/014. Final Award, 10 March 2017, para. 127 f; SCC Arbitration, *Anglia Auto v Czech Republic*. Case V 2014/181. Final Award, 10 March 2017, para. 127 f; PCA, *WNC Factoring v Czech Republic*. Case N° 2014–34. Award, 22 February 2017, para. 309 f; SCC Arbitration, *PL Holdings v Poland*. V 2014/163.

interpreted in harmony with one another. [...] if the BIT and [EU law] were considered to have the same subject matter, the BIT would not be terminated under Art. 59 VCLT, [...] neither in such hypothesis, would the application of Art. 30 (3) VCLT compel the inapplicability of [the BIT's arbitration clause], as the Tribunal could trace no EU rule which would be violated by such application.[216]

Accordingly, the *Achmea* tribunal found that "there is no incompatibility in circumstances where an obligation under the BIT can be fulfilled by Respondent without violating EU law."[217] According to the tribunal, Art. 30 (3) VCLT could hardly deprive an arbitral tribunal of its jurisdiction which is based upon the Parties' consent as even an incompatibility between EU law and a BIT "would be a question of the effect of EU law as part of the applicable law and, as such, a matter for the merits and not jurisdiction".[218] Nonetheless, the tribunal anticipated that the situation might change if the arbitration clause contained in the BIT was found to be itself incompatible with EU law. This would, according to the tribunal, "at least arguably, deprive the Tribunal of jurisdiction".[219]

Two questions arise, regarding the applicability of Art. 30 (3) VCLT to intra-EU BIT investor-State arbitration clauses, namely the question of 'same subject matter' and the question of incompatibility.

Against the background of the analysis carried out regarding the identically worded 'same subject matter' condition of Art. 59 VCLT, one could argue that Art. 30 (3) VCLT is not applicable. Accordingly, if intra-EU BITs do not relate to the 'same subject matter' pursuant to Art. 59 VCLT, they could hardly meet the 'same subject matter' condition of Art. 30 (3) VCLT. However, while the 'same subject matter' constitutes an explicit condition of Art. 59 VCLT, it is only part of the heading of Art. 30 VCLT and not reproduced as an explicit legal condition in the text of the article itself. This could justify an interpretation of Art. 30 (3) VCLT which neglects the 'same subject matter' condition contained in the article's heading or interprets it in a wide way. Also, with view to the legal consequence of Art. 30 (3) VCLT, which does not affect the entire treaty's validity but only the applicability of certain norms in a precedent treaty, it has convincingly been argued that the precondition of 'same subject matter' should be construed extensively in

---

Partial Award, 28 June 2017, para. 311; Ad Hoc Arbitration, *Wirtgen v Czech Republic*. PCA Case No. 2014–03. Final Award, 11 October 2017, para. 261.

216 PCA, *European American Investment Bank v Slovakia*. PCA Case No. 2010–17. Award on Jurisdiction, 22 October 2012, para. 280.

217 PCA, *Eureko v Slovakia*. Case No. 2008–13. Award on Jurisdiction, Arbitrability and Suspension, 26 October 2010, para. 271.

218 Ibid., para. 272.

219 Ibid., para. 273, hinting at the same result in case of an ECJ decision finding an incompatibility, SCC Arbitration, *PL Holdings v Poland*. V 2014/163. Partial Award, 28 June 2017, para. 316. With a similar view, see also B. Hess, *The Fate of Investment Dispute Resolution after the Achmea Decision of the European Court of Justice*, MPILux Research Paper Series (2018), at 12 f.

difference to the narrow interpretation in Art. 59 VCLT.[220] Otherwise, most cases such as "conflicts between environmental and trade treaties, or conflicts between human rights and humanitarian law treaties" would no longer fall under Art. 30 (3) VCLT and the article's scope of application would be severely limited.[221] In other words, 'same subject matter' should be interpreted in a much broader way in case of Art. 30 (3) VCLT than in case of Art. 59 VCLT. Thus for Art. 30 (3) VCLT to be applicable it would only be necessary that "all the parties to the earlier treaty are parties also to the later treaty but the earlier treaty is not terminated or suspended in operation under Art. 59" and that provisions of the earlier treaty are incompatible with those of the later treaty.

Against this backdrop, the ECJ's *Achmea* decision which explicitly found an incompatibility of investor-State arbitration provisions in intra-EU BITs with the EU Treaties could not only confirm the inapplicability of the former from an EU legal perspective but also lead to an inapplicability from an international legal perspective on the basis of Art. 30 (3) VCLT. Accordingly, the *Achmea* arbitration tribunal would be proven correct in assuming that the ECJ's finding that intra-EU investor-State arbitration clauses are incompatible with EU law would deprive investor-State arbitration tribunals from their jurisdiction.

The problem, however, persists that every arbitral tribunal called upon to decide an intra-EU investor-State arbitration, will have to assess on its own whether Art. 30 (3) VCLT is applicable to the relationship between EU law and intra-EU BITs, and whether the tribunal itself is bound by the interpretation of the ECJ in *Achmea*. It is doubtful that the arbitral practice, which so far has rather been rejecting the EU legal reasoning, will adapt to the ECJ's *Achmea* judgment without much ado and once and for all abandon its role as an independent international adjudicator of intra-EU investor-State arbitration disputes.[222] Thus, without major legal reforms, investor-State arbitration tribunals might just continue to deal with intra-EU investor-State disputes, even if the enforcement of possible awards might become increasingly difficult. Such reforms have now been announced by the EU Member States in their declarations regarding the legal consequences of the *Achmea* judgment[223] and partly been implemented in the Agreement for the Termination

---

220 ILC, *Fragmentation of International Law*, 13 April 2006, para. 253. See in a similar vein, PCA, *Eureko v Slovakia*. Case No. 2008–13. Award on Jurisdiction, Arbitrability and Suspension, 26 October 2010, para. 241, affirmed by the tribunal in *Wirtgen*, cf. Ad Hoc Arbitration, *Wirtgen v Czech Republic*. PCA Case No. 2014–03. Final Award, 11 October 2017, para. 260. See also K. von der Decken, *Art. 30* in O. Dörr and K. Schmalenbach (eds.), *Vienna Convention on the Law of Treaties* (Berlin: Springer, 2018), para. 13, who argues that the 'same subject matter' may be left aside "since the notion of (in)compatibility remains the issue of crucial importance."

221 ILC, *Fragmentation of International Law*, 13 April 2006, para. 253.

222 See for example, ICSID, *UP and C.D. v Hungary*. Case No. ARB/13/35. Award, 9 October 2018, paras. 254 ff. rejecting any effect of the ECJ's *Achmea* judgment on the proceeding pending before it. See also ICSID, *Marfin v Cyprus*. Case No. ARB/13/27. Award, 26 July 2018, para. 580.

223 Representatives of 22 EU Member States, *Declaration on the Legal Consequences of the Judgment of the ECJ in Achmea and on Investment Protection in the EU*, 15 January 2019; Representatives of Finland, Luxembourg, Malta, Slovenia and Sweden, *Declaration on the Enforcement of*

of Bilateral Investment Treaties between the Member States of the European Union, signed on May 5, 2020, by 23 EU Member States.

As will be shown in the next chapter, the *Achmea* decision has a major political impact on the future of intra-EU investor protection in general and investor-State arbitration proceedings in particular, regardless of the question whether Art. 30 (3) VCLT is applicable or not.

IV Energy Charter Treaty and EU law

So far, the ECJ has never been requested to rule on questions regarding the ECT and its relation to intra-EU investments.[224] In difference to CETA, the ECJ was neither asked to render an Opinion on the Energy Charter Treaty's compatibility with the EU Treaties before its ratification in accordance with Art. 218 (11) TFEU.[225] According to Advocate General Wathelet, this is due to the fact that at the time of negotiation of the ECT none of the Member States "had the slightest suspicion that it might be incompatible" with EU law.[226] This has changed over time and the EU Commission as well as different Member States being respondents in ECT based investor-State arbitration proceedings have repeatedly raised the argument of the ECT's inapplicability to intra-EU investor-State relations.

Many questions regarding intra-EU BITs also arise with regard to the relationship between the ECT and EU law. The following section will therefore consider whether the conclusion of the Lisbon Treaty by the EU Member States affected the validity of the Energy Charter Treaty according to Art. 59 VCLT (1.), whether the *Achmea* decision is applicable to the ECT (2.) and whether the ECT is compatible with the EU's non-discrimination principle codified in Art. 18 TFEU (3.). Finally, other possible grounds of incompatibility will be assessed both from an EU legal perspective (4.) and an international law perspective (5.).

the Judgement of the ECJ in Achmea and on Investment Protection in the EU, 16 January 2019; Representative of Hungary, *Declaration on the Legal Consequences of the Judgment of the ECJ in Achmea and on Investment Protection in the EU*, 16 January 2019. On these declarations, see in great detail Chapter IV.

224 However, the Paris Court of Appeal decided to suspend the proceedings to set aside the UNCITRAL ad hoc arbitration award in *Energoalliance v Moldova* under the ECT and to submit a preliminary reference to the ECJ, Cour d'Appel de Paris, *Energoalliance v Moldova*. N° 18/14721, 24 September 2019.

225 Art. 218 (11) TFEU grants the possibility for Member States and some EU institutions to request an Opinion of the ECJ as to whether an agreement envisaged is compatible with the EU Treaties. The aim is to prevent the EU from being bound internationally by a treaty which is incompatible with EU law. The proceeding has thus a preventive character and can only be initiated before the EU's consent to be bound by the treaty in question is finally expressed, i.e. before its ratification. A Belgium request has led to the CETA Opinion, ECJ, *CETA*. 1/17. Opinion, 30 April 2019, ECLI:EU:C:2019:341.

226 ECJ, *Achmea*. C-284/16. Opinion of Advocate General Wathelet, 19 September 2017, para. 43.

1 Art. 59 VCLT and the Energy Charter Treaty

As shown previously, the validity of intra-EU BITs is not affected by the subsequent entry into force of the Lisbon Treaty. Just like most BITs, the ECT entered into force for all EU Member States long before the Lisbon Treaty.[227] In difference to intra-EU BITs, however, Art. 59 VCLT is evidently not applicable to the ECT, as not *all* the parties to the earlier treaty, namely the Energy Charter Treaty, have also concluded the later treaty, the Lisbon Treaty. Currently 20 non-EU States are parties to the ECT. Hence, an automatic termination by application of the *lex posterior* rule of Art. 59 VCLT does not come into question. The ECT's validity was not affected by the later conclusion of the Lisbon Treaty.

2 Applicability of the Achmea *decision to the Energy Charter Treaty*

The effects of the *Achmea* decision on intra-EU BITs has been analysed previously. The applicability of this decision to intra-EU ECT proceedings remains highly controversial and has been assessed differently among the Member States, the EU Commission and arbitral tribunals. This section will start by presenting the declarations issued by the EU Commission and the Member States in regard of the ECT's applicability in intra-EU investor-State relations (a) and present the post-*Achmea* arbitral practice (b), before assessing whether the ECJ's *Achmea* decision can be applied to intra-EU ECT disputes (c).

a) Declarations of the EU Commission and the EU Member States

In reaction to the *Achmea* judgment, the EU Commission published its "Communication on the Protection of intra-EU Investments" on June 19, 2018, in which it found the *Achmea* decision to be applicable to the investor-State arbitration provision in Art. 26 ECT as regards intra-EU relations. According to the Commission, this provision

> if interpreted correctly, does not provide for an investor-State arbitration clause applicable between investors from a Member State of the EU and another Member State of the EU. Given the primacy of Union law, that clause, if interpreted as applying intra-EU, is incompatible with EU primary law and thus inapplicable. Indeed, the reasoning of the Court in Achmea applies equally to the intra-EU application of such a clause which, just like the clauses of intra-EU BITs, opens the possibility of submitting those disputes to a body which is not part of the judicial system of the EU. The fact that the EU is also a party to the ECT does not affect this conclusion: the participation of the EU in that Treaty has only created rights and obligations

---

227 For most EU Member States as well as the European Union, the ECT entered into force on 16 April 1998. France and Ireland, however, only joined in 1999 and Malta and Poland in 2001.

between the EU and third countries and has not affected the relations between the EU Member States.[228]

For the EU Commission, the *Achmea* judgment also applies to ECT based intra-EU disputes and arbitral tribunals thus lack jurisdiction to decide such disputes.

The majority of EU Member States expressed a similar view also understanding the ECJ's findings in *Achmea* to apply to ECT based arbitration proceedings. As stated by 22 Member States in their declaration on the legal consequences of *Achmea* in January 2019:

> Arbitral tribunals have interpreted the Energy Charter Treaty as also containing an investor-State arbitration clause applicable between Member States. Interpreted in such a manner, that clause would be incompatible with the Treaties and thus would have to be disapplied.[229]

Finland, Luxembourg, Malta, Slovenia and Sweden, however, came to a different conclusion and found that "it would be inappropriate, in absence of a specific judgment on this matter, to express views as regards the compatibility with Union law of the intra-EU application of the Energy Charter Treaty."[230] Hungary took an even stronger position. In its view, the *Achmea* judgment "concerns only the intra-EU bilateral investment treaties. The *Achmea* judgment is silent on the investor-State arbitration clause in the [ECT] and it does not concern any pending or prospective arbitration proceeding initiated under the ECT."[231]

Due to this dissent among the Member States the Agreement terminating intra-EU BITs among the 23 signatories explicitly excludes the ECT from its ambit and expresses in its preamble that the EU and its Member States will deal with the matter of intra-EU proceedings based on the ECT at a later stage.[232]

b) *Post-*Achmea *arbitral practice*

The arbitral practice has taken a different approach than the Member States. In light of the *Achmea* judgment, several intra-EU investor-State arbitration tribunals invited the parties to the dispute to submit observations on possible impacts of the *Achmea* judgment on pending proceedings.[233] Against this backdrop,

---

228 EU Commission, *Protection of intra-EU investment – COM (2018) 547/2: Communication from the Commission to the European Parliament and the Council*, 19 June 2018, at 3 f.

229 Representatives of 22 EU Member States, *Declaration on the Legal Consequences of the Judgment of the ECJ in Achmea and on Investment Protection in the EU*, 15 January 2019.

230 Representatives of Finland, Luxembourg, Malta, Slovenia and Sweden, *Declaration on the Enforcement of the Judgement of the ECJ in Achmea and on Investment Protection in the EU*, 16 January 2019.

231 Representative of Hungary, *Declaration on the Legal Consequences of the Judgment of the ECJ in Achmea and on Investment Protection in the EU*, 16 January 2019, para. 8.

232 The four non-signatories are: Austria, Finland, Ireland and Sweden.

233 Cf. ICSID, *Masdar Solar v Spain*. Case No. ARB/14/1. Award, 16 May 2018, para. 672; ICSID, *Vattenfall v Germany*. Case No. ARB/12/12. Decision on the Achmea Issue, 31 August 2018,

Spain, the respondent in the *Masdar Solar* proceeding argued that the *Achmea* judgment was also applicable to ECT proceedings as it referred to 'international agreements' in general and was not confined to bilateral treaties.[234] It thus requested the arbitral tribunal to interpret the ECT in line with the ECJ's *Achmea* interpretation, and to reach the conclusion that an EU investor was not entitled to initiate an investor-State arbitration proceeding against an EU Member State under the ECT with the effect that the tribunal should ultimately reject its own jurisdiction.[235]

In the first publicly know intra-EU ECT award rendered after *Achmea*, the *Masdar Solar* tribunal denied Spain's application and concluded "that the *Achmea* judgment [had] no bearing upon the present case," as it specifically dealt with the Netherlands–Czechoslovakia BIT and "in a more general perspective" with investor-State arbitration provisions such as the one contained in that BIT.[236] Against this background, the tribunal emphasized that while the ECJ had had the opportunity to address the question of the relationship between EU law and the ECT, the *Achmea* judgment was – in difference to the Advocate General's Opinion – "simply silent on the subject of the ECT".[237] For the tribunal, *Achmea* was thus not applicable to the multilateral ECT as the latter was not comparable to a BIT, also because the EU itself is a party to it.[238]

In *Vattenfall v Germany*, the respondent raised an objection to the tribunal's jurisdiction, claiming that the *Achmea* rationale was not limited to intra-EU BITs,

> but must also be applied to multilateral agreements to which EU Member States are party, such as the ECT. The ECJ Judgment, thus, applies erga omnes, with ex tunc effect, and in respect of all international agreements

para. 15; SCC Arbitration, *Greentech Energy Systems v Italy*. V (2015/095). Final Award, 23 December 2018, para. 356; SCC Arbitration, *Foresight Luxembourg Solar v Spain*. V (2015/150). Final Award, 14 November 2018, para. 39. In *Antaris v Czech Republic* and *Antin v Spain*, however, the arbitral tribunals rejected the respondents' applications to reopen the proceedings in order to discuss the effects of the *Achmea* judgment and did not consider the ECJ's decision in their awards, PCA, *Antaris v Czech Republic*. 2014–01. Award, 2 May 2018, para. 73; ICSID, *Antin v Spain*. Case No. ARB/13/31. Award, 15 June 2018, paras. 56 ff.

234 Position of Spain, as cited in ICSID, *Masdar Solar v Spain*. Case No. ARB/14/1. Award, 16 May 2018, para. 675.

235 Position of Spain, as cited in ibid., paras. 674, 676.

236 Ibid., para. 678 f. See also SCC Arbitration, *Foresight Luxembourg Solar v Spain*. V (2015/150). Final Award, 14 November 2018, para. 220.

237 ICSID, *Masdar Solar v Spain*. Case No. ARB/14/1. Award, 16 May 2018, para. 682. See also ICSID, *Vattenfall v Germany*. Case No. ARB/12/12. Decision on the Achmea Issue, 31 August 2018, para. 163.

238 ICSID, *Masdar Solar v Spain*. Case No. ARB/14/1. Award, 16 May 2018, para. 679 f. The tribunal emphasized its position by referring to the Opinion of the Advocate General which explicitly described the *Achmea* proceeding as the ECJ's "first opportunity to express its views on the thorny question of the compatibility of bilateral investment treaties," cf. ECJ, *Achmea*. C-284/16. Opinion of Advocate General Wathelet, 19 September 2017, para. 2 and by referring to the BGH, which had framed its preliminary question to the ECJ in a way applying only to BITs, cf. ECJ, *Achmea*. C-284/16. Judgment, 6 March 2018, para. 23.

between EU Member States under which an investor from one Member State may bring arbitration proceedings against another Member State.[239]

In light of this new objection, the arbitral tribunal rendered a separate "Decision on the Achmea Issue" which considered only the effects of *Achmea* on the applicability of the ECT to intra-EU disputes. The *Vattenfall* tribunal noted that Germany only relied on the argument of inapplicability *after* the publication of the ECJ's *Achmea* judgment, i.e. six years after the proceedings were initiated, even though this point had already been raised in the proceedings by the EU Commission acting as *amicus curiae*.[240] Similar to the *Masdar Solar* tribunal, the *Vattenfall* tribunal then reached the conclusion that EU law in general and the *Achmea* judgment in particular were not applicable in assessing whether an arbitral tribunal has jurisdiction under the ECT.[241] According to the arbitral tribunal,

> the ECT is not an agreement concluded "between Member States," as referred to by the ECJ. The ECT is a multilateral treaty, to which the EU itself is a party, alongside its Member States. Unlike the Dutch-Slovak BIT, the ECT is a "mixed agreement" between both Member States and third States, in addition to the EU itself. The wording of Art. 26 ECT is different to Art. 8 of the Dutch-Slovak BIT.[242]

Finally, in *Greentech Energy Systems v Italy*, the respondent State argued that the rationale *Achmea* equally applied to ECT proceedings – notwithstanding the EU being a Contracting Party to the ECT – as an arbitral tribunal constituted under the ECT might also be required to apply EU law in an intra-EU proceeding without having the possibility to refer a preliminary question to the ECJ and thus not being capable of "ensuring the proper application and full effectiveness of EU law."[243] These arguments, however, were rejected by the arbitral tribunal, which found to derive its jurisdiction from Art. 26 ECT and not an intra-EU BIT.[244] Furthermore, the choice of law provision of Art. 26 (6) ECT could not "be stretched to include EU law, absent doing violence to the text which would be impermissible under the VCLT".[245] And finally, that the

> ECJ in *Achmea* was careful to confine its ruling to agreements 'concluded between Member States', thereby leaving open the possibility of dispute

---

239 Position of Germany, as reported in ICSID, *Vattenfall v Germany*. Case No. ARB/12/12. Decision on the Achmea Issue, 31 August 2018, para. 49.
240 Ibid., para. 18.
241 Ibid., paras. 130 ff.
242 Ibid., para. 162.
243 Position of Italy as referred to in, SCC Arbitration, *Greentech Energy Systems v Italy*. V (2015/095). Final Award, 23 December 2018, para. 367 f.
244 Ibid., para. 396.
245 Ibid., para. 397.

resolution pursuant to international agreements that were not 'intra-EU' in the sense of being concluded by Member States as among themselves,

which is not the case for the ECT which includes the EU, EU Member States and third States as Contracting Parties.[246]

No ECT intra-EU investor-State tribunal has recognized any effect of the *Achmea* judgment on its jurisdiction yet.[247]

c) Assessment

Achmea's effect on intra-EU ECT proceedings continue to be highly controversial. Prima facie, the ECJ's judgment seems applicable to the ECT. Art. 26 ECT provides for investor-State arbitration proceedings in which by virtue of Art. 26 (6) ECT the arbitral tribunal "shall decide the issues in dispute in accordance with this Treaty and applicable rules and principles of international law." Hence, regarding the applicable law, the situation is similar to most intra-EU BITs: An intra-EU investor-State arbitration tribunal based on the ECT might be called upon to apply or interpret EU law.[248] It will however, not be able to refer a preliminary question to the ECJ, as just like a tribunal constituted under a BIT, it is exceptional in nature and has no sufficient links to the Member States' domestic judicial system. In light of the ECJ's considerations, the autonomy of the EU legal order could thus be just as jeopardized by intra-EU investor-State proceeding based on the ECT, as by proceedings based on an intra-EU BIT. The rationale of the *Achmea* decision is thus without any doubt transferable to investor-State arbitration proceedings initiated under the ECT.

Nonetheless, there is a fundamental difference between the ECT and intra-EU BITs. The EU itself is a party to the ECT, which is a mixed agreement under EU law and thus "binding upon the institutions of the Union and on its Member States" according to Art. 216 (2) TFEU. While intra-EU BITs have no link to the

---

246 Ibid., para. 398.

247 See also in this regard, ICSID, *Stadtwerke München GmbH v Spain.* Case No. ARB/15/1. Award, 2 December 2019, paras. 123 ff. and ICSID, *Belenergia v Italy.* Case No. ARB/15/40. Award, 6 August 2019, paras. 288 ff.

248 According to the *Charanne* and the *Isolux* tribunals, arbitral tribunals do not only have the power but also the duty to apply EU law, ICSID, *Charanne v Spain.* Arb. No. 062/2012. Final Award, 21 January 2016, para. 443; SCC Arbitration, *Isolux Infrastructure v Spain.* Case No. 2013/153. Final Award, 21 January 2016, para. 654. See also, ICSID, *Blusun v Italy.* ICSID Case No. ARB/14/3. Award, 27 December 2016, para. 277 f. Dissenting, on the question of application and interpretation of EU law by arbitral tribunals based on the ECT, P. Eeckhout, *The Law Applicable to the Dispute Under the Energy Charter Treaty 1994: Expert Opinion in the Matter of ICSID Case No. ARB/07/22 AES Summit Generation v Hungary,* 30 October 2008, at para. 21. See also the position of Germany, as reported in ICSID, *Vattenfall v Germany.* Case No. ARB/12/12. Decision on the Achmea Issue, 31 August 2018, para. 51 f.

EU legal order as they were neither concluded by the EU nor on its behalf,[249] the ECT actually forms an integral part of the EU legal order.[250] Thus, in case of conflict the ECT as a treaty concluded by the EU would even prevail over secondary EU law and the domestic law of Member States.[251] As explained by the EU Commission given that the ECT is part of EU law, the Commission could even initiate infringement proceedings against Member States which fail to comply with their obligations under the ECT.[252] The ECJ's *Achmea* decision must be read against this background. The court emphasized the fact that the intra-EU BITs have not been concluded by the EU but only by its Member States:

> In the present case, however, apart from the fact that the disputes falling within the jurisdiction of the arbitral tribunal [...] may relate to the interpretation both of that agreement and of EU law, the possibility of submitting those disputes to a body which is not part of the judicial system of the EU is provided for by an agreement which was concluded not by the EU but by Member States.[253]

The ECJ clearly differentiates between international courts and tribunal based on agreements which have been concluded by the EU itself on the one hand and agreements to which the EU is not a party on the other hand. The ECT falls under the former category, intra-EU BITs under the latter. Even though it is hard to perceive any practical difference between the arbitral proceedings based on BITs and the ECT regarding their potential effects on the EU legal order, their legal nature is not alike.

For all these reasons, an intra-EU BIT arbitration clause such as the one analysed in *Achmea* is not comparable to Art. 26 ECT, even if the rationale of *Achmea* to protect the autonomy of the EU legal order might be transferable to ECT based arbitrations.

In sum, the *Achmea* judgment does not apply to the ECT. Thus, in absence of an ECJ decision stating the opposite, the ECT, as part of EU law, must be understood to be compatible with the EU legal order. In other words, it must be assumed that the investor-State arbitration provision of Art. 26 ECT is compatible with Art. 344 and Art. 267 TFEU, even if such an understanding is in clear contradiction to the

---

249 Cf. T. Lock, *The European Court of Justice and International Courts* (Oxford: Oxford University Press, 2015), p. 139.

250 Cf. the submissions of the EU Commission in its *amicus curiae* brief in *Electrabel* ICSID, *Electrabel v Hungary*. Case No. ARB/07/19. Decision on Jurisdiction, Applicable Law and Liability, 30 November 2012, para. 4.170. See also ECJ, *Haegeman*. Case 181/73. Judgment, 30 April 1974, para. 8; ECJ, *MOX Plant*. C-459/03. Judgment, 30 May 2006, para. 82; ECJ, *CETA-Opinion*. 1/17. Opinion of Advocate General Bot, 29 January 2019, para. 60.

251 This is the result of the application of Arts. 218 (11) and 216 (2) TFEU, cf. M. Möldner, *European Community and Union, Mixed Agreements*, (May 2011) in *MPEPIL (Online-Edition)* at para. 29.

252 Position of the EU Commission, as quoted in ICSID, *Blusun v Italy*. ICSID Case No. ARB/14/3. Award, 27 December 2016, para. 220.

253 ECJ, *Achmea*. C-284/16. Judgment, 6 March 2018, para. 58.

rationale of the *Achmea* decision. There are, however, other possible grounds for an incompatibility of the ECT with the EU Treaties, which will be analysed in the following.

3 Art. 18 TFEU and the Energy Charter Treaty

Until Italy's withdrawal from the ECT the question of an incompatibility of the ECT with the non-discrimination principle codified in Art. 18 TFEU did not arise. Until then, every EU Member State was also a State party to the ECT and thus every EU investor could in theory enjoy the same level of substantive protection and initiate an investor-State arbitration proceeding against another Member State based on the ECT. This, however, changed with Italy's withdrawal from the treaty, which took effect on January 1, 2016.

The sovereign decision of the Italian State to withdraw from an international treaty cannot, however, have the effect of third States discriminating Italian investors abroad. Otherwise, a unilateral act of a Member State, namely Italy's withdrawal, could have detrimental effects on other Member States triggering their responsibility for a breach of international law.

Denmark for example, could hardly be accused of discriminating Italian investors because those are precluded from initiating investor-State arbitration proceedings under the ECT against Denmark due to the unilateral decision of the Italian government to withdraw from the treaty. In other words, even if *arguendo* one were to take the view that Italian investors are discriminated as they can no longer initiate intra-EU investor-State arbitration proceedings based on the ECT, this discrimination could not be attributable to other EU Member States but only to Italy, which according to Art. 18 (1) TFEU is only prohibited to discriminate other (non-Italian) EU citizens on grounds of their nationality. As discussed previously,[254] so-called reverse discrimination does not fall under Art. 18 TFEU but concerns the domestic legal order of the respective Member State.

On the other hand, it could be argued that other European investors could be discriminated by Italy. The latter's withdrawal from the ECT precludes them from initiating investor-State arbitration proceedings against Italy.[255] However, as already discussed with regard to intra-EU BITs, a discrimination cannot consist of one Member State acting in a different way than another, as the standard of comparison can only be the acts of the same public authority, i.e. those of one specific Member State. Italy does not grant preferential treatment to any investor but treats every single European investor the same way. It does therefore not act in violation of Art. 18 TFEU.

Hence, while intra-EU BITs are incompatible with the non-discrimination provision contained in Art. 18 TFEU, this is not the case for the Energy Charter Treaty as neither Italy, nor the other Member States discriminate foreign investors.

---

254 Cf. Chapter III: III. 3. b).
255 Notwithstanding, investments which were made before Italy's withdrawal enjoy an additional protection for 20 years due to the ECT's sunset clause in Art. 47 (3) ECT.

4 Other possible reasons of incompatibility from an EU perspective

Another ground of inapplicability raised in the context of intra-EU BITs was that of 'mutual trust'.[256] But just like intra-EU BITs, the ECT is neither incompatible with the principle of 'mutual trust'. As the treaty was concluded jointly by the EU and all EU Member States a violation of the concept of 'mutual trust' is excluded. On the contrary, the conclusion of the ECT could rather be understood as an expression of sincere cooperation and in that sense of 'mutual trust', since the ECT was a joint European endeavour to ensure the EU's energy supply and security.

Another potential reason for the arbitral tribunals' lack of jurisdiction and the inapplicability of the ECT to intra-EU investor-State relations could be the lack of clarity regarding the respondent in intra-EU investor-State disputes based on the ECT. In ECT investor-State disputes, a claim brought against an EU Member State could in theory also fall under the responsibility of the EU. Under a mixed agreement such as the ECT, both the EU and the Member States can be responsible for a violation of a treaty obligation. Hence, the risk of a claimant bringing a cause "against the wrong respondent before the wrong forum",[257] thereby interfering with the internal division of competences and responsibilities between the EU and its Member States.[258] To prevent such an external interference with the internal division of competences, the EU Commission has argued that when an ECT dispute is initiated against an EU Member State or the EU itself, it needs to be determined from the outset whether the subject-matter falls under the competence and responsibility of the EU or of that of the Member States.[259] The lack of a general declaration determining the competences among the EU and its Member States in ECT cases does not mean that both are internally competent and responsibly for all matters falling under the ECT. As explained by the EU Commission,

> if the Member States were competent for all matters covered by the ECT, it would have sufficed if they alone had concluded the ECT. This is not the case. Rather, in particular for intra-European disputes, it always needs to be determined whether the EC or the Member State is internationally responsible for a certain conduct in accordance with their respective competences.[260]

---

256 On 'mutual trust' in general, cf. Chapter III: III. 4.
257 Position of the EU Commission, as cited in ICSID, *Electrabel v Hungary*. Case No. ARB/07/19. Decision on Jurisdiction, Applicable Law and Liability, 30 November 2012, para. 5.20 at 49.
258 On this, see also the line of jurisprudence in ECJ, *European Economic Area*. 1/91. Opinion, 14 December 1991, paras. 33 ff; ECJ, *EU accession to the ECHR*. 2/13. Opinion, 18 December 2014, para. 201; ECJ, *Kadi*. Joined Cases C-402/05 P and C-415/05 P. Judgment, 3 September 2008, para. 282.
259 Position of the EU Commission, as cited in ICSID, *Electrabel v Hungary*. Case No. ARB/07/19. Decision on Jurisdiction, Applicable Law and Liability, 30 November 2012, para. 5.20 at 42.
260 Position of the EU Commission, as cited in ibid., para. 5.20 at 46.

While Art. 8.21 CETA requires a Canadian investor to deliver to the EU "a notice requesting a determination of the respondent" before being able to initiate a CETA-based investor-State arbitration proceeding, no similar provision is included in the treaty text of the ECT. However, the Council and Commission published a Statement pursuant to Art. 26 (3) lit. b) (ii) ECT in 1997 in which it explicitly stated that the EU and the Member States will, if necessary,

> determine among them who is the respondent party to arbitration proceedings initiated by an investor of another Contracting Party. In such cases, upon request of the investor, the Communities and the Member States concerned will make such determination within a period of 30 days. (This is without prejudice to the right of the investor to initiate proceedings against both the Communities and their Member States.)[261]

This declaration applies only upon request of an investor. Whether this lack of an 'automatic' referral regarding the right respondent suffices for the ECT to be incompatible with EU law, however, seems more than doubtful. The choice to leave the determination of competences and responsibility open and thus do decide on a case by case basis was a sovereign decision of the Member States and the EU, which does not affect the ECT's applicability to intra-EU investor-State disputes even if a dispute would be initiated against 'the wrong' respondent from an EU legal perspective.

This question remained of purely academic character until recently as no investor-State dispute falling under the ECT had ever been reported in which a proceeding was initiated against the EU itself or in which the EU would have been the correct respondent instead of one of its Member States. The situation has changed as Nordstream 2 initiated an ECT-based arbitration proceeding against the EU in September 2019.[262] Nonetheless, in sum, the possibility of an investor-State arbitration directed 'against the wrong respondent' from an internal EU legal perspective does not lead to an incompatibility of the ECT's investor-State arbitration provision with EU law.

5 EU–ECT relationship from an international law perspective

The question of the compatibility of the ECT and EU law and in particular the question of the applicability of the ECT to intra-EU investor-State relations can also be raised from an international law perspective. As the jurisdiction of an intra-EU investor-State arbitration tribunal based on the ECT "is derived from the express terms of the ECT, a binding treaty under international law", such a

---

261 Council and Commission of the European Communities, *Statement pursuant to ECT Art. 26 (3) (b) (ii)*, 17 November 1997.
262 PCA, *Nord Stream 2 AG v the European Union*. Case No. 2020-07. Toronto (Canada) has been chosen as seat of arbitration.

tribunal "is not an institution of the European legal order and is not subject to the requirements of that legal order."[263]

Against this backdrop, specific international legal arguments regarding the interpretation and application of the ECT have been raised by the EU Commission and several Member States to demonstrate the ECT's possible inapplicability in the intra-EU context. The following section will analyse whether intra-EU disputes were excluded from the ECT's scope of application *ab initio* through so-called disconnection clauses (a) or whether in the case of intra-EU disputes a so-called conflict clause applies (b) before assessing whether arbitral tribunals may lack jurisdiction over intra-EU disputes because of a so-called lack of territorial diversity (c).

a) 'Ab initio *disconnection'*

Arbitral tribunals could be precluded from exercising their jurisdiction over intra-EU investor-State disputes initiated under the ECT, if the latter was not applicable due to a so-called disconnection clause, be it explicit or implicit. In case of a 'disconnection', intra-EU investors could not rely on arbitration to solve their dispute with EU host States but would have to rely on the domestic judiciary of the respective EU Member States.

'Disconnection clauses' are "conflict clauses added to treaties" in order to regulate potential conflicts between EU law and the treaty they are contained in.[264] As explained by Cremona,

> Where some or all Member States conclude a Convention with third countries which may impact on the sphere of application of Union law, a particular technique may be used which is designed to ensure the primacy of Union law obligations in relations between the Member States themselves and to render this more transparent to other parties [...] – the disconnection clause.[265]

A typical 'disconnection clause' can be found in Art. 26 (3) of the 2005 Council of Europe Convention on the Prevention of Terrorism, which reads:

> Parties which are members of the EU shall, in their mutual relations, apply [...] EU rules in so far as there are [...] EU rules governing the particular subject concerned and applicable to the specific case, without prejudice to the object and purpose of the present Convention and without prejudice to its full application with other Parties.[266]

---

263 ICSID, *Eiser Infrastructure v Spain*. Case No. ARB/13/36. Award, 4 May 2017, para. 199.
264 ILC, *Fragmentation of International Law*, 13 April 2006, para. 292.
265 M. Cremona, *Disconnection Clauses in EU Law and Practice* in C. Hillion and P. Koutrakos (eds.), *Mixed Agreements Revisited: The EU and Its Member States in the World* (Oxford: Hart, 2010), pp. 160–86, at p. 161.
266 See also Art. 27 (1) of the 1989 European Convention on Transfrontier Television, Council of Europe and Art. 47 (1) of the 2005 Prüm Convention on the stepping up of cross-border

In the Declaration made in respect of this article, the Contracting Parties emphasized that

> The disconnection clause is necessary for those parts of the Convention which fall within the competence of the [...] Union, in order to indicate that EU Member States cannot invoke and apply the rights and obligations deriving from the Convention directly among themselves [...]. This does not detract from the fact that the Convention applies fully between the [...] EU and its Member States on the one hand, and the other Parties to the Convention, on the other hand.[267]

The drafters and negotiators of the ECT were aware of possible conflicts arising out of the co-existence of the ECT and other treaty regimes. The ECT thus contains two 'disconnection clauses', one regarding conflicts between the ECT and the Svalbard Treaty concerning Spitsbergen,[268] according to which the latter shall prevail to the extent of the conflict. The other 'disconnection clause' is reflected in the declaration of the European Communities on the one side and the Russian Federation, Ukraine, Kazakhstan, Kyrgyzstan, Tajikistan and Uzbekistan on the other side that trade in nuclear materials between them shall be exclusively governed by different prior agreements on cooperation, until they reach another agreement.[269]

No such clause, however, addresses intra-EU relations, nor does the wording of Art. 26 ECT exclude intra-EU situations from its scope of application. One could thus even make the *e contrario* argument that the ECT is supposed to cover intra-EU investor-State disputes just like any other dispute arising within its scope of application. Accordingly, in view of the *Vattenfall* tribunal, "a disconnection clause was intentionally omitted from the ECT", which "confirms that the treaty was intended to create obligations between Member States of the EU, including in respect of potential investor-State dispute settlement."[270] Another possibility, however, is that the Member States representatives did just not realise the possibility of intra-EU investor-State arbitration proceedings. In any case, no explicit 'disconnection clause' prevents arbitral tribunals from having jurisdiction over intra-EU investor-State arbitration proceedings based on the ECT.

---

cooperation, particularly in combating terrorism, cross-border crime and illegal migration, concluded between Belgium, Germany, Spain, France, Luxembourg, the Netherlands and Austria.

267 Declaration formulated by the European Community and the EU Member States upon the adoption of the Convention by the Committee of Ministers of the Council of Europe, on 3 May 2005.

268 Decision 1 with respect to the Energy Charter Treaty (Annex 2 to the Final Act of the European Energy Charter Conference).

269 Declaration with Respect to Annex [W(4)] to the Final Act of the European Energy Charter Conference.

270 ICSID, *Vattenfall v Germany*. Case No. ARB/12/12. Decision on the Achmea Issue, 31 August 2018, para. 206. See also ICSID, *Electrabel v Hungary*. Case No. ARB/07/19. Decision on Jurisdiction, Applicable Law and Liability, 30 November 2012, para. 4.163 f.

As there is no explicit 'disconnection clause' covering intra-EU investor-State relations, the EU Commission and several Member States have repeatedly argued that the ECT contains an implicit 'disconnection clause' regarding intra-EU situations.[271] Accordingly, the ECT would not be applicable to intra-EU disputes, but only to disputes involving either an investor from an EU Member State as claimant and a third State as respondent, or an investor from a third State and an EU Member State as respondent.

This argument is inter alia based on the alleged parallelism of Arts. 26 and 27 ECT. The later provides for State-to-State arbitration in case of a dispute between Contracting Parties. As ECT State-to-State disputes among EU Member States might be excluded by virtue of Art. 344 TFEU and the ECJ's MOX Plant decision,[272] one could assume the existence of an implicit 'disconnection clause' between EU Member States, which would not only exclude State-to-State disputes from its scope of application, but also intra-EU investor-State arbitration proceedings.[273] Accordingly, the ECT could not "create new rights and obligations for EU investors vis-à-vis EU Member States", as the EU legal order provides for a "complete set of rules for the protection of investments" and because Art. 344 TFEU precludes Member States from agreeing on dispute settlement proceedings concerning the interpretation of EU law which are different from those provided in the EU Treaties.[274] In other words, Member States would have only created

---

271 Position of Spain, Italy and the EU Commission as referred to in ICSID, *Charanne v Spain*. Arb. No. 062/2012. Final Award, 21 January 2016, paras. 440 ff; ICSID, *RREEF Infrastructure v Spain*. Case No. ARB/13/30. Decision on Jurisdiction, 6 June 2016, paras. 81 ff; ICSID, *Blusun v Italy*. ICSID Case No. ARB/14/3. Award, 27 December 2016, para. 242 f., 280. See also the EU Commission's *amicus curiae* briefs in the arbitration cases *Antaris v Czech Republic*, PCA Case No. 2014–01; *Natland Investment Group v Czech Republic; I.C.W. Europe Investments v Czech Republic; Photovoltaik Knopf Betriebs-GmBH v Czech Republic; WA Investments-Europa Nova Limited v Czech Republic*.

Remarkably, in *Masdar Solar*, however, the parties to the dispute concurred that there is no 'disconnection clause', be it explicit or implicit, contained in the ECT, which precludes intra-EU disputes from its scope of application, ICSID, *Masdar Solar v Spain*. Case No. ARB/14/1. Award, 16 May 2018, para. 312 f. Spain also clarified in *Antin Infrastructure* "that it does not claim that an explicit or implicit disconnection clause exists," position of Spain as reported in ICSID, *Antin v Spain*. Case No. ARB/13/31. Award, 15 June 2018, para. 180.

272 ECJ, *MOX Plant*. C-459/03. Judgment, 30 May 2006.

273 Cf. position of Spain, as referred to in ICSID, *Charanne v Spain*. Arb. No. 062/2012. Final Award, 21 January 2016, para. 434.

274 Position of the EU Commission as cited in, ICSID, *Masdar Solar v Spain*. Case No. ARB/14/1. Award, 16 May 2018, para. 305, see also position of Spain, as reported in ICSID, *Charanne v Spain*. Arb. No. 062/2012. Final Award, 21 January 2016, para. 208. In *Masdar Solar*, Spain took an even stronger position, arguing that EU law is applicable to intra-EU situations "in preference to or prevailing over any other law, displacing any other national or international provision. The preference given to community law does not admit comparisons with other laws. It does not demand that it be proven that other laws are more or less favourable. Simply put, EU law is given preference over any other dealing with regulating internal EU relations," position of Spain as cited in, ICSID, *Masdar Solar v Spain*. Case No. ARB/14/1. Award, 16 May 2018, para. 325.

obligations regarding investment protection under the ECT with respect to third countries but not among themselves.[275]

These arguments are also supported by the fact that the leading idea underlying the drafting of the ECT was the enhancement of East-West cooperation in the energy sector and the attraction of FDI in Eastern Europe from Western European investors. With the explicit goal to assure the energy supply for Western European States and to improve the EU's energy security,[276] but not the enhancement of intra-EU energy trade and investments.[277]

The argument of an implicit disconnection has so far, however, always been dismissed by intra-EU arbitral tribunals constituted under the ECT.[278] Several tribunals took the position that a 'disconnection clause' would only be necessary in case of a conflict between EU law and the ECT, which the tribunals rejected, as in their view only the ECT provides for investor-State dispute settlement, and as EU law does not prevent Member States to resolve investor-State disputes through arbitration.[279] The *RREEF* tribunal went so far to note that even if one day an irreconcilable inconsistency between EU law and the ECT would be determined, arbitral tribunals constituted under the ECT would be obliged under public international law to apply the ECT even to the detriment of EU law, as the latter could not trump public international law.[280]

See also position of the EU Commission, as cited in ICSID, *Blusun v Italy*. ICSID Case No. ARB/14/3. Award, 27 December 2016, paras. 217 ff.

275 Cf. Position of the EU Commission as cited in, ICSID, *Masdar Solar v Spain*. Case No. ARB/14/1. Award, 16 May 2018, para. 304 and in ICSID, *Blusun v Italy*. ICSID Case No. ARB/14/3. Award, 27 December 2016, para. 222.

276 With further references, J. R. Basedow, *The EU in the Global Investment Regime: Commission Entrepreneurship, Incremental Institutional Change and Business Lethargy* (London: Routledge, 2018), at 114 ff.

277 Cf. position of Spain, as reported in SCC Arbitration, *Novenergia II v Spain*. Arbitration 2015/063. Final Arbitral Award, 15 February 2018, paras. 423 ff. See also the submissions of the EU Commission in its *amicus curiae* brief in SCC Arbitration, *Greentech Energy Systems v Italy*. V (2015/095). Final Award, 23 December 2018, para. 283 f.

278 See for example, ICSID, *Charanne v Spain*. Arb. No. 062/2012. Final Award, 21 January 2016, paras. 435 ff; ICSID, *Eiser Infrastructure v Spain*. Case No. ARB/13/36. Award, 4 May 2017, para. 207; SCC Arbitration, *Greentech Energy Systems v Italy*. V (2015/095). Final Award, 23 December 2018, para. 338. Supportive, Eeckhout, *The law Applicable to the Dispute Under the Energy Charter Treaty 1994*, 30 October 2008, paras. 64 ff; Hess, *The Fate of Investment Dispute Resolution after the Achmea Decision of the European Court of Justice*, MPILux Research Paper Series (2018), 15.

279 ICSID, *Electrabel v Hungary*. Case No. ARB/07/19. Decision on Jurisdiction, Applicable Law and Liability, 30 November 2012, para. 4.175; ICSID, *Charanne v Spain*. Arb. No. 062/2012. Final Award, 21 January 2016, para. 438 f; ICSID, *RREEF Infrastructure v. Spain*. Case No. ARB/13/30. Decision on Jurisdiction, 6 June 2016, para. 83; ICSID, *Eiser Infrastructure v Spain*. Case No. ARB/13/36. Award, 4 May 2017, para. 199; ICSID, *Masdar Solar v Spain*. Case No. ARB/14/1. Award, 16 May 2018, para. 340; ICSID, *Blusun v Italy*. ICSID Case No. ARB/14/3. Award, 27 December 2016, paras. 286 ff.

280 ICSID, *RREEF Infrastructure v Spain*. Case No. ARB/13/30. Decision on Jurisdiction, 6 June 2016, para. 87.

Notwithstanding these positions, an implicit 'disconnection clause' would need to be read into the ECT's treaty text. In other words, the question arises whether Art. 26 ECT could be interpreted to contain an implicit 'disconnection clause'. Art. 31 VCLT provides the general rule of interpretation of international treaties, according to which a treaty should be interpreted "in good faith in accordance with the ordinary meaning to be given to the terms of the treaty in their context and in the light of its object and purpose." The historic circumstances of the conclusion of a treaty, however, are by virtue of Art. 32 VCLT only subsidiary in order to confirm the meaning from the application of Art. 31 VCLT or to determine the meaning of a norm when an interpretation according to Art. 31 VCLT leaves the meaning ambiguous or obscure. Arguments relying on the drafting history of the ECT would thus only play a subsidiary role for the treaty's interpretation, if the meaning of Art. 26 ECT would remain 'ambiguous or obscure' with an interpretation based on its wording, context and telos.

Against this backdrop, the *Eiser Infrastructure* tribunal emphasized that as a corollary to the interpretation of a treaty in good faith, "treaty makers should [also] be understood to carry out their function in good faith, and not to lay traps for the unwary with hidden meanings and sweeping implied exclusions."[281] It therefore rejected the implicit 'disconnection clause' argument, relying on the *RREEF* tribunal's findings that in a case in which

> the very essence of a treaty to which the EU is a party is at issue, such as it would be for the ECT [...], then precisely because the EU is a party to the treaty a formal warning that EU law would prevail over the treaty, such as that contained in a disconnection clause, would have been required under international law.

> This follows from the basic public international law principle of pacta sunt servanda. If one or more parties to a treaty wish to exclude the application of that treaty in certain respect or circumstances, they must either make a reservation (excluded in the present case by Art. 46 of the ECT) or include an unequivocal disconnection clause in the treaty itself. The attempt to construe an implicit clause into Art. 26 of the ECT is untenable, given that that article already contains express exceptions to the "unconditional consent to submission of a dispute to international arbitration or conciliation in accordance with the provisions of this Article" that had been agreed amongst the States Party.[282]

---

281 ICSID, *Eiser Infrastructure v Spain*. Case No. ARB/13/36. Award, 4 May 2017, para. 186. In the same vein, see also ICSID, *Antin v Spain*. Case No. ARB/13/31. Award, 15 June 2018, para. 225.
282 ICSID, *RREEF Infrastructure v Spain*. Case No. ARB/13/30. Decision on Jurisdiction, 6 June 2016, para. 84 f. The *Blusun* tribunal took a similar position, requiring "an express provision or very clear understanding between the negotiating parties" for a disconnection or inter-se exclusion of intra-EU disputes from the ECT's scope of application, ICSID, *Blusun v Italy*. ICSID Case No. ARB/14/3. Award, 27 December 2016, para. 280. See also ICSID, *Antin v Spain*. Case No. ARB/13/31. Award, 15 June 2018, para. 215; ICSID, *Vattenfall v Germany*. Case No. ARB/12/12. Decision on the Achmea Issue, 31 August 2018, para. 202; SCC Arbitration, *Greentech Energy Systems v Italy*. V (2015/095). Final Award, 23 December 2018, para. 342.

The tribunal's reflection is reinforced by the fact that the ECT provides for several exceptions regarding its scope of application, namely the explicit 'disconnection clauses' analysed previously.

These arguments are convincing. The ECT's treaty text is clear regarding its scope of application. It provides for investor-State dispute settlement between an investor from one State party and another State party. No exception regarding intra-EU investor-State relations can be found in the treaty, nor can a 'disconnection clause' be based on other means of treaty interpretation. The implicit disconnection argument rather seems to be an attempt to rectify the failure to introduce an explicit 'disconnection clause' at the time of the ECT's negotiation, which led to an unexpected wave of intra-EU investor-State arbitrations within the last years. In sum, there is no disconnection of intra-EU investor-State relations from the ECT, neither through an explicit, nor through an implicit 'disconnection clause'.

b) 'Conflict clauses' in Art. 30 VCLT and Art. 16 ECT

The jurisdiction of arbitral tribunals in intra-EU investor-State disputes could, however, be precluded through so-called conflict clauses. As already seen regarding the relationship of intra-EU BITs and the EU Treaties, Art. 30 VCLT applies to successive treaties, which relate to the 'same subject matter'. Accordingly, the EU Commission has argued that the ECT's rules on investment protection and investor-State dispute settlement are inapplicable to intra-EU investor-State relations, as

> for purposes of Art. 30 of the VCLT, the ECT and EU Treaties relate to the same subject matter, namely energy. Accordingly, while the ECT is an earlier treaty compared to the EU Treaties, the ECT only applies to the extent that its provisions are not incompatible with the EU treaties. On that basis, [...] the Tribunal should conclude that Chapter III and Art. 26 of the ECT are not applicable between Member States pursuant to Art. 30 VCLT.[283]

Art. 30 (3) VCLT is not directly applicable to the ECT, as not "all the parties to the earlier treaty are parties also to the later treaty." The earlier treaty is the ECT with today 47 Member States and the later the Lisbon Treaty with 27 Member States post Brexit. Nonetheless, as the parties to the later treaty do not include all the parties to the earlier one, Art. 30 (4) lit. a) VCLT applies according to which in such a situation as between States Parties to both treaties the same rule applies as in Art. 30 (3) VCLT.

---

283 Position of the EU Commission, as cited in ICSID, *Blusun v Italy*. ICSID Case No. ARB/14/3. Award, 27 December 2016, para. 229. See also the position of Germany as referred to in ICSID, *Vattenfall v Germany*. Case No. ARB/12/12. Decision on the Achmea Issue, 31 August 2018, para. 216.

Art. 30 (3) VCLT could, however, be inapplicable to intra-EU situations due to the existence of a 'conflict-clause' within the meaning of Art. 30 (2) VCLT.[284] Art. 16 ECT represents such a 'conflict clause'. It seeks to regulate the ECT's relationship with other treaties regarding investment protection and investor-State dispute settlement and reads:

> Where two or more Contracting Parties [...] enter into a subsequent international agreement, whose terms [...] concern the subject matter of Part III or V of this Treaty,
>
> (1) nothing in Part III or V of this Treaty shall be construed to derogate from any provision of such terms of the other agreement or from any right to dispute resolution with respect thereto under that agreement; and
> (2) nothing in such terms of the other agreement shall be construed to derogate from any provision of Part III or V of this Treaty or from any right to dispute resolution with respect thereto under this Treaty, where any such provision is more favourable to the Investor or Investment.

In other words, in case of conflict with an international treaty subsequent to the ECT, which also covers investment protection and/or investor-State dispute settlement, the provisions of the treaty more favourable to the investor or investment shall be applied. The Lisbon Treaty is a subsequent international agreement concluded by the EU Member States. Thus, if it covers the 'subject matter' of Part III or V of the ECT, Art. 16 ECT would be applicable to determine the rules on investor protection to be applied in the relationship between the ECT and the EU Treaties.

Many different positions on the 'subject matter' of the ECT and the EU Treaties have been expressed. Italy, for example, argued in *Greentech* that the EU Treaties and the ECT relate to the 'same subject matter' as they

> factually cover the same situation of an investor entering a foreign market in the hope of not being unduly discriminated or frustrated in its investment, as well as being duly protected by fair judicial or quasi-judicial mechanisms against misuse of power.[285]

In *Blusun*, Italy argued in a similar way and found Art. 16 ECT to be applicable, leading to the inapplicability of the ECT to intra-EU investor-State relations, as

> EU law guarantees better protection to an investor or an investment than the ECT, and therefore the coverage of intra-EU situations regarding FDI by EU law is compatible with the ECT by virtue of Art. 16 of the ECT.[286]

---

284 On conflict clauses, cf. in greater detail, Chapter III: II. 2. b).

285 Position of Italy, as cited in SCC Arbitration, *Greentech Energy Systems v Italy*. V (2015/095). Final Award, 23 December 2018, para. 267.

286 Position of Italy, as referred to in ICSID, *Blusun v Italy*. ICSID Case No. ARB/14/3. Award, 27 December 2016, para. 247. According to Italy, the same conclusion would also be reached – regardless of Art. 16 ECT – by applying Art. 30 (4) VCLT, cf. ibid., para. 248.

This position, however, was rejected by the tribunals in both proceedings, without giving any further interpretation on the 'subject matter' of the respective treaties.[287]

As seen previously, EU law does not cover the protection of already established investments in an identical manner to the ECT and has a significantly wider scope than the latter.[288] Whereas EU law regulates the entire EU common market and the interaction and cooperation between the EU Member States, the ECT covers only the very specific field of energy investments. There is an overlap between EU law and the ECT. However, several key features of the latter are not provided for in the former, namely the investor-State arbitration mechanism, the most-favoured nation treatment or the protection of contractual undertakings through umbrella clauses. Hence, it is more than doubtful that the ECT and EU law concern the 'same subject matter' regarding investment protection. Furthermore, there are strong arguments that the substantive and procedural rules of investor protection provided by the ECT are more favourable to foreign investors and their investments than those provided by EU law.[289] In any case the ECT's rules would remain applicable in intra-EU situations even if they concerned the 'same subject matter'.[290] As convincingly explained by an arbitral tribunal,

> To the extent that provisions of European law may in some manner provide protections more favorable to Investors or Investments than those under the ECT, Art. 16 (2) makes clear that they do not detract from or supersede other ECT provisions, in particular the right to dispute settlement under ECT Part V. By its terms, Art. 16 assures Investors or their Investments the greatest protection available under either the ECT or the other agreement. Thus, an agreement covered by Art. 16 (2) may improve upon particular protections available to Investors or their Investments, but it cannot lessen rights or protections under the ECT that are in other respects more favorable.[291]

Thus, in sum, Art. 16 ECT does not exclude the applicability of the ECT to intra-EU investor-State disputes.

---

287 SCC Arbitration, *Greentech Energy Systems v Italy*. V (2015/095). Final Award, 23 December 2018, para. 346; ICSID, *Blusun v Italy*. ICSID Case No. ARB/14/3. Award, 27 December 2016, para. 303. See on the 'subject matter' also in a similar vein, ICSID, *Electrabel v Hungary*. Case No. ARB/07/19. Decision on Jurisdiction, Applicable Law and Liability, 30 November 2012, para. 4.176.
288 See Chapter II.
289 See Chapter II. See also ICSID, *Vattenfall v Germany*. Case No. ARB/12/12. Decision on the Achmea Issue, 31 August 2018, para. 194.
290 See also Eeckhout, *The law Applicable to the Dispute Under the Energy Charter Treaty 1994*, 30 October 2008, para. 74 and the tribunal in ICSID, *RREEF Infrastructure v Spain*. Case No. ARB/13/30. Decision on Jurisdiction, 6 June 2016, para. 75, which stated that "if there must be a 'hierarchy' between the norms to be applied by the Tribunal, it must be determined from the perspective of public international law, not of EU law. Therefore, the ECT prevails over any other norm (apart from those of ius cogens [...])."
291 ICSID, *Eiser Infrastructure v Spain*. Case No. ARB/13/36. Award, 4 May 2017, para. 202.

c) Lack of 'territorial diversity'

Notwithstanding the existence of a 'conflict' or 'disconnection clause', arbitral tribunals could have no jurisdiction due to a lack of 'territorial diversity' in intra-EU investor-State relations.

Art. 26 ECT applies to "disputes between a Contracting Party and an Investor of another Contracting Party relating to an investment of the latter in the Area of the former." 'Area' is defined in Art. 1 (10) ECT with respect to a State as "the territory under its sovereignty" and with respect to an REIO as the "Areas of the member States of such Organisation, under the provisions contained in the agreement establishing that Organisation." The geographical scope of application of the EU is defined in Art. 52 TEU and Art. 355 TFEU and comprises the territories of the 27 Member States after Brexit. In other words, the 'area' of the EU in the sense of Art. 26 ECT comprises the territories of all EU Member States.

According to the EU Commission and some Member States, Art. 26 ECT is not applicable to a case initiated by an EU investor against another EU Member State, as the ECT's requirement of 'territorial diversity' is not met, i.e. the investor initiating an arbitral proceeding must be a national of a Contracting Party other than the respondent and the investment must have been undertaken in a territory different to the investor's home State.[292] Accordingly, an investor stemming from an EU Member State could be understood to be "both an investor of that State and of the EU", which is a REIO within the meaning of Art. 1 (3) ECT,[293] and which covers the territory of all Member States with the effect that the "diversity criteria between the territory of an investor and territory of the other Contracting Party receiving the investment is absent."[294] According to this position in case of intra-EU investment activities, European investors are not foreign investors, i.e. investors *of* 'another Contracting Party' in the meaning of Art. 26 ECT. They are understood to be investors from the EU not investors *from* an EU Member State, and are in that sense 'nationals' of the Contracting Party they bring a claim

---

292 See for example, the position of Spain, as reported in, ICSID, *Charanne v Spain.* Arb. No. 062/2012. Final Award, 21 January 2016, para. 213. See also the position of Spain as reported in, SCC Arbitration, *Foresight Luxembourg Solar v Spain.* V (2015/150). Final Award, 14 November 2018, paras. 159 ff.

293 Art. 1 (3) ECT reads: "'Regional Economic Integration Organisation' means an organization constituted by states to which they have transferred competence over certain matters a number of which are governed by this Treaty, including the authority to take decisions binding on them in respect of those matters."

294 Position of Spain as reported in, ICSID, *Charanne v Spain.* Arb. No. 062/2012. Final Award, 21 January 2016, para. 213 f; ICSID, *Antin v Spain.* Case No. ARB/13/31. Award, 15 June 2018, para. 163. See also the position of the EU Commission, as reported in ICSID, *Electrabel v Hungary.* Case No. ARB/07/19. Decision on Jurisdiction, Applicable Law and Liability, 30 November 2012, para. 5.10, in ICSID, *Blusun v Italy.* ICSID Case No. ARB/14/3. Award, 27 December 2016, para. 227, in SCC Arbitration, *Greentech Energy Systems v Italy.* V (2015/095). Final Award, 23 December 2018, para. 280 and in ICSID, *Vattenfall v Germany.* Case No. ARB/12/12. Decision on the Achmea Issue, 31 August 2018, para. 179.

against, namely the EU.[295] This situation is understood to be similar to that of an investor initiating an ISDS proceeding against its own home State, which is excluded under Art. 26 ECT.[296]

Against this background, the EU Commission argues that the EU would be disadvantaged compared to any other party to the ECT if intra-EU proceedings were admissible, as other State parties to the ECT can turn down "any international litigation request" of their own investors against home State measures.[297] The EU, however, could not "do the same vis-à-vis international arbitration requests under the ECT" from companies incorporated under the domestic legal systems of the EU Member States and would thus not only grant international litigation rights to foreign, but also to domestic investors.[298] According to the EU Commission, the ECT was certainly not intended to create alternative fora for EU investors regarding measures attributable to the EU as this would create a "considerable disadvantage by comparison to other non-EU contracting parties".[299]

Arbitral tribunals have taken a different position. So far, every arbitral tribunal confronted with that question found Art. 26 ECT to be applicable. As paradigmatically emphasized by the tribunal in *Charanne v Spain*:

> Although the EU is a Contracting Party of the ECT, the States that compose it have not ceased to be Contracting Parties as well. Both the EU, and its Member States, may have legal standing as Respondents in an action based on the ECT.
>
> Art. 1 (10) ECT, [...] refers to both the territory of the Contracting States [...] and the EU territory [...]. Therefore, it appears reasonable to deduce that, in referring to investments made 'in the territory' of a contracting party, Art. 26 (1) refers to both, in the case of a EU member State, to the territory of a national State as well as the territory of the EU. There is no rule in the ECT according to which a different interpretation can be inferred.
>
> To know if the term 'territory' refers to one or the other depends on the content of the claim and the entity against which the claim is directed. An investor may well sue the EU based on allegedly unlawful acts committed by

---

295 Position of Spain, as cited in ICSID, *Eiser Infrastructure v Spain*. Case No. ARB/13/36. Award, 4 May 2017, para. 161 f; ICSID, *RREEF Infrastructure v Spain*. Case No. ARB/13/30. Decision on Jurisdiction, 6 June 2016, para. 37 f; ICSID, *Masdar Solar v Spain*. Case No. ARB/14/1. Award, 16 May 2018, para. 269, 299 f. See also the position of Spain and the EU Commission, as reported in SCC Arbitration, *Novenergia II v Spain*. Arbitration 2015/063. Final Arbitral Award, 15 February 2018, para. 449 f.

296 See also the position of the EU Commission, as cited in ICSID, *Electrabel v Hungary*. Case No. ARB/07/19. Decision on Jurisdiction, Applicable Law and Liability, 30 November 2012, para. 5.20 at 62.

297 Position of the EU Commission, as cited in ibid., para. 5.20 at 63.

298 Ibid.

299 Ibid.

it. In this case, it could be considered that for the purposes of Art. 26 ECT, the dispute is related to an investment made in the territory of the EU.[300]

The *Charanne* tribunal differentiated between intra-EU disputes in which the EU itself is the respondent and such disputes in which an EU Member State is the respondent. In other words, the tribunal found that in the case of an intra-EU '*investor-EU*' arbitration proceeding, i.e. a proceeding directed against the EU itself by a European investor, the argument of a lack of 'territorial diversity' should be considered. In a typical intra-EU *investor-State* dispute, however, it is clear for the tribunal that Art. 26 ECT is applicable as the Member States continue to be Contracting Parties to the ECT with all rights and obligations arising out of that treaty.[301] Accordingly, arbitral tribunals would have jurisdiction to decide investor-State arbitration claims initiated by investors from one Member State and directed against another EU Member State, i.e. all the ECT-based proceedings discussed so far.

Another approach was taken by the *Eiser* tribunal. It found that an 'Investor of the EU' could not satisfy the definition of investor in Art. 1 (7) (a) ECT, which defines 'investor' as

i   a natural person having the citizenship or nationality of or who is permanently residing in that Contracting Party in accordance with its applicable law;
ii a company or other organisation organised in accordance with the law applicable in that Contracting Party

Accordingly, there could be no 'investor of the EU' within the framework of the definition, as "there is no trans-national body of European law regulating the organization of business units, a matter that remains subject to member countries' domestic law."[302] The tribunal relied on the fact that also within the EU the 'nationality' of corporations is determined by their incorporation in a Member State's domestic legal system or based on the fact that the corporation's seat is located within a specific Member State. In other words, an investor could not be labelled 'EU investor' but only be understood as an investor from one specific EU

---

300 ICSID, *Charanne v Spain*. Arb. No. 062/2012. Final Award, 21 January 2016, paras. 429 ff. See also ICSID, *Vattenfall v Germany*. Case No. ARB/12/12. Decision on the Achmea Issue, 31 August 2018, para. 183; ICSID, *Antin v Spain*. Case No. ARB/13/31. Award, 15 June 2018, paras. 218 ff.; ICSID, *Stadtwerke München GmbH v Spain*. Case No. ARB/15/1. Award, 2 December 2019, paras. 126 ff; ICSID, *Belenergia v Italy*. Case No. ARB/15/40. Award, 6 August 2019, para. 292.

301 See also SCC Arbitration, *Novenergia II v Spain*. Arbitration 2015/063. Final Arbitral Award, 15 February 2018, para. 453.

302 ICSID, *Eiser Infrastructure v Spain*. Case No. ARB/13/36. Award, 4 May 2017, para. 196. See also ICSID, *Vattenfall v Germany*. Case No. ARB/12/12. Decision on the Achmea Issue, 31 August 2018, para. 183.

Member State. In sum, the arbitral practice has unanimously recognized the standing of both investors from EU Member States as claimants and EU Member States as respondents in intra-EU investor-State arbitration proceedings as it understands the 'territory', Art. 26 (1) ECT refers to as the respective territory of the Member States, respondent to a dispute, and not the territory of the EU.[303]

The position taken by the arbitral tribunals is convincing. Art. 26 ECT refers to disputes between a 'Contracting Party' and an investor of 'another Contracting Party' relating to an investment of the latter in the 'Area' of the former. Clearly, the EU Member States themselves are contracting parties to the ECT. The fact that they are also Member States of the EU, a REIO within the meaning of Art. 1 (3) ECT does not alter this fact.

Art. 1 (7) ECT defines 'investor' as a "natural person having the citizenship or nationality of or who is permanently residing in" a Contracting Party or a company that is organised in accordance with the law applicable in a Contracting Party of the ECT.

The EU Commission and some Member States have argued that intra-EU investors are 'EU investors' and could thus not initiate an investor-State arbitration proceeding against an EU Member State as this would amount to a proceeding against the investor's 'home Contracting Party', namely the EU. There is, however, no 'pure' EU citizenship. According to Art. 9 TEU and Art. 20 TFEU, the EU citizenship is additional to and does not replace the national citizenship of the respective Member States. When the citizens of an EU Member State lose their citizenship, they also lose their EU citizenship. The latter does further only apply to individuals and not to corporations.[304] It is possible to establish a *Societas Europaea*, which is a European limited liability company. Its purpose, however, is only a limited one, namely "to enable companies incorporated in different Member States to merge or form holding companies or joint subsidiaries while avoiding the legal and practical difficulties arising from the existence of the Member States' different legal systems."[305] The *Societas Europaea* structure can only be chosen by publicly traded companies and is thus not accessible to common European investors. Furthermore, even a *Societas Europaea* would in an arbitral proceeding be considered as a company of the State in which it has its seat and not as an 'actual' European company. Thus, European investors remain nationals of their home States and do not become 'actual' nationals of the European Union.

---

303 Cf. ICSID, *Charanne v Spain*. Arb. No. 062/2012. Final Award, 21 January 2016, para. 431, concurring, ICSID, *Eiser Infrastructure v Spain*. Case No. ARB/13/36. Award, 4 May 2017, para. 194; SCC Arbitration, *Isolux Infrastructure v Spain*. Case No. 2013/153. Final Award, 21 January 2016, paras. 633 ff; ICSID, *Masdar Solar v Spain*. Case No. ARB/14/1. Award, 16 May 2018, para. 323; PCA, *The PV Investors v Spain*. Case No. 2012–14. Preliminary Award on Jurisdiction, 13 October 2014, para. 179 f.

304 For a great overview on the EU citizenship, cf. P. Craig and G. de Búrca, *EU Law: Text, Cases and Materials*, 6. ed. (Oxford: Oxford University Press, 2015), at 852 ff.

305 T. Roe and M. Happold, *Settlement of Investment Disputes Under the Energy Charter Treaty* (Cambridge: Cambridge University Press, 2011), at 93.

Hence, if investors operate in another Member State and initiate an arbitration proceeding against this host State, the respondent State is not the investors' State of nationality, i.e. their home State.

Any time an EU Member State is facing a claim brought by an investor under the ECT, the arbitral tribunal will have to assess whether this investor is from a Contracting Party different to that respondent State, and whether an investment has been made in the 'area' of the respondent State. As has been convincingly shown by arbitral practice, the coincidental membership of the host State and the home State of the investor in the same REIO does not affect the jurisdiction of the arbitral tribunal. Arbitral tribunals are competent to hear the claim brought against an EU Member State by an investor from another EU Member State. This might only be different in a case in which the REIO, i.e. the EU itself, is the respondent to such a proceeding initiated by an EU investor. Such a case, however, has not yet arisen. Even the recently initiated proceeding in *Nord Stream 2 v the European Union* does not fall under this category, as the Nord Stream 2 AG is registered in Switzerland and does therefore not represent an EU investor.[306]

6 Interim findings on the ECT–EU relationship

The ECT has always had a particular relationship to the EU legal order. In difference to intra-EU BITs, which were concluded as extra-EU BITs and only became intra-EU treaties through the later accession of several Member States, the ECT was already concluded as a multilateral treaty among EU Member States and other States. The later accession of new EU Member States had thus no particular effect on the ECT's relationship to the EU legal order.

The unique feature of the ECT is that the EU itself is a Contracting Party to that treaty. Hence, the ECT has also become an integral part of EU law. It is mainly for this reason that the ECJ's *Achmea* judgment is not transferable to the ECT, even though its rationale seems to apply to ECT based intra-EU investor-State arbitration without any restrictions. Furthermore, the ECT does not collide with the non-discrimination principle codified in Art. 18 TFEU or the principle of 'mutual trust' among EU Member States, as until Italy's withdrawal every EU Member State was a State party to the ECT.

It is true that the lack of a specific proceeding regarding the determination of the respondent in potential investor-State arbitration proceedings against EU Member States or the EU itself could potentially affect the internal division of competences and responsibilities within the EU. This, however, does not preclude the jurisdiction of arbitral tribunals over intra-EU investor-State arbitration proceedings. The same is true with regard to the alleged lack of 'territorial diversity' due to the fact that the EU's 'area' comprises the territory of all EU Member States and that there is an EU citizenship, which is additional to the national citizenship. There

---

306 Cf. D. Charlotin, *Russian Backed Project Investor, Nord Stream 2, Files Arbitration Against European Union Under the Energy Charter Treaty*, IA Reporter, 26 September 2019.

is no 'disconnection clause' excluding the applicability of the ECT in intra-EU disputes. Furthermore, the 'conflict clause' in Art. 16 ECT explicitly determines the rules to be applicable in case of conflict, which are the most favourable to the investor and the investment. Thus, as long as there is no ECJ decision to the contrary, the ECT is – unlike intra-EU BITs – applicable to intra-EU investor-State relations.

V Result

After an assessment of the nature of EU law and its position in the classical dichotomy between domestic law and international law, the present chapter has analysed the relationship between intra-EU BITs and EU law as well as between the ECT and EU law. The argument of the intra-EU BITs' invalidity due to the *lex posterior* principle has been rejected. The BITs continue to be valid treaties until their termination by the EU Member States. They have not been terminated by the entry into force of the Lisbon Treaty, nor by the accession of new Member States to the EU as they do not relate to the 'same subject matter' as the EU Treaties.

The ECJ, however, has found in its long awaited *Achmea* judgment, that investor-State arbitration provisions in intra-EU BITs are incompatible with EU law as they potentially undermine the autonomy of the EU legal order and the ECJ's monopoly in giving final and binding decisions regarding EU law, enshrined in Arts. 267 and 344 TFEU. Furthermore, as determined in this chapter, such provisions also discriminate European investors which do not fall under intra-EU BITs providing for investor-State arbitration and thus violate Art. 18 TFEU. The principle of 'mutual trust', however, does not affect their compatibility with EU law.

With regard to the ECJ's line of jurisprudence and especially its *Exportur* judgment,[307] the provisions of these BITs, namely their investor-State arbitration clauses, cannot apply in the relations between the respective Member States, as they were found to be contrary to the EU legal order.

According to Art. 30 (3) VCLT, this finding of incompatibility has to be considered and applied by arbitral tribunals, in case they consider EU law and intra-EU BITs to relate to the 'same subject matter'. This, however, is open to interpretation. Considering the current arbitral practice, it is rather likely that also future investors-State arbitration tribunals will reject the 'same subject matter' of both regimes.

The ECT is a particular case considering the fact that it is the only multilateral intra-EU IIA and that the EU itself is a Contracting Party to it. For these reasons, there is no incompatibility between both the ECT and EU law, even though the rationale of the *Achmea* judgment, namely the protection of the autonomy of the

---

307 ECJ, *Exportur*. C-3/91. Judgment, 10 November 1992, para. 8. See also ECJ, *American Bud.* C-478/07. Judgment, 8 September 2009, para. 98; ECJ, *Commission v Germany*. C-546/07. Judgment, 21 January 2010, para. 44; ECJ, *Ravil*. C-469/00. Judgment, 20 May 2003, para. 37.

EU legal order would also apply to investor-State arbitration proceedings based on the ECT.

The future of intra-EU investor protection and especially of investor-State arbitration remains an open question. The *Achmea* judgment was only able to provide some answers regarding the relationship between the 'international investment protection regime' and EU law. The following chapter will thus assess the effects of the *Achmea* decision and of the other findings made in this chapter and will offer solutions to the already existing and possibly arising challenges.

References

Aust, Anthony, *Modern Treaty Law and Practice*, 3. ed. (Cambridge: Cambridge University Press, 2013).

Aust, Helmut P., *Eine völkerrechtsfreundliche Union? Grund und Grenze der Öffnung des Europarechts zum Völkerrecht*, Europarecht 52 (2017), 106–21.

Basedow, Johann R., *The EU in the Global Investment Regime: Commission Entrepreneurship, Incremental Institutional Change and Business Lethargy* (London: Routledge, 2018).

Berger, Julien, *Intra-EU Investor-State Arbitration – The Uncertainty Continues: Unpacking the Advocate General's Opinion in Case C-284/16 (Achmea)*, Zeitschrift für Schiedsverfahren 15 (2017), 282–91.

Berger, Julien, *Die Bundesrepublik Deutschland – Internationaler Investitionsschutz und das Vattenfall-Verfahren*, Europäische Zeitschrift für Wirtschaftsrecht 31 (2020), 229–33.

Bermann, George A., *Navigating EU Law and the Law of International Arbitration*, Arbitration International 28 (2012), 397–445.

Bermann, George A., *International Arbitration and Private International Law*, Hague Academy of International Law (Leiden: Brill, 2017).

Binder, Christina, *A Treaty Law Perspective on Intra-EU BITs*, Journal of World Investment & Trade 17 (2016), 964–83.

Blackaby, Nigel, Partasides, Constantine, Redfern, Alan and Hunter, Martin, *Redfern and Hunter on International Arbitration*, 6. ed. (New York, London: Oxford University Press, 2015).

Bogdandy, Armin von and Ioannidis, Michael, *Das systemische Defizit: Merkmale, Instrumente und Probleme am Beispiel der Rechtsstaatlichkeit und des neuen Rechtsstaatlichkeitsverfahrens*, Zeitschrift für ausländisches öffentliches Recht und Völkerrecht 74 (2014), 283–328.

Chalmers, Damian, Davies, Gareth and Monti, Giorgio, *European Union Law*, 3. ed. (Cambridge: Cambridge University Press, 2014).

Craig, Paul and Búrca, Gráinne de, *EU Law: Text, Cases and Materials*, 6. ed. (Oxford: Oxford University Press, 2015).

Crawford, James, *Brownlie's Principles of Public International Law*, 8. ed. (Oxford: Oxford University Press, 2012).

Cremona, Marise, *Disconnection Clauses in EU Law and Practice* in C. Hillion and P. Koutrakos (eds.), *Mixed Agreements Revisited: The EU and Its Member States in the World* (Oxford: Hart, 2010), pp. 160–86.

Delgado Casteleiro, Andrés, *The International Responsibility of the European Union: From Competence to Normative Control* (Cambridge: Cambridge University Press, 2016).

Finke, Jasper, *Regime-collisions* in C. J. Tams, et al. (eds.), *Research Handbook on the Law of Treaties* (Cheltenham: Edward Elgar, 2014), pp. 415–46.

García-Castrillón, Carmen O., *Spain and Investment Arbitration* in A. de Mestral (ed.), *Second Thoughts: Investor State Arbitration Between Developed Democracies* (Montreal: McGill-Queen's University Press, 2017), pp. 285–308.

Gáspár-Szilágyi, Szilárd, *A Standing Investment Court Under TTIP from the Perspective of the Court of Justice of the European Union*, Journal of World Investment & Trade 17 (2016), 701–42.

Hess, Burkhard, *The Fate of Investment Dispute Resolution after the Achmea Decision of the European Court of Justice*, MPILux Research Paper Series (2018).

Hindelang, Steffen, *Repellent Forces*: *The CJEU and Investor-State Dispute Settlement*, Archiv des Völkerrechts 53 (2015), 68–89.

ILC, *Most-Favoured-Nation Clause: Final Report of the Study Group on the Most-Favoured-Nation Clause* (New York: United Nations, 2015).

Kaddous, Christine, *Arbitrage, Union européenne et accords bilatéraux d'investissement*, Swiss Review of International and European Law (2013), 3–8.

Kjos, Hege E., *Applicable Law in Investor-State Arbitration* (Oxford: Oxford University Press, 2013).

Lock, Tobias, *Why the European Union Is Not a State*: *Some Critical Remarks*, European Constitutional Law Review 5 (2009), 407–20.

Lock, Tobias, *The European Court of Justice and International Courts*, International Courts and Tribunals Series (Oxford: Oxford University Press, 2015).

Mariani, Paola, *The Future of BITs Between EU Member States* in G. Sacerdoti, et al. (eds.), *General Interests of Host States in International Investment Law* (Cambridge: Cambridge University Press, 2014), pp. 265–86.

McLachlan, Campbell, *Investment Treaty Arbitration* in A. J. van den Berg (ed.), *50 Years of the New York Convention* (Alphen aan den Rijn: Kluwer Law International, 2009), pp. 95–145.

Meyer, Frank, *Der Grundsatz gegenseitigen Vertrauens*: *Konzeptualisierung und Zukunftsperspektiven eines neuen Verfassungsprinzips*, Europarecht 52 (2017), 163–86.

Möldner, Mirka, *European Community and Union, Mixed Agreements*, (May 2011) in *MPEPIL (Online-Edition)* (Oxford: Oxford University Press).

Nagy, Csongor I., *Central European Perspectives on Investor-State Arbitration* in A. de Mestral (ed.), *Second Thoughts: Investor State Arbitration Between Developed Democracies* (Montreal: McGill-Queen's University Press, 2017), pp. 309–31.

Nagy, Csongor I., *Intra-EU Bilateral Investment Treaties and EU Law After Achmea*: "*Know Well What Leads You Forward and What Holds You Back*", German Law Journal 19 (2018), 981–1015.

Papp, Konstanze von, *Clash of "Autonomous Legal Orders"*: *Can EU Member State Courts Bridge the Jurisdictional Divide Between Investment Tribunals and the ECJ?* Common Market Law Review 50 (2013), 1039–81.

Reinisch, August, *Articles 30 and 59 of the Vienna Convention on the Law of Treaties in Action*: *The Decisions on Jurisdiction in the Eastern Sugar and Eureko Investment Arbitrations*, Legal Issues of Economic Integration 39 (2012), 157–77.

Reinisch, August, *Most Favoured Nation Treatment* in M. Bungenberg, et al. (eds.), *International Investment Law: A Handbook* (Baden-Baden: Nomos, 2015), pp. 807–45.

Roe, Thomas and Happold, Matthew, *Settlement of Investment Disputes Under the Energy Charter Treaty*, Law Practitioner Series (Cambridge: Cambridge University Press, 2011).

Rudolf, Walter, *Federal States*, (May 2011) in *MPEPIL (Online-Edition)* (Oxford: Oxford University Press).

Sasson, Monique, *Substantive Law in Investment Treaty Arbitration: The Unsettled Relationship Between International Law and Municipal Law*, 2. ed. (Alphen aan den Rijn: Wolters Kluwer, 2017), vol. 21.

Shaw, Malcolm N., *International Law*, 7. ed. (Cambridge: Cambridge University Press, 2014).

Spiermann, Ole, *Investment Arbitration: Applicable Law* in M. Bungenberg, et al. (eds.), *International Investment Law: A Handbook* (Baden-Baden: Nomos, 2015), pp. 1373–90.

Thürer, Daniel and Burri, Thomas, *Secession*, (June 2009) in *MPEPIL (Online-Edition)* (Oxford: Oxford University Press).

Thürer, Daniel and Burri, Thomas, *Self-Determination*, (December 2008) in *MPEPIL (Online-Edition)* (Oxford: Oxford University Press).

Tietje, Christian and Wackernagel, Clemens, *Enforcement of Intra-EU ICSID Awards: Multilevel Governance, Investment Tribunals and the Lost Opportunity of the Micula Arbitration*, Journal of World Investment & Trade 16 (2015), 205–47.

Watts, Arthur, *The International Law Commission 1949–1998: Volume Two: The Treaties Part II* (New York: Oxford University Press, 1999).

Weller, Matthias, *Mutual Trust: In Search of the Future of European Union Private International Law*, Journal of Private International Law 11 (2015), 64–102.

Witte, Bruno de, *The European Union as an International Legal Experiment* in G. de Búrca and J. Weiler (eds.), *The Worlds of European Constitutionalism* (Cambridge: Cambridge University Press, 2012), pp. 19–56.

Ziegler, Katja S., *Beyond Pluralism and Autonomy: Systemic Harmonization as a Paradigm for the Interaction of EU Law and International Law*, Yearbook of European Law 35 (2016), 667–711.

IV What future for intra-EU investor protection?

I Introduction

The preceding chapters have retraced the development of intra-EU investment protection through EU law and IIAs, compared the different regimes and analysed the lines of conflict among them. The present chapter, based on these findings, assesses the consequences of the *Achmea* decision and tries to answer the question as to the future of intra-EU investment protection.

The *Achmea* decision has clarified the interpretation of EU norms. The decision itself, however, has had no direct effect on the BITs in force. They remain valid international treaties applicable between the Contracting States and remain the legal basis for potential investor-State arbitration proceedings until the Member States amend or terminate them.

The Member States, however, are obliged to give legal effect to the *Achmea* judgment, which according to the EU Commission

> implies that all investor-State arbitration clauses in intra-EU BITs are inapplicable and that any arbitration tribunal established on the basis of such clauses lacks jurisdiction due to the absence of a valid arbitration agreement. As a consequence, national courts are under the obligation to annul any arbitral award rendered on that basis and to refuse to enforce it. Member States that are parties to pending cases, in whatever capacity, must also draw all necessary consequences from the Achmea judgment. Moreover, pursuant to the principle of legal certainty, they are bound to formally terminate their intra-EU BITs.[1]

Against this background, the EU Member States published three different declarations on the legal consequences of the *Achmea* judgment in January 2019.[2] On

---

1 EU Commission, *Protection of intra-EU investment – COM (2018) 547/2: Communication from the Commission to the European Parliament and the Council*, 19 June 2018, at p. 3.
2 Representatives of 22 EU Member States, *Declaration on the Legal Consequences of the Judgment of the ECJ in Achmea and on Investment Protection in the EU*, 15 January 2019, signed by Austria, Belgium, Bulgaria, Croatia, Cyprus, the Czech Republic, Denmark, Estonia, France,

May 5, 2020, 23 of the remaining 27 EU Member States signed an "Agreement for the Termination of Bilateral Investment Treaties between the Member States of the European Union" (in the following Multilateral Agreement for the Termination of intra-EU BITs).[3]

This chapter analyses the scope of the *Achmea* judgment and its effect on intra-EU BITs (II.) and on the Energy Charter Treaty (III.). It then assesses the impact on domestic courts which are faced with challenges of intra-EU investor-State arbitration awards as well their recognition and enforcement (IV.) and on pending and potentially upcoming intra-EU investor-State arbitration proceedings (V.). In the following, the need for a possible substitute for the current 'international investment protection regime' within the EU is discussed (VI.), before developing potential policy solutions to the open challenges (VII.). The chapter ends with a general assessment (VIII.).

II Termination of intra-EU BITs

The *Achmea* decision has provided clarity in so far that intra-EU BIT arbitration clauses 'such as' the one contained in Art. 8 of the Netherlands–Czechoslovakia BIT are incompatible with EU law. However, an ECJ decision cannot terminate international treaties, regardless whether they have been concluded by Member States or by the EU itself. The finding of intra-EU BIT investor-State arbitration provisions being incompatible with EU law, does therefore not affect the Member States' obligation under international law to comply with the intra-EU BITs' provisions according to the principle of *pacta sunt servanda* codified in Art. 26 VCLT.

Nonetheless, every Member State that is a party to an intra-EU BIT providing for investor-State arbitration is obliged by virtue of Art. 4 (3) TEU to adapt to the ECJ's decision. Thus, as just shown in this chapter's introduction, the EU Commission has in reaction to the *Achmea* judgment reiterated its request vis-à-vis the EU Member States to terminate the intra-EU BITs and announced that it will monitor the progress and if necessary pursue existing or initiate new infringement proceedings against non-complying Member States.[4] In the event of non-compliance with the ECJ's decision, Member States could face infringement

---

Germany, Greece, Ireland, Italy, Latvia, Lithuania, the Netherlands, Poland, Portugal, Romania, Slovakia, Spain and the United Kingdom. Two other declarations were signed the following day by five other Member States, Representatives of Finland, Luxembourg, Malta, Slovenia and Sweden, *Declaration on the Enforcement of the Judgement of the ECJ in Achmea and on Investment Protection in the EU,* 16 January 2019. Hungary issued a separate declaration, Representative of Hungary, *Declaration on the Legal Consequences of the Judgment of the ECJ in Achmea and on Investment Protection in the EU,* 16 January 2019.

3 The four non-signatories are Austria, Finland, Ireland and Sweden.

4 EU Commission, *Protection of intra-EU investment – COM (2018) 547/2: Communication from the Commission to the European Parliament and the Council,* 19 June 2018, 2 f.

proceedings leading to important lump sums or penalty payments.[5] While all Member States had declared their intention to terminate all existing intra-EU BITs in January 2019,[6] only 23 Member States have signed the Multilateral Agreement for the Termination of intra-EU BITs in May 2020, among them Poland, that had already terminated 18 of its 23 intra-EU BITs in reaction to the *Achmea* judgment before signing the Multilateral Agreement.[7] The four non signatories are Austria, Finland, Ireland and Sweden. Ireland, however, is not party to any intra-EU BIT and thus not directly affected neither by this Agreement nor the *Achmea* judgment.

The EU Commission has sent a letter of formal notice to Finland on May 14, 2020, for failing to effectively remove intra-EU BITs from its legal order. In this letter the Commission expressed its regret that Finland did not sign the plurilateral treaty alongside other Member States and announced to initiate an infringement proceeding against Finland if it continued to fail to terminate its intra-EU BITs.[8] On the same date the EU Commission sent a similar letter of formal notice to the United Kingdom for not terminating its intra-EU BITs, as under the Withdrawal Agreement, EU law continues to apply to the United Kingdom during the transition period. It is, however, very unlikely that the United Kingdom will comply with this request, as in light of Brexit the United Kingdom has a genuine interest in maintaining its ten formerly intra-EU BITs.[9] These BITs could become interesting gateways for British investors to the European market after Brexit, in case they are not terminated in result of the negotiations on the future EU–UK relationship.

---

5 Infringement proceedings can lead to penalty payments of up to 852,642 € per day and/or a one-time lump sum of up to 10,610,000 € depending on various factors inter alia a Member State's GDP, cf. W. Cremer, *Art. 260 AEUV* in C. Calliess and M. Ruffert (eds.), *EUV/AEUV – Kommentar*, 5. ed. (München: Beck, 2016), at paras. 13 ff.

6 Representatives of 22 EU Member States, *Declaration on the Legal Consequences of the Judgment of the ECJ in Achmea and on Investment Protection in the EU*, 15 January 2019, paras. 5 and 8. With a very similar wording, Representatives of Finland, Luxembourg, Malta, Slovenia and Sweden, *Declaration on the Enforcement of the Judgement of the ECJ in Achmea and on Investment Protection in the EU*, 16 January 2019, paras. 5 and 8; Representative of Hungary, *Declaration on the Legal Consequences of the Judgment of the ECJ in Achmea and on Investment Protection in the EU*, 16 January 2019, paras. 4 and 7.

7 Poland unilaterally denounced its BITs with Austria, Finland, France, Germany, Greece, the Netherlands, Portugal, Spain, Sweden, Croatia, Cyprus and Slovenia, as well as with the United Kingdom. The BITs with Denmark, the Czech Republic, Estonia, Latvia and Romania were terminated by consent. Thus, before the entry into force of the Termination Agreement only the Polish intra-EU BITs with the Belgium-Luxembourg Economic Union, Bulgaria, Hungary, Lithuania and Slovakia remain in force. See in detail, UNCTAD, *Investment Policy Hub: International Investment Agreements Navigator – Poland.* https://investmentpolicy.unctad.org/international-investment-agreements/countries/168/poland (21 May 2020).

8 EU Commission, *May Infringements Package: Key Decisions: INF 20/859*, 14 May 2020. https://ec.europa.eu/commission/presscorner/detail/en/INF_20_859 (21 May 2020).

9 The UK has concluded BITs with the following EU Member States: Bulgaria, Croatia, the Czech Republic, Estonia, Hungary, Latvia, Lithuania, Malta, Slovakia and Slovenia. They all provide for investor-State arbitration.

Under public international law, the termination of a treaty has no specific conditions. According to Art. 54 VCLT, "the termination of a treaty or the withdrawal of a party may take place in conformity with the provisions of the treaty; or at any time by consent of all the parties after consultation with the other contracting States." Every intra-EU BIT contains a termination clause. Although these clauses differ from treaty to treaty, they generally provide for the possibility of a unilateral denunciation of the treaty.[10] Art. 10 (2) of the 2002 Sweden–Romania BIT contains an exemplary termination clause:

> This Agreement shall remain in force for a period of twenty years. Thereafter it shall remain in force until the expiration of twelve months from the date that either Contracting Party in writing notifies the other Contracting Party of its decision to terminate this Agreement.

Similar to that provision, most BITs have an initial minimum term of application of ten to 20 years, which serves to create a certain degree of stability for foreign investors and guarantees that they can rely on the BIT for at least that period of time.[11] After that period, BITs generally provide for a tacit renewal, which keeps the treaty in force after completion of the initial term of duration.

The initial duration period of the great majority of intra-EU BITs has already expired as most of these treaties have entered into force in the 1990s and early 2000s. There are only six exceptions known to the author, in which the initial duration of an intra-EU BIT has not yet lapsed.[12] After the lapse of the initial lifetime of a BIT, the renewal clause is activated if the parties to the treaty have not denounced it on time or terminated it by mutual consent. Some renewal clauses provide for an indefinite continuation of a BIT's lifetime, limited by the State

---

10 While 'denunciation' and 'withdrawal' are often used synonymously, this study uses the term 'denunciation' regarding bilateral treaties and the term 'withdrawal' regarding multilateral treaties. In that sense, cf. K. von der Decken, *Art. 42* in O. Dörr and K. Schmalenbach (eds.), *Vienna Convention on the Law of Treaties: A Commentary*, 2. ed. (Berlin: Springer, 2018), at para. 19; A. Aust, *Modern Treaty Law and Practice*, 3. ed. (Cambridge: Cambridge University Press, 2013), at 245.

11 Cf. J. Harrison, *The Life and Death of BITs: Legal Issues Concerning Survival Clauses and the Termination of Investment Treaties,* Journal of World Investment & Trade (2012), 928–50, at 933 ff.

12 This is the case regarding the following treaties: The 1999 Croatia–Finland BIT, which entered into force on 1 November 2002, and provides for an initial duration of 20 years, ending on 31 October 2022. The 2000 Croatia–Denmark BIT, which entered into force on January 12th, 2002, and provides for an initial duration of 20 years, ending on 11 January 2022. The 2000 Croatia–Sweden BIT, which entered into force on 1 August 2002, and provides for an initial duration period of 20 years, ending on 31 July 2022. The 2001 BLEU–Bulgaria BIT, which entered into force on 29 December 2003, and provides for an initial duration of 20 years, ending on 28 December 2023. The 2002 Sweden–Romania BIT, which entered into force on 1 April 2003, and provides for an initial duration of 20 years, ending on 31 March 2023 and the 2005 Bulgaria–Lithuania BIT, which entered into force on 25 April 2006 and provides for an initial duration of 15 years, ending on 24 April 2021.

parties' right to terminate it by prior written notice. Other renewal clauses prolong a BIT's lifetime for an additional fixed-time period, excluding a unilateral termination prior to the completion of the new period.[13] In any case a BIT remains applicable until it is terminated. There are two possible ways to terminate a BIT: Either through a unilateral denunciation (1.) or through a termination by mutual agreement (2.). The latter can take either the form of a multilateral treaty as chosen by the 23 signatory States of the Multilateral Agreement for the Termination of intra-EU BITs or take the form of a bilateral agreement which might be accompanied by a previous renegotiation of the treaty. Both unilateral and consent-based termination, however, might trigger sunset clauses which can potentially prolong a BIT's protection for several years after the termination becomes effective (3.).

1 Unilateral termination or denunciation

The denunciation of a treaty does generally not face major obstacles. However, as just shown, most BITs contain a clause which temporarily prohibits the denunciation of a BIT and stipulates a minimum period of application. After this initial term, a unilateral denunciation is possible in accordance with the VCLT and the BIT's respective termination clause, which often requires a denunciation in writing which will take effect after a certain period of time, often 12 months. The particularity of a denunciation, however, is that it will always trigger the BIT's sunset clause, which will extend the BITs protection for already established investments for a certain period of time.[14]. Notwithstanding the announcement of all Member States to mutually terminate the existing intra-EU BITs, Poland unilaterally denounced 12 of its intra-EU BITs in reaction to the *Achmea* judgment.[15]

2 Termination by mutual agreement

Party autonomy is the central principle governing the termination of a treaty according to the VCLT. The States parties to a BIT are the 'masters of the agreement' and can terminate it at any time by mutual consent.[16] This mutual consent can take the form of both a bilateral agreement between both States Parties to a BIT or the form of a multilateral treaty, such as the Multilateral Agreement for the

---

13 See also F. M. Lavopa, L. E. Barreiros and V. M. Bruno, *How to Kill a BIT and not Die Trying: Legal and Political Challenges of Denouncing or Renegotiating Bilateral Investment Treaties*, Journal of International Economic Law (2013), 869–91, at 879; K. Nowrot, *Termination and Renegotiation of International Investment Agreements* in S. Hindelang and M. Krajewski (eds.), *Shifting Paradigms in International Investment Law: More Balanced, Less Isolated, Increasingly Diversified* (Oxford: Oxford University Press, 2016), pp. 227–65, at 239 ff.

14 See in detail, Chapter IV: II. 3.

15 UNCTAD, *Investment Policy Hub*. https://investmentpolicy.unctad.org/international-investment-agreements/countries/168/poland (21 May 2020).

16 See also ILC, *Draft Articles on the Law of Treaties with commentaries* – Yearbook of the ILC, 1966, at Commentary on Art. 51 VCLT, at 249.

Termination of intra-EU BITs, the purpose of which is to terminate the previously concluded BITs in accordance with Art. 59 (1) lit. a) VCLT.

In that sense, Art. 2 of the Multilateral Agreement for the Termination of intra-EU BIT provides that the intra-EU BITs listed in Annex A of the Agreement as well as the sunset clauses contained therein "are terminated according to the terms set out in this Agreement". Pursuant to Art. 4 (2) of the Multilateral Agreement for the Termination of intra-EU BITs this termination shall take effect, for each of these BITs, as soon as this Agreement enters into force for the relevant Contracting Parties.

The timing of termination is decisive for ISDS proceedings. If a tribunal is seized before the termination of the BIT, its jurisdiction remains unaffected by the BIT's termination. A retroactive extinguishment of exercised rights is excluded.[17] Furthermore, once investors have initiated an arbitration proceeding under a BIT, they have accepted the standing offer to arbitrate and thus concluded an arbitration agreement with the host State which is detached from the IIA and cannot unilaterally be revoked.[18] Thus, the mutual termination of a BIT does in principle not affect previously initiated investor-State arbitration proceedings and an arbitral tribunal's jurisdiction.[19] Against this backdrop, the signatories of the Multilateral Agreement for the Termination of intra-EU BITs drafted Art. 7 of that Agreement. It provides that if Contracting States are party to a BIT on the basis of which an intra-EU arbitration proceeding has been initiated, which is still pending, the States shall

> inform, in cooperation with each other [...] arbitral tribunals about the legal consequences of the *Achmea* judgment [...] and where they are party to judicial proceedings concerning an arbitral award issued on the basis of a BIT, ask the competent national court, including in any third country, as the case may be, to set the arbitral award aside, annul it or refrain from recognising and enforcing it.

---

17 Cf. C. Binder, *A Treaty Law Perspective on Intra-EU BITs*, Journal of World Investment & Trade 17 (2016), 964–83, at 981; T. Voon, A. Mitchell and J. Munro, *Parting Ways: The Impact of Mutual Termination of Investment Treaties on Investor Rights,* ICSID Review 29 (2014), 451–73, at 464. See also ICJ, *Nottebohm (Liechtenstein v Guatemala).* Judgment on Preliminary Objection, 18 November 1953, ICJ Rep 111, p. 123.

18 See for example, Art. 25 (1) ICSID Convention. See also C. Binder, *A Treaty Law Perspective on Intra-EU BITs,* Journal of World Investment & Trade 17 (2016), 982. The validity of such an arbitration agreement in case of intra-EU investor-State arbitration is discussed in detail in Chapter IV: IV. 1. a) and Chapter IV: IV. 2.

19 This, however, has to be distinguished from the doctrine of separability in commercial arbitration according to which the arbitration clause is a separate and autonomous agreement from the contract in which it is contained. On this doctrine, cf. N. Blackaby, C. Partasides, A. Redfern and M. Hunter, *Redfern and Hunter on International Arbitration,* 6th ed. (New York, London: Oxford University Press, 2015), at paras. 5.100 ff. It is, however, not applicable to intra-EU BITs as these treaties do not contain an arbitration clause in the sense of an actual agreement to arbitrate, but just an offer to arbitrate, which the investor still needs to accept.

While this approach might deter investors from initiating new investor-State arbitration proceedings, it has, however, no effect on the jurisdiction of arbitral tribunals in already pending proceedings.

The Contracting States are indeed the 'masters of the agreement'. It has, nonetheless, been argued that the States' right to terminate a BIT could be limited by a direct or analogous application of the principle of 'third party rights' codified in Art. 37 VCLT.[20] According to Art. 37 (2) VCLT,

> when a right has arisen for a third State [...], the right may not be revoked or modified by the parties if it is established that the right was intended not to be revocable or subject to modification without the consent of the third State.

Art. 37 (2) VCLT is not directly applicable to investors as it explicitly refers to third States. An analogous application to investors would require a legal lacuna regarding investor's rights granted through a treaty and that in this regard the investors' situation is similar to that of third States.[21] In the present case, however, the investors' situation is not comparable to that of third States. In difference to States, investors are no subjects of public international law and generally do not have international legal personality, even though the creation and further development of investor-State arbitration and directly accessible human rights courts are an expression of the continuing move from a purely State-centric international law towards a more inclusive international legal order increasingly recognizing the role and position of non-State actors within the international legal order. Nonetheless, while especially large corporations often conclude concession agreements with foreign States, these contracts are not governed by the law of treaties.[22] According to Art. 36 (1) VCLT, third States have to assent for a treaty between other States to provide rights for them. No similar condition exists for foreign investors. Even if BITs created direct legal entitlements for foreign investors,[23] their consent would be no condition for the mutual termination of an intra-EU BIT by the contracting States.[24] Such a precondition of investors' consent to a

---

20 Arguing that Art. 37 (2) VCLT "represents a general principle which is applicable to all third party right holders" and thus also to foreign investors falling under a BIT, cf. with further references, J. Harrison, *The Life and Death of BITs: Legal Issues Concerning Survival Clauses and the Termination of Investment Treaties,* Journal of World Investment & Trade (2012), at 944 ff. See also accepting the possibility of an analogous application of Art. 37 (2) VCLT, C. Wackernagel, *The Twilight of the BITs? EU Judicial Proceedings, the Consensual Termination of intra-EU BITs and Why that Matters for International Law,* Beiträge zum Transnationalen Wirtschaftsrecht (2016), at 16 f.

21 Cf. S. Vöneky, *Analogy in International Law,* (February 2008) in *MPEPIL (Online-Edition).*

22 Cf. J. Crawford, *Brownlie's Principles of Public International Law,* 8th ed. (Oxford: Oxford University Press, 2012), at 121 f.

23 On this question, see Chapter IV: II. 3.

24 See also C. Binder, *A Treaty Law Perspective on Intra-EU BITs,* Journal of World Investment & Trade 17 (2016), 979; Y.-I. Kim, *Investment Law and the Individual* in M. Bungenberg, et al. (eds.), *International Investment Law: A Handbook* (Baden-Baden: Nomos, 2015), pp. 1585–601,

BIT termination would also practically be impossible to observe considering the inifinte number of potential investors falling under a BIT.

3 Sunset clauses

EU Member States could technically terminate all intra-EU BITs in the twinkling of an eye. A difficulty or rather a challenge regarding the termination of intra-EU BITs, however, is the fact that every single one of them contains a 'sunset clause',[25] which extends the BIT's protection for already established investments for a certain period of time after the termination has become effective, generally ten to 20 years.

Sunset clauses are aimed at protecting the legitimate expectations of the investors of both parties, avoiding that the investment suddenly loses its protection because of a unilateral decision of the host State, i.e. a denunciation of the treaty. This is of particular relevance for foreign investors, as their investments are generally cost-intensive and planed long-term and thus require a certain degree of risk mitigation.[26] While a sunset clause does not extend a BIT's protection for an infinite time, the idea behind it is to give the investor a further period of protection to restructure and rearrange the investment and to adapt it to the new circumstances.

An exemplary clause is Art. 27 (3) of the 2002 Austria–Malta BIT:

> In respect of investments made prior to the date of termination of the present Agreement the provisions [...] of the present Agreement shall continue to be effective for a further period of ten years from the date of termination of the present Agreement.

This clause does not differentiate between mutual termination and denunciation but is linked to the 'termination' in general. Some sunset clauses, however, only apply to unilateral denunciations.[27] Those, are not triggered by a mutual termination of the BIT which thus has an immediate effect without any prolongation of protection for already established foreign investors and their investments. Most sunset clauses, however, have a wide wording like the one in the 2002

---

at 1599 ff; A. Roberts, *Triangular Treaties: The Extent and Limits of Investment Treaty Rights,* Harvard International Law Journal 57 (2015), 353–417, at 404; K. Nowrot, *Termination and Renegotiation of International Investment Agreements* in S. Hindelang and M. Krajewski (eds.), *Shifting Paradigms in International Investment Law* (Oxford: Oxford University Press, 2016), at 245 f.

25 Sometimes also referred to as 'survival clause' or 'grandfathering clause'.

26 Cf. Y.-I. Kim, *Investment Law and the Individual* in M. Bungenberg, et al. (eds.), *International Investment Law: A Handbook* (Baden-Baden: Nomos, 2015), p. 1599; T. Voon, A. Mitchell and J. Munro, *Parting Ways: The Impact of Mutual Termination of Investment Treaties on Investor Rights,* ICSID Review 29 (2014), 466.

27 See for example, Art. 12 (2) of the 1994 Croatia–Romania BIT. See also C. Binder, *A Treaty Law Perspective on Intra-EU BITs,* Journal of World Investment & Trade 17 (2016), 977; T. Voon, A. Mitchell and J. Munro, *Parting Ways: The Impact of Mutual Termination of Investment Treaties on Investor Rights,* ICSID Review 29 (2014), 466.

Austria–Malta BIT and could thus potentially be interpreted also to apply to mutual terminations, thereby practically creating a suspensive effect for the termination, regarding already existing investments.

In their political declaration the EU Member States have taken a different position and unanimously explained that as a direct consequence of the *Achmea* judgment, sunset clauses contained in intra-EU BITs do not produce any effect with regard to intra-EU investor-State arbitration provisions.[28]

It seems, however, at least questionable whether investor-State arbitration tribunals, that will ultimately be responsible to determine the sunset clauses' effects, will follow this line of argument. So far, they have taken the view that their jurisdiction is solely based on the BIT in question and could thus possibly ignore the ECJ's interpretation when establishing their own jurisdiction. In that scenario, sunset clauses contained in intra-EU BITs could thus prevent the ECJ's *Achmea* decision from unfolding its full effects and create very long transition periods for investor-State protection within the EU. In other words, the 'risk' of further investor-State arbitration proceedings might not vanish with the intra-EU BIT's termination. The respective sunset clauses would rather continue to provide the possibility for investors to initiate proceedings for up to 10, 15 or 20 years regarding investments made before the termination of a BIT.[29]

To avoid this scenario of sunset clauses undermining the *Achmea* decision and unnecessarily prolonging the intra-EU BITs' lifetime, the EU Commission suggested a way to neutralize these clauses or to prevent them from taking effect. It envisaged a two-step approach, starting with the renegotiation or amendment of the BITs, abolishing the sunset clauses, followed by the mutual termination of the BIT, a 'legal second' after the amendment took effect.[30] This approach was originally

---

28 Representatives of 22 EU Member States, *Declaration on the Legal Consequences of the Judgment of the ECJ in Achmea and on Investment Protection in the EU*, 15 January 2019; Representatives of Finland, Luxembourg, Malta, Slovenia and Sweden, *Declaration on the Enforcement of the Judgement of the ECJ in Achmea and on Investment Protection in the EU*, 16 January 2019; Representative of Hungary, *Declaration on the Legal Consequences of the Judgment of the ECJ in Achmea and on Investment Protection in the EU*, 16 January 2019. See also in a similar way, K. Nowrot, *Termination and Renegotiation of International Investment Agreements* in S. Hindelang and M. Krajewski (eds.), *Shifting Paradigms in International Investment Law* (Oxford: Oxford University Press, 2016), at 256 ff., according to whom even broadly phrased sunset clauses do not cover terminations based on the mutual consent of the Contracting States, as this would contravene the Contracting States' original intention.

29 The sunset clauses contained in intra-EU BITs either provide for a transition period of ten years, see for example Art. 14 (3) of the 2005 Bulgaria–Lithuania BIT, for 15 years, see for example Art. 13 (3) of the 1999 Sweden–Slovenia BIT or for 20 years, see for example Art. 14 (2) of the 2001 BLEU–Croatia BIT. Most Italian BITs provided for transition periods of only five years; they all have already been terminated.

30 See also J. K. Schäfer and J. P. Gaffney, *Intra-EU BITs: Toothless Tigers or Do They Still Bite?: The OLG Frankfurt Considers the Impact of EU Law on the Investor-State Dispute Resolution Mechanism*, Zeitschrift für Schiedsverfahren (2013), 68–78, at 71; C. Wackernagel, *The Twilight of the BITs? EU Judicial Proceedings, the Consensual Termination of intra-EU BITs and Why that Matters for International Law*, Beiträge zum Transnationalen Wirtschaftsrecht (2016), 14; T. Voon,

adopted by some Member States,[31] but rejected by the majority of Member States.[32] Eventually, the Member States agreed on a different approach. Article 2 (2) and Article 3 of the Multilateral Agreement for the Termination of intra-EU BITs provide that the sunset clauses of the BITs listed in Annex A and Annex B are terminated by this Agreement and shall not produce legal effects.

The approach taken by the 23 signatories of the Multilateral Agreement for the Termination of intra-EU BITs is, however, not uncontroversial. While the termination of a treaty by the States party to it can in principle be seen as an expression of the exercise of these States' sovereignty, for some authors a mutual termination of a BIT that circumvents its sunset clause, could amount to a violation of the States' commitments vis-à-vis foreign investors, especially regarding the doctrine of acquired rights and the principle of legitimate expectations.[33] Whether States could potentially violate the rights and expectations of foreign investors by terminating a BIT, however, depends on the lively debated question whether BITs grant rights to investors and if so whether these rights are directly conferred to them or are only derivative rights, i.e. arising out of the reciprocal rights and obligations of the States parties as determined in the BIT.[34]

A. Mitchell and J. Munro, *Parting Ways: The Impact of Mutual Termination of Investment Treaties on Investor Rights,* ICSID Review 29 (2014), at 467 f.

31　See for example, the Czech position, as cited in, SCC Arbitration, *Eastern Sugar B.V. v Czech Republic.* SCC No. 088/2004. Partial Award, 27 March 2007, para. 127, to terminate BITs by means of mutual agreements, which should "eliminate the application of transitional investment treaty provisions that enable the application of investment treaties for additional, typically ten-year, periods." The Czech Republic followed this 'two-step' approach in the mutually agreed intra-EU BIT termination processes with Denmark, Italy, Malta and Slovenia. With further references, K. Nowrot, *Termination and Renegotiation of International Investment Agreements* in S. Hindelang and M. Krajewski (eds.), *Shifting Paradigms in International Investment Law* (Oxford: Oxford University Press, 2016), p. 263.

32　See for example, *2007 Annual EFC Report to the Commission and the Council on the Movement of Capital and the Freedom of Payments,* 23 November 2007, at para. 15.

33　Cf. E. Gaillard, *L'Avenir des Traités de Protection des Investissements* in C. Leben (ed.), *Droit international des investissements et de l'arbitrage transnational* (Paris: Editions Pedone, 2015), pp. 1027–47, at 1032 f. See also with a slightly more moderate view, J. Harrison, *The Life and Death of BITs: Legal Issues Concerning Survival Clauses and the Termination of Investment Treaties,* Journal of World Investment & Trade (2012), at 948 f. For a great overview, see finally also K. Nowrot, *Termination and Renegotiation of International Investment Agreements* in S. Hindelang and M. Krajewski (eds.), *Shifting Paradigms in International Investment Law* (Oxford: Oxford University Press, 2016), at 252 f.

34　On the debate see in great detail and with further references, C. Binder, *A Treaty Law Perspective on Intra-EU BITs,* Journal of World Investment & Trade 17 (2016), at 980 f; A. Roberts, *Power and Persuasion in Investment Treaty Interpretation: The Dual Role of States,* American Journal of International Law 104 (2010), 179–225, at 184; A. K. Bjorklund, *Private Rights and Public International Law: Why Competition Among International Economic Law Tribunals is Not Working,* Hastings Law Journal 59 (2007), 241–307, at 263 ff; Y.-I. Kim, *Investment Law and the Individual* in M. Bungenberg, et al. (eds.), *International Investment Law: A Handbook* (Baden-Baden: Nomos, 2015), at 1599 ff; T. Voon, A. Mitchell and J. Munro, *Parting Ways: The Impact of Mutual Termination of Investment Treaties on Investor Rights,* ICSID Review 29 (2014), at 454 ff; F. M. Lavopa, L. E. Barreiros and V. M. Bruno, *How to Kill a BIT and Not Die Trying,* Journal

With regard to the position of the individual, international investment law can be situated between human rights law and the law of diplomatic protection.[35] In case of diplomatic protection, an individual's claim regarding an alleged violation of another State's international legal obligations is taken up by the individual's State of nationality and becomes that State's own claim.[36] On the other hand, human rights treaties grant individual rights to all individuals under a certain jurisdiction based on the principle of universality and in certain circumstances even allow individuals direct access to and standing before an international court, as it is the case for example with the ECHR and the European Court of Human Rights.[37] As discussed earlier, most IIAs contain a standing offer to arbitrate which every investor falling under the scope of the treaty can accept by initiating an ISDS proceeding.[38] In difference to human rights law, which is founded on the principle of universality, international investment law, however, is based on the principle of reciprocity and consent.[39] International investment law can thus be positioned between diplomatic protection and human rights law as only nationals of the States parties to an IIA enjoy the protection guaranteed in the treaty but can also invoke these rights against the host State without the home State needing to become active. However, the only direct relationship between an investor and the host State is created through the investor-State arbitration provision.[40] Substantive protection standards on the other hand are only conferred upon the investors through the agreement between the States parties.[41] Thus, if an investor accepts the host State's offer by initiating arbitration proceedings, "the result is the creation of an entirely new, direct, relationship between that investor and the State Party concerned."[42]

of International Economic Law (2013), at 886 ff; J. Harrison, *The Life and Death of BITs: Legal Issues Concerning Survival Clauses and the Termination of Investment Treaties,* Journal of World Investment & Trade (2012), at 948 f. See also Advocate General Wathelet, according to whom it is firmly established that the provisions of a BIT may confer rights on investors, ECJ, *Achmea.* C-284/16. Opinion of Advocate General Wathelet, 19 September 2017, ECLI:EU:C:2017:699, para. 156.

35 C. Binder, *A Treaty Law Perspective on Intra-EU BITs,* Journal of World Investment & Trade 17 (2016), 980.

36 Cf. PCIJ, *The Mavrommatis Palestine Concessions.* Series A No 2. Judgment, 30 August 1924, p. 12. See also Chapter I: II. 2. b).

37 Cf. Chapter I: III. 4. See also C. Binder, *A Treaty Law Perspective on Intra-EU BITs,* Journal of World Investment & Trade 17 (2016), 980.

38 Cf. Chapter II: IV. 1. a).

39 Cf. T. Voon, A. Mitchell and J. Munro, *Parting Ways: The Impact of Mutual Termination of Investment Treaties on Investor Rights,* ICSID Review 29 (2014), 458.

40 Cf. J. Paulsson, *Arbitration Without Privity,* ICSID Review 10 (1995), 232–57.

41 See also PCA, *European American Investment Bank v Slovakia.* PCA Case No. 2010–17. Award on Jurisdiction, 22 October 2012, para. 445.

42 Ibid.

However, even human rights treaties do generally not "confer acquired rights to individuals that continue to exist even if the treaty is denounced."[43] Although human rights treaties grant subjective rights to the individuals falling under their scope of application,[44] many of them do not protect these individuals against the termination of the treaty by a State party, but often even contain explicit withdrawal clauses such as Art. 58 ECHR.[45] An exception in this regard is the International Covenant on Civil and Political Rights (ICCPR), which does not contain any provision on its termination or withdrawal. Thus, when the Democratic People's Republic of Korea, better known as North Korea, attempted to withdraw from the ICCPR in 1997, the Human Rights Committee found that a withdrawal was not possible, as the Covenant had created irrevocable rights for the people of North Korea.[46] According to the General Comments adopted by the Human Rights Committee,

> The rights enshrined in the Covenant belong to the people living in the territory of the State party. [...] once the people are accorded the protection of the rights under the Covenant, such protection devolves with territory and continues to belong to them, notwithstanding change in government of the State party, including dismemberment in more than one State or State succession or any subsequent action of the State party designed to divest them of the rights guaranteed by the Covenant.[47]

While the UN Secretary General, as the ICCPR's treaty depositary, took a different position on this question accepting a withdrawal if all other treaty parties agreed to it,[48] the ICCPR's case can according to Roberts, not be transposed to BITs as these are reciprocal treaties, providing rights of lesser normative quality than human rights,[49] and providing for treaty denunciation and termination.

---

43 S. Wittich, *Art. 70* in O. Dörr and K. Schmalenbach (eds.), *Vienna Convention on the Law of Treaties: A Commentary*, 2. ed. (Berlin: Springer, 2018), at para. 30.

44 For a great overview, see A. Peters, *Jenseits der Menschenrechte: Die Rechtsstellung des Individuums im Völkerrecht* (Tübingen: Mohr Siebeck, 2014), at 387 ff.

45 Another example is Art. 78 of the *1969 American Convention on Human Rights* – 1144 UNTS 143. In greater detail, C. Binder, *A Treaty Law Perspective on Intra-EU BITs*, Journal of World Investment & Trade 17 (2016), 980.

46 Human Rights Committee, *General Comment 26 (61) – CCPR/C/21/Rev.1/Add.8/Rev.1*, 8 December 1997, at para. 5. See also A. Roberts, *Triangular Treaties: The Extent and Limits of Investment Treaty Rights*, Harvard International Law Journal 57 (2015), at 405 f.

47 Human Rights Committee, *General Comment 26 (61) – CCPR/C/21/Rev.1/Add.8/Rev.1*, 8 December 1997, para. 4.

48 UN Secretary General, *C. N. 4 6 7 .19 9 7. TREATIES -10 (Depositary Notification*, 12.11.1997.

49 A. Roberts, *Triangular Treaties: The Extent and Limits of Investment Treaty Rights*, Harvard International Law Journal 57 (2015), 406. See also C. Wackernagel, *The Twilight of the BITs? EU Judicial Proceedings, the Consensual Termination of intra-EU BITs and Why that Matters for International Law*, Beiträge zum Transnationalen Wirtschaftsrecht (2016), at 25 ff.

This is convincing. Even though BITs guarantee a specific level of protection and give an investor the right to initiate an investor-State arbitration proceeding, the States remain the masters of the treaties and the investor's legal position cannot hinder them to terminate the treaty by a mutual agreement which abolishes its sunset clause, be it bilateral or multilateral.[50] As long as an investor has not accepted the standing offer to arbitration contained in a BIT, no special relationship arises between the investor and the host State. From the moment the investor has accepted the offer to arbitrate and initiated an investor-State arbitration proceeding a later termination of the BIT does not affect the pending proceeding. Hence, there is no reason to interpret the BITs to grant rights to investors that would prevent a consent-based termination or an amendment of the treaty by the States parties to it. As aptly put by Wackernagel,

> while BITs might establish international individual rights that are not subordinated to the investor's home State's interests, as they used to be in the traditional concept of diplomatic protection, the individual investor remains subject to the State interest as soon as States act in concert.[51]

Thus, even though, the clarification in Art. 2 (2) and Art. 3 of the Multilateral Agreement for the Termination of intra-EU BITs might not have been necessary, they clearly express the intention of the 23 signatories regarding the abolishment and non-applicability of the sunset clauses and thus help to avoid ambiguities and uncertainty regarding the legal situation of investors falling under the intra-EU BITs in Annex A and Annex B of the Agreement.

4 Interim findings

In sum, the Member States can terminate the BITs through a subsequent multilateral treaty pursuant to Art. 59 VCLT, which explicitly provides the termination of the existing BITs and states that the sunset-clauses will no longer take effect. With the entry into force of the Multilateral Agreement for the Termination of intra-EU BITs most intra-EU BITs will seize to exist. It, however, remains to be seen, whether Austria, Finland and Sweden will follow their fellow Member States or

---

50 See in this regard also, C. Binder, *A Treaty Law Perspective on Intra-EU BITs,* Journal of World Investment & Trade 17 (2016), 981; Y.-I. Kim, *Investment Law and the Individual* in M. Bungenberg, et al. (eds.), *International Investment Law: A Handbook* (Baden-Baden: Nomos, 2015), at 1599 ff; T. Voon, A. Mitchell and J. Munro, *Parting Ways: The Impact of Mutual Termination of Investment Treaties on Investor Rights,* ICSID Review 29 (2014), 468; F. M. Lavopa, L. E. Barreiros and V. M. Bruno, *How to Kill a BIT and not Die Trying,* Journal of International Economic Law (2013), at 888 ff; H. Ascensio, *Art. 70 of the 1969 Convention* in O. Corten and P. Klein (eds.), *The Vienna Conventions on the Law of Treaties: A Commentary* (Oxford: Oxford University Press, 2011), at para. 22.

51 C. Wackernagel, *The Twilight of the BITs? EU Judicial Proceedings, the Consensual Termination of intra-EU BITs and Why that Matters for International Law,* Beiträge zum Transnationalen Wirtschaftsrecht (2016), 18.

rely on a different approach regarding their intra-EU BITs. In case they rely on a bilateral termination without the conclusion of a subsequent bilateral treaty, they could amend the sunset clauses before terminating these BITs to prevent them from prolonging the lifetime of the BITs' protection standards and remedies. Finally, another alternative for the three remaining Member States to comply with the *Achmea* judgment could also be an amendment of the BITs abolishing the investor-State arbitration provisions while maintaining the substantive protection provisions.

III Energy Charter Treaty

More than 70 intra-EU investor-State arbitration proceedings have so far been initiated on basis of the Energy Charter Treaty. It has become by far the most invoked intra-EU IIA. The ECT's future, however, remains uncertain. Even though the *Achmea* decision does not directly affect the ECT, the Member States will soon also need to 'deactivate' the ECT's intra-EU ISDS mechanism to guarantee a coherence in intra-European investor protection. It would be inconsistent to abolish the possibility of investor-State arbitration based on intra-EU BITs, while maintaining this possibility with regard to the ECT. This would arbitrarily favour investors in the energy sector. Thus, the EU Member States have announced to discuss together with the EU Comission, "whether any additional steps are necessary to draw all the consequences from the *Achmea* judgment in relation to the intra-EU application of the Energy Charter Treaty".[52] This is also emphasized in the preamble of the Multilateral Agreement for the Termination of intra-EU BITs. Against this backdrop, the Member States can choose among different courses of action: an amendment or the termination of the ECT (1.), the unilateral withdrawal from the ECT by all EU Member States (2.) or the conclusion of a subsequent treaty among the Member States (3.).

1 Mutual termination, suspension and renegotiation of the ECT

In order to achieve a coherent approach towards intra-EU IIAs, the EU Member States could either try to terminate or suspend the ECT (a) or to amend it in order to render it inapplicable to intra-EU investor-State relations and to exclude the possibility of intra-EU investor-State arbitration proceedings (b).

---

52 Representatives of 22 EU Member States, *Declaration on the Legal Consequences of the Judgment of the ECJ in Achmea and on Investment Protection in the EU*, 15 January 2019, para. 9. In a similar way, even though not explicitly referring to the ECT, Representatives of Finland, Luxembourg, Malta, Slovenia and Sweden, *Declaration on the Enforcement of the Judgement of the ECJ in Achmea and on Investment Protection in the EU*, 16 January 2019, para. 9. For Hungary, finally, "the ongoing and future applicability of the ECT in intra-EU relations requires further discussions and individual agreement amongst the Member States", cf. Representative of Hungary, *Declaration on the Legal Consequences of the Judgment of the ECJ in Achmea and on Investment Protection in the EU*, 16 January 2019, para. 9.

a) Mutual termination or suspension of the ECT

As already shown with regard to intra-EU BITs, a treaty can be terminated according to Art. 54 VCLT in conformity with its provisions or by consent of all the parties after consultation with the other contracting States. In difference to intra-EU BITs, the ECT does not contain a termination clause. Its Art. 47 only covers the withdrawal from the treaty. Thus, the consent of all 47 contracting States to the ECT would be needed to terminate the treaty.[53] In light of the ECT's success story with a growing number of Contracting Parties and over 120 investor-State dispute settlement proceedings initiated on the basis of the ECT, it is, however, more than unlikely that there is any political will to terminate the treaty.

The same is true regarding a suspension of the operation of the ECT. By virtue of Art. 57 VCLT, a suspension is possible in conformity with the provisions of the treaty or by consent of all the parties. The ECT contains a suspension clause in Art. 32 ECT. It provides for transitional agreements for States in order to adapt to the requirements of a market economy. This clause, however, is not applicable to the EU Member States, as all States must prove prior to their accession to the EU that they satisfy the economic accession criterion of a functioning market economy and the capacity to cope with competition and market forces.[54]

b) Amendment of the ECT

An alternative approach could be the amendment of the ECT. An amendment could either delete the ISDS clause or introduce a 'disconnection clause', excluding intra-EU investments from the ECT's scope of application or at least from its ISDS provision in Art. 26 ECT.

According to Art. 42 (3) ECT an amendment would need to be adopted by the Energy Charter Conference, in which each Contracting Party is entitled to have one representative.[55] By virtue of Art. 36 (1) lit. a) ECT, unanimity of the Contracting Parties present and voting is required to adopt an amendment to the ECT, i.e. every Contracting Party present needs to agree on an amendment. The EU Member States – post-Brexit – account for 26 of the 47 Contracting States to the ECT. While the European Union and Euratom are also a Contracting Party to the ECT they have no independent voting rights. Rather, according to Art. 42 (7) ECT, a REIO such as the EU and Euratom shall,

> when voting, have a number of votes equal to the number of its member states which are Contracting Parties to this Treaty; provided that such an Organisation shall not exercise its right to vote if its member states exercise theirs, and vice versa.

---

53 47 States as well as the EU and Euratom have ratified the ECT. According to Art. 42 (7) ECT, however, the EU and Euratom would not be allowed to vote if the Member States exercise their right to vote.

54 EU Commission, *Copenhagen Accession Criteria*. https://ec.europa.eu/neighbourhood-enlargement/policy/glossary/terms/accession-criteria_en (2 May 2020).

55 Art. 34 (1) ECT.

In other words, the EU and its Member States have regardless whether the EU exercises the vote or whether the Member States exercise it on their own 26 votes in total, since Italy is no longer a Contracting Party to the ECT. Therefore, in order to reach the required unanimity regarding an ECT amendment, the EU and its Member States would need to convince 21 other Contracting Parties, among them such disparate nations as Afghanistan, Bosnia and Herzegovina, Liechtenstein, Mongolia and Japan.

In case the EU would reach an unanimity in the Energy Charter Conference, the amendment would only enter into force between the Contracting Parties which ratified it, on the 90th day after deposit of at least three fourths of the Contracting Parties.[56] In other words, at least 36 Contracting Parties to the ECT would have to ratify an ECT amendment for it to reach the quorum of Art. 42 (4) ECT and to enter into force among the ratifying States. Hence, for a possible amendment of the ECT to enter into force and become binding, all EU Member States and at least ten further Contracting States would need to ratify it. As it is extremely unlikely to convince all State Parties to the ECT to amend it, other options seem more promising.

2 Unilateral withdrawal from the ECT

Art. 47 ECT provides for unilateral withdrawal from the treaty. If a State wants to withdraw from the ECT, as Italy did in 2014, it must notify the depository of the ECT, which is the government of Portugal.[57] The withdrawal takes effect a year later. Like a unilateral denunciation of intra-EU BITs, a withdrawal from the ECT would, however, trigger the ECT's sunset clause, which according to Art. 47 (3) ECT provides for a continued protection of 20 years. It would allow investors to continue to initiate intra-EU investor-State arbitration proceedings based on the ECT regarding already existing investments.[58] A withdrawal would, however, not only exclude intra-EU investor-State arbitration proceedings based on the ECT but also preclude European investors from benefiting from the substantive protection guaranteed under the ECT and from initiating investor-State arbitration proceedings against third States, that are Contracting Parties to the ECT. It is thus not a viable option for the EU Member States.

---

56 Art. 42 (4) ECT.
57 Art. 49 ECT.
58 Italy, for instance continues to be the respondent in intra-EU investor-State arbitration proceedings. Since its withdrawal from the ECT, which took effect in January 2016, at least six new intra-EU proceedings have been initiated, which are all still pending: SCC Arbitration, *Sun Reserve v Italy*. Case No. 132/2016; ICSID, *ESPF v Italy*. Case No. ARB/16/5; ICSID, *VC Holding v Italy*. Case No. ARB/16/39; ICSID, *Rockhopper Italia v Italy*. Case No. ARB/17/14; ICSID, *Veolia v Italy*. Case No. ARB/18/20); ICSID, *Hamburg Commercial Bank AG v Italy*. Case No. ARB/20/3.

3 Subsequent treaty among the Member States

As the renegotiation, termination or suspension of the ECT is not promising and does not reflect the political will within the EU and as a unilateral withdrawal, even if concerted among the Member States, would trigger the ECT's sunset clause and terminate the protection of European energy investors in third States, the most promising way for the EU Member States seems to be the disconnection of intra-EU investor-State relations from the ECT through a subsequent treaty modifying the ECT as between them. However, in light of the general interest in the integrity of treaties, the possibility to conclude such a modifying later treaty is strictly limited. It is governed by Art. 41 (1) VCLT, which deals with "agreements to modify multilateral treaties between certain of the parties only". It reads:

> Two or more of the parties to a multilateral treaty may conclude an agreement to modify the treaty as between themselves alone if:
>
> (a) The possibility of such a modification is provided for by the treaty; or
> (b) The modification in question is not prohibited by the treaty and:
>
> > (i) Does not affect the enjoyment by the other parties of their rights under the treaty or the performance of their obligations;
> > (ii) Does not relate to a provision, derogation from which is incompatible with the effective execution of the object and purpose of the treaty as a whole.

The ECT does not provide for a modification among certain Contracting Parties pursuant to Art. 41 (1) lit. a) but does neither prohibit a modification. Thus, Art. 41 (1) lit. b) VCLT would apply to an intra-EU agreement disconnecting intra-EU investor-State relations from the ECT.

Accordingly, a modification of the ECT would be permissible if both substantive conditions of that article, which apply cumulatively,[59] are met, namely that the modification "does not affect the enjoyment by the other parties of their rights under the treaty or the performance of their obligations" and that the modification "does not relate to a provision, derogation from which is incompatible with the effective execution of the object and purpose of the treaty as a whole."

A new agreement among some Contracting Parties of a multilateral treaty is *res inter alios acta* for the parties to the original multilateral treaty that are not parties to the new modifying agreement. Their rights cannot be affected, or their obligations transformed without them giving their consent.[60] A modification of the

---

59 K. von der Decken, *Art. 41* in O. Dörr and K. Schmalenbach (eds.), *Vienna Convention on the Law of Treaties: A Commentary*, 2. ed. (Berlin: Springer, 2018), at para. 14; A. Rigaux and D. Simon, *Art. 41 of the 1969 Convention* in O. Corten and P. Klein (eds.), *The Vienna Conventions on the Law of Treaties: A Commentary* (Oxford: Oxford University Press, 2011), at paras. 30 ff.

60 K. von der Decken, *Art. 41* in O. Dörr and K. Schmalenbach (eds.), *Vienna Convention on the Law of Treaties* (Berlin: Springer, 2018), para. 15; A. Rigaux and D. Simon, *Art. 41 of the 1969*

ECT precluding its applicability for intra-EU investments would, however, not affect the enjoyment of third States of their rights under the ECT. Their investors would continue to be protected by the substantive standards contained in the ECT and continue to be able to initiate investor-State dispute settlement proceedings against the EU and EU Member States on the basis of the ECT. In other words, the modifying treaty would not create any obligations or rights for third States which are Contracting Parties to the ECT, but just remain *res inter alios acta* for these States. The first condition of Art. 41 (1) lit. b) VCLT would thus be met.

The second condition, however, raises more difficulties for potential treaty drafters. Art. 41 (1) lit. b) ii) VCLT focusses on "the object and purpose of the treaty as a whole". A modification is precluded if these can no longer be executed effectively.[61] This condition reflects the findings of the ICJ in its Advisory Opinion on the *Reservation to the Genocide Convention*:

> It is also a generally recognized principle that a multilateral convention is the result of an agreement freely concluded upon its clauses and that consequently none of the contracting parties is entitled to frustrate or impair, by means of unilateral decisions or particular agreements, the purpose and raison d'être of the convention.[62]

Notwithstanding, the referral to the "treaty as a whole" in Art. 41 VCLT, is not absolute but allows minor modifications, if they are detachable from the treaty and do not compromise the treaty's general object and purpose.[63] Against this backdrop, the assessment whether a modification of the ECT is compatible with Art. 41 (1) lit. b) VCLT, can be sustained relying on the distinction between 'reciprocal' and 'absolute' treaties.[64] A 'reciprocal' treaty is a treaty in which the Contracting

---

Convention in O. Corten and P. Klein (eds.), *The Vienna Conventions on the Law of Treaties: A Commentary* (Oxford: Oxford University Press, 2011), para. 31.

61 K. von der Decken, *Art. 41* in O. Dörr and K. Schmalenbach (eds.), *Vienna Convention on the Law of Treaties* (Berlin: Springer, 2018), para. 16.

62 ICJ, *Reservations to the Convention on the Prevention and Punishment of the Crime of Genocide*. Advisory Opinion, 28 May 1951, ICJ Reports 1951, p. 21. See also A. Rigaux and D. Simon, *Art. 41 of the 1969 Convention* in O. Corten and P. Klein (eds.), *The Vienna Conventions on the Law of Treaties: A Commentary* (Oxford: Oxford University Press, 2011), para. 32.

63 Cf. K. von der Decken, *Art. 41* in O. Dörr and K. Schmalenbach (eds.), *Vienna Convention on the Law of Treaties* (Berlin: Springer, 2018), para. 17; A. Rigaux and D. Simon, *Art. 41 of the 1969 Convention* in O. Corten and P. Klein (eds.), *The Vienna Conventions on the Law of Treaties: A Commentary* (Oxford: Oxford University Press, 2011), para. 32.

64 K. von der Decken, *Art. 41* in O. Dörr and K. Schmalenbach (eds.), *Vienna Convention on the Law of Treaties* (Berlin: Springer, 2018), para. 18; A. Rigaux and D. Simon, *Art. 41 of the 1969 Convention* in O. Corten and P. Klein (eds.), *The Vienna Conventions on the Law of Treaties: A Commentary* (Oxford: Oxford University Press, 2011), paras. 35 ff. Von der Decken, further differentiates among absolute treaties between interdependent treaties like disarmament conventions and integral treaties like human rights conventions, cf. K. von der Decken, *Art. 41* in O. Dörr and K. Schmalenbach (eds.), *Vienna Convention on the Law of Treaties* (Berlin: Springer, 2018), para. 18.

Parties "engage in a reciprocal way", "grant each other advantages and subscribe to obligations between one another, in a quasi-bilateral fashion".[65] In such a 'reciprocal' treaty, "States engage vis-à-vis others, but a derogation between two or several of them will not necessarily entail a restriction of rights granted to other States and will not affect the realization of the object and purpose of the treaty," a typical example being conventions on diplomatic relations.[66] 'Absolute' treaties, on the other hand, "oblige States parties in an interdependent fashion, the effectiveness of the treaty being dependent on compliance with all its provisions," examples being human rights treaties or nuclear non-proliferation treaties.[67]

A modification of an absolute treaty among several parties is most likely incompatible with the object and purpose of the treaty, as it would actually constitute a modification to the treaty itself and thus affects the other parties as well.[68] For example, the object and purpose of a nuclear non-proliferation treaty could hardly be compatible with an inter-se agreement of certain Contracting Parties allowing them the use of nuclear weapons in their reciprocal relations.[69] On the other hand, modifications of reciprocal treaties, like the 1961 Vienna Convention on Diplomatic Relations or the 1994 Marrakesh Agreement establishing the WTO, would generally meet the condition of Art. 41 (1) lit. b) VCLT, especially if they aim at enforcing a higher standard than that required in the original treaty.[70] The ECT is comparable to such treaties as the Contracting Parties grant each other advantages in a reciprocal way. The ECT is thus a reciprocal treaty,[71] and can thus in principle be modified by a subsequent treaty among certain Contracting Parties.

Notwithstanding, it has been argued that an agreement modifying the ECT in intra-EU relations would not satisfy the condition of Art. 41 (1) lit. b) VCLT, as the ISDS mechanism, which would be abolished, is a key element to the liberalization objective of the ECT and would thus be incompatible with the effective execution of the object and purpose of the treaty as a whole.[72] In a similar way, the *Vattenfall* tribunal argued against the disconnection of intra-EU investor-State

---

65 A. Rigaux and D. Simon, *Art. 41 of the 1969 Convention* in O. Corten and P. Klein (eds.), *The Vienna Conventions on the Law of Treaties: A Commentary* (Oxford: Oxford University Press, 2011), para. 36.

66 Ibid., para. 36.

67 Ibid., para. 37.

68 Ibid., para. 37.

69 K. von der Decken, *Art. 41* in O. Dörr and K. Schmalenbach (eds.), *Vienna Convention on the Law of Treaties* (Berlin: Springer, 2018), para. 18; A. Rigaux and D. Simon, *Art. 41 of the 1969 Convention* in O. Corten and P. Klein (eds.), *The Vienna Conventions on the Law of Treaties: A Commentary* (Oxford: Oxford University Press, 2011), para. 37.

70 K. von der Decken, *Art. 41* in O. Dörr and K. Schmalenbach (eds.), *Vienna Convention on the Law of Treaties* (Berlin: Springer, 2018), paras. 17 f. See also J. Pauwelyn, *The Role of Public International Law in the WTO: How Far Can We Go?* American Journal of International Law 95 (2001), 535–78, at 547 ff.

71 See also in a similar vein with regard to the reciprocal nature of CETA, ECJ, *CETA-Opinion. 1/17.* Opinion of Advocate General Bot, 29 January 2019, ECLI:EU:C:2019:72, para. 82.

72 F. Montanaro, *Ain't no Sunshine* in G. Adinolfi, et al. (eds.), *International Economic Law: Contemporary Issues* (Cham: Torino, 2017), pp. 211–30, at p. 224.

relations from the ECT and stated that the ECT's aim is to promote "cooperation and the flow of international investments in the energy field" in order "to serve the ultimate goal of creating and maintaining a stable and efficient energy market".[73] Thus, for the tribunal "depriving EU Investors of the right to invoke the arbitration provision of the ECT, where the respondent State is an EU Member State, would be counterproductive to the flow of international investments in the energy field."[74]

In light of these views, a modifying agreement excluding intra-EU investments from the ECT, would run counter to its object and purpose and thus be precluded by virtue of Art. 41 (1) VCLT. These positions, however, must be rejected. The object and purpose of the ECT is described in its Art. 2 as the promotion of "long-term cooperation in the energy field, based on complementarities and mutual benefits, in accordance with the objectives and principles of the [Energy] Charter". The ECT's preamble is more detailed and describes the object and purpose of the ECT inter alia as the broadening of cooperation among the States parties in order to create economic growth through the liberalization of investment and trade in the energy sector, and the removal of technical, administrative and other barriers to trade in the energy sector.

An agreement between the Member States excluding the ECT's application in intra-EU investor-State relations would not affect the goals of the treaty. The latter would not be undermined within the EU, which itself has a highly integrated and liberalized energy market. The abolishment of intra-EU investor-State disputes based on the ECT would further not affect the general goals of the ECT, as the possibility of ISDS is no precondition for the achievement of economic growth and the liberalization of investment and trade in the energy sector but only one means to achieve it. A subsequent treaty among the EU Member States disconnecting the ECT or its investor-State arbitration provision from intra-EU investor-State relations would thus be compatible with Art. 41 (1) VCLT.

The conclusion of a treaty disconnecting intra-EU investor-State relations from the ECT is thus a highly promising approach the Member States and the EU could take in order to implement the rationale of the *Achmea* judgment to the Energy Charter Treaty.

IV Effects on EU Member State courts and other domestic courts

What effects will the *Achmea* decision have on the EU judiciary? The judgment does not treat the question of investor-State arbitration awards but refers only to the ISDS clause in intra-EU BITs. As already discussed, the enforcement

73 ICSID, *Vattenfall v Germany.* Case No. ARB/12/12. Decision on the Achmea Issue, 31 August 2018, para. 198.
74 Ibid., para. 198.

jurisdiction is strictly territorial. Recognition and enforcement of awards is solely possible through the domestic judiciary.[75] Therefore, the question arises how domestic courts in EU Member States will treat intra-EU awards.

The effects of an ECJ decision in an Art. 267 TFEU proceedings are *ex tunc*. It is settled case-law that an interpretation of the ECJ of a rule of EU law must be understood as applicable to that rule from the time of its entry into force. In other words, the ECJ's interpretation must be "applied by the courts even to legal relationships which arose and were established before the judgment ruling on the request for interpretation".[76] Accordingly, intra-EU BIT arbitration provision 'such as' the one in the Netherlands–Czechoslovakia BIT must be interpreted as having been incompatible with EU law at least since the entry into force of the Lisbon Treaty.

Under exceptional circumstances, "in application of a general principle of legal certainty", "the Court may decide to restrict the right to rely upon a provision, which it has interpreted, with a view to calling in question legal relations established in good faith."[77] In *Achmea*, however, no such decision is apparent. The judgment can thus be understood as determining the *ex tunc* incompatibility of all intra-EU BIT investor-State arbitration provisions with EU law. While the decision has no direct effect on the validity of these provisions, it does, create a ground for non-enforcement of awards, as will be shown in the following.

In this light, Art. 7 of the Multilateral Agreement for the Termination of intra-EU BITs signed by 23 Member States provides that Member States being respondents to an intra-EU investor-State arbitration proceeding, shall

> where they are party to a judicial proceeding concerning an arbitral award issued on the basis of an [intra-EU BIT], ask the competent national court, including in any third country, as the case may be, to set the arbitral award aside, annul it or to refrain from recognising and enforcing it.

In a similar way all EU Member States had previously announced in their political declarations that respondent Member States "will request the courts, including in any third country, which are to decide in proceedings relating to an intra-EU investment arbitration award, to set these awards aside or not to enforce them due to a lack of valid consent."[78] The six Member States that published different declarations, however, limited this decision to request the setting aside or

---

75 On this in greater detail, cf. Chapter II: IV. 1. c).

76 With further references, ECJ, *Meilicke*. C-292/04. Judgment, 6 March 2007, ECLI:EU:C:2007:132, para. 34.

77 With further references, ibid., para. 35; ECJ, *Linneweber*. Joined Cases C-453/02 and C-462/02. Judgment, 17 February 2005, ECLI:EU:C:2005:92, para. 42.

78 Representatives of 22 EU Member States, *Declaration on the Legal Consequences of the Judgment of the ECJ in Achmea and on Investment Protection in the EU*, 15 January 2019, para. 2.

non-enforcement to proceedings or awards relating to investment arbitration under BITs, thus excluding ECT proceedings and ECT awards.[79]

Regardless of the effect of the *Achmea* decision, parties to an investor-State dispute can no longer challenge an award once the time limit for a review has lapsed, which is generally three months after the reception of the award.[80] The same is true for ICSID awards, which can only be challenged before an ICSID 'ad hoc Committee'.[81] The lapse of time to challenge an award, however, does not affect the possibility for a domestic court to deny the enforcement of a non-ICSID award, if the grounds for non-enforcement are met.[82]

The present part will start by analysing the direct effects of the ECJ's *Achmea* decision on the *Achmea* proceeding before the German BGH, which had led to the preliminary reference to the ECJ in the first place (1.), before assessing its impact on the EU Member States' domestic judiciary in general (2.).

1 Proceeding before the German BGH

The ECJ's *Achmea* judgment was an answer to the preliminary reference submitted by the German BGH. In reaction to the *Achmea* judgment of the ECJ, the BGH annulled the *Achmea* arbitration award on October 31st, 2018 on the basis of Section 1059 (2) Nr. 1 lit. a) ZPO according to which an award can be annulled if the "arbitration agreement is invalid under the laws to which the parties to the dispute have subjected it, or, if the parties to the dispute have not made any determinations in this regard, that it is invalid under German law".[83] The BGH's reasoning will be presented (a) before assessing another ground of annulment under German law on the basis of which award could also have been annulled (b); namely Section 1059 (2) Nr. 1 lit b) ZPO according to which an award can be annulled if its recognition or enforcement "will lead to a result contrary to the public order".

---

79 Cf. Representatives of Finland, Luxembourg, Malta, Slovenia and Sweden, *Declaration on the Enforcement of the Judgement of the ECJ in Achmea and on Investment Protection in the EU*, 16 January 2019, para. 2; Representative of Hungary, *Declaration on the Legal Consequences of the Judgment of the ECJ in Achmea and on Investment Protection in the EU*, 16 January 2019, para. 2.

80 Section 1059 (3) ZPO for example, states that unless there exists a different agreement among the parties to the dispute, the petition for reversal must be filed with the court within a period of three months after the day on which the petitioner has received the arbitration award. See also Art. 34 (3) UNCITRAL Model Law.

81 The review of an ICSID award can only be requested within 90 days after the discovery of a fact of such nature to decisively affect the award, however no later than three years after the award was rendered, Art. 51 ICSID Convention. The application to annul an award must in principle be made within 120 days after the date on which the award was rendered, Art. 52 (2) ICSID Convention. On the challenge of ICSID awards, see also Chapter II: IV. 1. d).

82 Cf. Section 1060 (2) ZPO, Art. 36 (1) lit. b) UNCITRAL Model Law and Art. V (2) New York Convention.

83 BGH, *Achmea*. I ZB 2/15. Beschluss, 31 October 2018.

a) No valid arbitration agreement

In its decision the BGH found that the parties to the dispute, namely the Achmea company and Slovakia, had not concluded any valid arbitration agreement and that the award thus had to be annulled pursuant to Section 1059 (2) Nr. 1 lit. a) ZPO.[84]

In the initial *Achmea* proceeding the arbitral tribunal had only been constituted after Slovakia's accession to the EU. Thus, the BGH found EU law to be of relevance in that proceeding especially regarding the question whether the arbitration agreement between the parties could establish the arbitral tribunal's jurisdiction or whether the arbitration agreement was invalid because of its incompatibility with EU law.[85]

The BGH reiterated that the Netherlands–Czechoslovakia BIT had become an intra-EU treaty with Slovakia's accession to the EU on May 1, 2004, and that according to the ECJ's established line of jurisprudence,[86] EU law takes precedence in matters governed by the EU Treaties over treaties concluded between Member States before the EU Treaties' entry into force. Accordingly, the BGH found that a bilateral treaty between two EU Member States could, from the moment of the second State's accession to the EU, no longer be applicable insofar as it is incompatible with EU law.[87] As such an incompatibility was found by the ECJ in its *Achmea* judgment regarding the investor-State arbitration provision in the Netherlands–Czechoslovakia BIT,[88] this provision was inapplicable and accordingly no valid arbitration agreement between the Achmea company and Slovakia could have been concluded on basis of that provision.[89] Indeed, the ECJ judgment did not address the question of the validity of the arbitration agreement but only dealt with the BIT's compatibility with the EU Treaties. According to the BGH, however, the BIT and the arbitration agreement were inextricably linked in the case at hand as the only possible basis for a Slovakian offer to arbitrate vis-à-vis the Achmea company could be found in Art. 8 (2) of the Netherlands–Czechoslovakia BIT. As according to the ECJ's *Achmea* judgment this provision is not applicable, there was no offer to arbitrate by Slovakia which the Achmea company could have accepted by initiating an investor-State arbitration proceeding.[90] In other words, due to the ISDS provision's incompatibility with EU law, Slovakia could not have made a valid offer to arbitrate and thus no arbitration agreement on which the arbitral tribunal could base its jurisdiction on had been concluded.

84 Ibid., para. 14.
85 Ibid., para. 18.
86 ECJ, *Matteucci.* Case 235/87. Judgment, 27 September 1988, ECLI:EU:C:1988:460, para. 22; ECJ, *Exportur.* C-3/91. Judgment, 10 November 1992, ECLI:EU:C:1992:420, para. 8; ECJ, *American Bud.* C-478/07. Judgment, 8 September 2009, ECLI:EU:C:2009:521, para. 98; ECJ, *Commission v Germany.* C-546/07. Judgment, 21 January 2010, ECLI:EU:C:2010:25, para. 44.
87 BGH, *Achmea.* I ZB 2/15. Beschluss, 31 October 2018, para. 20.
88 ECJ, *Achmea.* C-284/16. Judgment, 6 March 2018, ECLI:EU:C:2018:158, para. 60.
89 BGH, *Achmea.* I ZB 2/15. Beschluss, 31 October 2018, para. 25.
90 Ibid., para. 28.

b) Violation of the ordre public

Even if the *Achmea* award had been based on a valid arbitration agreement within the meaning of Section 1059 (2) Nr. 1 lit. a) ZPO, the award could still have been reversed based on Section 1059 (2) Nr. 2 lit. b) ZPO and the argument that its recognition or enforcement would lead to a result contrary to the *ordre public*.

An arbitral award violates the German *ordre public* when it contravenes a rule that regulates the bases of the public or commercial sphere or if it contradicts fundamental ideas of justice.[91] However, going beyond the purely national scope of *ordre public*, the ECJ has confirmed that within the EU the *ordre public* of the place of arbitration does not only comprise domestic but also fundamental rules of EU law, which are essential for the fulfilment of the EU's goals and the functioning of the common market.[92] Against this background, the EU Commission convincingly explained in its *amicus curiae* brief in the intra-EU *European American Investment Bank* arbitration proceeding that

> the fundamental elements of the EU legal order and its judicial system, as designed by the founding Treaties and developed by the case-law of the Court of Justice of the EU, form part of the public order of all its Member States and therefore of the law to be applied by the arbitrators. Member States that have concluded agreements conferring jurisdiction on courts or tribunals which rule on the scope of obligations imposed on EU Member States pursuant to EU law but are not bound to respect EU law are in breach of this public order. An arbitral award that breaches these principles cannot be recognised or enforced in the EU.[93]

These findings are transferable to the *Achmea* proceeding. The ECJ has determined that the autonomy of the EU legal order is jeopardized through intra-EU investor-State arbitration proceedings based on intra-EU BITs. The importance of this autonomy as a fundamental element of the EU legal order has been repeatedly emphasized by the ECJ and must thus be understood as being part of the EU's *ordre public*.

Hence, the recognition or enforcement of the *Achmea* arbitration award by the German BGH would have led to a result jeopardizing the autonomy of the EU

---

91 Cf. BGH. III ZR 174/89, 12 July 1990. See also G. Born, *International Commercial Arbitration*, 2nd ed. (New York, Alphen aan den Rijn, 2014), at 3666 ff.

92 ECJ, *Eco Swiss*. C-126/97. Judgment, 1 June 1999, ECLI:EU:C:1999:269, paras. 35 ff; ECJ, *Mostaza Claro*. C-168/05. Judgment, 26 October 2006, ECLI:EU:C:2006:675, para. 37; ECJ, *Asturcom Telecomunicaciones*. C-40/08. Judgment, 6 October 2009, ECLI:EU:C:2009:615, paras. 51 f. See also J. Münch, *§ 1059* in *Münchener Kommentar ZPO*, 5th ed. (München: Beck, 2016), at para. 47; G. A. Bermann, *Navigating EU Law and the Law of International Arbitration*, Arbitration International 28 (2012), 397–445, at 410.

93 EU Commission, *Observation on jurisdiction regarding the PCA Case No. 2010–17 – European American Investment Bank v Slovakia: L. Romero Requena, Director General EU Commission Legal Service*, 13 October 2011, at p. 2.

legal order and would thus have been contrary to the *ordre public*. In other words, the ground of annulment codified in Section 1059 (2) Nr. 1 lit. a) ZPO is also met. The BGH could thus have annulled the *Achmea* award because of its violation of the *ordre public*.[94]

2 General effect on intra-EU investor-State arbitration awards

As provided for in Art. 7 lit. b) of the Multilateral Agreement for the Termination of intra-EU BITs, most Member States respondent to intra-EU investor-State arbitration proceedings will increasingly challenge arbitral awards before domestic courts, both at the seat of arbitration as well as at the place where enforcement of the awards is sought.

A respondent State has two possibilities: either to file an application for the setting aside or annulment of the award, as Slovakia did in the BGH *Achmea* proceedings, or to request the non-recognition or non-enforcement of the award.

The actual enforcement of an award is only necessary if the debtor, i.e. generally the respondent State, is not willing to pay. This has so far, rather been the exception than the rule in investor-State arbitration. It might, however, change with the recent developments in connection with the ECJ's *Achmea* judgment. As expressed in their declarations on the legal consequences of the *Achmea* decision, all Member States understand investor-State arbitration tribunals established on the basis of an intra-EU BIT to lack jurisdiction over intra-EU investor-State disputes.[95] This has also been reiterated in Arts. 4 and 5 of the Multilateral Agreement for the Termination of intra-EU BITs.

The Member States will thus not only be inclined to refuse to comply with intra-EU investor-State arbitration awards, but also to challenge the awards' validity and bindingness at the seat of arbitration or before an ICSID 'ad hoc Committee'. Regarding pending arbitration proceedings, the 23 signatories of the Multilateral Agreement for the Termination of intra-EU BITs have created the possibility of a settlement procedure in Art. 9. Furthermore, pursuant to Art. 10 investors get

> access to judicial remedies under national law against a measure contested in a pending arbitration proceeding even if national time limits for bringing actions have expired [...] on condition that the investor withdraws the pending arbitration proceeding and waives all rights and claims pursuant to the

---

94 In that sense, see also B. Hess, *The Fate of Investment Dispute Resolution after the Achmea Decision of the European Court of Justice*, MPILux Research Paper Series (2018), at 11 f.

95 Representatives of 22 EU Member States, *Declaration on the Legal Consequences of the Judgment of the ECJ in Achmea and on Investment Protection in the EU*, 15 January 2019; Representatives of Finland, Luxembourg, Malta, Slovenia and Sweden, *Declaration on the Enforcement of the Judgement of the ECJ in Achmea and on Investment Protection in the EU*, 16 January 2019; Representative of Hungary, *Declaration on the Legal Consequences of the Judgment of the ECJ in Achmea and on Investment Protection in the EU*, 16 January 2019.

relevant BIT or renounces execution of an award already issued, but not yet definitively enforce or executed, and commits to refrain from instituting new arbitration proceedings.

A refusal of enforcement and the challenge of arbitral awards is also likely to happen with regard to intra-EU investor-State arbitration awards based on the ECT, at least in case the respondent is one of the 22 Member States which have signed the first Declaration of January 15, 2019, which found *Achmea's* effect to apply as well to ECT based arbitration proceedings.[96] The challenge of a non-ICSID ECT award as well as an ECT award enforcement request could allow a domestic court of a Member State to refer the question of the ECT's compatibility with EU law to the European Court of Justice pursuant to Art. 267 TFEU and finally allow the Court to provide clarity in this regard.

In any case, successful claimants are likely to be obliged to seek the enforcement of awards, which is only possible through domestic courts. Those can hinder the enforcement under very narrow conditions, depending on the question whether they are dealing with a non-ICSID award (a) or with an ICSID award (b).

a) Non-ICSID awards

Regarding non-ICSID awards, the grounds for non-recognition and non-enforcement are generally almost identical to those for the annulment of an award.[97] As just seen with regard to the proceedings before the BGH, the most important grounds for annulment and non-recognition in the intra-EU investor-State context are the lack of a valid arbitration agreement between the investor and the host State as well as the award's incompatibility with the *ordre public*. It is very likely that domestic courts will base their review on either of these grounds.

Both are inscribed in the New York Convention and the 1985 *UNCITRAL Model Law on International Commercial Arbitration* (UNCITRAL Model Law).[98] Several domestic arbitration laws in the EU Member States have been inspired by the latter.[99]

The *ordre public* is in principle subject to narrow interpretation, in order to prevent domestic courts from easily rejecting arbitral awards they disapprove on the merits and to protect the effectiveness and the functioning of international

---

96 Representatives of 22 EU Member States, *Declaration on the Legal Consequences of the Judgment of the ECJ in Achmea and on Investment Protection in the EU*, 15 January 2019.

97 See for example Art. 34 and 36 of the UNCITRAL Model Law and Sections 1059, 1060 and 1061 ZPO in conjunction with Art. V New York Convention.

98 Cf. Art. V New York Convention and Art. 34 UNCITRAL Model Law.

99 This is the case for 18 of the EU Member States, which have adopted legislation based on this Model law, cf. UNCITRAL, *1985 Model Law on International Commercial Arbitration – Status.* https://uncitral.un.org/en/texts/arbitration/modellaw/commercial_arbitration/status (4 May 2020).

arbitration as a whole.[100] In that context, the ECJ has developed an EU *ordre public* which covers certain legal norms that are so essential for the fulfilment of the EU's goals and objectives, that they have the status of public policy and cannot be compromised by arbitral proceedings and arbitral awards.[101] As just shown with regard to the BGH *Achmea* proceeding, this 'European' *ordre public* encompasses the autonomy of EU law and is thus be affected by every single intra-EU investor-State arbitration award based on a BIT.[102]

In difference to the challenge of an award because of an invalid arbitration agreement, the question of the compatibility of the award's enforcement with the *ordre public* can be raised *ex officio* by domestic courts.[103]

It could thus become almost impossible to enforce an intra-EU investor-State arbitration award in EU Member States as the domestic court will with great probability at least raise the issue of the award's incompatibility with the *ordre public*. Hence, successful claimants might try to enforce the awards outside the EU. This is not an unusual approach, as the enforcement attempts regarding the *Micula* award have shown.[104] An enforcement outside the EU could, however, potentially be impeded if the award has been set aside at the seat of arbitration. In other words, an award that has been annulled can also become unenforceable in other States, as Art. V (1) lit. e) of the New York Convention provides that

> Recognition and enforcement of the award may be refused, at the request of the party against whom it is invoked, [...] if [...] the award [...] has been set aside or suspended by a competent authority of the country in which, or under the law of which, that award was made.[105]

Thus, investors could face major difficulties to enforce their awards not only in other European Member States but in any of the 161 States party to the New York Convention. However, as the wording indicates, domestic courts have a discretion whether or not to enforce an award that has been set aside at the seat of arbitration. Several European domestic courts have thus enforced international

---

100 Cf. G. A. Bermann, *Navigating EU Law and the Law of International Arbitration*, Arbitration International 28 (2012), 409.

101 ECJ, *Eco Swiss*. C-126/97. Judgment, 1 June 1999, paras. 35 ff; ECJ, *Mostaza Claro*. C-168/05. Judgment, 26 October 2006, para. 37; ECJ, *Asturcom Telecomunicaciones*. C-40/08. Judgment, 6 October 2009, paras. 51 f. See also J. Münch, *§ 1059* in *Münchener Kommentar ZPO* (München: Beck, 2016), para. 47; G. A. Bermann, *Navigating EU Law and the Law of International Arbitration*, Arbitration International 28 (2012), 410.

102 See in this regard, Chapter IV: IV. 1. b).

103 See for example, Art. V (2) lit. b) New York Convention and Arts. 34 (2) lit. b) ii) and 36 (1) lit. b) ii) UNCITRAL Model law. See also G. Born, *International Commercial Arbitration* (New York: Alphen aan den Rijn, 2014), p. 3445.

104 ICSID, *Ioan Micula, Viorel Micula and others v Romania*. Case No. ARB/05/20. Award, 11 December 2013. On this proceeding and the enforcement attempts, see in greater detail Chapter III: III. 5.

105 See also with almost identical wording, Art. 36 (1) lit. a) v) of the UNCITRAL Model Law.

commercial arbitration awards notwithstanding their annulment at the seat of arbitration.[106] Especially French courts have understood awards as being independent from the legal system of the country of the seat of arbitration, with the effect that only the law at the place of enforcement, i.e. French law, is applicable to the setting aside of an award or the refusal of its enforcement.[107] This, however, remains an absolute exception. In principle, courts called upon to enforce an award "treat a decision of a foreign court with due deference" and do not enforce set aside awards.[108] Furthermore, even if a French or other EU Member State court would not recognize the annulment decisions of another Member State court, it could nonetheless refuse recognition and enforcement of an intra-EU award due to the lack of a valid arbitration agreement as well as the award's incompatibility with the *ordre public*.

The signatories of the Multilateral Agreement for the Termination of intra-EU BITs have agreed in Art. 7 lit. b) that a Member State respondent in an intra-EU investor-State arbitration will also challenge an award before third country courts if the tribunal was seated in that country or enforcement is sought in the State of the court. The case of the intra-EU *EDF International v Hungary* award,[109] based on the UNCITRAL arbitration rules and administered by the PCA, however, shows that non-EU courts might be reluctant in applying a European *ordre public*. Hungary being the respondent to that dispute, tried to have set aside the award rendered by a Zurich-seated arbitral tribunal, before Swiss courts. Reportedly, the Swiss Federal Supreme Court denied this request in its ruling of October 6, 2015, rejecting Hungary's claim that its compliance with the award would violate the *ordre public* as it would force Hungary to breach EU law on State aid.[110] In other words, it will depend on the respective domestic courts outside the EU, whether they will consider and accept the argument of incompatibility of the award with EU law, in an enforcement proceeding or whether they will reject it.

Finally, it remains open how domestic courts will react to ECT based awards. Even though, the *Achmea* judgment is not directly transferable to ECT arbitration, and thus the argument of an invalid arbitration clause in the meaning of Art. V

---

106 See in great detail D. Solomon, *International Commercial Arbitration* in S. Balthasar (ed.), *International Commercial Arbitration: International Conventions, Country Reports and Comparative Analysis* (München: C. H. Beck, 2016), pp. 45–157, at para. 198 ff; G. Born, *International Commercial Arbitration* (New York: Alphen aan den Rijn, 2014), at 3625 ff; C. Liebscher, *Article V (1) (e)* in R. Wolff (ed.), *New York Convention – Commentary* (München: C. H. Beck, 2012), pp. 356–80, at 369 f.

107 With further references, C. Liebscher, *Article V (1) (e)* in R. Wolff (ed.), *New York Convention – Commentary* (München: C. H. Beck, 2012), p. 370.

108 Ibid., 370 f.

109 PCA, *EDF International v Hungary.* Award, 4 December 2014.

110 Cf. Swiss Federal Supreme Court, *EDF v Hungary.* 4A_34/2015. Decision on Set-Aside of Award, 6 October 2015, paras. 5.1. ff. See also J. Hepburn, *In Upholding intra-EU Energy Charter Award, Swiss Court Considers EU State Aid Issue, as Well as Umbrella Clause Reservation and Tribunal's Damages Methodology,* IA Reporter, 23 October 2015.

(1) lit. a) New York Convention is not applicable, domestic courts could refuse the recognition and enforcement of a non-ICSID ECT award based on the *ordre public* argument. As shown earlier, ECT arbitration is just as jeopardizing the autonomy of the EU legal order as intra-EU BIT proceedings are. It is thus perfectly arguable to refuse the enforcement of an intra-EU ECT decision.

b) ICSID awards

The situation is more complex regarding ICSID proceedings, which account for the great majority of intra-EU arbitration proceedings. ICSID provides for 'delocalized' arbitration and creates a quasi-autonomous, self-contained system of review of awards, which are directly enforceable in all ICSID Member States. Each contracting State to the ICSID Convention must recognize an ICSID award as if it was a final judgment of its own national courts and enforce the obligation imposed by the award.[111]

Whereas the New York Convention and domestic law provide for the possibility to review an arbitral award, the ICSID Convention totally excludes domestic courts from the review process. According to Art. 53 (1) ICSID Convention, an award "shall be binding on the parties and shall not be subject to any appeal or to any other remedy except those provided for in this Convention." Accordingly, Art. 54 (1) ICSID Convention provides that "each Contracting State shall recognize an award rendered pursuant to this Convention as binding and enforce the pecuniary obligations imposed by that award within its territories as if it were a final judgment of a court in that State."

The only possibility to challenge an ICSID award is thus to initiate an annulment proceeding before an ICSID 'ad hoc Committee' according to Art. 52 ICSID Convention. While the *ordre public* cannot be considered by an 'ad hoc Committee' in such an annulment proceeding, a party to the dispute can request the annulment of the award on the ground that the arbitral tribunal has manifestly exceeded its powers.[112] An award rendered by a tribunal that lacks competence is "the most obvious example of an excess of powers".[113] Hence, EU Member States could try to challenge an ICSID award on the same ground that led to the annulment of the award in *Achmea* by the German BGH, namely that due to the incompatibility of a BIT's investor-State arbitration provision with the EU Treaties, no valid arbitration agreement could have been concluded between the investor and the host State and thus the arbitral tribunal that rendered the award in question had no jurisdiction. While it remains to be seen how ICSID 'ad hoc Committees' will react to this line of argument regarding intra-EU BIT awards, it is more than unlikely that they will annul intra-EU ECT awards based on this reasoning.

---

111 See on this in greater detail, Chapter II: IV. 1.
112 Art. 52 (1) lit. b) ICSID Convention.
113 C. Schreuer, *The ICSID Convention: A Commentary*, 2nd ed. (Cambridge: Cambridge University Press, 2009), at Art. 52, para. 155.

Notwithstanding, just like it is the case regarding non-ICSID awards, the recognition and enforcement of ICSID awards is left to the domestic courts. But, as explained by Schreuer, a domestic court

> before which recognition and enforcement is sought is restricted to ascertaining the award's authenticity. It may not re-examine the ICSID tribunal's jurisdiction. It may not re-examine the award on the merits. Nor may it examine the fairness and propriety of the proceedings before the ICSID tribunal.[114]

In other words, an EU Member State court called upon to enforce an intra-EU ICSID award, could not reject it based on the *Achmea* judgment, neither because of a lack of jurisdiction nor because of the violation of the *ordre public*. Nonetheless, Member State courts might be inclined or pressured to deny the enforcement of an ICSID award on the – non-codified – basis that it conflicts with the autonomy of the EU legal order. Such a decision, however, would run counter to the State's international obligations arising out of the ICSID Convention.

This would even be the case if the Member States' courts denied enforcement because of State immunity from execution.[115] The impossibility to enforce an ICSID award because of State immunity from execution does not affect the respondent State's obligation to comply with the award in accordance with Arts. 53 (1) and 54 ICSID Convention.[116] Hence, a State's non-compliance with an ICSID award would trigger its responsibility under international law and would allow the investor's home State according to Art. 27 (1) ICSID Convention to provide diplomatic protection. As explained by Schreuer,

> diplomatic protection for the purpose of securing compliance with the award may be exercised by the State of nationality of the aggrieved natural or juridical person [...] through negotiations, the institution of judicial proceedings between the two States or by any other means of dispute settlement that may be available. [...] [T]he protecting State may threaten to take or may actually take countermeasures such as withholding payments due to the recalcitrant award debtor, offsetting the claim arising from the award against claims that the award debtor may have against the protecting State or the freezing of assets that belong to the award debtor.[117]

---

114 Ibid., Art. 54, para. 81.

115 While the Contracting States to the ICSID Convention have waived their immunity from jurisdiction, they have not waived their immunity from execution as is explicitly stated in Art. 55 ICSID Convention. See also ibid., Art. 55, paras. 5 ff.

116 Cf. ibid., Art. 54, para. 115; S. A. Alexandrov, *Enforcement of ICSID Awards* in C. Binder, et al. (eds.), *International Investment Law for the 21st Century: Essays in Honour of Christoph Schreuer* (Oxford: Oxford University Press, 2009), pp. 322–37, at p. 325. See also on respondent State's successful and unsuccessful attempts to hinder enforcement due to State immunity, A. K. Bjorklund, *State Immunity and the Enforcement of Investor-State Arbitral Awards* in C. Binder, et al. (eds.), *International Investment Law for the 21st Century: Essays in Honour of Christoph Schreuer* (Oxford: Oxford University Press, 2009), pp. 302–21.

117 C. Schreuer, *The ICSID Convention: A Commentary*, 2nd ed. (Cambridge: Cambridge University Press, 2009), Art. 53, para. 43.

A possible means regarding dispute settlement between the home and the host State would be the referral of the dispute to the International Court of Justice. In the situation of deliberate non-enforcement, the investor's home State would be entitled to initiate a proceeding before the ICJ, pursuant to Art. 64 ICSID Convention in accordance with Art. 36 (1) of the ICJ Statute, which establishes the ICJ's 'compulsory' jurisdiction "in the sense that no further agreement between the States parties to a dispute is needed".[118] A dispute regarding an EU Member State's non-compliance with an intra-EU investor-State arbitration award would be a dispute "concerning the interpretation or application" of the ICSID Convention as required by its Art. 64. It could thus be invoked by any EU Member State against the host State of one of its investors which is not complying with an ICSID award. As such a dispute would solely focus on the interpretation and application of the ICSID Convention and not concern the interpretation or application of the EU Treaties, it would not affect the autonomy of the EU legal order and thus not fall under the EU law prohibition of Art. 344 TFEU. In other words, the rationale of the ECJ's MOX Plant decision would not be transferable to a dispute between two Member States on the interpretation of the ICSID Convention brought before the ICJ. In difference to such a dispute regarding the ICSID Convention, the MOX Plant dispute covered rules which formed part of the EU legal order, especially because the EU itself had become a Contracting Party to the UNCLOS, which is a mixed agreement under EU law.[119] In difference to UNCLOS, however, the ICSID Convention is according to its Art. 67 only open for signature on behalf of States member of the World Bank. The EU can thus not become a Contracting Party to the ICSID Convention. Hence, the ECJ's ruling that the provisions of UNCLOS in issue in the MOX Plant dispute form an integral part of the EU legal order as they fall within the scope of EU competence which the EU exercised by acceding to the UNCLOS and that consequently the MOX Plant dispute is a dispute concerning the interpretation or application of the EU Treaty in accordance with Art. 344 TFEU,[120] is not transferable to an inter-State ICSID dispute before the ICJ.

Notwithstanding the risk of a possible ICJ proceeding, an EU Member State's refusal to enforce an ICSID award could also lead to enforcement attempts abroad, i.e. in third States in which the domestic courts are not bound by EU law and the ECJ's jurisdiction. Such third State courts are not bound by the *Achmea* decision and could thus enforce an award according to their State's international legal obligations arising out of the ICSID Convention. The most notorious example in this respect is the *Micula* award, which has been discussed previously and in which the Swedish investors have sought enforcement outside the EU as a reaction to the EU Commission's attempts to prevent Romania from paying the damages awarded to them.[121]

---

118 Ibid., Art. 64, para. 2.
119 ECJ, *MOX Plant.* C-459/03. Judgment, 30 May 2006, paras. 82 ff.
120 Ibid., paras. 126 f.
121 Cf. in greater detail, Chapter III: III. 5.

c) Interim findings

In light of the ECJ's *Achmea* judgment the EU Member States will refuse to comply with upcoming awards granting damages to intra-EU investors. With the high number of pending intra-EU investor-State arbitration proceedings, the EU Member States' judiciaries might thus face many upcoming enforcement proceedings in the near future.

With regard to non-ICSID awards, the Member States' domestic courts have effective means to prevent enforcement based on the New York Convention and the domestic civil procedural laws, which are often inspired by the UNCITRAL Model Law. The German BGH has shown the way in determining the effects of the ECJ's *Achmea* judgment, namely that no valid arbitration agreement between an EU Member State and a European investor could be concluded on the basis of an intra-EU BIT investor-State provision due to the latter's incompatibility with the EU Treaties. Such awards could thus be set aside at the seat of arbitration or their enforcement could be prevented by the courts of the EU Member State in which enforcement is sought. An annulment of an award could also prevent the award's enforcement abroad, due to the general principle codified in Art. V (1) lit. e) New York Convention. Furthermore, intra-EU investor-State arbitration awards are incompatible with the *ordre public* of the EU Member States, which could also lead to their annulment or non-enforcement.

With regard to ICSID awards, however, the situation seems more complicated. While from an EU legal perspective an ICSID arbitral tribunal would neither have jurisdiction in an intra-EU investor-State dispute settlement, the Member States' domestic courts are precluded from reviewing such awards. It thus remains to be seen how ICSID 'ad hoc Committees' will interpret the effects of the ECJ's *Achmea* judgment on intra-EU ICSID awards. In the meantime, in order not to force their own courts into political decision making and to prevent a massive flight abroad regarding the enforcement of awards, the Member States should either try to settle the pending ICSID proceedings or to comply with the awards already rendered. Against this backdrop, Art. 9 of the Multilateral Agreement for the Termination of intra-EU BITs provides a settlement procedure open to investors in intra-EU arbitration proceedings.

Regarding ECT awards, it remains to be seen how the domestic judiciary will react. It is, however, very likely that the ECJ will soon be requested through a preliminary reference in accordance with Art. 267 TFEU to rule on the compatibility of the ECT with the EU Treaties and to provide clarity in this regard.

V Effects on investment arbitration proceedings

In principle, arbitral tribunals are not bound by a judgment of the ECJ, especially as – according to the ECJ's own *Achmea* decision – they are not 'courts or tribunals of the Member States'.[122] Nonetheless, the decision will affect current and future intra-EU investor-State disputes.

---

122 ECJ, *Achmea*. C-284/16. Judgment, 6 March 2018, paras. 45 f.

With regard to already concluded arbitral proceedings, the Member States have made clear that "settlements and arbitral awards in intra-EU investment arbitration cases that can no longer be annulled or set aside and were voluntarily complied with or definitively enforced before the *Achmea* judgment should not be challenged."[123] This is also reflected in Art. 6 (1) of the Multilateral Agreement for the Termination of intra-EU BITs which explicitly provides that concluded arbitration proceedings based on an intra-EU BIT, i.e. proceedings which ended with a settlement agreement or with a final award issued prior to the *Achmea* judgment, shall not be reopened.

The present section will analyse the effects of the ECJ's *Achmea* judgment on pending and upcoming intra-EU investor-State arbitration proceedings (1.). Its effects depend to a large degree on whether an arbitral tribunal has already been constituted, still must be constituted or whether the parties to the dispute still have to choose the arbitration rules and the seat of arbitration. Once the BITs have been terminated, however, no further investor-State arbitration proceedings can be initiated on their basis, unless a sunset clause applies (2.).

1 Pending and upcoming investor-State arbitration proceedings

As of May 23, 2020, there are at least 67 pending intra-EU investor-State arbitration proceedings. In most of these cases, the arbitral tribunal has already been constituted and many proceedings are expected to come to an end in the near future. Several proceedings, however, have only been initiated after the *Achmea* judgment,[124] which suggests that at least some investors do not believe that the arbitral tribunals will reject their claims because of the ECJ's decision.

The EU Member States have declared to inform, "investment arbitration tribunals about the legal consequences of the Achmea judgment [...] in all pending intra-EU investment arbitration proceedings [...] brought under bilateral treaties concluded between Member States", and to "inform the investor community that no new intra-EU investor-State arbitration proceedings" based on an intra-EU

---

123 Representatives of 22 EU Member States, *Declaration on the Legal Consequences of the Judgment of the ECJ in Achmea and on Investment Protection in the EU*, 15 January 2019, para. 7; Representatives of Finland, Luxembourg, Malta, Slovenia and Sweden, *Declaration on the Enforcement of the Judgement of the ECJ in Achmea and on Investment Protection in the EU*, 16 January 2019, para. 7. Differing in the wording of its declaration which only covers "awards in intra-EU bilateral investment treaty arbitration cases", however, Representative of Hungary, *Declaration on the Legal Consequences of the Judgment of the ECJ in Achmea and on Investment Protection in the EU*, 16 January 2019, para. 6.

124 See for example, ICSID, *LSG Building Solutions v Romania*. Case No. ARB/18/19; ICSID, *Veolia v Italy*. Case No. ARB/18/20); ICSID, *Bladon Enterprises v Romania*. Case No. ARB/18/30; ICSID, *Olegs Roščins v Lithuania*. Case No. ARB/18/37; ICSID, *European Solar Farms v Spain*. Case No. ARB/18/45; ICSID, *Canepa Green Energy v Spain*. Case No. ARB/19/4; ICSID, *Petrochemical Holding GmbH v Romania*. Case No. ARB/19/21; ICSID, *Sapec v Spain*. Case No. ARB/19/23; ICSID, *Strabag v Germany*. Case No. ARB/19/29; ICSID, *VM Solar Jerez v Spain*. Case No. ARB/19/30; ICSID, *Société Générale v Croatia*. Case No. ARB/19/33; ICSID, *Marko Mihaljevic v Croatia*. Case No. ARB/19/35; ICSID, *Hamburg Commercial Bank AG v Italy*. Case No. ARB/20/3; ICSID, *Adria Group v Croatia*. Case No. ARB/20/6; ICSID, *EP Wind Project v Romania*. Case No. ARB/20/15.

BIT should be initiated.[125] While the great majority of EU Member States also plans to inform investment arbitration tribunals constituted under the ECT about *Achmea's* effects on their proceeding and to inform the investor community that also no new intra-EU investment arbitration proceedings under the ECT should be initiated,[126] Finland, Hungary, Luxembourg, Malta, Slovenia and Sweden omitted to include ECT proceedings in their declarations.[127] The dissent among Member States becomes also apparent with regard to the Member States' recent commitments regarding intra-EU investor-State arbitration proceedings that have been initiated by State-owned companies or undertakings. While the 22 Member States issuing the Declaration of January 15, 2019, declared that they will "take steps under their national laws governing such undertakings in compliance with Union law, so that those undertakings withdraw pending investment arbitration cases" against other Member States,[128] Finland, Luxembourg, Malta, Slovenia and Sweden expressed a similar intention, however, limited only to investment arbitration proceedings under a BIT.[129] In other words, the latter States made a less expansive commitment, announcing only to terminate arbitration proceedings initiated under BITs, thus excluding ECT proceedings such as the one initiated by the Swedish State-owned company Vattenfall against Germany.[130] In a similar way, Hungary did not announce any intention to make its State-owned companies withdraw from investor-State arbitration proceedings under any intra-EU IIA,[131]

---

125 Representatives of 22 EU Member States, *Declaration on the Legal Consequences of the Judgment of the ECJ in Achmea and on Investment Protection in the EU*, 15 January 2019, paras. 1 ff; Representatives of Finland, Luxembourg, Malta, Slovenia and Sweden, *Declaration on the Enforcement of the Judgement of the ECJ in Achmea and on Investment Protection in the EU*, 16 January 2019, paras. 1 ff; Representative of Hungary, *Declaration on the Legal Consequences of the Judgment of the ECJ in Achmea and on Investment Protection in the EU*, 16 January 2019, paras. 1 ff.

126 Cf. Representatives of 22 EU Member States, *Declaration on the Legal Consequences of the Judgment of the ECJ in Achmea and on Investment Protection in the EU*, 15 January 2019, para. 3, which does not differentiate between BITs and the ECT but refers to "intra-EU investment arbitration proceedings" in general, thus implicitly comprising ECT proceedings.

127 Cf. Representatives of Finland, Luxembourg, Malta, Slovenia and Sweden, *Declaration on the Enforcement of the Judgement of the ECJ in Achmea and on Investment Protection in the EU*, 16 January 2019, paras. 1, 3. Hungary even explicitly stated that the *Achmea* judgment had no effect on ECT proceedings, cf. Representative of Hungary, *Declaration on the Legal Consequences of the Judgment of the ECJ in Achmea and on Investment Protection in the EU*, 16 January 2019, paras. 1, 3, 8 f.

128 Representatives of 22 EU Member States, *Declaration on the Legal Consequences of the Judgment of the ECJ in Achmea and on Investment Protection in the EU*, 15 January 2019, para. 4.

129 Representatives of Finland, Luxembourg, Malta, Slovenia and Sweden, *Declaration on the Enforcement of the Judgement of the ECJ in Achmea and on Investment Protection in the EU*, 16 January 2019, para. 4.

130 ICSID, *Vattenfall v Germany*. Case No. Arb/12/12.

131 Representative of Hungary, *Declaration on the Legal Consequences of the Judgment of the ECJ in Achmea and on Investment Protection in the EU*, 16 January 2019.

thereby preventing the proceedings of the Hungarian partly State-owned energy firm MOL against Croatia from being abandoned.[132]

Against this backdrop, it is worth differentiating between investor-State arbitration proceedings based on intra-EU BITs (a) and such proceedings based on the ECT (b).

a) Intra-EU BIT proceedings

It could be suggested that arbitral tribunals should bring pending intra-EU BIT proceedings to an end due to the incompatibility of the arbitration clause with EU law found by the ECJ. It is, however, more likely that already established tribunals will continue their work and not abandon the pending proceedings as they are only bound by the ECJ's decision as to the content of EU law, and because a termination of the proceedings would restrict the procedural rights guaranteed to the investor in the respective BIT. Furthermore, as discussed previously, once investors have initiated an arbitration proceeding, they have accepted the host State's standing offer to arbitrate and thus concluded an arbitration agreement, which is separate from the IIA.[133]

Arbitral tribunals, however, face the obligation to make every possible effort to render enforceable awards.[134] While this is an obligation to perform and a not an obligation to achieve a defined result, "in principle the outcome of every arbitration is intended to be a final, enforceable, award – as opposed to the outcome of a mediation, which is intended to be an agreement between the parties."[135] Thus, in order to render an enforceable award, an arbitral tribunal has to ensure that it has jurisdiction to decide the case and must comply with the procedural rules and the applicable law chosen by the parties to the arbitration.[136] The failure to abide by the law of the seat of arbitration can easily lead to the non-enforcement of a possible award. This is especially the case for territorialized or 'non-ICSID' tribunals, which have to consider the public policy of the State of their seat of arbitration and of the States where enforcement is potentially sought in order to render an

---

132 ICSID, *MOL Hungarian Oil and Gas Company Plc v Republic of Croatia.* Case No. ARB/13/32.

133 Cf. Chapter IV: II. 2.

134 Cf. N. Blackaby, C. Partasides, A. Redfern and M. Hunter, *Redfern and Hunter on International Arbitration* (New York, London: Oxford University Press, 2015), paras. 9.14 ff; B. Hess, *The Fate of Investment Dispute Resolution after the Achmea Decision of the European Court of Justice,* MPILux Research Paper Series (2018), 14; ICSID, *Vattenfall v Germany.* Case No. ARB/12/12. Decision on the Achmea Issue, 31 August 2018, para. 230. This idea is also reflected in Art. 42 of the ICC Arbitration Rules: "In all matters not expressly provided for in the Rules, the Court and the arbitral tribunal shall act in the spirit of the Rules and shall make every effort to make sure that the award is enforceable at law."

135 N. Blackaby, C. Partasides, A. Redfern and M. Hunter, *Redfern and Hunter on International Arbitration* (New York, London: Oxford University Press, 2015), para. 9.14.

136 Cf. ibid., para. 9.15.

enforceable award.[137] In other words, non-ICSID tribunals which have their seat of arbitration within the EU and base their jurisdiction on an intra-EU BIT need to consider the *lex arbitri* of the country of the seat of arbitration, and especially the latter's *ordre public*. A tribunal that applies EU rules, has to consider them as a part of the EU legal order and as falling under the ECJ's exclusive competence. It thus cannot "substitute its own judgment" for that of the ECJ "regarding the normative content of EU law."[138] As shown in the previous chapter, an arbitral tribunal could thus need to reject its own jurisdiction based on Art. 30 (3) VCLT due to the incompatibility of the investor-State arbitration provision with EU law. To reach such a conclusion it would, however, need to reconsider the established line of intra-EU arbitration jurisprudence and come to the conclusion that intra-EU BITs and EU law relate to the 'same subject matter' and conflict with each other.

The *Achmea* judgment, however, only found investor-State arbitration clauses *such* as the one in the Netherlands–Czechoslovakia BIT to be incompatible with EU law. Whether a specific BIT, a tribunal bases its jurisdiction upon, contains *such* a clause, and thus whether there is a conflict between the BIT in dispute and EU law, is ultimately for the arbitral tribunal to determine. As the previous chapter has shown,[139] there is much to suggest that the *Achmea* decision is transferable to every intra-EU BIT. Nonetheless, some tribunals might reject any link to EU law in cases pending before them (as many intra-EU arbitral tribunals have done so far) and continue the proceedings. Arbitral tribunals have the *competence de la competence*[140] to decide whether or not they have jurisdiction over a particular dispute and as just shown, the BITs continue to be valid treaties as long as they are not terminated by the Member States. It is thus unlikely that currently pending proceedings based on intra-EU BITs will be terminated by the tribunals themselves. A recent example of the reluctance of arbitral tribunals to implement the ECJ decision can be found in the award in *Magyar Farming v Hungary* rendered in November 2019 in which the tribunal rejected the applicability of the *Achmea* decision to the case at hand.[141]

Notwithstanding, it is probable that already established arbitral tribunals will at least follow the example of the arbitral tribunals in the ECT disputes in *Masdar*

---

137 Cf. B. Hess, *The Fate of Investment Dispute Resolution after the Achmea Decision of the European Court of Justice*, MPILux Research Paper Series (2018), 14; H. E. Kjos, *Applicable Law in Investor-State Arbitration* (Oxford: Oxford University Press, 2013), at 260.

138 C. Wackernagel, *The Twilight of the BITs? EU Judicial Proceedings, the Consensual Termination of intra-EU BITs and Why that Matters for International Law*, Beiträge zum Transnationalen Wirtschaftsrecht (2016), 9.

139 Cf. Chapter III: III. 2.

140 See also C. Brown, *Inherent Powers in International Adjudication* in C. Romano, et al. (eds.), *The Oxford handbook of International Adjudication* (Oxford: Oxford University Press, 2014), pp. 828–47, at p. 831.

141 ICSID, *Magyar Farming v Hungary*. Case No. ARB/17/27. Award, 13 November 2019, paras. 205 ff.

Solar and *Vattenfall*,[142] and reopen hearings to address the new situation after the *Achmea* decision. This would provide the parties to the proceeding with the possibility to reconsider their case and assess the effects and the enforceability of a possible award and possibly allow the disputing parties to reach a settlement and discontinue the proceedings.

Regarding possible upcoming proceedings but also those already pending, in which the seat of arbitration has not yet been determined, the arbitrators might – unless there is an agreement to the contrary among the parties – choose a seat outside the EU and try to enforce potential awards in States outside the EU in which the respondent Member State has some assets. This would allow to circumvent the *ordre public* of the State of the tribunal's seat of arbitration and thus increase the likelihood of rendering an enforceable award. In order to avoid the effects of the *Achmea* decision, it is further likely that that investors initiating new ISDS proceedings will, whenever it is possible, rely on the ICSID Convention.[143] As in the case of ICSID proceedings, domestic courts are excluded from reviewing an award and can only verify its authenticity at the enforcement stage, without being allowed to re-examine the tribunal's jurisdiction or the decision on the merits.[144]

b) ECT proceedings

As of May 23, 2020, out of the 67 pending intra-EU investor-State arbitration proceedings, 46 are based on the ECT. These proceedings are most likely to be continued. As extensively discussed in the previous chapter, the *Achmea* decision has no direct effect on investor-State arbitration proceedings based on the ECT, even though the rationale of the decision, i.e. the protection of the EU's autonomy applies to ECT proceedings just as it applies to proceedings based on intra-EU BITs. This becomes apparent with the recent 'post-*Achmea*' arbitral decisions in *Stadtwerke München v Spain*,[145] *Belenergia v Italy*,[146] *Masdar Solar v Spain*[147] and *Vattenfall v Germany*,[148] which all rejected the argument

---

142 ICSID, *Masdar Solar v Spain*. Case No. ARB/14/1. Award, 16 May 2018; ICSID, *Vattenfall v Germany*. Case No. ARB/12/12. Decision on the Achmea Issue, 31 August 2018.

143 The recourse to ICSID could not be prevented by the EU Member States by notifying the Centre that intra-EU investor-State disputes are no longer considered to be submitted to its jurisdiction in accordance with Art. 25 (4) ICSID Convention, as such a notification has no direct effect on the jurisdiction of an arbitral tribunal, cf. C. Schreuer, *The ICSID Convention: A Commentary*, 2nd ed. (Cambridge: Cambridge University Press, 2009), Art. 25, paras. 928 ff.

144 See on this, in greater detail Chapter II: IV. 1. d).

145 ICSID, *Stadtwerke München v Spain*. Case No. ARB/15/1. Award, 2 December 2019, paras. 136 ff.

146 ICSID, *Belenergia v Italy*. Case No. ARB/15/40. Award, 6 August 2019, paras. 323 ff.

147 ICSID, *Masdar Solar v Spain*. Case No. ARB/14/1. Award, 16 May 2018, para. 638.

148 ICSID, *Masdar Solar v Spain*. Case No. ARB/14/1. Award, 16 May 2018, para. 638; ICSID, *Vattenfall v Germany*. Case No. ARB/12/12. Decision on the Achmea Issue, 31 August 2018, para. 232.

that due to the *Achmea* decision the arbitral tribunal would lack jurisdiction to decide the dispute. In fact, it is even possible that the number of cases initiated under the ECT will rise. As the era of intra-EU BITs is coming to an end especially due to the Multilateral Agreement for the Termination of intra-EU BITs, which, however, does not affect ECT arbitration, investors in the energy sector might try to increasingly rely on the ECT to initiate investor-State arbitration proceedings.[149]

2 Effects of a BIT termination on pending proceedings

Most intra-EU BITs will be terminated through the Multilateral Agreement for the Termination of intra-EU BITs. The termination of these treaties will extinguish the possibility to rely on investor-State arbitration by abolishing the standing offer to arbitrate contained in the investor-State arbitration provision. It will, however, not affect pending proceedings. A respondent State cannot unilaterally stop a pending investor-State arbitration proceeding by terminating the BIT, the tribunal's jurisdiction is based upon. This becomes also clear with regard to Art. 25 (1) ICSID Convention according to which the parties to an investor-State dispute cannot withdraw their consent to the jurisdiction of an ICSID tribunal unilaterally after the consent has been perfected among the parties to the dispute. Once an investor has accepted the offer to arbitrate contained in the investor-State arbitration clause of the BIT the arbitral tribunal set up for this purpose has jurisdiction over the specific disputes, i.e. the consent of the host State becomes irrevocable and is insulated from any attempt by the host State to terminate the BIT.[150] This general principle can be transferred to non-ICSID proceedings as well, even in the absence of explicit provisions in other arbitration rules. Also, with regard to the ECT, a termination, withdrawal or the conclusion of a subsequent treaty would not affect pending investor-State arbitration proceeding based on the ECT.[151]

---

149 See in this regard the ECT-based intra-EU investor-State arbitration proceedings initiated after the *Achmea* judgment: ICSID, *LSG Building Solutions v Romania*. Case No. ARB/18/19; ICSID, *Veolia v Italy*. Case No. ARB/18/20); ICSID, *European Solar Farms v Spain*. Case No. ARB/18/45; ICSID, *Canepa Green Energy v Spain*. Case No. ARB/19/4; ICSID, *Petrochemical Holding GmbH v Romania*. Case No. ARB/19/21; ICSID, *Sapec v Spain*. Case No. ARB/19/23; ICSID, *Strabag v Germany*. Case No. ARB/19/29; ICSID, *VM Solar Jerez v Spain*. Case No. ARB/19/30; ICSID, *Hamburg Commercial Bank AG v Italy*. Case No. ARB/20/3; ICSID, *EP Wind Project v Romania*. Case No. ARB/20/15.

150 Cf. C. Schreuer, *The ICSID Convention: A Commentary*, 2nd ed. (Cambridge: Cambridge University Press, 2009), Art. 25, para. 619.

151 In the *Vattenfall* proceeding, Germany, however, argued that as an effect to the ECJ's *Achmea* judgment the investor-State arbitration clause in Art. 26 ECT would have become inapplicable ex tunc, with the effect that arbitral tribunals based on this clause would lack jurisdiction, ICSID, *Vattenfall v Germany*. Case No. ARB/12/12. Decision on the Achmea Issue, 31 August 2018, para. 56.

3 Interim findings

The great majority of pending investor-State arbitration proceedings will not be discontinued in reaction to the ECJ's *Achmea* judgment, neither by arbitral tribunals whose jurisdiction is based on an intra-EU BIT nor by those whose jurisdiction is based on the ECT. It is even possible that the *Achmea* decision might lead to an important increase in case numbers, as many intra-EU investors currently facing disputes with EU host States may develop a 'last-minute panic'. They could be incited to profit from the possibility of investor-State arbitration, before this procedural tool is excluded from intra-EU relations. It, however, remains to be seen whether investors in pending intra-EU BIT proceedings will make use of the structured dialogue provided for in Art. 9 of the Multilateral Agreement for the Termination of intra-EU BITs and try to settle the disputes amicably.

Regarding newly initiated and upcoming investor-State disputes, it is likely that investors will increasingly rely on ICSID arbitration proceedings due to the very limited State control and in in case of non-ICSID proceedings advocate for a seat of arbitration outside the EU to avoid conflicts with the lex arbitri.

Thus, the signatory EU Member States of the Multilateral Agreement for the Termination of intra-EU BITs should quickly ratify the Agreement in order to terminate all intra-EU BITs. For a coherent approach within the EU, Austria, Finland and Sweden should follow suit. Furthermore, the Member States should start negotiating a way to disconnect the ECT from intra-EU investor-State relations in order to avoid new proceedings being initiated. Regarding already pending ECT proceedings, the Member States could also consider their discontinuation through settlements with the investors, in order to prevent further complications regarding investors' attempts to enforce intra-EU awards within the EU and abroad, i.e. outside the reach of the EU legal order.

VI Why a substitute might be necessary

Achmea will eventually lead to the termination of all intra-EU BITs and with great probability also lead to a disconnection of intra-EU investor-State relations from the ECT. Thus, without the creation of any substitute, the 'additional' substantive protection of investors guaranteed through intra-EU IIAs and the remedy of ISDS will vanish and all intra-EU investors will be subject to the domestic jurisdiction of the host State only. This is not a problem *per se*. It even reflects the principle of 'mutual trust' among EU Member States. Turning away from the long-established 'international investor-protection regime' within the EU might, however, create a regulatory gap or a decline of investor protection in certain Member States. Against this backdrop, the EU Member States have announced in their declarations regarding the legal consequences of the *Achmea* judgment that they will – together with the EU Commission – intensify discussions

> with the aim of better ensuring complete, strong and effective protection of investments within the European Union. Those discussions include the

assessment of existing processes and mechanisms of dispute resolution, as well as of the need and, if the need is ascertained, the means to create new or to improve existing relevant tools and mechanisms under Union law.[152]

The sole abolishment of intra-EU ISDS proceedings through disconnection from or termination of intra-EU IIAs might create new difficulties or reinforce existing ones. In certain cases, for example diplomatic protection could experience a new rise within the EU. Diplomatic protection does not fall under the prohibition of Art. 344 TFEU and is thus in principle compatible with the EU Treaties.[153] Compared to the legal settlement of disputes by arbitral tribunals, this mode of dispute settlement is often highly politicized and thus contradicts the purpose of international investment law as it is known today. Diplomatic protection bears the inherent risk of the home State pressuring the host State or vice versa. This could undermine the idea of settling disputes based on transparent legal procedures. In other words, it might be in the interest not only of investors but also of the respective home States and especially the host States to have clear standards on the protection of intra-EU foreign investments and at least the option to rely at a certain point in a dispute settlement procedure on a neutral transnational body of adjudication.

The following section will analyse the challenges the EU might be facing after the termination of the 'international investment protection regime' within the EU. It starts by revisiting the principle of 'mutual trust' and judicial independence within the EU, which seem to be rather normative goals than stable achievements (1.). It then analyses the possible reaction of certain investors to the abolishment of the intra-EU investor-State dispute settlement regime, namely the risk of intensified forum shopping and restructuring of investment activities (2.). Finally, it assesses whether the developments on the intra-EU level could weaken the EU's position on the global level and its attempts to 'shape the rules of globalization' (3.).

1 Mutual trust and judicial independence within the EU

In the ECJ's understanding, intra-EU investor-State arbitration proceedings stand in contradiction to the principle of 'mutual trust'.[154] It has always been a general principle that only the domestic judiciary is competent to decide cases

---

152 Representatives of 22 EU Member States, *Declaration on the Legal Consequences of the Judgment of the ECJ in Achmea and on Investment Protection in the EU*, 15 January 2019; Representatives of Finland, Luxembourg, Malta, Slovenia and Sweden, *Declaration on the Enforcement of the Judgement of the ECJ in Achmea and on Investment Protection in the EU*, 16 January 2019; Representative of Hungary, *Declaration on the Legal Consequences of the Judgment of the ECJ in Achmea and on Investment Protection in the EU*, 16 January 2019.

153 Cf. M. Athen and O. Dörr, *Art. 344 AEUV* in E. Grabitz and M. Hilf (eds.), *Das Recht der Europäischen Union* (München: C. H. Beck, 2018), at paras. 2, 22 ff.

154 Cf. ECJ, *Achmea*. C-284/16. Judgment, 6 March 2018, para. 58.

that fall under its jurisdiction. This has changed with the proliferation of international courts and tribunals. In this context, investor-State arbitration emerged as a potential safeguard against a host State's arbitrary behaviour and as forum 'of last resort' for disputes in which an investor could not or did not want to rely on the domestic judiciary, which was understood to be – at least potentially biased in favour of the State and thus partial. Against this backdrop, investor-State arbitration developed with – at least in theory – the arbitrators' impartiality as one of its main features. In difference to domestic proceedings, arbitrators are not part of an organ of any of the disputing parties. Thus, in case of an arbitral proceeding, an alleged violation of a State's obligation is not assessed by its 'own' judges but by a truly detached dispute settlement body.

From an EU legal perspective, investor-State arbitration, which is based on the assumption of a potential risk of partially acting domestic courts is not compatible with the EU's general principle of 'mutual trust'. EU law is rather influenced by the idea that a particular regime granting special remedies to foreign investors is not necessary but rather dispensable between democracies that abide by the rule of law, which is also reflected in the relatively low number of investor-State disputes.[155] This assumption, however, needs to be questioned. First of all, the high compliance rates of host States with substantive investor protection standards could precisely be linked to the risk for Member States of otherwise facing an investor-State arbitration proceeding. Furthermore, a functioning legal system which complies with basic rule of law principles but also provides for independent dispute settlement proceedings outside the domestic judiciary is far more attractive for foreign investors, than a system which lacks such attributes.[156] But, above all, the EU is facing different crises in the last years. The Brexit decision has shocked the Union and its former cohesion is increasingly questioned. Some Member States have weak institutions and several developments reveal fundamental deficits regarding compliance with the EU's fundamental values and principles, most notably with the rule of law.[157] In other words, one can observe that

---

155 See especially A. de Mestral, *Investor State Arbitration Between Developed Democratic Countries* in A. de Mestral (ed.), *Second Thoughts: Investor State Arbitration Between Developed Democracies* (Montreal: McGill-Queen's University Press, 2017), pp. 9–56.

156 See also M. Bungenberg, *A History of Investment Arbitration and Investor-State Dispute Settlement in Germany* in A. de Mestral (ed.), *Second Thoughts: Investor State Arbitration Between Developed Democracies* (Montreal: McGill-Queen's University Press, 2017), pp. 259–83, at p. 276.

157 Cf. with further references, A. von Bogdandy and M. Ioannidis, *Das systemische Defizit: Merkmale, Instrumente und Probleme am Beispiel der Rechtsstaatlichkeit und des neuen Rechtsstaatlichkeitsverfahrens*, Zeitschrift für ausländisches öffentliches Recht und Völkerrecht 74 (2014), 283–328, at 284 ff; T. T. Andersen and S. Hindelang, *The Day after: Alternatives to Intra-EU BITs*, Journal of World Investment & Trade 17 (2016), 984–1014, at 989 f. See also the decision of the European Parliament to request the Member States to determine in accordance with Art. 7 TEU whether Hungary is at risk of breaching the EU's founding values, European Parliament, *Rule of Law in Hungary: Parliament Calls on the EU to Act*. www.europarl.europa.eu/news/en/press-room/20180906IPR12104/rule-of-law-in-hungary-parliament-calls-on-the-eu-to-act

there is not necessarily a symmetry regarding substantive and especially procedural levels of protection among all EU Member States. This is also reflected in several studies and indicators which have been published in recent years.

Already in 2013, the Council had defined country-specific recommendations in respect of ten Member States concerning deficiencies in independence, quality and efficiency of their judicial systems.[158] One attempt to improve the situation has been the EU Commission's permanent "Mechanism for Cooperation and Verification for Bulgaria and Romania,"[159] which was created in 2007 and assesses the progress with judicial reform and the fight against corruption in these two States. Its sole existence demonstrates that judicial standards are far from being totally equivalent all over the EU. The most recent reports show an improvement of the general situations but also imply that there is still a long way to go for both countries before achieving all the goals set by the EU Commission in the field of judicial independence, high level corruption and organized crime.[160]

Another EU source which reveals the great divergence among judicial systems in the EU and the independence of the respective judiciary, is the EU Justice Scoreboard, an information tool aiming to assist the EU and its Member States to achieve more effective justice by providing objective, reliable and comparable data with regard to three indicators, namely the quality, independence and efficiency of justice systems in all Member States.[161] Efficiency is connected to the length of proceedings, the clearance rate and the number of pending cases. The quality is assessed on the base of accessibility, resources and quality standards of the judiciary. The independence criterion focusses on structural independence. While the EU Commission stresses the importance of an independent judiciary, the EU Justice Scoreboard 2019, shows an alarmingly low level of perceived judicial independence in several Member States. Only 20 per cent of the general public perceives the independence of the Croatian judiciary to be good. Bulgarian and Slovakian courts and judges only reach an approval rate of 30 per cent regarding their independence.[162] The perception among companies is similarly bad and mainly linked to the perceived interference or pressure from government

---

(23 May 2020). See finally, also the recent ECJ decision on the reform of the Polish judicial system, ECJ, *Minister for Justice and Equality v LM (Deficiencies in the system of justice).* C-216/18 PPU. Judgment, 25 July 2018, ECLI:EU:C:2018:586.

158 Cf. M. Weller, *Mutual Trust: In Search of the Future of European Union Private International Law,* Journal of Private International Law 11 (2015), 64–102, at 66 f.

159 EU Commission, *Mechanism for Cooperation and Verification for Bulgaria and Romania.* http://ec.europa.eu/cvm/progress_reports_en.htm (23 May 2020).

160 EU Commission, *Report to the European Parliament and the Council on Progress in Bulgaria Under the Co-operation and Verification Mechanism: COM(2017) 750 final,* 15.11.2017; EU Commission, *Report to the European Parliament and the Council on Progress in Romania Under the Co-operation and Verification Mechanism: COM(2017) 751 final,* 15.11.2017. See also EU Commission, *EU Justice Scoreboard 2018* (Brussels, 2018), at 6.

161 Cf. EU Commission, *The 2016 EU Justice Scoreboard* (Brussels, 2016); E. Mak and S. Taekema, *The European Union's Rule of Law Agenda: Identifying Its Core and Contextualizing Its Application,* Hague Journal on the Rule of Law 8 (2016), 25–50, at 31.

162 EU Commission, *Justice Scoreboard 2019* (Brussels, 2019), at p. 44, figure 47.

and politicians.[163] Furthermore, there is "a clear risk of a serious breach of the rule of law" in Poland[164] and Hungary.[165] The perception of a lack of rule of law abidance by Poland has recently been confirmed by the ECJ in its judgment of the deficiencies of the Polish justice system.[166] In a similar vein, the European Parliament has requested the EU on September 12, 2018, to act with regard of the clear risk of a "serious breach of the EU founding values in Hungary", especially due to the perception of inter alia a lack of judicial independence in the country.[167] Other independent reports have reached similar conclusions,[168] even though many reports reflect surveys of business leaders or experts and not empirical scientific studies, they show that the judicial independence among EU Member States is at least perceived to be everything but uniform. In sum, the 'mutual trust' within the EU is currently facing a major crisis. This principle of EU law appears to be more a normative goal than a stable achievement and established reality.

The EU, however, is not only a group of nation States with the common goal of promoting the economy. It is also a legal and a value community. A decline of the rule of law and the independence of the judiciary in some Member States does therefore not only affect the specific Member State, but the entire EU. The common market is at risk if the trust in the respective domestic legal systems vanishes.

While ISDS is definitely not the solution to these challenges, its abolishment without the creation of a substitute will neither improve the current situation but might even worsen it. With regard to a decreasing rule of law compliance in some Eastern EU Member States and a decline of judicial independence, investors might tend to avoid investing in specific Member States, especially if no independent transnational dispute settlement mechanisms are guaranteed, which could protect the investment against arbitrary and discriminatory State acts. Hence, the need for a harmonized substitute of the current ISDS regime, which could enhance the 'mutual trust' and the compliance with the rule of law in all EU Member States.

2 Forum shopping and restructuring

The perceived lack of judicial independence and the non-compliance with basic principles of the rule of law in connection with the abolishment of the intra-EU investor protection regime may lead to another unwanted effect: an increased

---

163 Ibid., p. 45 f., figures 49 and 50.
164 EU Commission, *EU Justice Scoreboard 2018* (Brussels, 2018), p. 6.
165 EU Commission, *Justice Scoreboard 2019* (Brussels, 2019), p. 9.
166 ECJ, *Minister for Justice and Equality v LM (Deficiencies in the system of justice)*. C-216/18 PPU. Judgment, 25 July 2018.
167 Cf. European Parliament, *Rule of Law in Hungary: Parliament Calls on the EU to Act*. www. europarl.europa.eu/news/en/press-room/20180906IPR12104/rule-of-law-in-hungary-parlia ment-calls-on-the-eu-to-act (23 May 2020).
168 Cf. World Economic Forum, *The Global Competitiveness Report 2017–2018*. www.weforum. org/reports/the-global-competitiveness-report-2017-2018 (23 May 2020), at 75, 99, 119, 219, 265, 301; Transparency International, *Corruption Perception Index 2017*. www.transparency.org/ news/feature/corruption_perceptions_index_2017 (23 May 2020).

forum shopping and company restructuring, which in turn could entail the risk of rerouting of financial flows and the reduction of jobs in the EU.

In a globalized world with huge MNEs controlling the global markets, the State loses its importance as connecting factor and reference value for companies active in many different States. As convincingly summarized by Moon, companies generally "behave on behalf of their own interests, not by national allegiances, unless the company is closely tied to their nation's economic development, either through direct public ownership or through financial intermediaries."[169] The 'international investment protection regime', however, like many other international law regimes, remains based on rather static assumptions of State borders and nationalities. Thus, many MNEs try to remain flexible vis-à-vis their nationality in order to profit from different tax or investment protection regimes.

As an effect of the *Achmea* judgment and the termination of intra-EU BITs and a possible disconnection from the ECT regarding intra-EU investment activities, an investor stemming from one Member State could be less protected when acting within the EU than when acting outside the EU, while an extra-European investor falling under an extra-EU BIT or an EU FTA providing for investor protection would remain as protected as before or receive new level of protections through the EU treaties to be concluded in the near future.

As a result, many observers have predicted serious competitive distortions and a wave of restructuring of EU companies. Investors could try to profit from the extra-EU investment protection regime and initiate new investments via subsidies based outside the EU. In that case they could fall under extra-EU BITs and FTAs and thus maintain the high level of protection guaranteed in these treaties for their own investments.[170] For example, a German company investing in Romania, could structure its investment through a subsidiary incorporated in Australia, to profit from the protection offered by the 1993 Australia–Romania BIT and thus to maintain the possibility to rely on investor-State dispute settlement in case of a conflict with Romania. So far, however, foreign investors have not accorded too much importance to the legal investment protection framework when deciding whether to invest in a specific country. As explained by Schreuer:

> For the typical investor the availability of international protection does not seem to be decisive when making investment decisions. Rather they will

169 H.-C. Moon, *Foreign Direct Investment: A Global Perspective* (Hackensack, NJ: World Scientific, 2016), at 3.

170 Cf. J. K. Schäfer and J. P. Gaffney, *Intra-EU BITs: Toothless Tigers or Do They Still Bite?* Zeitschrift für Schiedsverfahren (2013), 78; C. Schreuer, *The Future of International Investment Law* in M. Bungenberg, et al. (eds.), *International Investment Law: A Handbook* (Baden-Baden: Nomos, 2015), pp. 1904–11, at 1907 f; S. Wilske and C. Edworthy, *The Future of Intra-European Union BITs: A Recent Development in International Investment Treaty Arbitration against Romania and Its Potential Collateral Damage,* Journal of International Arbitration 33 (2016), 331–52, at 346; T. T. Andersen and S. Hindelang, *The Day after,* Journal of World Investment & Trade 17 (2016), 987. In a similar way, see also E. Gaillard, *L'Avenir des Traités de Protection des Investissements* in C. Leben (ed.), *Droit international des investissements et de l'arbitrage transnational* (Paris: Editions Pedone, 2015), at 1032 f.

discover the potential of BIT arbitration after problems have arisen. Only some major investors contemplate corporate structuring at the time of the investment so as to avail themselves of the protection of particular treaties.[171]

Nonetheless, it is likely that the unawareness of investors regarding the possibility of ISDS has vanished due to recent prominent media coverage of investment disputes and the highly politicized debates around international investment law. The rise of investor-State arbitration proceedings is a sign that the possibility to rely on an independent international dispute settlement mechanism might increasingly gain importance for foreign investors when making their investment decisions – especially in the intra-EU context.

Corporate restructuring and ownership complexity are no new phenomena. The UNCTAD World Investment Report 2016 revealed that "between 1/7 (TTIP) and 1/3 (TPP) of apparently intraregional foreign affiliates in major megaregional treaty areas are ultimately owned by parents outside the region."[172] Thus, it is not surprising that so-called nationality-mismatch cases are gaining relevance. Between 2010 and 2016 about one-third of the publicly known ISDS proceedings were initiated by corporations which were ultimately owned by a parent company based in a third State, i.e. not a State party to the IIA, or which was based in the host State itself, i.e. domestic investors invested in their home State through foreign subsidies, so-called round-tripping investment.[173]

According to Schreuer, such a corporate restructuring is "a promising way to obtain protection if only it is undertaken early enough"; however, "once the dispute with the host State has broken out it is too late to obtain the protection of a favourable treaty by changing the investor's nationality."[174] Of the accessible 78 cases in which jurisdiction was denied between 2000 and 2015, the question of 'time-sensitive restructuring', i.e. the restructuring for the purpose of initiating an investor-State arbitration proceeding, was an issue in at least eight cases.[175] The most famous of these cases, was *Philip Morris v Australia*, in which the tribunal found that

> the commencement of treaty-based investor-State arbitration constitutes an abuse of right (or abuse of process) when an investor has changed its corporate structure to gain the protection of an investment treaty at a point in time where a dispute was foreseeable. A dispute is foreseeable when there is

171 C. Schreuer, *The Future of International Investment Law* in M. Bungenberg, et al. (eds.), *International Investment Law: A Handbook* (Baden-Baden: Nomos, 2015), p. 1905.
172 UNCTAD, *World Investment Report 2016: Investor Nationality: Policy Challenges* (New York, Geneva: United Nations, 2016), at 185.
173 Cf. ibid., p. 171.
174 C. Schreuer, *The Future of International Investment Law* in M. Bungenberg, et al. (eds.), *International Investment Law: A Handbook* (Baden-Baden: Nomos, 2015), p. 1910.
175 UNCTAD, *World Investment Report 2016: Investor Nationality: Policy Challenges* (New York, Geneva: United Nations, 2016), p. 179.

a reasonable prospect that a measure that may give rise to a treaty claim will materialise.[176]

However, if planned carefully, restructuring is not unlawful and it generally suffices to create a company with the right nationality somewhere in the corporate chain to profit from an IIA.[177] Thus, as explained by UNCTAD, essentially as long as one country has a broadly worded IIA, investors from any country can potentially benefit from it by structuring their investments into that country through entities established in another Contracting Party.[178] This is mostly due to the fact that so far, most arbitral tribunals have refused to 'pierce the corporate veil',[179] but have rather taken a formalistic approach to assess a company's nationality, sticking to the express wording of the respective IIAs, which seldomly require substantive links between the company and the 'alleged' home State. Whether the tribunals should rather concentrate on other conditions such as the origin of capital or significant operational activities in the home State, even if not expressly mentioned in an IIA, is a highly controversial issue.[180] As put by the arbitrators in the 'transition case'[181] *Saluka v Czech Republic*:

> The Tribunal has some sympathy for the argument that a company which has no real connection with a State party to a BIT, and which is in reality a mere shell company controlled by another company which is not constituted under the laws of that State, should not be entitled to invoke the provisions of that treaty. Such a possibility lends itself to abuses of the arbitral procedure, and to practices of "treaty shopping" [...]. However, [...] the predominant factor which must guide the Tribunal's exercise of its functions is the terms

---

176 PCA, *Philip Morris Asia v Australia*. Case No. 2012–12. Award on Jurisdiction and Admissibility, 17 December 2015, para. 585. See also ICSID, *Levy v Peru*. Case No. ARB/11/17. Award, 9 January 2015, para. 185.

177 See also C. Schreuer, *The Future of International Investment Law* in M. Bungenberg, et al. (eds.), *International Investment Law: A Handbook* (Baden-Baden: Nomos, 2015), p. 1910; UNCTAD, *World Investment Report 2016: Investor Nationality: Policy Challenges* (New York, Geneva: United Nations, 2016), p. 180; ICSID, *Levy v Peru*. Case No. ARB/11/17. Award, 9 January 2015, para. 184.

178 UNCTAD, *World Investment Report 2016: Investor Nationality: Policy Challenges* (New York, Geneva: United Nations, 2016), p. 185.

179 See for example, ICSID, *ADC v Hungary*. Case No. ARB/03/16. Award of the Tribunal, 2 October 2006, paras. 332 ff; ICSID, *Rompetrol v Romania*. Case No. ARB/06/3. Decision on Respondent's Preliminary Objections, 18 April 2008, paras. 78 ff. The *Charanne* tribunal found that piercing the corporate veil is only conceivable in the event of a jurisdictional fraud, cf. ICSID, *Charanne v Spain*. Arb. No. 062/2012. Final Award, 21 January 2016, paras. 415 ff.

180 For an extended overview see with further references, M. Perkams, *Protection for Legal Persons* in M. Bungenberg, et al. (eds.), *International Investment Law: A Handbook* (Baden-Baden: Nomos, 2015), pp. 638–52, at 641 f; N. Blackaby, C. Partasides, A. Redfern and M. Hunter, *Redfern and Hunter on International Arbitration* (New York, London: Oxford University Press, 2015), paras. 8.20 ff.

181 On the classification of ISDS proceedings within the EU as pre-accession, transition and intra-EU cases, see Chapter I: III. 5.

in which the parties to the Treaty now in question have agreed to establish the Tribunal's jurisdiction. [...] That agreed definition required only that the claimant-investor should be constituted under the laws of [a State party], and it is not open to the Tribunal to add other requirements which the parties could themselves have added but which they omitted to add.[182]

The tribunal in *Yukos v Russia* took an even more general approach, explaining that

the Tribunal knows of no general principles of international law that would require investigating the structure of a company or another organization when the applicable treaty simply requires it to be organized in accordance with the laws of a Contracting Party.[183]

Even though there is a risk of restructuring and treaty shopping, the advantages for companies are not as clear as often claimed. The protection of non-EU investments in Germany for example, is less developed than that of domestic and European investors. This becomes clear regarding the access to fundamental rights. The German State can rather easily influence non-EU investments compared to intra-EU investment which receive a high protection under the German constitution.[184]

Nonetheless, in sum, the creation of a substitute for the current 'international investment protection regime' within the EU seems the most promising way to circumvent the considerable risk of restructuring and treaty shopping, which could undermine the effects of the *Achmea* judgment.

3 Weakening of the EU's position as a global player

The outright termination of intra-EU BITs and the disconnection from the ECT could also affect the EU's external trade policy and cast doubts regarding the need of investor protection in FTAs between the EU and developed partner States.[185]

One of the core objectives of the EU's foreign and trade policy in the last two decades was to strengthen its position as a global actor, while 'shaping the rules' of a globalisation.[186] In pursuit of this objective, the EU attempted to create greater

---

182 PCA, *Saluka Investments v Czech Republic.* Partial Award, 17 March 2006, paras. 240 f.
183 PCA, *Yukos v The Russian Federation.* Case No. AA 227. Interim Award on Jurisdiction and Admissibility, 30 November 2009, para. 415. See also ICSID, *Charanne v Spain.* Arb. No. 062/2012. Final Award, 21 January 2016, para. 417.
184 Cf. S. Schill, *Investitionsschutz in EU-Freihandelsabkommen: Erosion gesetzgeberischer Gestaltungsmacht?,* Zeitschrift für ausländisches öffentliches Recht und Völkerrecht 78 (2018), 33–92, at 50.
185 Cf. the concerns expressed in, Austria, Finland, France, Germany and the Netherlands, *Non-Paper on Intra-EU Investment Treaties,* 7 April 2016. www.bmwi.de/Redaktion/DE/Downloads/I/intra-eu-investment-treaties.pdf?__blob=publicationFile&v=4 (23 May 2020), at para. 6.
186 See among others, P. Craig and G. de Búrca, *EU Law: Text, Cases and Materials,* 6th ed. (Oxford: Oxford University Press, 2015), at 316; C. Titi, *International Investment Law and the European Union: Towards a New Generation of International Investment Agreements,* European Journal of International Law 26 (2015), 639–61, at 641. See also the speech of EU Trade Commissioner,

consistency and coherence in its external relations and introduced several novelties in the Lisbon Treaty, in particular the transfer of competence on international investment protection in Art. 207 TFEU.[187]

While the TTIP negotiations between the EU and the United States have been interrupted, the EU continues to be an active participant in the field of international investment law. In this context, it has started to propagate, together with other States, the replacement of investor-State arbitration with a Multilateral Investment Court (MIC) or an Investment Court System, providing for an appellate mechanism.[188] This goal, however, could become more difficult to achieve without a clear-cut transition towards a new regime of investor-protection within the EU. It will be difficult for the EU to argue that ISDS instruments are needed in the relation with third States in order to guarantee the compliance with investor-protection rules, while at the same time arguing that such a mechanism is not necessary with regard to the Member States judiciary. This could be perceived as implying that the neutrality and impartiality of the domestic judiciary is guaranteed in all EU Member States while one cannot rely on it with regard to States like Japan or Canada.[189] It could even be understood to imply that these States "do not, from an EU perspective, comply with the international rule of law" and thus compromise the EU's efforts to promote FTAs with a reformed investor-State dispute settlement mechanism.[190]

Thus, if no coherent way to tackle the issue of intra-EU IIAs and intra-EU ISDS proceedings is found and the EU and its Member States prevent the enforcement of arbitral awards based on such treaties or even encourage the non-recognition and non-enforcement of intra-EU awards by other actors like third-State domestic courts, the EU's position in the international sphere could be weakened. In other words, if the EU does not 'play by the rules' of international law in its internal affairs, its credibility in its external relations might suffer.[191] A coherent approach towards intra-EU protection and intra-EU investor-State settlement is

---

C. Malmström, *The Next Transatlantic Project: John D. Greenwald Memorial Lecture, Georgetown University*, 7 March 2019. http://trade.ec.europa.eu/doclib/docs/2019/march/tradoc_157721.pdf (23 May 2020).

187 P. Craig and G. de Búrca, *EU Law: Text, Cases and Materials*, 6th ed. (Oxford: Oxford University Press, 2015), p. 316; C. Titi, *International Investment Law and the European Union: Towards a New Generation of International Investment Agreements*, European Journal of International Law 26 (2015), 641.

188 Cf. A. Roberts, *Incremental, Systemic, and Paradigmatic Reform of Investor-State Arbitration*, American Journal of International Law 112 (2018), 410–32, at 416. See also ECJ, *CETA-Opinion*. 1/17. Opinion of Advocate General Bot, 29 January 2019, paras. 7 f.

189 See for example, Art. 8.27 ff. CETA.

190 Cf. M. Bungenberg, *A History of Investment Arbitration and Investor-State Dispute Settlement in Germany* in A. de Mestral (ed.), *Second Thoughts* (Montreal: McGill-Queen's University Press, 2017), p. 276. See also Austria, Finland, France, Germany and the Netherlands, *Non-Paper on Intra-EU Investment Treaties*, 7 April 2016. www.bmwi.de/Redaktion/DE/Downloads/I/intra-eu-investment-treaties.pdf?__blob=publicationFile&v=4 (23 May 2020), para. 6.

191 In a similar vein, see also H. P. Aust, *Eine völkerrechtsfreundliche Union? Grund und Grenze der Öffnung des Europarechts zum Völkerrecht*, Europarecht 52 (2017), 106–21, at 120.

thus needed, not only with regard to intra-EU investments but also with regard to the EU's credibility and reliability vis-à-vis its global partners. This does not mean that intra-EU investor-State arbitration must be maintained, but it implies that the EU should consider a concerted approach to investor protection which transcends the domestic judiciary and aims at transnational control mechanisms.

4 Interim findings

With regard to the current crisis of 'mutual trust' and judicial independence within the EU, the increasing risk of forum shopping and restructuring of companies as well as the possible weakening of the EU's position in the international legal sphere, it seems promising to substitute the current system of investor protection in the EU with a coherent and harmonized European approach and to align the protection standards of extra-EU and intra-EU investments to a certain degree, in order to avoid the favouring of extra-EU investors. The different options in this regard will be discussed in the following section.

VII Possible substitutes

Louis Henkin's famous quote that "almost all nations observe almost all principles of international law and almost all of their obligations almost all of the time",[192] is transferable to the EU Member States with regard to investor protection. It could thus be argued that – even in light of rule of law impairments in some Member States – there is no major need within the EU for an independent control mechanism of the States' compliance with their obligations similar to the one provided through investor-State arbitration provisions.

However, one must keep in mind that a core reason for the existence of international investment law is its preventive character aiming at securing the legal environment even if a State develops in an arbitrary direction. One cannot be too sure that achievements such as widespread respect for the rule of law and the protection of foreigners are set in stone; the recent developments in some Member States can be seen a *menetekel* or a warning sign in this regard.

As has been developed in this chapter, there are many indications that a termination *pur et dur* of the current international intra-EU investor protection regime could create new legal and political challenges for the EU and its Member States. It would lead to a situation in which the EU would propagate classical, albeit 'improved', international investment law in its external relations but initiate a 'renaissance' of an adapted and 'Europeanized Calvo Doctrine' in intra-EU relations,[193] i.e. the exclusion of any preferential treatment of EU investors compared to the host State's nationals (a part from provisions of EU law) and the

---

192 L. Henkin, *How Nations Behave: Law and Foreign Policy*, 2nd ed. (New York: Columbia University Press, 1979), at 47.
193 On the 'Calvo Doctrine', see in greater detail Chapter I: II. 1.

reliance on the domestic judiciary of the EU host State as the only competent forum for investor-State dispute resolution.

Indeed, the alternative of a uniform framework of investment protection within the EU, which is proposed here, has not a supreme value on its own. Diversity as well as the competition of different domestic regimes are not bad as such and might even lead to unexpected and advantageous developments. In case of intra-EU investor protection, however, a concerted effort among Member States could have beneficial effects for all stakeholders and thus seems a promising approach to be taken.

As shown previously,[194] the EU guarantees fundamental freedoms and fundamental rights, which, however, must be invoked by investors before the domestic courts of the respective Member States, without having direct access to the ECJ. The latter can only be addressed through the preliminary reference procedure of Art. 267 TFEU. Furthermore, the domestic law of the Member States continues to regulate the greatest part of foreign investments, with the effect that the actual protection of intra-EU investments may significantly differ among the respective host States to an investment.

Against this backdrop, the effectiveness and predictability of the investment protection system as well as the confidence in the EU legal system could be strengthened through a substitute for the current 'international investment protection regime' within the EU. Such a substitute could be based on public international law (1.) or on EU law (2.) and could cover substantive standards of protection as well as procedural protection standards. In any case, the substitute would need to be compatible with EU law and the ECJ's jurisprudence, especially the principles reflected in the *Achmea* judgment.

1 International law substitute

There are several possibilities for substitutes based in the international legal sphere such as the strengthening of the European Court of Human Rights as an investment dispute resolution body (a) or the creation of a multilateral investment protection treaty among the EU Member States, which could refer disputes to a multilateral international investment court (b).

a) New role for the ECtHR

As already touched upon in Chapter I, the ECHR has been suggested by several authors as a possible alternative set of substantive investment protection with the ECtHR as an alternative forum for investor-State dispute settlement.[195] The ECtHR has already proven its capacity to deal with investor-State disputes, inter alia in the notorious *Yukos v Russia* case, in which it ordered Russia to pay

---

194 Cf. Chapter II.
195 Cf. Chapter I: III. 4.

damages of more than 1.8 billion euro.[196] A possibility for the EU Member States and especially intra-EU investors could thus be to increasingly rely on the ECtHR as a proper venue for investor-State disputes.

The requirement of exhaustion of local remedies to access the ECtHR codified in Art. 35 (1) ECHR, however, could prevent capital exporting States from pushing the ECtHR to develop into a *new* transnational European investment court, especially as it could significantly extend the duration of proceedings. But first and foremost, such a reliance on the ECtHR as *the* new remedy for intra-EU investor-State dispute settlement could be incompatible with the EU Treaties. It could quickly lead to an *'Achmea II'* decision, i.e. a transmission of the *Achmea* reflections on the decision making of the ECtHR. The ECtHR is precluded from referring preliminary questions to the ECJ.[197] Thus, a situation similar to the one of the ECJ's *Achmea* judgment could arise. The ECJ could come to the conclusion that the ECtHR is potentially applying and interpreting EU law without having access to the Art. 267 TFEU procedure, which could have the effect that such rulings of the ECtHR would be found to be incompatible with the autonomy of the EU legal order, based on the rationale applied in the *Achmea* judgment. Thus, the ECtHR remains a potential alternative forum for intra-EU disputes but cannot be relied upon to serve as a proper substitute for the current intra-EU IIA investment protection regime.

b) *Multilateral treaty and the international investment court*

Most EU Member States will terminate their intra-EU BITs through the Multilateral Agreement for the Termination of intra-EU BIT. In a similar way, the Member States could also conclude a multilateral treaty to create a substitute for the current net of intra-EU IIAs. Multilateral treaties among EU Member States outside the EU legal sphere are not uncommon and have been on the rise in the last years, examples are the treaty-based European Stability Mechanism or the European Fiscal Compact.[198] For the EU Member States to be competent to conclude such a treaty the matter regulated by it may not fall under the EU's exclusive competence. As an intra-EU investment protection treaty would regulate economic activities in the area of the internal market, it would fall under the shared competence of the EU under Art. 4 (2) lit. a) TFEU.[199] Hence, by virtue of Art. 2 (2) TFEU, the Member States could exercise this shared competence "to the extent that the Union has not exercised its competence" and "to the extent that the Union has decided to cease exercising its competences". Notwithstanding the Member States'

---

196 ECtHR, *Yukos v Russia.* Application no. 14902/04. Judgment, 31 July 2014.
197 Cf. K. Lenaerts, I. Maselis and K. Gutman, *EU Procedural Law* (Oxford: Oxford University Press, 2014), at para. 3.14.
198 Cf. H. P. Aust, *Eine völkerrechtsfreundliche Union? Grund und Grenze der Öffnung des Europarechts zum Völkerrecht,* Europarecht 52 (2017).
199 Cf. T. T. Andersen and S. Hindelang, *The Day after,* Journal of World Investment & Trade 17 (2016), 1002.

competence to conclude such a treaty, it should be drafted in compliance with EU law to avoid further collisions. A possibility to avoid such collisions, could be to introduce a clause that any obligations of an EU Member State arising out of that subsequent treaty would be subject to the limitations of EU law.[200] In case such treaty provided for dispute settlement, the body competent to decide investor-State disputes would need to comply with the ECJ's *Achmea* judgment. Different options are conceivable with regard to dispute settlement, either to refer disputes to domestic courts, arbitral tribunals or to an international investment court. The sole referral to domestic courts, however, would not actually create a substitute and guarantee for a fully independent transnational dispute settlement body. The referral to classical investor-State arbitration tribunals would face the same difficulties the current net of intra-EU BITs is facing with regard to its relationship to the EU legal order. The most promising adjudicatory substitute could thus be the creation of an international investment court, which could become competent to decide disputes based on the multilateral investment treaty concluded among the EU Member States.

On March 20, 2018, the Council of the EU adopted the negotiating directives authorizing the EU Commission to negotiate, on behalf of the EU, a Convention establishing a permanent Multilateral Investment Court (MIC), which could eventually replace the current bilateral investment court system.[201] Paragraph 7 of the negotiating directives explains that "the Convention should also allow the Member States of the Union and third countries to bring agreements to which they are or will be Parties to under the jurisdiction of the multilateral court." However, a footnote is attached to this paragraph, which explicitly excludes intra-EU BITs and the ECT from the scope of application of the negotiating directives. It reads:

> Without prejudice to the question of their validity or applicability under EU law, bilateral investment treaties concluded among Member States (i.e. intra-EU BITs), as well as the intra-EU application of the Energy Charter Treaty shall not fall within the scope of these directives.[202]

In other words, the MIC shall not cover disputes arising out of intra-EU IIAs. It could, however, cover agreements concluded in the future covering intra-EU investor-State disputes. Thus, disputes arising out of a potential subsequent multilateral intra-EU investment treaty, as the one discussed here, could potentially fall under the MICs competence. In any case, the MIC presupposes the adoption of a multilateral treaty by many States. It is not clear whether this further body of international adjudication would pool sufficient political will and thus ever or at least

200 Ibid.
201 Council of the EU, *Negotiating Directives for a Convention Establishing a Multilateral Court for the Settlement of Investment Disputes: 12981/17 ADD 1 DCL 1*, 20 March 2018.
202 Ibid.

soon see the light of the day,[203] especially regarding the manifold interests of the different States and the so far unsuccessful attempts to create a multilateral investment regime.[204] But primarily, there are many reasons to be sceptical whether and how such an international adjudicative body could be compatible with EU law. In its *Achmea* decision the ECJ emphasized that the establishment of an international adjudicatory body rendering decisions binding on the EU institutions, "is not in principle incompatible with EU law", provided that "the autonomy of the EU and its legal order is respected".[205] How a permanent international investment court, competent to decide intra-EU investor-State disputes, could respect the autonomy of the EU and its legal order, however, remains to be seen.

2 EU law substitute

The creation of substitutes based in the international legal order are a conceivable path to take for the EU Member States. Such approaches, however, bear the risk to collide with EU law and eventually to be found to be incompatible with the autonomy of the EU legal order. A substitute to the current intra-EU IIA protection regime enshrined in the EU legal order thus appears more promising and feasible. EU legislators could either concentrate on substantive standards of protection or on the procedural elements. Against this backdrop, the present section will assess the prospects of an intra-EU investment court integrated into the EU judiciary (a) and then focus on the possibility of secondary EU legislation, namely a regulation or directive covering intra-EU investments (b).

a) Intra-EU investment court

With the difficulties a standing multilateral investment court might be facing in its relationship with EU law and especially the ECJ, it seems more feasible to create an intra-EU dispute settlement mechanism, in conformity with the EU Treaties as they stand. Such a court could be integrated into the EU judiciary as a new specialized body of adjudication, i.e. an EU Investment Court. According to Art. 257 (1) TFEU a specialized court may be established by the European Parliament and the Council "attached to the General Court to hear and determine at first

---

203 Very sceptical, C. Schreuer, *The Future of International Investment Law* in M. Bungenberg, et al. (eds.), *International Investment Law: A Handbook* (Baden-Baden: Nomos, 2015), p. 1908 para. 20; A. de Mestral, *Investor State Arbitration Between Developed Democratic Countries* in A. de Mestral (ed.), *Second Thoughts* (Montreal: McGill-Queen's University Press, 2017), at 21 f.; J. Ketcheson, *Investment Arbitration* in S. Hindelang and M. Krajewski (eds.), *Shifting Paradigms in International Investment Law: More Balanced, Less Isolated, Increasingly Diversified* (Oxford: Oxford University Press, 2016), pp. 97–127, at 118 f.

204 Cf. Chapter I: II. 2. a). See also A. Roberts, *Incremental, Systemic, and Paradigmatic Reform of Investor-State Arbitration,* American Journal of International Law 112 (2018), at 419 ff.

205 ECJ, *Achmea*. C-284/16. Judgment, 6 March 2018, para. 57. On the other conditions the ECJ has developed in its jurisprudence for an international court or tribunal to be compatible with EU law, cf. Chapter III: I. 2.

instance certain classes of action or proceedings brought in specific areas". An appeal mechanism involving the General Court would also be possible by virtue of Art. 257 (3) TFEU.

Nonetheless, such a newly created court would be powerless and rather useless without any substantive provisions to rely on. The substantive investment protection already guaranteed under EU law already falls under the jurisdiction of the ECJ. In other words, a set of substantive investment protection rules would be needed for the court as a judicial basis for its decisions. As will be shown in the next subsection, however, such rules might be more than sufficient to guarantee an effective intra-EU investment protection, so that no new body of adjudication would be needed within the EU.

b) Act of secondary legislation

EU secondary law has not been taken into consideration in most contributions reflecting on possible reactions to the *Achmea* decision. However, of all possible ways to handle the termination of the intra-EU BIT regime, it seems the most promising approach, especially as it is the one which is both politically and legally the least complicated to implement.

The harmonization of substantive investment protection among EU Member States could be the answer to the current conflicts and difficulties. The obligation for all Member States' legislative, administrative and judicial bodies to treat EU investors in a fair and non-arbitrary manner, enshrined in EU law would not only reduce the risk of disputes among EU Member States and between investors and EU Member States, but also strengthen the rule of law within the EU. A harmonized approach could guarantee the compliance with these standards and impose the same obligations on all EU Member States with regard to intra-EU investments. All Member States' organs would be required to apply and consider the common rules on investment protection. Domestic courts could submit preliminary references to the ECJ, regarding the interpretation of the new instrument and the ECJ would guarantee a uniform interpretation of the legal text. Furthermore, Member States not complying with the common rules could face infringement proceedings, which could be initiated either by the EU Commission or by another EU Member State pursuant to Arts. 258 and 259 TFEU.

To initiate infringement proceedings, the EU Commission often relies on initiatives of EU citizens or companies based in the EU. Accordingly, the EU Commission has made the commitment to consider every individual complaint submitted in written form and concerning alleged infringements of EU law committed by EU Member States.[206] Thus, even without the creation of specific fora, the possibility for intra-EU investors to inform the EU Commission, could be understood

---

206 Cf. P. Craig and G. de Búrca, *EU Law: Text, Cases and Materials*, 6th ed. (Oxford: Oxford University Press, 2015), at 431 ff; D. Chalmers, G. Davies and G. Monti, *European Union Law*, 3rd ed. (Cambridge: Cambridge University Press, 2014), at 368 ff.

as a potential remedy available to them in order to ensure the Member States' compliance with the secondary act of legislation.

With the creation of secondary EU legislation on intra-EU investment protection, the EU Member States' domestic courts would become the only original fora for the settlement of intra-EU investor-State disputes. In difference to the rather inconsistent system of investor-State arbitration, this approach could provide for a more consistent and predictable regime, especially through the preliminary reference mechanism to the ECJ.

The adoption of EU secondary law requires a competence of the EU in this policy field.[207] As discussed, the Lisbon Treaty conferred FDI to the exclusive competence of the EU, codified in Art. 207 TFEU. This competence, however, covers extra-EU investments only and has no effects on FDI in intra-EU relations.[208] Intra-EU investments form part of the internal market,[209] they thus fall under the EU's shared competence of Art. 4 (2) lit. a) TFEU. Hence, Art. 114 TFEU which aims at the establishment and development of a functioning internal European market through harmonization, could be relied on as the competence for a harmonization of intra-EU investment protection, especially as there is no other legislative competence provided for in the Treaties concerning intra-EU investments.[210]

According to the principle of subsidiarity codified in Art. 5 (3) TEU,

> in areas which do not fall within its exclusive competence, the Union shall act only if and in so far as the objectives of the proposed action cannot be sufficiently achieved by the Member States, either at central level or at regional and local level, but can rather, by reason of the scale or effects of the proposed action, be better achieved at Union level.[211]

The need for a concerted effort to harmonize intra-EU investment protection has been discussed in the last chapters. The Member States could hardly achieve this goal acting on their own. Thus, a secondary act of EU legislation would comply with the principle of subsidiarity. Furthermore, according to the principle of proportionality, codified in Art. 5 (4) TEU, "the content and form of Union action shall not exceed what is necessary to achieve the objectives of the Treaties." In fact, the EU legislator enjoys a wide discretion in this regard. The ECJ intervenes only if the action taken "is manifestly inappropriate to the objective sought by

---

207 Art. 2 TFEU.
208 Cf. Chapter I: III.
209 As shown in Chapter II, FDI is covered by both the freedom of establishment enshrined in Art. 49 TFEU and the free movement of capital enshrined in Art. 63 TFEU.
210 See also T. T. Andersen and S. Hindelang, *The Day After,* Journal of World Investment & Trade 17 (2016), 1003.
211 See also K. S. C. Bradley, *Legislating in the European Union* in C. Barnard and S. Peers (eds.), *European Union Law*, 2nd ed. (Oxford: Oxford University Press, 2017), pp. 97–142, at 111 ff.

the measure."[212] The principle, however, requires the legislator to opt for the least intrusive form, which would still allow the achievement of the desired aim.[213]

As long as the principle of subsidiarity and proportionality would be respected, the EU legislator could freely choose the form of the legal act to attain its goal of creating a harmonized intra-EU investment protection regime, as Art. 114 TFEU does not require a certain type of legislative instrument to be used. Two types of legislation come into question, regulations and directives. By virtue of Art. 288 TFEU a regulation is "binding in its entirety and directly applicable in all Member States", while a directive "shall be binding, as to the result to be achieved, upon each Member State to which it is addressed, but shall leave to the national authorities the choice of form and methods."

While a regulation has legal effect in the Member States without any need of domestic transformation, directives have to be transposed into the respective domestic legal systems of the Member States.[214] Directives, thus allow smoother legislative changes and the harmonization of legal standards in specific areas, as they leave discretion to the respective Member States with regard to the implementation.[215] In case a State does not implement a directive, it can develop direct effect allowing individuals to invoke it before domestic courts.[216] Furthermore, States can be held liable for non-complying with the implementation of a directive and thus ordered to pay damages.[217]

A regulation on the other hand, would constitute a fundamental policy shift in the EU, obliging all Member States to comply with one specific established set of investor protection rules. Thus, a European investment directive providing for a minimum harmonization is more expedient. The directive would guarantee a minimum level of investor protection, leaving an important margin of discretion to the Member States regarding the balance between public and private interests and allowing the Member States to grant higher standards of protection. Thus, a European investment protection directive would not only allow the Member States to uphold their domestic particularities with regard to FDI but would also enhance the competition among Member States to attract FDI from other EU States.

Regarding the definition of standards, the new EU investment directive should be oriented on the directives that authorized the FTA negotiations with

212 See also ibid., p. 117.
213 Ibid., p. 99. See also Art. 296 (1) TFEU.
214 Cf. P. Craig and G. de Búrca, *EU Law: Text, Cases and Materials*, 6th ed. (Oxford: Oxford University Press, 2015), at 107 f.
215 Ibid., p. 108.
216 Cf. ECJ, *Becker*. Case 8/81. Judgment, 19 January 1982, ECLI:EU:C:1982:7, para. 25; D. Chalmers, G. Davies and G. Monti, *European Union Law* (Cambridge: Cambridge University Press, 2014), at 308 ff; P. Craig and G. de Búrca, *EU Law: Text, Cases and Materials*, 6th ed. (Oxford: Oxford University Press, 2015), at 200 ff.
217 Cf. ECJ, *Andrea Francovich*. Joined Cases C-6/90 and C-9/90. Judgment, 19 November 1991, ECLI:EU:C:1991:428. See also D. Chalmers, G. Davies and G. Monti, *European Union Law* (Cambridge: Cambridge University Press, 2014), at 325 ff; P. Craig and G. de Búrca, *EU Law: Text, Cases and Materials*, 6th ed. (Oxford: Oxford University Press, 2015), p. 222.

third-countries, and guarantees the Member States the right to pursue their legitimate public policy objectives in a non-discriminatory manner.[218] Besides, the Member States should negotiate which substantive standards of protection contained in already existing IIAs and Model BITs should be transferred or adapted to the directive. In this light, it seems advisable, in case the FET standard is chosen to be maintained, to enumerate in a quasi-exhaustive manner the measures incompatible with the fair and equitable treatment standard, as it was done in the treaty texts adopted with Singapore and Canada.[219]

In any case, an EU directive would need to thoroughly define the coverage of investment protection to avoid granting benefits to investors that are not intended to be covered, namely non-EU investors. The same is true regarding the phenomenon of round-tripping investments and mailbox companies. Under EU law, investors are generally free to incorporate new companies or to set up subsidies in any Member State, irrespective of the place of their main business as the Member States have to recognize companies that have been validly created according to the laws of other Member States.[220] The ease with which companies can be incorporated in EU Member States should be explicitly considered while drafting the investment protection directive, in order to prevent free riding of non-EU companies and the creation of mailbox companies, and other artificial corporate structures.[221] Against this backdrop, a possible approach could be to limit the protection provided for in the investment directive to investments and investors owned or effectively controlled by nationals of EU Member States. Another possibility could be to require substantive business activities within the territory of the EU and the respective EU host State to the investment for an investor to fall

---

218 See for example, Council of the European Union, *Directives for the negotiation of a Free Trade Agreement with Japan: 15864/12 ADD1 REV2,* 29 November 2012, at para. 24. See also C. Titi, *International Investment Law and the European Union: Towards a New Generation of International Investment Agreements,* European Journal of International Law 26 (2015), at 654 ff.

219 See for example, EU – Singapore Investment Protection Agreement, at Art. 2.4; Comprehensive Economic and Trade Agreement (CETA) between Canada and the EU and its Member States, at Art. 8.10. See also C. Titi, *International Investment Law and the European Union: Towards a New Generation of International Investment Agreements,* European Journal of International Law 26 (2015), at 656 f.

220 Cf. ECJ, *Überseering.* Case C-208/00. Judgment, 5 November 2002, ECLI:EU:C:2002:632, para. 95; EU Commission, *Protection of intra-EU investment – COM (2018) 547/2: Communication from the Commission to the European Parliament and the Council,* 19 June 2018, p. 7.

221 According to UNCTAD's World Investment Report 2016, around 1/3 of investor-State dispute have been filed by entities "that are ultimately owned by parent companies in countries that are not party to the treaty on which the claim is based." UNCTAD, *World Investment Report 2016: Investor Nationality: Policy Challenges* (New York, Geneva: United Nations, 2016), p. 175. Furthermore, regarding mailbox companies, "of the ISDS claims filed by claimants whose ultimate owners have a different nationality, more than a quarter do not engage in substantial business activities in the country whose nationality they claim," cf. ibid., 178. See also M. Feldman, *Setting Limits on Corporate Nationality Planning in Investment Treaty Arbitration,* ICSID Review 27 (2012), 281–302.

under the directive's scope of application.[222] Regarding the condition of substantive business activities, purely objective criteria such as a certain minimum period of establishment would be too rigid and exclude and discriminate newly created enterprises. The requirement of a company having its seat in the EU, i.e. the location of its real operations be they administrative or managerial, could thus be more promising.[223] In any case an EU investor bringing a claim before a domestic Member State's court on the basis of the protection standards contained in the newly created European investor protection directive, would have the onus to proof that its investment is owned or effectively controlled by a national of an EU Member States and has substantive business activities within the EU.

With the creation of an intra-EU investment-protection directive, all Member States' organs would be obliged to treat EU investors according to the minimum substantive standards contained therein and transformed into domestic legislation. The domestic courts and tribunals would have the obligation together with the ECJ to ensure the full application of this directive in all Member States and to ensure judicial protection of the rights of individuals provided therein. This new system of investor-protection would be based on primary legal protection and allow Member States to correct unlawful acts and thus to build a clear legal situation for all investors, instead of only compensating individual investors for specific unlawful State acts.

In case of doubts regarding for example the conditions for an investor to fall under the directive or regarding the content of specific substantive standards, domestic courts could refer the question to the ECJ. Courts "against whose decisions there is no judicial remedy under national law" would even be obliged to do so by virtue of Art. 267 (3) TFEU. If a Member State organ, however, violated the directive and was not penalized for it by a domestic court, the Member State could face an infringement proceeding initiated either by the EU Commission or by another Member State pursuant to Art. 258 and 259 TFEU.

In sum, the ECJ would indirectly control the implementation of intra-EU investment protection. The Court, however, would only be seized in case of uncertainties regarding the interpretation of the directive and massive violations of its principles, which are not stopped by the domestic judiciary of the investors host State. This would guarantee a high level of protection combined with a greater leeway for the respective Member States. While the possibility to rely on investor-State arbitration would have been abolished, intra-EU investors could still rely on a transnational court, namely the ECJ, in cases in which a domestic judicial

---

222 For greater detail on the substantial business activities criterion, cf. UNCTAD, *World Investment Report 2016: Investor Nationality: Policy Challenges* (New York, Geneva: United Nations, 2016), p. 174. This condition is also enshrined in Art. 17 (1) ECT, according to which each Contracting Party reserves the right to deny the advantages of the ECT to "a legal entity if citizens or nationals of a third state own or control such entity and if that entity has no substantial business activities in the Area of the Contracting Party in which it is organized."

223 Such an approach was also suggested by UNCTAD with regard to new IIA standards in its World Investment Report 2016, cf. ibid., 178 f.

system becomes partial and starts acting arbitrarily. In light of the EU Commission's confident statement that within the EU there is no suspicion of "a structural bias" of the European Courts but rather a "strong confidence" in the European judiciary,[224] this approach should be acceptable for the great majority of stakeholders in intra-EU investments.

VIII Assessment

The question asked at the beginning of this chapter was that of the future of intra-EU investment protection after the *Achmea* judgment.

At the end of the day, the *Achmea* decision might lead to the 'end 'of the 'international investment protection regime' within Europe and to an alleged victory of EU law over its international law 'competitor' in the field of intra-EU investment protection. However, as EU law focusses primarily on market access questions and does not cover the protection of already established investments in a way comparable to the existing IIAs, the domestic law of the Member States will again become the main legal system governing intra-EU investments. This could potentially lead to a situation in which European investors are less protected than extra-EU investors while investing within the EU, as the latter will continue to be protected under both domestic law and extra-EU BITs as well as EU Free Trade Agreements.

The EU should therefore try to use the new-found freedom to create an adequate and carefully considered harmonized substitute for investor-State arbitration and BITs at the European level. Such harmonized approach would not only guarantee a high protection standard for intra-EU investments and improve the rule of law within the EU but could especially hinder multinational investors to proceed to nationality planning, namely to invest through non-EU subsidiaries in order to fall under the scope of application of extra-EU investment protection agreements. Finally, it could also counter the increasing doubts concerning the 'mutual trust' and judicial independence in several Member States, and thus strengthen the integration of the common European market.

Regarding the overall development of international markets and FDI, the connecting factor of nationality for investment protection appears to be outdated and needs to be questioned. The significance of the nation-State seems to be constantly eroding and even key elements of State sovereignty like the citizenship have become available for purchase in several Member States.[225] The main role

---

224 Position of the EU Commission, as cited in ICSID, *Electrabel v Hungary*. Case No. ARB/07/19. Decision on Jurisdiction, Applicable Law and Liability, 30 November 2012, para. 5.20 at 65.

225 The possibility to purchase a Member State's nationality is possible for example in Malta and Cyprus, other Member States like Bulgaria, Latvia and Greece allow a buy-in into fast track citizenship programs, cf. J. Henley, *Citizenship for Sale,* The Guardian, 2 June 2018. www.theguardian.com/world/2018/jun/02/citizenship-by-investment-passport-super-rich-nationality (23 May 2020). See also A. Shachar, *Citizenship for Sale?* in A. Shachar, et al. (eds.), *The Oxford Handbook of Citizenship* (New York: Oxford University Press, 2016), pp. 789–816, at 795 f.

for the nation-State remains its legislative competence and its budgetary powers. Within the EU, however, and especially regarding the rules regulating the protection of foreign investments, a common and harmonized approach seems more promising than an 'everyone-for-themselves' approach of the – post-Brexit – 27 EU Member States. In difference to investor-State arbitration tribunals, the domestic courts will consider a claim initiated by a foreign investor against the background of their domestic legal system and the legal system of the EU, which both reflect the democratically elaborated and complex balance between private and public interests.

The settlement of investor-State disputes through domestic courts will also mitigate the raising criticism of discrimination of domestic investors vis-à-vis foreign ones. While there always remains the risk of domestic courts failing to adjudicate in an impartial way, or even being corrupt, this risk is mitigated through the triple control mechanism by the ECJ which has the last word on the directive's interpretation, the EU Commission which might initiate infringement proceedings or the other Member States, especially the home States which can also rely on this remedy.

References

Alexandrov, Stanimir A., *Enforcement of ICSID Awards* in C. Binder, et al. (eds.), *International Investment Law for the 21st Century: Essays in Honour of Christoph Schreuer* (Oxford: Oxford University Press, 2009), pp. 322–37.

Andersen, Teis T. and Hindelang, Steffen, *The Day After: Alternatives to Intra-EU BITs*, Journal of World Investment & Trade 17 (2016), 984–1014.

Aust, Anthony, *Modern Treaty Law and Practice*, 3. ed. (Cambridge: Cambridge University Press, 2013).

Aust, Helmut P., *Eine völkerrechtsfreundliche Union? Grund und Grenze der Öffnung des Europarechts zum Völkerrecht*, Europarecht 52 (2017), 106–21.

Bermann, George A., *Navigating EU Law and the Law of International Arbitration*, Arbitration International 28 (2012), 397–445.

Binder, Christina, *A Treaty Law Perspective on Intra-EU BITs*, Journal of World Investment & Trade 17 (2016), 964–83.

Bjorklund, Andrea K., *Private Rights and Public International Law: Why Competition Among International Economic Law Tribunals Is Not Working*, Hastings Law Journal 59 (2007), 241–307.

Bjorklund, Andrea K., *State Immunity and the Enforcement of Investor-State Arbitral Awards* in C. Binder, et al. (eds.), *International Investment Law for the 21st Century: Essays in Honour of Christoph Schreuer* (Oxford: Oxford University Press, 2009), pp. 302–21.

Blackaby, Nigel, Partasides, Constantine, Redfern, Alan and Hunter, Martin, *Redfern and Hunter on International Arbitration*, 6. ed. (New York, London: Oxford University Press, 2015).

Bogdandy, Armin von and Ioannidis, Michael, *Das systemische Defizit: Merkmale, Instrumente und Probleme am Beispiel der Rechtsstaatlichkeit und des neuen Rechtsstaatlichkeitsverfahrens*, Zeitschrift für ausländisches öffentliches Recht und Völkerrecht 74 (2014), 283–328.

Born, Gary, *International Commercial Arbitration*, 2. ed. (New York, Alphen aan den Rijn: Wolters Kluwer Law & Business; Kluwer Law International, 2014).

Bradley, Kieran S. C., *Legislating in the European Union* in C. Barnard and S. Peers (eds.), *European Union Law*, 2. ed. (Oxford: Oxford University Press, 2017), pp. 97–142.

Brown, Chester, *Inherent Powers in International Adjudication* in C. Romano, et al. (eds.), *The Oxford Handbook of International Adjudication* (Oxford: Oxford University Press, 2014), pp. 828–47.

Bungenberg, Marc, *A History of Investment Arbitration and Investor-State Dispute Settlement in Germany* in A. de Mestral (ed.), *Second Thoughts: Investor State Arbitration Between Developed Democracies* (Montreal: McGill-Queen's University Press, 2017), pp. 259–83.

Chalmers, Damian, Davies, Gareth and Monti, Giorgio, *European Union Law*, 3. ed. (Cambridge: Cambridge University Press, 2014).

Craig, Paul and Búrca, Gráinne de, *EU Law: Text, Cases and Materials*, 6. ed. (Oxford: Oxford University Press, 2015).

Crawford, James, *Brownlie's Principles of Public International Law*, 8. ed. (Oxford: Oxford University Press, 2012).

EU Commission, *The 2016 EU Justice Scoreboard* (Brussels, 2016).

EU Commission, *EU Justice Scoreboard 2018* (Brussels, 2018).

EU Commission, *Justice Scoreboard 2019* (Brussels, 2019).

Feldman, Mark, *Setting Limits on Corporate Nationality Planning in Investment Treaty Arbitration*, ICSID Review 27 (2012), 281–302.

Gaillard, Emmanuel, *L'Avenir des Traités de Protection des Investissements* in C. Leben (ed.), *Droit international des investissements et de l'arbitrage transnational* (Paris: Editions Pedone, 2015), pp. 1027–47.

Harrison, James, *The Life and Death of BITs: Legal Issues Concerning Survival Clauses and the Termination of Investment Treaties*, Journal of World Investment & Trade (2012), 928–50.

Henkin, Louis, *How Nations Behave: Law and Foreign Policy*, 2. ed. (New York: Columbia University Press, 1979).

Hess, Burkhard, *The Fate of Investment Dispute Resolution after the Achmea Decision of the European Court of Justice*, MPILux Research Paper Series (2018).

Ketcheson, Jonathan, *Investment Arbitration* in S. Hindelang and M. Krajewski (eds.), *Shifting Paradigms in International Investment Law: More Balanced, Less Isolated, Increasingly Diversified* (Oxford: Oxford University Press, 2016), pp. 97–127.

Kim, Yun-I, *Investment Law and the Individual* in M. Bungenberg, et al. (eds.), *International Investment Law: A Handbook* (Baden-Baden: Nomos, 2015), pp. 1585–601.

Kjos, Hege E., *Applicable Law in Investor-State Arbitration* (Oxford: Oxford University Press, 2013).

Lavopa, Federico M., Barreiros, Lucas E. and Bruno, Victoria M., *How to Kill a BIT and Not Die Trying: Legal and Political Challenges of Denouncing or Renegotiating Bilateral Investment Treaties*, Journal of International Economic Law (2013), 869–91.

Lenaerts, Koen, Maselis, Ignace and Gutman, Kathleen, *EU Procedural Law* (Oxford: Oxford University Press, 2014).

Liebscher, Christoph, *Article V (1) (e)* in R. Wolff (ed.), *New York Convention – Commentary* (München: C.H. Beck, 2012), pp. 356–80.

Mak, Elaine and Taekema, Sanne, *The European Union's Rule of Law Agenda: Identifying Its Core and Contextualizing Its Application*, Hague Journal on the Rule of Law 8 (2016), 25–50.

Mestral, Armand de, *Investor State Arbitration Between Developed Democratic Countries* in A. de Mestral (ed.), *Second Thoughts: Investor State Arbitration Between Developed Democracies* (Montreal: McGill-Queen's University Press, 2017), pp. 9–56.

Montanaro, Francesco, *Ain't no Sunshine* in G. Adinolfi, et al. (eds.), *International Economic Law: Contemporary Issues* (Cham, Torino: Springer, 2017), pp. 211–30.

Moon, Hwi-Chang, *Foreign Direct Investment: A Global Perspective* (Hackensack, NJ: World Scientific, 2016).

Nowrot, Karsten, *Termination and Renegotiation of International Investment Agreements* in S. Hindelang and M. Krajewski (eds.), *Shifting Paradigms in International Investment Law: More Balanced, Less Isolated, Increasingly Diversified* (Oxford: Oxford University Press, 2016), pp. 227–65.

Paulsson, Jan, *Arbitration Without Privity*, ICSID Review 10 (1995), 232–57.

Pauwelyn, Joost, *The Role of Public International Law in the WTO: How Far Can We Go?* American Journal of International Law 95 (2001), 535–78.

Perkams, Markus, *Protection for Legal Persons* in M. Bungenberg, et al. (eds.), *International Investment Law: A Handbook* (Baden-Baden: Nomos, 2015), pp. 638–52.

Peters, Anne, *Jenseits der Menschenrechte: Die Rechtsstellung des Individuums im Völkerrecht* (Tübingen: Mohr Siebeck, 2014).

Roberts, Anthea, *Power and Persuasion in Investment Treaty Interpretation: The Dual Role of States*, American Journal of International Law 104 (2010), 179–225.

Roberts, Anthea, *Triangular Treaties: The Extent and Limits of Investment Treaty Rights*, Harvard International Law Journal 57 (2015), 353–417.

Roberts, Anthea, *Incremental, Systemic, and Paradigmatic Reform of Investor-State Arbitration*, American Journal of International Law 112 (2018), 410–32.

Schäfer, Jan K. and Gaffney, John P., *Intra-EU BITs: Toothless Tigers or Do They Still Bite? The OLG Frankfurt Considers the Impact of EU Law on the Investor-State Dispute Resolution Mechanism*, Zeitschrift für Schiedsverfahren (2013), 68–78.

Schill, Stephan, *Investitionsschutz in EU-Freihandelsabkommen: Erosion gesetzgeberischer Gestaltungsmacht?* Zeitschrift für ausländisches öffentliches Recht und Völkerrecht 78 (2018), 33–92.

Schreuer, Christoph, *The ICSID Convention: A Commentary*, 2. ed. (Cambridge: Cambridge University Press, 2009).

Schreuer, Christoph, *The Future of International Investment Law* in M. Bungenberg, et al. (eds.), *International Investment Law: A Handbook* (Baden-Baden: Nomos, 2015), pp. 1904–11.

Shachar, Ayelet, *Citizenship for Sale?* in A. Shachar, et al. (eds.), *The Oxford Handbook of Citizenship* (New York: Oxford University Press, 2016), pp. 789–816.

Solomon, Dennis, *International Commercial Arbitration* in S. Balthasar (ed.), *International Commercial Arbitration: International Conventions, Country Reports and Comparative Analysis* (München: C.H. Beck, 2016), pp. 45–157.

Titi, Catharine, *International Investment Law and the European Union: Towards a New Generation of International Investment Agreements*, European Journal of International Law 26 (2015), 639–61.

UNCTAD, *World Investment Report 2016: Investor Nationality: Policy Challenges*, United Nations Publication (New York, Geneva: United Nations, 2016).

Vöneky, Silja, *Analogy in International Law*, (February 2008) in *MPEPIL (Online-Edition)* (Oxford: Oxford University Press).

Voon, Tania, Mitchell, Andrew and Munro, James, *Parting Ways: The Impact of Mutual Termination of Investment Treaties on Investor Rights*, ICSID Review 29 (2014), 451–73.

Wackernagel, Clemens, *The Twilight of the BITs? EU Judicial Proceedings, the Consensual Termination of Intra-EU BITs and Why That Matters for International Law*, Beiträge zum Transnationalen Wirtschaftsrecht (2016).

Weller, Matthias, *Mutual Trust: In Search of the Future of European Union Private International Law*, Journal of Private International Law 11 (2015), 64–102.

Wilske, Stephan and Edworthy, Chloe, *The Future of Intra-European Union BITs: A Recent Development in International Investment Treaty Arbitration against Romania and Its Potential Collateral Damage*, Journal of International Arbitration 33 (2016), 331–52.

General conclusion

The world is facing a crisis of multilateralism, an increasing loss of faith in liberal economic policies and the comeback of a self-confident but often exclusive statehood, with the 45th US president as a nationalist role model for many actors. These developments have not stopped at the gates of the EU. The Union is internally facing major challenges ranging from Brexit and mass migration, to difficulties with budgetary discipline, the compliance with fundamental principles of the rule of law and the effects of the Covid-19 pandemic. Increasingly, nationalist tendencies are observable at the heart of the EU. However, because of the 'globalization', every State and its domestic economy are more than ever before depending on good relations to other States. In order to benefit from steadily rising financial flows and foreign direct investments, States need to cooperate and develop well balanced investor-protection regimes, which provide for both a predictbale and stable investment environment but especially take into consideration the public interest.

The present study has revealed that the legal regimes surrounding international investments have been and still are highly influenced by the EU Member States and increasingly also the EU itself. With regard to intra-EU investments, however, the picture is gloomier. The duality of investment protection regimes applicable within the EU will soon come to an end at the cost of the diverse net of intra-EU BITs and the Energy Charter Treaty. This 'international investment protection regime' as it stands has proven no longer to represent the most appropriate legal framework for the protection of intra-EU investments. Whether the EU, however, will rely on the remaining 'European investment protection regime', i.e. all domestic rules of the Member States and of the EU legal order which cover foreign direct investments and their protection, or whether it will seize the opportunity for a far-reaching reform or further development of European rules in this field, remains to be seen. The present study has expressed a clear stance in this regard. But before summarizing the policy recommendations developed in the last chapter, let us review the principal findings.

Rise of investment protection in Europe

Two totally separate investment protection regimes have emerged after World War II in the same rather small geographic region of central Europe. While these regimes did originally not interact with each other, the EU legal order played a major role in the creation of the intra-EU BIT network, which it actively promoted in its 'Europe Agreements' with potential accession candidates. The currently observable clash of both investor protection regimes in Europe would not have arisen if the BITs had not been promoted or the accession treaties and the negotiators involved in their creation would have foressen the possible collision. This, however, did not happen. On the contrary more than 200 BITs were concluded before the Member States joined the EU and then maintained after their accession.

Apart from the BITs, another increasingly important IIA has seen the light of the day in the early 1990s. In an attempt to enhance the economic exchange between Western European States and the States of the former Communist bloc and to secure a stable energy supply for the former, the Energy Charter Treaty was concluded in 1994, again without considering any possible clash between its investment protection rules and the EU legal order.

As there was no considerable investor-State arbitration practice with regard to intra-EU investments until around 2008, the relationship between the two regimes resembled for a long time an unnoticed smouldering conflict. Only slowly the EU Commission together with some Member States started to realize the possible implications of the parallel existence of both regimes and began to challenge the international investment regime, which it found not only to be outdated and incompatible with the EU legal order but also superfluous as the latter was allegedly providing for a comparable level of investor protection. Another argument was that of an 'automatic' termination of the BITs due to the Member States' conclusion of the Lisbon Treaty. Allegedly the *lex posterior* rule in Art. 59 VCLT would have been applicable and would have had the effect of the BITs' termination. This argument has been rejected in Chapter III. It is true that both investment protection regimes cover intra-European investment flows in the widest sense. Their legal sources, however, do not relate to the 'same subject matter' in the sense of Art. 59 VCLT, even though they share some common goals such as non-discrimination, the stability and predicatbiliy of the judicial system, proportionality, protection of private property and the prohibition of arbitrariness. The BITs' validity has thus not been affected by the conclusion of the later Lisbon Treaty among all EU Member States.

Comparable but not similar regimes

Chapter II has analysed and compared both investment protection regimes. It revealed that many standards contained in intra-EU IIAs are reflected in EU law, some other, however, such as the most-favoured nation treatment or the concept of umbrella clauses are unkown to the EU legal order. Both EU law and international investment law operate with loose legal terms. In EU law, they have generally been clarified by the ECJ's jurisprudence. In international investment law, however, due to the inapplicability of the *stare decisis* principle and because of the different wordings in many treaties, the legal terms remain open to manifold interpretations as every single arbitral tribunal can interpret the same treaty text in a different way. The fragmented net of intra-EU IIAs is thus – unlike the EU legal order – not capable to build a coherent and integrated system and can therefore hardly create any legal certainty and predictability, especially due to the decentralized practice of arbitral tribunals.

The main difference, however, regarding substantive protection is that EU law provides for a sophisticated and careful balance of public and private interests, which is created through different exception clauses, that allow for the justification of restrictions of fundamental freedoms and fundamental rights under certain circumstances. While there is an observable trend in a similar direction in more recent IIAs on the global level, the old intra-EU IIAs, do generally not provide for such balancing. This does not preclude arbitrators from taking conflicting interests into consideration but makes it rather unlikely that these are comprehensively taken into account by an arbitral tribunal. Thus, in sum, EU law provides for a more carefully weighed substantive protection of intra-EU investments than intra-EU IIAs.

With regard to the remedies provided by the two different regimes, the disparities are even more important. The European Court of Justice has no competence to decide on individual claims initiated by investors against Member States for their non-compliance with EU law. Investors have no direct access to the ECJ but must rely on the Member States' judiciary, which might submit a preliminary reference to the European Court by virtue of Art. 267 TFEU. The EU Commission or other Member States can, however, initiate infringement proceedings against a Member State that is violating EU law. This, however, is generally a lengthy and unpredictable road to take, which cannot be influenced by the European investors themselves. The remedies provided by the 'European investment protection regime' are thus not comparable to the investor-State arbitration mechanism, which allows foreign investors to directly bring a claim against a host State before an independent international tribunal, detached from any State.

Another fundamental difference is that under international investment law, the State's responsibility for a breach of an IIA obligation is purely determined by international law, which is interpreted and applied by investor-State arbitration tribunals. Under EU law, questions of liability are assessed through domestic rules and domestic courts and secondary remedies are only subsidiary to primary remedies which aim at creating a lawful situation instead of compensating for an unlawful one.

All in all, EU law and international investment law share many commonalities but have differing goals. Some aspects of investment protection as they are typical for IIAs can be found in EU law. But the law of the European Union has a more comprehensive normativity, seeking to establish an increasingly integrated continent with a common market and social exchanges. In other words, EU law covers a broad range of policy areas, aspiring to bring them in accordance with each other in order to build a functioning and strong European Union. It is led by the goal to balance public and private interests to the advantage of all stakeholders within the Union.

Intra-EU IIAs on the other hand have a far more specialized and thereby also normatively limited field of application: the attraction of foreign investments and their protection against unlawful State behaviour. They do hardly ever envisage the balancing of public interests and individual investor protection. For this reason, it is possible that a Member State is compliant with EU law while violating its obligations arising out of an intra-EU IIA.

While the high level of economic integration within the EU is a crucial aspect for every investor operating in another EU country, the actual investment still takes place in a specific Member State and is governed by the rules and regulations of that State. In other words, even though EU law forms an integral part of the legal orders of its Member States, these domestic legal orders remain the legal fundament for all economic and other activities in the host State, also with regard to intra-EU investments. Hence, in principle disputes between an investor and the host State concerning an investment fall under the competence of the domestic courts of the respective State. The domestic courts protect foreign property rights especially through the respective national constitutional fundamental right to property and national legislation. Thus, the advantages and downsides of the respective EU Member States' domestic legal orders and their administrative practice are of the utmost significance for every intra-EU investor, which makes forum and treaty shopping highly relevant within the EU as the national investment protection systems may significantly differ among the different States.

In sum, Chapter II has revealed the commonalities and differences of intra-EU investor protection under EU law and international investment law. It has become clear that these two regimes are far from being identical. From an investor's perspective they might be considered complementary; from a State's perspective as absolutely incompatible. In difference to the intra-EU IIAs, the EU legal order does not grant high levels of protection independent and detached from the respective host State's legal system. It does, nonetheless, effectively influence the respective domestic legal orders and has created effective control mechanisms of the States' actions, without allowing direct access for individuals to its supranational European courts.

In the end, the question whether the differences in the level of protection between EU law and intra-EU IIAs can be translated into a deficit of protection by the EU legal order, remains rather a political than a legal question, which is also emphasized by the fact that of the possible 325 intra-EU BITs that could have been concluded among EU Member States post-Brexit, only 184 were in force when the ECJ rendered its *Achmea* judgment.

Total clash

The 'innocent' coexistence of the two investment protection regimes ended abruptly with the unexpected rise of intra-EU investor-State arbitration proceeding within the last decade. Especially the occurrence of countless intra-EU 15 investor-State disputes, i.e. disputes between investors from the traditionally capital-exporting EU 15 States against other EU 15 Member States, has further fuel the already existing backlash against the 'international investment protection regime'. The counter-reaction by the EU Commission and several Member States was to promote treaty termination and the abolishment of the remedy of investor-State arbitration as well as the rejection of the arbitral tribunals' jurisdiction. The EU Commission started to assert the control over investment protection in Europe in general.

A decisive moment in this conflict was the ECJ's *Achmea* judgment in which the Court in clear contradiction to its Advocate General gave a forceful support to the EU Commission's attempts to abolish the non-EU investment protection system. The ECJ found an intra-EU investor-State arbitration provision contained in a BIT to be incompatible with the autonomy of the EU legal order and the ECJ's monopoly in giving final and binding decisions regarding EU law, enshrined in Arts. 267 and 344 TFEU. As developed in Chapter III, this decision is transferable to all other intra-EU BITs with the effect that from a purely EU legal perspective investor-State arbitration tribunals are not competent to decide disputes arising out of these BITs. The present study has also revealed the incompatibility of the arbitration provisions with the principle of non-discrimination codified in Art. 18 TFEU.

The ECJ's judgment, however, only interprets the provisions of the EU Treaties and thus has no effect on the validity of the BITs, which remain valid under international law until their termination by the Member States. Most intra-EU BITs will now be terminated through the Multilateral Agreement for the Termination of intra-EU BITs signed by 23 Member States in May 2020.

Notwithstanding the BITs' termination, arbitral tribunals adopting a broad understanding of the 'same subject matter' criterion in Art. 30 (3) VCLT could reach the conclusion that the arbitration provision they base their jurisdiction upon is not applicable under international law due to its incompatibility with EU law. This could also lead to the end of BIT based intra-EU investor-State arbitration as accordingly all intra-EU investor-State arbitration tribunals applying this interpretation would lack jurisdiction to decide intra-EU investor-State disputes. At the present stage, however, this development seems more than doubtful. The most recent arbitral awards indicate that arbitral tribunals are not willing to follow the ECJ's interpretation and to deny their own jurisdiction but rather tend to a narrow understanding of Art. 30 (3) VCLT, excluding any incompatibility between the EU Treaties and the intra-EU BITs.

The situation is even more complicated regarding the relationship between EU law and the Energy Charter Treaty. In difference to intra-EU BITs, which only became intra-EU through the later accession of some Member States, the ECT was already concluded as a multilateral treaty among EU Member States and other third States as well as the EU itself. It became an integral part of the EU legal order. The later accession of new States to the EU had no effect on the ECT. The present study argues that the *Achmea* judgment is not transferable to the ECT's investor-State arbitration clause, even if its rationale, the protection of the autonomy of the EU legal order, is without any doubt applicable to intra-EU investor-State disputes based on the ECT. Just like it is the case in BIT based intra-EU arbitration proceedings, there is an inherent risk in ECT arbitrations of arbitral tribunals interpreting and applying EU legal rules without being able to submit preliminary references to the ECJ as these tribunals are not 'courts or tribunals of a Member State'. This bears the risk of a binding interpretation of EU law by the arbitral tribunal which could threaten the autonomy of the EU legal order. Notwithstanding, as the EU is a party to this mixed treaty it has become an integral part of the EU legal order and is thus legally not comparable to the BITs. Hence, as long as the ECJ does not render an explicit decision on this matter, the ECT continues to be applicable even from an EU legal perspective.

Other grounds for the inapplicability of the ECT have been raised by the EU Commission and some Member States. These have all been rejected in Chapter III. There is especially no implicit disconnection of the ECT from intra-EU investments and no lack of 'territorial diversity' in disputes concerning such investments, which could prevent an arbitral tribunal from having jurisdiction. Thus, in difference to the intra-EU BITs, the ECT remains compatible with EU law.

Foresight

As shown throughout this study, the international and the European regime protecting intra-EU investments conflict with each other. This conflict can only be solved through concerted political efforts. The 'international investment law regime' in Europe that consists of the intra-EU BITs and the Energy Charter Treaty is clearly outdated. It does no longer represent the most appropriate legal framework to address investment-related questions within this highly integrated Union, which does not only cover economic matters related to the common market but also social and cultural issues and influences all spheres of life within the territory of its – post-Brexit – 27 Member States. This raises the question of the future of investment protection within Europe.

The ECJ's *Achmea* decision forces the Member States to become active in order to comply with their obligation of 'sincere cooperation' codified in Art. 4 (3) TEU. But this is not the only reason to take action. Many intra-EU investors that currently face disputes with EU host States may develop a 'last-minute panic' and be incited to profit from the remaining possibility of investor-State arbitration, before this procedural remedy is excluded from intra-EU relations. EU Member States could thus face an important increase of investor-State arbitration proceedings.

Notwithstanding, the EU Member State courts will be able to review and annul non-ICSID awards and to deny the enforcement of intra-EU arbitration awards in general. The German BGH has shown the way. It found in its *Achmea* decision that the arbitral tribunal that had rendered the award in question lacked jurisdiction as due to the inapplicability of the BIT's investor-State arbitration provision no valid arbitration agreement between the investor and the host State could have been concluded. Furthermore, this study has shown that intra-EU awards could also be understood to be incompatible with the European *ordre public*, which would also allow their annulment or the denial of enforcement. The annulment of intra-EU investor-State arbitration awards rendered by an arbitral tribunal seated in an EU Member State could also prevent further enforcement attempts abroad according to Art. V (1) lit. e) New York Convention. The situation, however, is more complicated with regard to ICSID proceedings, arbitral tribunals seated in third States and attempts to enforce awards outside the EU. To avoid the Member States' influence on the review and enforcement proceedings of potential awards, investors and arbitral tribunals might thus tend to base their seat of arbitration outside the EU or to rely on ICSID proceedings. This could eventually lead to increasing enforcement attempts outside the EU and further deepen the collision between the two regimes. Especially with regard to ICSID proceedings the Member States thus have two possibilities if they do not want to infringe their international legal obligations, they can either try to settle the disputes or comply with possible awards until the legal basis for new proceedings has been abolished.

The Member States will terminate their intra-EU BITs. The future of the ECT in intra-EU investor-State relations, however, remains open. In this light, the EU and its Member States face the question whether or not to create a substitute, compatible with the EU legal order and to fill the lacunae of the current 'European investment protection regime'. In the author's view, the EU should seize the opportunity and create a harmonized, coherent and predictable investment protection substitute for the current 'international investment protection regime'.

Such a substitute is needed for several reasons. Turning away from the long-established investor-State arbitration system without creating a substitute could create regulatory gaps and potentially lead to a decline of investor protection in certain Member States. While there is a 'mutual trust' among Member States at least on paper, the present study has revealed that this principle seems to be rather a normative goal than a stable achievement. The independence of the judiciary in many Member States is under pressure just like the compliance rates with fundamental principles of the rule of law. Against this background, it is also likely that without a substitute, investors could start to restructure their investments in order to fall under specific extra-EU BITs and FTAs. This could totally circumvent the EU's assertion of control over investment protection. Finally, a weakened investor protection system within the EU could undermine the EU's attempts to create a multilateral and at best global investment protection regime in its external relations and weaken its negotiating position in the international sphere.

As most EU Member States comply with most of their international legal obligations most of the time, one could argue that there is no need for an independent control mechanism such as the one provided through international investor-State arbitration. But this is a misleading approach. One key rationale behind international investment law has always been its preventive character aimed at securing the legal environment even if a State develops in an arbitrary direction. The gloomy developments in some European Member States especially regarding the independence of the judiciary are warning signs in this regard and emphasize the importance of transnational compliance control mechanism in such politically and economically sensitive fields as foreign direct investment. Thus, against the backdrop of the current crisis of 'mutual trust' and judicial independence, the increasing risk of forum shopping and restructuring of companies as well as the possible weakening of the EU's negotiation position in the international legal sphere, a substitute seems more than promising.

As discussed in Chapter IV, the termination of most BITs through a multilateral agreement among the Member States will allow them to circumvent the risk of the triggering of sunset clauses, which could otherwise lead to transition periods of up to 20 years in which the current level of substantive and procedural investment protection would be maintained. While the Energy Charter Treaty has not yet been found to be incompatible with EU law, it nevertheless jeopardizes the autonomy of the EU legal order through intra-EU investor-State arbitration proceedings and thus eventually will have to be disconnected from intra-EU investments. Such a disconnection could also take the form of a multilateral treaty among the Member States.

The study concludes that the most effective and implementable approach to substitute this 'international investment protection regime' would be a secondary legislative act of EU law, namely an 'intra-EU investment protection directive'. It could strengthen the effectiveness and predictability of the investment protection system as well as the confidence in the EU legal order. The new investment protection directive would create a system of investor-protection based on primary legal protection and thus allow the Member States to correct unlawful acts and thereby to build a clear legal situation for all investors, instead of only compensating individual investors for specific violations. The directive could thus help to develop a coherent and effective system of investor protection within the EU legal order.

The envisaged directive would further oblige all EU Member States and their organs to treat European investors according to the minimum substantive standard provided therein and transformed into the domestic legal framework. Domestic courts would need to ensure the full application of the directive and in case of doubts submit preliminary questions to the ECJ. In case of non-compliance, i.e. the violation of the investment protection provisions contained in the directive, Member States could face infringement proceedings initiated by the EU Commission or other Member States, e.g. the investor's home State. The ECJ would thus become the new independent transnational control instance of intra-EU investment protection. It could, however, only be seized in case of uncertaitnties regarding the interpretation and application of the directive or in cases of infringement proceedings for Member State's non-compliance, i.e. in the case of massive violations, which are not remedied by the domestic judiciary. In sum, the new regime created by such an 'intra-EU investment protection directive' would provide a high level of investor protection combined with a substantive leeway for the respective Member States. Investor-State arbitration proceedings within the European Union would no longer be necessary, as investors could continue to rely on the ECJ as an independent and transnational instance of control.

Index

Printed in the United States
By Bookmasters